The Hominid Individual i

This volume explores new approaches to the remarkably detailed information that archaeologists have for the study of our earliest ancestors. Previous investigations of human evolution in the Palaeolithic period have conventionally been from an ecological and behavioural point of view. The emphasis has been on how our early ancestors made a living, decided what to eat, adapted through their technology to the conditions of existence and reacted to changing ice age climates. *The Hominid Individual in Context* takes a different approach.

Rather than explaining the archaeology of stones and bones as the product of group decisions, the contributors investigate how individual action created social life. This challenge to the accepted standpoint of the Palaeolithic brings new models and theories into the period; innovations that are matched by the resolution of the data that preserve individual action among the artefacts. The book brings together examples from recent excavations at Boxgrove, Schöningen and Blombos Cave, and the analyses of findings from Middle and Early Upper Pleistocene excavations in Europe, Africa and Asia. The results will revolutionise the Palaeolithic as archaeologists search for the lived lives among the empty spaces that remain.

Clive Gamble is Professor of Geography in the Centre for Quaternary Research at Royal Holloway, University of London. He spent many years at the University of Southampton, where he founded the Centre for the Archaeology of Human Origins. He is the author of many books, including *Archaeology, The Basics* (Routledge, 2001), and *The Palaeolithic Societies of Europe* (1999).

Martin Porr is based at the Landesmuseum für Vorgeschichte in Halle, Germany. There he has been involved as a project manager for the high-profile exhibition of the Bronze Age Sky Disc of Nebra, in co-operation with the National Museum of Denmark.

The Hominid Individual in Context

Archaeological investigations
of Lower and Middle Palaeolithic
landscapes, locales and artefacts

**Edited by Clive Gamble
and Martin Porr**

Routledge
Taylor & Francis Group

LONDON AND NEW YORK

First published 2005
by Routledge
2 Park Square, Milton Park, Abingdon, Oxon OX14 4RN

Simultaneously published in the USA and Canada
by Routledge
270 Madison Ave, New York, NY 10016

Routledge is an imprint of the Taylor & Francis Group

Typeset in Garamond
by Keystroke, Jacaranda Lodge, Wolverhampton
Printed and bound in Great Britain
by Cromwell Press, Trowbridge, Wiltshire

British Library Cataloguing in Publication Data
A catalogue record for this book is available from the British Library

Library of Congress Cataloging in Publication Data
The hominid individual in context : archaeological investigations of
lower and middle Palaeolithic landscapes, locales, and artefacts /
edited by Clive Gamble and Martin Porr.
   p. cm.
Includes bibliographical references and index.
1. Paleolithic period. 2. Fossil hominids. 3. Human evolution.
4. Social evolution. 5. Hominids. I. Gamble, Clive. II. Porr, Martin.
GN771.I53 2005
930.1′2–dc21

                                        2004014096

ISBN 0–415–28432–5 (hbk)
ISBN 0–415–28433–3 (pbk)

Contents

Figures

Tables

Contributors

D. S. Adler's current research centres on Neanderthal and Modern human lifeways and interactions in the southern Caucasus. To date he has conducted excavations in the Georgian Republic at the late Early Pleistocene locality of Akhalkalaki, the Middle-Upper Palaeolithic rockshelter of Ortvale Klde, the late Middle Pleistocene open-air site of Mashavera Gorge 3, and a series of Palaeolithic open-air sites identified during a recent survey of the Dmanisi region. Daniel Adler is currently a Lecturer at Harvard University.

Nicholas J. Conard is Professor of Early Prehistory and Quaternary Ecology at the University of Tübingen, Germany. He has directed numerous excavations in Germany, Syria and South Africa. He is especially interested in human behaviour during the Middle Palaeolithic, the processes related to the Middle-to-Upper-Palaeolithic transition and the rise of cultural modernity. Most recently he presented new finds of mobiliary Aurignacian art from Hohle Fels Cabe in the Swabian Jura.

Marcia-Anne Dobres studies late Pleistocene technology and cave art in France and South Africa. She is author of *Technology and Social Agency: Outlining a Practice Framework for Archaeology* (Blackwell, 2000), senior editor of *Agency in Archaeology* (Routledge, 2000), and senior editor of *The Social Dynamics of Technology: Practice, Politics, and World Views* (Smithsonian Institution Press, 1999).

F. d'Errico is Director of Research at the Centre National de la Recherche Scientifique (CNRS) and Research Professor at the Department of Anthropology, The George Washington University. He has focused his scientific investigations upon the evolution of human cognitive abilities. He currently directs a EUROCORE project of the European Science Foundation in the archaeology of the origin of language and its early diversification and a French Ministry of Research project on the linguistics, genetics, and environments of the Upper Palaeolithic.

A. S. Field completed her PhD at the University of Southampton in 2002 on the topic of 'The Middle Pleistocene in transition: lithic assemblages between OIS12 and 6 in Europe and Africa'. She has extensive Palaeolithic field experience in South Africa where she worked and published with Dr Kathy Kuman of the University of Witwatersrand. An expert lithic technologist, she is currently studying for a law degree.

Clive Gamble is Professor of Geography in the Centre for Quaternary Research at Royal Holloway, University of London. He spent many years at the University of Southampton, where he founded the Centre for the Archaeology of Human Origins. He is author of several books, including *In Search of the Neanderthals* with Christopher Stringer (1993), *Timewalkers: The Prehistory of Global Colonisation* (1993) and *The Palaeolithic Societies of Europe* (1999) which won the Society for American Archaeology Book Award in 2000. In 2002 he was the presenter of a six-part television documentary for Channel Five, *Where Do We Come From?* He is a co-director of the British Academy Centenary Research Project 'Lucy to Language – the Archaeology of the Social Brain'.

Sabine Gaudzinski is Professor of Prehistory at the University of Mainz, Germany, and Director of the Palaeolithic Research Centre of the Römisch-Germanisches Zentralmuseum at Monrepos, Germany. She has been involved in numerous research projects in Germany and Israel, such as the excavations of the Lower Palaeolithic site of 'Ubeidiya. She specializes in the analysis of faunal remains and their potential for the reconstruction of Palaeolithic economic behaviour.

J. A. J. Gowlett is Professor of Archaeology at the School of Archaeology, Classics and Egyptology at the University of Liverpool. John Gowlett's areas of expertise are Palaeolithic or Evolutionary Archaeology, and Evolutionary Anthropology. He is one of the three Directors of the British Academy's Centenary Research Project 'Lucy to Language – the Archaeology of the Social Brain'. He works with a research group which is particularly concerned with the form and dynamics of early artefacts, and also with investigating the early history of human fire use and control. In addition, he has developed studies in artefact form, and in relating early technology to social action and communication.

C. Henshilwood is Professor of Archaeology at the Centre for Development Studies, University of Bergen in Norway and Director of the African Heritage Research Institute in Cape Town, South Africa. He currently directs the Blombos Cave Project, a major archaeological research initiative at the southern tip of Africa that is contributing significantly to the international debate on the origins of what is considered 'modern' human behaviour.

Terry Hopkinson is currently a Lecturer at the School of Archaeology and Ancient History at the University of Leicester. He read Archaeology as a mature student at St John's College, Cambridge, obtaining his first degree in 1995 and completing his PhD in 2001. He was a Research Fellow at St John's for three years before joining the School in 2002. His research interests centre on Lower and Middle Palaeolithic landscapes and technologies in the context of climatic and environmental change, with an emphasis on the Middle Palaeolithic of Central Europe.

Robert Hosfield is a Lecturer at the School of Human and Environmental Sciences, University of Reading. He recently completed 'The Archaeological Potential of Secondary Contexts' project (funded by English Heritage through the Aggregates Levy Sustainability Fund), which re-assessed the archaeological value of the Lower Palaeolithic stone tools scattered throughout Britain's Pleistocene river landscapes.

Dietrich Mania was Professor for Prehistory at the University of Jena, Germany, and Director of the Bilzingsleben research project, until his retirement in 2003. For more than thirty years he has conducted pioneering research on Palaeolithic sites in Central Germany. He has published numerous academic and popular books and articles on Palaeolithic archaeology, human evolution and Pleistocene ecology and chronology.

Ursula Mania has been a member of the Bilzingsleben research group at the University of Jena for the last thirty years. She was involved in numerous excavations of important Palaeolithic sites in Central Germany, including Bilzingsleben and Neumark-Nord, and has published widely on Palaeolithic archaeology and human evolution.

John McNabb is a member of the Centre for the Archaeology of Human Origins at the University of Southampton. He is interested in the social aspects of technology and material culture with special reference to the Acheulean and the Lower Palaeolithic/Earlier Stone Age. He has worked extensively in Europe and Africa.

K. Paddayya is Director of Deccan College and Head of the Department of Archaeology. He has carried out archaeological investigations in the Hunsgi and Baichbal Valleys of Karnataka, India, for more than thirty years, identifying sites dating from the Lower to the Upper Palaeolithic. He has edited *Recent Studies in Indian Archaeology* (2002) and he has authored *The New Archaeology and Aftermath: A View from Outside the Anglo-American World* (1991).

Michael D. Petraglia is Lecturer in Human Evolution at the University of Cambridge. He has carried out Palaeolithic archaeology in South Asia and Arabia, the research centering on hominin adaptations and evolution of cognition and behaviour. He has edited *Early Human Behaviour in Global Context* (with Ravi Korisettar, 1998) and he has recently published the book

The Old World Paleolithic and the Development of a National Collection (with Richard Potts, 2004).

Matt Pope is a Research Fellow at the Institute of Archaeology, University College London and Deputy Director of the Boxgrove Research Project. He is interested in patterning the use, transportation and discard of artefacts by early humans, taphonomic processes and the geological context of Middle Pleistocene human occupation. He is currently exploring the role of bifacial technology and tool curation behaviour in Lower Palaeolithic hunting strategies and social organization.

Martin Porr is based at the Landesmuseum für Vorgeschichte in Halle, Germany. Most recently he has been involved as a project manager for a high-profile exhibition of the Bronze Age Sky Disc of Nebra, in co-operation with the National Museum of Denmark. He has published on theoretical issues of archaeology, Palaeolithic art and has edited *Ethno-Analogy and the Reconstruction of Prehistoric Artefact Use and Production* (with Linda R. Owen, 1999).

Mark Roberts is Principal Research Fellow at the Institute of Archaeology, University College London and has been Director of the Boxgrove Research Project since 1984. His research interests are the colonisation of Europe, Middle Pleistocene chronostratigraphy and its impact upon archaeological theory, and hominin behaviour during the Middle Pleistocene. He is currently undertaking the geological mapping of the Boxgrove sediments across the landscape of southern England. In 1994/95, he was awarded the Stopes medal for services to Quaternary geology and Palaeolithic archaeology.

Ceri Shipton is currently a PhD student in the Leverhulme Centre for Human Studies, University of Cambridge. He is currently carrying out archaeological investigations on the Acheulean assemblages of the Hunsgi and Baichbal Valleys, measuring the three-dimensional coordinates of bifaces. He is interested in the evolution of hominin cognition and sociality.

Anthony Sinclair is a Senior Lecturer at the School of Archaeology, Classics and Egyptology at the University of Liverpool. He is especially interested in the archaeology of the Palaeolithic and Mesolithic, with particular reference to technological planning and landscape use by gatherer-hunter groups in southern Europe, southern Africa and East Asia (Japan). He is co-director of the Makapansgat Middle Pleistocene Research Project, South Africa, and of a research project on the Archaeology of Carden Park, Cheshire.

Hartmut Thieme is employed at the Niedersächsisches Landesamt für Denkmalpflege at Hannover and is Director of the Department of Palaeolithic and Mesolithic Archaeology. Between 1973 and 1981 he conducted several excavations at the Middle Palaeolithic site of Rheindahlen (Germany). In 1982 he initiated and subsequently directed the large-scale excavation project at the open-cast mine of Schöningen, where from 1992 a number of Lower Palaeolithic sites were discovered and excavated. These sites have also yielded the oldest wooden hunting weapons from anywhere in the world.

Mark J. White is a Lecturer in Palaeolithic Archaeology at the University of Durham, UK. He is a core member of the Ancient Human Occupation of Britain Project (funded by the Leverhulme Trust) and has published widely on the British Lower and Middle Palaeolithic, including papers on handaxe variability, the Clactonian, palaeogeography and the emergence of Levallois technology.

Preface
Hominids and hominins

The idea for an edited book on the individual in the Palaeolithic started with a session on this topic, organised by the editors, at the Bournemouth meeting of the European Association of Archaeologists held in 1999. Several of the contributors to the present volume participated in this session. It was, however, soon apparent that the scope and scale needed broadening if we were to meet our two aims. These were to present the high-resolution data that Palaeolithic archaeologists have been recovering over the last three decades and to ask what can we do with them? Our focus on the individual as an appropriate unit of analysis raises many questions about how we currently approach the interpretation of Palaeolithic data. The challenge, we believe, is to existing concepts and theories of hominid behaviour precipitated by the virtuoso recovery of spatial evidence in many parts of the world. It is also a challenge to our perception and interpretation of the great range of hominin and hominid species. In this volume we have sampled such work in Africa, Asia and Europe during the Middle and Early Upper Pleistocene. We have included work from open and cave locales and in particular drawn attention to the spectacular but less well-known results from Germany. Neither have we opted for the easy ride by concentrating upon Palaeolithic Pompeiis. Instead, we have included palimpsest locales in caves and open contexts to demonstrate that looking for the individual is not confined to picking the plums from the tree.

We thank all our contributors for wrestling hard with the concept of the individual and for giving us their particular views on the issue supported by site, assemblage and artefact data. We are also very grateful to the efforts of our editing team at the Centre for the Archaeology of Human Origins at the University of Southampton: Natalie Uomini, Fiona Coward (who also compiled the index), Carina Buckley and Farina Sternke. Penny Copeland expertly redrafted some of the figures and Karol Schauer illustrated the individual hominids for our cover.

Finally, we make no editorial apology for any apparent lack of consistency between the chapters which follow over the use of hominid and hominin. The terms have been selected by authors as they see fit to classify and describe all our ancestors prior to the appearance of an equally contentious category, modern humans. If there is inconsistency it only serves to show how important the individual has always been in the interpretation of our earliest activities.

Chapter 1

From empty spaces to lived lives

Exploring the individual in the Palaeolithic

Clive Gamble and Martin Porr

Introduction

For too long the Palaeolithic was regarded by archaeologists as the most un-promising of all periods for the reconstruction of society and economy (e.g. Childe 1951; Wheeler 1954). However, in the past fifty years it has been demonstrated that this widespread impression has no basis either in the supposed lack of evidence or in its quality. Well-preserved, high-resolution sites are known from all periods and regions of the Palaeolithic world (e.g. Carr 1984; Conard 2001b; Cziesla *et al*. 1990; Gamble and Boismier 1991; Goring-Morris 1987; Hietala 1984; Kind 1985; Kroll and Price 1991) and from these have come abundant artefacts and ecofacts to examine such issues as site structure, *chaînes opératoires* and contextual associations at the scale of both the site and region. The dictum that archaeologists should dig for relationships not facts (Binford 1964) has become standard Palaeolithic practice and the results, as this volume shows, are impressive.

However, while Palaeolithic archaeologists have made the case for the study of economic adaptation and social change at Pleistocene timescales, they are now faced with a wealth of detail requiring further analysis and inter-pretation. It is time to re-examine what those relationships we are excavating might be. In order to start this examination we have selected the individual hominid as the focus for this book. We are aware that such a focus may not be readily accepted, even by some of our contributors, since the Palaeolithic is predominantly seen as the preserve of group behaviour and selection, especially in the Earlier Palaeolithic which we concentrate upon here.

Moreover, even among those who champion the individual as the locus for selection in a Neo-Darwinian approach the prospects for the Palaeolithic are regarded as grim: 'Ethnographies record the behaviour of individuals, a capacity that is beyond the techniques of archaeology today, and in the forseeable future' (Kelly 1995: 340). While we disagree with Kelly's pessimism (see Mania and Mania, Thieme, Pope and Roberts, Petraglia, Shipton and Paddayya, Adler and Conard this volume), neither must we confuse a richly detailed record, where the shadow of the individual can often be seen among the stones and bones, with the concept of the individual agent as the source for social and economic life. It is the latter concept which is our ultimate target. But we acknowledge that seeing those shadows in the empty spaces were the inspiration to consider the lived lives we want to investigate through our data. Our aim in this introduction is to explore these issues and provide a framework for the contributions which follow. Our goal in this volume is to showcase spatial and artefactual data from the Earlier Palaeolithic that range in archaeological integrity and temporal resolution from high to low, fine to coarse grain (Gamble 1986: 22–4), and ask: What should we be doing with them?

The paradigm of the collective

> The first thing you must realise is that power is collective. The individual only has power in so far as he ceases to be an individual
>
> George Orwell, *1984*

With hindsight, no one doubted that the archaeology of modern humans would yield high-resolution results and, at an early stage, the models of Star Carr (Clark 1954), Kostenki (Efimenko 1958) and Pincevent (Leroi-Gourhan and Brézillon 1966) pointed the way for their social and economic interpretation. In the subsequent half century the archaeology of the Lower and Middle, or Earlier, Palaeolithic has extended the high-resolution record back to the earliest appearance of stone tools. Among many such studies the work of Mary Leakey (1971) at Olduvai Gorge deserves special mention. Her model of hominid living floors, and its elaboration by Isaac (1978b, 1980) into home bases with central place foraging, proved immensely influential in raising expectations about the social and economic inferences which could be made from simple stone tools and scatters of bones. Subsequently these models were criticised (Binford 1981a) and a greater role assigned to carnivores and hydraulic processes. However, while some of the key sites such as Olduvai and Ambrona have been unflatteringly subjected to the taphonomic lens, there have been others such as Boxgrove (Pope and Roberts this volume), Wallertheim (Adler and Conard this volume), Schöningen (Thieme this volume), Bilzingsleben (Mania and Mania this volume) and Hunsgi (Petraglia, Shipton and Paddayya this volume) which have retained their integrity.

While we can congratulate ourselves on these achievements we also need to take stock of the interpretive frameworks that are applied to such evidence. While the Earlier Palaeolithic has been investigated at ever finer spatial and temporal scales our interpretations generally use a traditional unit of analysis. Palaeolithic archaeologists continue to affirm the primacy of the group, and the wider organisational system of adaptation, when it comes to understanding patterns in the data. Altogether, the successes of Palaeolithic archaeology in the last fifty years have been achieved at the expense of the individual.

One reason was the reaction during this period to the explanations of variation by culture historians. As summed up by Binford (1978b: 2), 'for many years . . . the dynamic standing behind an archaeological fact was thought to be simply the maker of the artefact'. The preferred dynamic was the organisational system (Flannery 1967: 106) because the intentions, motives and indeed decisions of individuals were regarded as invisible to the archaeologist and hence not amenable to scientific investigation (Clark 1992: 107). The system is archaeologically visible because it summarises the decisions made by individuals in the interests of adaptation, reproductive success, risk minimisation, competitive advantage and any other process which ensured their survival. To paraphrase Orwell (1949: 276), quoted above: in the Palaeolithic the individual only exists in so far as he ceases to be an individual.

The paradigm of the collective has been traced by Bettinger (1991: 153) and Kelly (1995: 48–53) to the neo-functionalism of cultural ecology (Steward 1936) and the techno-environmental determinism of cultural materialism (Harris 1968), both of which shaped the New Archaeology of the 1960s. As Bettinger (1991: 213 ff.) has rightly argued, such approaches are not evolutionary in a Darwinian sense because they express only a theory of consequences that stem from adaptation. Significantly, cultural ecologists attributed groups and populations with decision-making capacities that can, in fact, only reside with the individual (Kelly 1995: 48). Archaeological examples would include the Cambridge Palaeoconomy school (Higgs 1972, 1975) and numerous case studies with an adaptive focus inspired by the New Archaeology (e.g. selected papers in Bailey 1983, Binford 1977). The collective paradigm is also much broader since it includes Marxist approaches, although few Palaeolithic case studies exist (Bender 1978; Gilman 1984).

Neither is the paradigm of the collective confined simply to the study of occupations in caves and open sites. It is also applied to the analysis of artefacts and minds. Two examples will suffice. First, the widespread application of trace analysis to stone tools has added considerably to our understanding of the frequency of edge use and the function of some tool types. When combined with re-fitting, *chaîne opératoire* studies and experimental technology, a dynamism is returned to those site plans with piece-plotted data (Cziesla *et al.* 1990). Former movements of artefacts can now be visualised, and can be turned into traceable, short-term biographies as they move from 'cradle' to 'grave' within the excavated area (Close 2000), and sometimes between sites (Scheer 1993).

But, as Dobres (2000) has commented, when it comes to interpretation it is as if the evidence takes on a life of its own. And although reference is often made to individuals they remain abstract – demiurges to the will of the stones and bones – reminiscent of Richard Dawkins' (1976) view that bodies are just vehicles for genes to reproduce themselves which translates, in a Palaeolithic setting, into the statement that a hominid is just a way for a stone tool to make more stone tools (*pace* Dennett 1991). In other words, we all know that individuals were responsible, but we prefer a collective summary of the evidence.

Our second example concerns two influential models of the development of hominid minds. In his pioneering work, Wynn (1989, 1993a, 1993b) made inferences about the development of hominid cognition most notably through the analysis of the shape and manufacture of stone tools. In Mithen's (1996b) important study, the Palaeolithic mind is analysed in terms of discrete mental modules. The characteristics of different hominid species emerge from the degree of linkage and feedback between these cognitive compartments. Such a systemic approach to the mind is a good example of how a universal approach to the question of hominid cognition is achieved. This is possible by reference to a paradigm of the collective rather than one based on the individual. The mind, in both Wynn and Mithen's approaches, may be a social one but it is corporately owned and applied. In both models individuals are not given an active role and serve only as a background idea rather than a foreground principle in our evolutionary history.

Explaining the paradox

> Whatever the Party holds to be truth, is truth.
>
> George Orwell, *1984*

The successes of high-resolution Palaeolithic archaeology have therefore contributed paradoxically to the disappearance of the individual hominid. On the one hand field methods and analytical advances provide information on land use and the technological strategies of hominids, so that very detailed site histories and artefact biographies can now be reconstructed. To this end the excavation of high-integrity, high-resolution contexts reveals traces of precise, individual activity between 1.5 million and ~60,000 years ago, the time frame covered in this volume. These traces are preserved primarily as knapping and butchering events set within environmental contexts, which on occasion can be shown to have also been ephemeral when measured on a Pleistocene timescale. But on the other hand, these dramatic signatures of individual action, equally well represented by the single stone tool, cut-marked bone or piece of shaped ochre, are routinely analysed as collective action. The quality of data is not at issue. In fact, the Palaeolithic is better off than many later periods in archaeology where, aside from graves, 'special' deposits and the floors of Pompeii, most evidence comes from so-called secondary contexts such as middens, ditches and pits. The mobility of Palaeolithic hominids is a positive advantage for a study of the direct traces of individual activity through the archaeological record. But the general consensus is that this approach is neither possible nor desirable. And herein lies the paradox between data relating to individuals and their interpretation.

Why is this the case? We identify two main reasons. In the first place the success of the Palaeolithic is founded on an interdisciplinary approach designed to illuminate adaptation to ecological processes and changing environmental conditions. This has not always been done within an evolutionary framework. As forcefully represented in the writings of Lewis Binford, a scientific approach to Palaeolithic hominids requires an understanding of group dynamics where patterning can be causally related to the properties and organisation of environmental systems (see Gamble and Gaudzinski this volume). The unit of analysis in such a framework is therefore an aggregate of behaviour, and the purpose of enquiry is to understand variation in that aggregate. In this conception, interpretation in the Palaeolithic depends on a frame of reference that is universal – hence the various 'world-models' of hunters and gatherers that exist (Binford 2001; Kelly 1995).

Second, we must consider the importance of origins research in the Palaeolithic (Gamble and Gittins 2004). Questions such as the origins of modern humans, the origins of art and the origins of the hominid lineage structure Palaeolithic investigations (Alexandri 1995). Within archaeology more generally, the Palaeolithic provides an origin point for the many different approaches to the interpretation and reconstruction of societies in later prehistory and the historic, text-aided, periods. To put it in another way: very often the Palaeolithic has not been studied in its own right, but rather for its potential to shed light on to issues in later periods. Its importance is as a complete point of contrast to the complexities of culture, technology, settlement, economy and society that followed agriculture. As a result there has not been much interest, until recently, in exploring a social archaeology for the Earlier Palaeolithic (Gamble 1999). Neither is the individual a useful focus for Palaeolithic analysis if questions such as the origins of language and the human mind are being pursued. Individuals, by themselves, did not evolve tools, language, symbolism, bipedal locomotion or modern behaviour and therefore the individual as a unit of analysis is not needed.

A fresh look at the individual

> Even a back can be revealing.
>
> George Orwell, *1984*

So far it might be said: 'Well, if it ain't broke don't fix it!' and probably many Palaeolithic archaeologists would agree. However, we are then faced with a fundamental problem: Why bother to investigate the composition of sites, assemblages and industrial traditions when all that is needed are broad collectives set within a more precise chronological framework? Do we really need the spatial detail that is currently being produced at great expense? What exactly is the place and value of 'those rare and precious moments of contact between the archaeologist and another human being across ages of time' (Roe 1981: 197) within the existing scientific and origins-based approaches?

Keeping this in mind, it is interesting to note the differences between excavation strategies in Europe and Australia (e.g. Julien and Rieu 1999; Smith *et al.* 1993). In Europe attention has focused, where possible, on spatially extensive excavations of *in situ* camp sites. The detailed recording of spatial information at the micro-level implies that archaeologists *are* interested in the individual. But further inspection reveals a greater interest in using these data to unravel taphonomy and site formation. In Australia the focus has been rather different. Many sites, often rock shelters, have been sampled with small 'telephone-booth' size trenches. Multiple radiocarbon samples are obtained and artefacts and ecofacts counted against age-depth curves. The goal is to acquire regional information about phases of settlement and to identify changes in technology. The individual is unnecessary to such goals and the phone-booth sampling strategy is therefore entirely appropriate.

European archaeologists seem to have opted for an excavation strategy that is cost *in*-effective when it comes to addressing the research questions that really occupy Palaeolithic specialists. Those 'telephone booths' are very well suited to describe the transition from the Middle to the Upper Palaeolithic and to establish criteria to see where and when hominid behaviour became human by finding the oldest art and the right kind of fossil skulls. Moreover, the extension of new chronometric dating techniques beyond the range of radiocarbon in Africa and Asia has led to a longer timescale for the introduction of many cultural items and behaviours once thought the exclusive preserve of the last 40,000 years (Henshilwood and d'Errico this volume). As a result, the timing, pattern and process of change have become more complex and not necessarily as a result of those large area excavations.

Our suggestion is to amend the questions enshrined in the existing framework and to find within it a place for the individual. Currently there are two main pathways illustrated by several chapters in this book. First there are approaches stemming from behavioural ecology with its emphasis on the individual as the unit of selection in neo-Darwinian evolution. A promising line of enquiry is raised by cultural transmission theory (Shennan 2002) and is here touched upon in chapters which deal with palimpsest (Hosfield), cave (Henshilwood and d'Errico) and landscape data (Petraglia, Shipton and Paddayya). These enquiries take into account Kelly's (1995: 340) view that 'coarse as it may be, the archaeological record was nevertheless produced by the behaviour of individuals'.

The second pathway would replace behaviour in Kelly's quote with social actions. The chapters in this volume address artefacts (Porr, Field, Hopkinson and White, Gowlett, Pope and Roberts) and fauna (Gamble and Gaudzinski). They stem from our proven ability to see individuals in our micro-level data and the requirement to conceptualise them as a social and economic agent who created those patterns and so structured the archaeological record from the earliest Palaeolithic.

At the moment there is little common ground between these two approaches which champion the individual. The Palaeolithic naturally inclines to the paradigm of behavioural ecology and we welcome a more explicit evolutionary approach to the period. But this can only be done by recasting the individual as our unit of analysis. Such methodological individualism does not, of course, imply the scale at which evolutionary processes operate (Bettinger 1991: 153). It only refers to the initial approach and ultimately explanation can be either collective or individual as revealed by analysis.

Our concern here is more with the other approach derived from a social theory of action since this is alien to the Palaeolithic. To extend it we need a concept of the individual which is very different to those currently employed and which, in consequence, utilises the archaeological evidence differently based on concepts of material culture. In the interests of fostering this development further we will concentrate on the following five aspects:

- Explaining change
- Practice rather than behaviour
- The body
- Defining the social
- Time and the individual.

Explaining change

In our view the individual needs to be seen as the centre of causality in order to understand why change and variation occur. It is individuals that make decisions and deal with choices (Mithen 1993: 396). It is individuals that are active agents in the historical process.

This fundamental orientation has significant consequences. In Palaeolithic archaeology it is very easy to ascribe causality to environmental forces or forget that hominids, as people we could engage and interact with, were indeed present in the past. We consequently want to question the implication that the artefact record reflects a response to selection pressure dependent upon environmental changes, without any mediation by social agents.

Our view of the individual is consequently not simply rational but also relational (Gamble and Gaudzinski this volume). We see every hominid as an individual agent, someone who has a history and potentially a sense of self and personhood. We follow this route because we think that this is clearly suggested by sociology, anthropology, material culture studies and modern primate studies (Porr this volume). In choosing this theoretical orientation we do not want to be guided and restricted by the prevailing view of the available material and where a consideration of the significance of past lives is usually ruled out.

Instead we are responding, albeit with a different set of principles, to the challenge issued by Binford thirty years ago that:

> The practical limitations on our knowledge of the past are not inherent in the nature of the archaeological record; the limitations lie in our methodological naiveté, in our lack of development for principles determining the relevance of archaeological remains to propositions regarding processes and events of the past.
>
> (Binford 1972: 96)

To update the challenge we have deliberately chosen to restrict this book to the Lower and Middle Palaeolithic periods whose archaeological remains are often seen as the most unsuitable for providing answers to social questions, particularly those involving the individual. We may not have many answers at this stage but we recognise a need for a new standpoint, and ignoring modern humans for the moment has its advantages for developing such a conceptual perspective. For example, why should we deny a *Homo erectus* her or his full endowment of cognitive capabilities just because we know a *Homo sapiens* would later paint the cave of Lascaux? Such denials rest on the prior assumptions which govern origins research, assumptions that seem incongruous given that primate studies have successfully questioned similar denials for other hominids (Boesch and Boesch-Achermann 2000). We prefer Shennan's solution since it can be extended to all hominids and hominins, and hence the choice of the former in the title of our book.

> Assumptions about individuals are in fact behind any attempts at understanding past socio-economic change, or indeed social evolution. The basic ingredients required are *social actors* with *intentions*, who may or may not stand for more than themselves; *conditions of action*, acknowledged and unacknowledged; and *consequences*, intended and unintended.
>
> (Shennan 1993: 56 our emphasis)

Practice rather than behaviour

It is therefore necessary to look critically at our understanding of the mechanisms which guide and change practice in actors, both hominids and humans. We think that these processes need to be seen as much more flexible and dynamic than has been the case in the past.

We therefore want to critically question the use of the term 'behaviour' because it often carries with it reductionist and deterministic connotations. Behaviour often implies that the actions of hominids can effectively, and solely, be described in evolutionary and biological terms and consequently as products of genetic adaptations (Ingold 2000b). Individual actions are simply reduced to passive and mechanistic reactions.

While it is clear that evolutionary mechanisms have to be taken into account (Shennan 2002), we want to question the primacy that has been ascribed to these theories and the corresponding vocabulary in Palaeolithic archaeology. As an alternative to the familiar evolutionary terminology we suggest that notions from the social and cultural sciences should be integrated. Therefore, instead of 'behaviour' we prefer to use the term 'practice' to describe and explain the actions of hominids.

With the notion of practice we want to stress the dual character of human interactions with the environment. Practice is both a reaction as well as action. The agent not only responds, he or she also actively manipulates the material environment, which, in turn, necessitates further actions and reactions. In this way increasingly complex networks of people and material objects were created by hominids over time and space. They necessitated choices which cannot be accounted for by biological concepts alone. The patterns in the data have to be seen as the products of habits that are inscribed into actors during everyday activities. They are not the product of abstract symbolic or cognitive structures, but are created as a result of the active involvement of hominids in the world. As Gosden (1994: 35) has said, 'life itself, in the short or the long term, is not primarily to do with consciousness and structures of meaning, but rather to do with a set of habits created in the body'.

The body

If our attention is to be directed at the actions of individuals and how individuals acted and reacted in their environment, then the body also gains a new significance (Hamilakis *et al.* 2002a). Practice depends upon the body and is implicated in every social act. Before we can talk about the significance of tools or fauna, we need to consider the primary means of interaction, the body itself. In this regard we see the 'individual' as an embodied actor with a material existence in the world. The body holds a special position in that it is dynamic and material at the same time. It consequently can be considered as part of the 'material environment' of the actor or the actor itself. In any case, the specific materiality of the body gives the individual certain potentials and limitations in their interaction with the world. It is here that the aspects of sex, age and gender have to be considered and integrated into our thinking.

Furthermore, artefacts need to be seen in relation to the scales of bodily practice which include gestures, movements and perceptions (Thomas 1996). At the scale of the body itself we have to consider objects that to the observer form a part of it. Important here are body ornaments, which interestingly have little significance in the time periods we are dealing with in this book. From the perspective of how individuals were constituted in the Palaeolithic we should ask why? However, even ordinary artefacts such as the abundant stone tools of the Earlier Palaeolithic have the potential to visually change the boundaries and shape of the body when they are being made, carried and used.

As a result skin is not necessarily the surface of the individual. Sometimes material objects are integrated into the body such as tattoos and piercings. Often the body forms a unity with objects that are carried, worn or used such as clothing and tools. Furthermore, these artefacts are also the objects of exchange and intentional fragmentation (Chapman 2000) and in this way an individual's 'body' is distributed through social networks.

These malleable bodies, constructed biologically and culturally, need to be fully integrated into the scales of locales and landscapes. However, the emphasis is currently on the cognitive dimension of living at these scales, the choices and decisions made by the mind. These have been at the expense of the corpo-reality of hominids which also needs to be addressed as a source of memory, experience and symbolic force (Gamble in press). The Palaeolithic archaeologist may be able to see the shadows of individuals among the flint scatters but such distributions are not the same as acknowledging embodied-enminded actors (Field this volume). It is of less interest to reconstruct the stature of an individual from such shadows, or the organisational system which led them to sit there, than to recognise their embodied presence. Such presence has implications for their experience of place and, through the performance of their social lives, their wider landscapes (Gamble 1999: Table 3.1).

Defining the social

The body is also a network for interaction. We discussed above how the individual moves through and with a material environment that involves other individuals, other hominids. Our concept of the individual is a social actor constituted by his/her relation to these other individuals. As individuals we do not necessarily stop-at-the-skin nor find ourselves, in a cartesian sense, opposed to another category as in nature:culture, human:animal, hominid:hominin to establish who we are and why our social lives differ. The anthropological debate about Western and Melanesian forms of personhood (Bird-David 1999; Gell 1998; LiPuma 1998; Strathern 1988) provides an example that constructions of personhood are dependent on context rather than universal (Field this volume). We can assume nothing in the Palaeolithic except a comparable variety either for *Homo sapiens* or for *Homo erectus/ergaster*.

It is this unwillingness to consider variety that characterises the group approach to Palaeolithic society. This approach classically adopts a top-down route to identify social institutions such as Band society and the nuclear family (Johnson and Earle 1987). The social individual is lost in the collective of society. Instead, we favour a bottom-up approach using ego-centred networks as an analytical device (Gamble 1999), where we aim to investigate how individuals formed social groups and were formed by them. Variation is expected as an outcome of personal ability in the encounters and occasions where negotiation and the construction of social life took place. A tension between 'the individual' and 'the group' will always remain and even needs to be regarded as a fundamental creative aspect in human evolution. While groups certainly exist what we question is their primacy as analytical devices for the social dimensions of Palaeolithic data.

Time and the individual

One of the central characteristics of Palaeolithic archaeology is the enormous difference that seems to separate human actions and processes on a geological scale. Episodes in daily life have to be linked to developments that took thousand, of years. The results of dealing with this problem within the discipline are often unsatisfactory. Usually the impression is that long-term and short-term processes were separate and that they developed independently. The perspective of the individual draws attention to the fact that we are only seeing different effects that are causally related to the same processes: the actions of individual hominids.

Consequently, we want to question the dichotomy of the 'long term' and the 'short term' (Bailey 1983). We believe that new notions and approaches are necessary to address the mechanisms which produce change and stability in the actions of hominids. The so-called 'long-term changes' have to be conceptualised as accumulations of individual changes in behaviour and practice, and their transmission from one individual to the other.

We therefore need a rethinking of the relations between 'long-term' effects that can be observed in the archaeological record and the actions of individuals who, in their lifetime, never consciously perceived any changes at all. Why and how did small changes initiated by the individual develop into recognisable changes? Why do these processes have stability and direction over long periods of time and across space? Palaeolithic archaeologists need to establish an understanding of the individual's perspective and the factors that influenced actions within human timescales. Only if processes at this scale are understood will it be possible to make temporal comparisons. Many Palaeolithic archaeologists hold that practical problems militate against this kind of approach. In Earlier Palaeolithic contexts science-based age estimates, such as U/Th, have standard errors that can span tens of thousands of years. Two scatters of flints and bones in the same geological layer might be separated by the time between the invention of agriculture and the fall of the Berlin Wall. While time-averaging is a fact of Palaeolithic enquiry (Hosfield this volume), on occasion the archaeological contents of a single paleosol, traced across a wide region, refers to no more than the average life span of an individual hominid (Pope and Roberts this volume).

We do not want to deny the issue of contemporaneity or temporal resolution. However, our solution is to consider temporality rather than time alone. Temporality refers to the activities and processes that occur within time. It forms a series of interlinked rhythms rather than the sequential measurement of age. Temporality provides a structure for the social life of the individual.

Palaeolithic archaeology, as the chapters in this volume abundantly show, has the resolution to move from the particular, the day-in-the-life (Sinclair and McNabb this volume) to the palimpsest of an isotope stage (Hosfield this volume).

Conclusion

> Reality exists in the human mind, and nowhere else. Not in the individual mind, which can make mistakes, and in any case soon perishes.
>
> George Orwell, *1984*

If Palaeolithic archaeologists ever had to enter George Orwell's infamous Room 101 most of them, we suspect, would encounter the threat of the individual. Why is this concept the bogeyman of the subject? Because once acknowledged the individual is difficult to accommodate within the existing paradigm. He/she suggests variance in spatial and artefact data (Gowlett this volume) that are normally regarded as lacking such attributes over vast territories and immense time periods. The individual therefore questions the current practice of the Palaeolithic, so better to hide the concept in the box marked 'scientifically unamenable'.

Our aim in this book is to use the individual to breathe some alternative social life back into the data of human ancestry. The Palaeolithic has many models and national traditions of research. Regional studies and the synthesis of diverse evidence on fauna, artefacts, art and environment characterise a truly global study endowed with some remarkably well-preserved and many horrendously ravaged data. The individual offers Palaeolithic archaeologists the means to expand their theoretical and analytical horizons with respect to this evidence. We can do this if we conceive of the individual as a unity of mind and body, collapse the taxonomy of hominid, hominin and human and so allow us to study those lived lives in the empty spaces before us.

Acknowledgements

We are grateful for comments from Claire Forshaw, John McNabb and the participants at the 1999 session presented to the European Association of Archaeologists at Bournemouth.

Chapter 2

The Acheulean and the handaxe

Structure and agency in the Palaeolithic

Terry Hopkinson and Mark J. White

Introduction

Palaeolithic archaeology is in large degree an exercise in generalisation. Our interpretive stocks-in-trade – lithic industrial cultures and their succession in time and space, adaptive hominid behaviour systems, and descriptive taxonomies of reduction strategies – are all devices for deriving systematic generalisations from the variability evident in the Palaeolithic record. These in turn direct our search for, and confer significance on, the kinds of patterns we find in our data. We are conditioned by our own discipline's history to produce narratives of Palaeolithic prehistory dealing exclusively with 'high-level' domains that transcend the individual in time and space. In consequence stone artefacts have been rendered the products first and foremost of the overarching entity to which we assign them. Handaxes, for example, have become products of 'the Acheulean', while the past individuals responsible for fabricating, transporting, using and discarding them are reduced to mere passive instruments of this higher power to which our gaze must be directed if the real causative factors that shaped handaxes are to be revealed.

The contributions to this volume express a growing unease with this disciplinary habit. Can we so readily dismiss the role played by the individual in shaping the character and trajectories of hominid experience in those distant times? We think not. Without real, acting individuals, there can be – in the past as in the present – no societies, traditions or culture systems (Gamble 1998a, 1999). Just as there can be no generalising disciplinary tradition without individual Palaeolithic archaeologists writing such narratives, so there could be no Acheulean without individuals that made handaxes. If we are to move beyond one-sided accounts of the deep past, an understanding of an active, rather than passive, role for individuals is required. Only exceptionally has this been a central focus of investigation (e.g. Schlanger 1996; Gamble 1998b, 1999).

This is especially true of the perennially intractable problem of the Acheulean handaxe. It is necessary to assert that making and using handaxes, and doing so in particular ways, is something that *individuals* in the Lower Palaeolithic sometimes *did*. The problem is therefore, at root, a behavioural one that can be reduced to two fundamental and closely related overarching questions: Why and how did hominids make, use and discard handaxes? Why and how did they do so as they did at particular times and places, and differently or similarly at other times and other places? We are, then, embroiled in a wider problem, that of why individuals do what they do. In other words, what are the factors and principles that generate, maintain and transform particular behaviours – or, if one dislikes the ethological tone of that term, *practices?*

A refocusing of attention on the Palaeolithic, and particularly the Acheulean, individual should not be taken to imply a denial of the importance of other scale domains of Pleistocene hominid history. The generalising imperative remains essential for the production of non-trivial archaeologies capable of making sense of the vast spatial, temporal and evolutionary sweep of Pleistocene. Here we consider how the problem of practice, the individual and the supra-individual in the Palaeolithic has been understood hitherto, and then offer our own thoughts on how the individual domain might be incorporated into our understanding of the Acheulean and of the handaxe.

Structured systems, individual agents and the problem of practice

Structure and the collective

From the perspective outlined here, the tendency to locate the dynamics responsible for shaping past practices in a domain beyond that of the individual can be seen as a disciplinary emphasis on structure, broadly understood to mean those properties of human collective entities that constrain or determine the way the individuals of which they are comprised act and interact. Over the last century this has most typically been expressed in terms of the normative culture. Structure here is conceived as a mentalistic or cognitive phenomenon, a prescribed set of beliefs, values and templates for action. The actions, including technical actions, perpetrated by an individual are governed by the normative prescriptions of the culture of which they are a member. The Acheulean culture is characterised by 'the handaxe' as an ideal type, a prehistoric *idea* of 'handaxe'. An individual knapper might have been the instrument that effected a particular handaxe, but as a specific practice it is a product of a transcendent behaviour-structuring power, the Acheulean culture, to which individuals and their actions are entirely subordinated. Particular handaxes are material expressions or exemplars of this culture. As with the handaxe, so with Palaeolithic artefacts generally; knappers are reduced to mere undifferentiated products of the cultural entity that created them, with no power to generate or transform the practices they themselves enact. This remains true even if one sees cultural norms as procedural, as opposed to formal, in character (e.g. Gowlett 1984, 1996a).

Processual and functionalist approaches in Palaeolithic archaeology reject this mentalism but are no less committed to the primacy of supra-individual structures in the shaping of hominid behaviour. The collective entity is instead generally understood in terms of the adaptive system and the network of causal relations between social and ecological system components. Although this perspective has in fact made little contribution to our understanding of the Acheulean, possibly because of the paucity of Acheulean sites with artefacts in primary depositional context, it has an important presence in the archaeology of the Oldowan (e.g. Isaac 1978a; papers in Oliver *et al.* 1994; Domínguez-Rodrigo 2001). Whatever the object of analysis, functionalism in Palaeolithic archaeology, as in archaeology more generally, presents behaviour as emerging from the structured organisation of a system understood as a thing-like working object immersed in a natural ambient to which it must adapt. Structure is understood as a material fact and the determination of behaviour by objective forces as comparable in status with natural law. The individual becomes no more than a cog in a functioning machine. The organising impulse is to follow Flannery (1967) in searching not for the Indian behind the artefact, but for the system or process behind both.

Resistance to the notion that individuals in the Lower and Middle Palaeolithic in particular possessed any creative or causative power is in part a consequence of a prior disciplinary dual standard, a conviction that non-modern hominids existed in an essentially animal-natural state with little capacity for purposive thought and action (Roebroeks and Corbey 2001). Taken together with the discipline's historical roots in geology and palaeontology, this underwrites a preference for interpretations from which past subjectivity is absent. More crucially, the coarse-grained and time-averaged nature of much of the Palaeolithic record, especially in the Acheulean, renders patterned regularities in the accumulated products of many individuals far more visible and robust than the particular individual act. This is one reason why the drive to generalisation ought not to be dismissed as mistaken. Normativism and functionalism both strive to reveal, describe and understand real archaeological data-patterning relating to enormously significant temporal and spatial domains of deep human history. Both make indispensible contributions to our understanding of early hominids. But their lack of interest in the individual limits their interpretive power. Of course, individuals are recognised as the entities that actually knapped the stone artefacts we recover; but *that* they knapped, *what* they knapped and *how*, are portrayed as determined by over-arching structural forces of which the individual was a passive instrument. The individual in the Palaeolithic has therefore been cast as a mere epiphenomenon (Hopkinson 2001).

The illusory individual

This seems quite out of kilter with our contemporary Western culture of individualism. We live today in the age of the apparently sovereign individual in pursuit of his or her own goals and believe ourselves to be the authors of our own fates, not the witless slaves of 'The System'. Why then should we deny this sovereignty to individuals in the past? We can choose instead to recognise the Acheulean individual as a knowledgeable subject possessing the property of agency, the power of the individual to perpetrate acts and bring about effects.

In fact, despite the powerful disciplinary presumption in favour of the primacy of structure, the past individual has indeed been present in some archaeologies of the Lower and Middle Palaeolithic. Intra-site spatial analysis and refitting of assemblages from high-resolution *in situ* deposits have permitted the reconstruction of, for example, particular handaxe-knapping events and their localisation in the space of real past individuals (Roberts and Parfitt 1999) and of the skilled, practical decisions taken in the course of reducing a single Levallois core (Schlanger 1996). The reconstruction of such action sequences is perhaps the most useful treatment of real individuals that the archaeology of the Lower and Middle Palaeolithic has yet achieved. But if we attempt to go beyond these single events to ask fundamental behavioural questions – why did the Boxgrove knappers make handaxes whereas those at Maastricht Belvedere used the Levallois method to produce flakes, for example – then we are forced to generalise from the particular and to make the individual act an essential expression of a regional industry or species-wide mode of behaviour. The Middle Pleistocene knappers at Boxgrove made handaxes, so they were Acheulean and their handaxe-making behaviour can be taken as read; being Acheuleans, they were bound to behave in this way. This circularity of reasoning leaves little room for the creative individual and amounts to an implicit assertion of the primacy of structure.

In addition, a kind of abstracted individual has been an important figure in some economic approaches to lithic-industrial variability in the Lower and Middle Palaeolithic. These proceed from the 'economic actor' premise that structural entities have no reality. Only individuals, and their disposition rationally to pursue economic self-interest, are real (Hayek 1949; Elster 1983). All patterned regularities in human life are simple aggregates of, and must therefore be reduced to, the activities of decision-making, ego-centred individuals. We can see such figures in Dibble and Rolland's work on Middle Palaeolithic industrial variability (Rolland and Dibble 1990; Dibble and Rolland 1992) in which individuals as conscious economic actors are confronted with a world of finite material resources unevenly distributed in time and space. Within this they make informed decisions about raw material procurement, transport, reduction and discard that depend on conscious knowledge of environmental constraints and proximate goals. The free individual makes choices which, when aggregated over time and space and over many individuals, incidentally generate the patterned typological and technological variability visible in Mousterian stone tool industries and which François Bordes famously interpreted in normative terms as the cultural markers of ethnically discrete Neanderthal tribes in the southwest of France (Bordes 1961; Mellars 1996a: 169–83).

In reality, however, Dibble and Rolland's Middle Palaeolithic knappers have no freedom of choice at all. In solving the problems posed by environmental forces and functional imperatives over which they have no control, they are governed by a universal decision-making economic logic deriving from their Malthusian status as organisms in a world of finite resources. Faced with specific conjunctures of local geology and geography, demography and climatically determined ranging territory size, they are disposed to respond in the same predictable and optimal way. Any individuals whose behaviour departs from this optimum are supplanted through universal forces such as natural selection (Torrence 1989a, b). The behaviour evidenced in the archaeological record therefore represents a central tendency towards a single 'best solution' visible to archaeologists through statistical analysis. Behavioural variation about this central tendency is simply trivial noise. Neanderthal knappers are reduced to passive conduits along which 'input signals' from external stimuli travel until a determined Bordian Mousterian facies 'output' emerges at the other end. Individual behaviour is therefore governed by the obligate application of a general structuring principle – economic rationalism – which disposes all individuals to respond in the same specified manner to given system conditions. Behaviour again emanates exclusively from structural constraints external to individual consciousness and purpose.[1] Several recent attempts to explain handaxe form, including McPherron's reduction model (1994), White's raw material model (1998) and Kohn and Mithen's sexual selection model (1999) similarly conform to a template in which apparently purposeful individual behaviour is in reality determined by functional calculations, whether conscious or otherwise, that brook only a single optimal solution to externally specified problems.

Structuration and the reconciliation of structure with agency

The marginalisation of the individual in the Palaeolithic – explicit or implicit – raises a number of problems. Structural entities like cultures and ecosystems are not physical objects, and their nature and reality are contentious. Not being sentient, embodied organisms they lack consciousness, purpose and knowledge and they have no capacity to engage physically with or impact upon the world, except through the agency of the individual. Neither the Acheulean nor *Homo heidelbergensis* as categories ever made a single handaxe; each one was created through the knowledgeable action of its individual maker(s). Yet we have seen that the entirely free individual, whose dispositions and decisions are utterly unprecedented and owe nothing to external constraints or received dispositions – like Nietzsche's Superman (Nietzsche 1954) or Sartre's revolutionary (Sartre 1962), recasting the world anew in a single bound of the unfettered will – is unimaginable, except as a philosophical aspiration, even for those who seek to place the individual at the centre of analysis. We have an apparent paradox: structure-centred explanations of the generation of practices fall because they do not account for the constant presence of the individual agent; but individual-centred approaches seem compelled to make appeals, even if clandestine, to determining structures that precede and transcend the individual.

A solution to this conundrum is offered by Giddens' concept of structuration (Giddens 1981, 1984). His central thesis is that: 'all human action is carried on by knowledgeable agents who both construct the social world through their action, but yet whose action is also conditioned or constrained by the very world of their creation' (Giddens 1981: 54). Action proceeds from a set of structuring principles deriving from a social domain that transcends and precedes the individual, equips them with a rationale for life and disposes them to act in particular ways. But at the same time these principles cannot be manifest except insofar as they are expressed in the acts of real individual agents and can only be reproduced and transmitted in time and space through such acts. What is more, not only do social individuals pursue their own particular goals, they are also positioned differently in the world, so there can be no invariant set of dispositions to act, no universal rationale for life. Actions have consequences that ripple out across social time and space, and some of these consequences are likely to be unforeseen and unintended. Consequently, action is chronically liable to throw up new contexts and circumstances for future action, and thus new practices. Much of the knowledge that guides action is habitual and intuitive rather than conscious and reflective, and is founded on routine and repetition (Gosden 1994). New practices, if repeated, therefore produce and reproduce new structuring principles of action. Practices might indeed *con*form to prior structures, but, reversing the direction of causality, they might equally *trans*form structure. Practices are said to be *structurated*.

From a structurationist standpoint, neither structure nor agency can be understood as prior to the other in the generation, reproduction and transformation of practices. In Giddens' terms, structure is both medium and outcome of practice. There is a duality of structure, a mutually determining dynamic relationship between the things people do and the things they are disposed to do. From this point of view it is no more useful to think of institutions, culture, or society as emerging from the individual in a 'bottom-up' process than it is to imagine the individual act as constituted entirely through the 'top-down' tyranny of the collective entity. Our actions and fates are not predestined, but neither are we free to 'construct the world and then live in it' (Gamble 1993: 19). After all, where would we live before it was finished? Life is rather a constant *re*construction and *re*production of a world in which we are already located and into which we were born. History is that process of constant reconstruction, reproduction and (intended or unintended) transformation of the terms and conditions of practical social life. Patterning in the archaeological record, including the Acheulean record, is a trace of specific dynamics of persistence and change that emerged from the interplay of structured dispositions and creative individual agents in experienced time and space.

Projects for living

Although the value of structuration theory for interpretation of the archaeology of later prehistory has been recognised for some time (Shanks and Tilley 1987b; Barrett 1987, 1994; Barrett *et al.* 1991) only recently has this begun to percolate into thinking about the Palaeolithic (e.g. Dobres 2000; Gamble 1999: 38–40; Hopkinson 2001; Sinclair 2000; Wobst 2000). It is essential that, from the outset, the limits of its applicability to Palaeolithic archaeology are understood. Giddens shows little interest in the relation between practices and the propertied material world or 'environment'. He is silent on how environmental variation in time and space might challenge and transform the structuring principles of action. These are central considerations in the Palaeolithic archaeology and should certainly remain so. Giddens also offers no specific investigation of the structuration of technical practices. He limits himself instead to asserting the centrality of *signification* to structurated practices (Giddens 1984: 31–3). Yet our concern here is precisely with the production of Acheulean handaxes, the incorporation of which into realms of signification or symbolism cannot be assumed. Finally, despite his interest in persistent social institutions, nowhere in his account of structuration does Giddens grapple with the timescales that confront Palaeolithic archaeology, nor with the kinds of processes that might be apparent only on such timescales. These shortcomings need to be addressed if structuration theory is to form the basis of an archaeology of the Palaeolithic individual.

Nevertheless, Gamble is correct in identifying structuration theory as a way forward to a more balanced understanding of the generation of practices in the Palaeolithic in that the interplay between received structuring principles and their manifestation in contextually appropriate individual action is plausibly a universal feature of all modes of learned behaviour acquired through socially mediated experience. Even chimpanzee technical practices might be thought of as structurated, given the growing evidence for learned and regionally specific chimp technical traditions (McGrew 1992; Whiten *et al.* 1999; van Schaik and Pradhan 2003).

The solution lies in broadening the concept of structure. Although Giddens does not acknowledge it, structuration theory can be seen as an expression in sociology of a much wider body of ideas concerned with the relationships between domains of scale in the natural world (Hopkinson 2001). Evolution through natural selection, for example, also deals with the structuring properties of a collective entity – the species or gene pool – which is manifest, reproduced and transformed only through its variable expression in behaving individuals. Grene has taken this even further and identified this 'dual asymmetry', in which 'high-level' constraints and 'low-level' constrained processes are mutually dependent, as a pervasive feature of ecological and other systems organised on multiple scales (Grene 1969; O'Neill *et al*. 1986).

So we are not compelled to operate within Giddens' narrow purview of the nature of structure. What we are interested in is structured and structuring dispositions to act in certain ways not only towards other people, *but also in and on the material world* of which other people are not the only components. But the material world has real properties, independent of human engagement and understanding. The character of the world impacts upon what people can do with and to it, and with what we can say about it (Gosden 1994). The things people do are indeed structured by the properties of the material ambient in which they are immersed.

This does not mean, however, that we can safely abandon our present concern with the knowlegeable handaxe-making individual in favour of an exclusive reliance on adaptive behavioural systems operating within objectified and determining ecological parameters, since the ecological properties of the material world are not unambiguous. Although the properties of substances and objects underwrite the opportunities and dangers that they afford to organisms (Gibson 1979), what those affordances are depends upon the organism itself. For example, a leaf is an object that affords eating to a deer. To a fly, the same leaf is a surface that affords rest, and to a caterpillar it is both (Hopkinson 2001). What the properties of the world mean to an organism is therefore a function of its own being, its mode of orientation to the world which is transmitted to it from its predecessors and which confers upon it a way of perceiving the world, of appropriating it into its own scheme and acting accordingly. Ingold has called this the *project for living* (Ingold 1986).

To a degree the project for living can be equated with 'lifeway' or with 'adaptation', in the sense that the latter is often used in Palaeolithic archaeology (e.g. Svoboda *et al*. 1996). Where it differs is in its conceptualisation of the relationship between organism and environment. Adaptation, understood to mean both a functioning way of life and the process that generates it, is predicated in contemporary neo-Darwinist evolutionary and ecological thinking on a radical separation between the organism and a recalcitrant environment that is external to it. The organism, population, community or species adapts to its environment and is therefore defined by it. The relationship is that of jelly to a mould. The project for living, on the other hand, recognises the ambiguity of the propertied material world. Each organism renders the world an environment by virtue of its own terms of engagement with it. Therefore, organisms themselves define the nature of their own environments, which emanate in part from within them (Rose *et al*. 1984: 275). For all organisms, their project for living is literally embodied in their cellular, physiological and anatomical architecture, which represents a historically transmitted store of knowledge. But for the higher vertebrates at least, and especially for human beings, the bodily property of mindedness adds another pole to the dynamic of the project for living, namely conscious knowledge acquired through socially mediated experience.[2]

Like Giddens' structure, projects for living are characterised by duality. They can be considered as structuring principles of action, residing in supra-individual domains and transmitted through and across supra-individual time and space, that equip individuals with a prior position in and precedented dispositions towards the world. On the other hand, these principles are expressed and reproduced only in such individuals and their life actions and are prone to transformation in reproduction since individuals, and the practical contexts for action that they encounter, vary in time and space. But the project for living departs from the structuration concept, which remains purely mentalistic in a normative or classic structuralist sense, in its additional incorporation of materiality into the historical dynamic of duality, mutuality and knowledgeability. In recognising the body as an anatomical and physiological entity with capabilities and requirements, and the material environment as a constraining and propertied physical ambient, the project for living embraces ecology and evolution precisely where Giddens is suspicious and even hostile. Environmental variation in space and change through time, by transforming the world that individuals encounter and their actions and fates within it, can impact upon the reproduction of a project for living and thus transform it. Structure conceived in this broader way is generated, expressed and transformed not only through practical social encounters between people, but also between people and things, including stone, stone tools and the things to which they were applied.

The Acheulean and the handaxe

We begin by drawing a fundamental distinction between the Acheulean and an individual handaxe. The Acheulean is a socially mediated, historically transmitted structuring principle, a technological aspect of a received project for living and acting in the world. An individual handaxe, on the other hand, is the outcome of one or more particular and purposeful acts perpetrated by one or more knowledgeable agents in specific social and material circumstances. It was produced because a Middle Pleistocene knapper, on encountering these circumstances and resolving on a purpose, was disposed to work stone in a way that produced an object we call a handaxe. They were so disposed by virtue of their socialisation into a project for living that organised the world and action in it in part through the knowledge, skill and practice of this mode of stone-working. The key point is that the knowledgeable disposition to sometimes work stone in this manner both structured the practice of handaxe fabrication and was structured and reproduced by it. Inherent in this is the possibility that, by producing handaxes differently, the knapper might transform the Acheulean. The extent to which the Acheulean was subject to transformation in this way is considered below. It is worth noting here, however, that by not producing handaxes at all for social or material reasons, individuals could effect the loss of this practice from the project for living. This may lie behind the absence of handaxes in some European Lower Palaeolithic assemblages, including virtually all known from east of the Rhine and north of the Alps, and those attributed to the Clactonian industry in Britain (Mithen 1994; White 2000).

A key implication of this approach is that both the individual agent *and* the structuring properties of the socially received project for living are always present in both the Acheulean and in the particular handaxe. Large-scale overviews of handaxe variability (e.g. Wynn and Tierson 1990) can address the stability or otherwise of the Acheulean as a phenomenon in space and time, but, without a recognition of the role of the agent as knowledgeable subject, they lack a convincing dynamic of behaviour to which variation and similarity can be referred. Equally, virtuoso reconstructions of handaxe-knapping and use events can illuminate a real individual, but without an explicit awareness of the role of structure simply cannot place the individual's actions in an adequate context.

Handaxe form and raw material

One of us (White 1998) has previously developed a model of handaxe morphological variation in the British Acheulean that proceeds essentially from 'economic actor' assumptions. A re-examination of this analysis may serve to illuminate the roles of received structure and individual agency in the handaxe phenomenon. White examined 1,300 handaxes from twenty-two British assemblages and was able to show that the well-known opposition between assemblages dominated by ovate handaxes and those dominated by pointed handaxes (Roe 1968, 1981) could be understood in terms of the size and shape of the blanks employed for handaxe fabrication. Point-dominated assemblages employed primarily small, elongate nodules derived from gravel sources, whereas ovate-dominated assemblages mainly exploited large nodules or flakes procured from primary flint sources, such as chalk. Analysis of the technological attributes characteristic of ovate and pointed handaxes suggested that hominids had employed different knapping strategies to deal with these different resources. Elongate nodules limited the technological choices open to the knapper, but at the same time afforded a path of least resistance though the material. By concentrating work at the tip, leaving a thick, minimally worked butt, a pointed handaxe was produced. Large nodules or flakes on the other hand presented fewer constraints and the knapper had greater freedom to impose desired form. In these situations they usually made ovates. Acheulean hominids had therefore tailored a flexible biface-making strategy to deal with the variety of raw materials they encountered as they moved through and engaged with their world.

White concluded that this apparent preference for ovates indicated a functional preference for that form, although he had previously considered that it might simply reflect the outcome of habitual rhythms of making in which the process of bifacial knapping was not compromised by the constraints imposed by elongate blanks (White 1996). We now reject this polarisation and see handaxe production and use instead as a complex interplay between social, material and functional factors, and as drawing upon both consciously thought-out and habituated knapping knowledge and skill. For present purposes, however, the significance of White's analysis lies in its demonstration that, *contra* Wenban-Smith (2000), handaxe variability in the British Acheulean is not to be understood in terms of subtly different and socially discrete 'pointed' and 'ovate' cultural entities, whose individual members were compelled to make handaxes of a single culturally determined form. Rather, pointed and ovate handaxes were underwritten by *the same* repertoire of knapping knowledge. Variation in handaxe form arose from the differential and contextually appropriate application of this received knowledgeability to diverse real-world situations *by individual knappers*. Handaxe fabrication and particular form emerged from the mutuality between the structuring principle and its variable realisation by knowledgeable individual agents in the course of their practical engagement with their environments. In fact the fine detail of formal variation and similarity among the ovate handaxes from Foxhall Road, Ipswich, England (Figure 2.1) may be evidence for knapping styles, 'hands' or 'signatures' unique to particular individuals (White and Plunkett in press).

Persistence and change in the Lower Palaeolithic

If handaxe fabrication in the British Acheulean was indeed a structurated practice as we suggest, it was nevertheless clearly of a different kind from those of contemporary Western societies on which Giddens' concept of structuration is based. The transformation of structure through practice discussed earlier is not much in evidence in White's dataset. The twenty-two sites considered cover a time span of 250–300,000 years between Oxygen Isotope Stages 13 and 8, and probably beyond. Yet the fabrication of handaxes, and the flexible responses to raw material constraints that generate their morphological variability, persist apparently unchanged through this immense period of time. The Lower Palaeolithic seems to have been very different from the modern world, in which technologies and technical practices are repeatedly transformed over much shorter time spans. Even by comparison with later prehistory the persistence of technical practices through time in the Lower Palaeolithic is remarkable.

Of course, stone tools alone do not constitute a project for living. Their fabrication, use and transport were links in chains of action that connected to

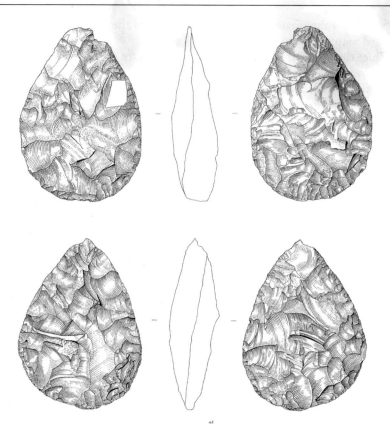

Figure 2.1 Two technologically and typologically identical handaxes found by Miss Nina Layard at Foxhall Road, Ipswich. The handaxes were found *in situ*, lying together around a supposed hearth in association with other paired groups. (Illustration by Yvonne Beadnell. White area = Layard's original paper label.)

all acts perpetrated in the lived landscape. To grasp the projects of which Lower Palaeolithic stone artefacts were a part, one must therefore take into account dimensions of the archaeological record other than stone tool typology and technology. But if we consider the European Lower Palaeolithic from the point of view of settlement and mobility, it becomes apparent that strategies in these realms showed an extraordinary persistence comparable to that of handaxe manufacture.

One of us (Hopkinson 2001), in a review of the evidence for the occupation of central Europe before 200,000 years ago, identified only thirteen robustly dated archaeological horizons with at least 100 unequivocal artefacts in the region east of the Rhine, north of the Alps and west of the Black Sea. Of these, nine (Memleben, Schöningen 12, Schöningen 13, Bilzingsleben II Travertine, Ehringsdorf, Markkleeberg, Wallendorf, Kärlich-Seeufer and Miesenheim I) are in Germany, at the westernmost edge of central Europe. Only Bilzingsleben II, Schöningen 13, Markkleeberg, Vérteszöllös and Korol'evo VI can be regarded as major sites. There are many more in southern England alone (Roe 1981). It seems that Lower Palaeolithic occupation in temperate Europe was strongly concentrated in the oceanic, low-seasonality west where the winter dearth was less severe and seasonal variations in food resource availability were less marked than to the east. Occupation of central Europe in this period seems to have been possible only in episodes of marked local and regional climatic oceanicity (Frenzel 1973: 104–11; Rousseau et al. 1990). Since systematic occupation of temperate western Europe was established no later than 500,000 years ago (Roebroeks 2001), this pattern represents the persistence for as much as 300,000 years of a particular mode of appropriating environmental heterogeneity in time into ways of life. Only with the advent of the Middle Palaeolithic does the systematic occupation of climatically continental, high-seasonality central and eastern Europe begin (Svoboda et al. 1996; Hoffecker 2002).

Hopkinson (2001) has also shown that, in addition to this persistent orientation towards low levels of seasonality, the Lower Palaeolithic inhabitants of Europe avoided regions of high topographical relief, even in the west of the continent. The Palaeolithic of the Dordogne is overwhelmingly of Upper Pleistocene age,[3] and the Lower Palaeolithic is absent, or virtually so, from the Cantabrian Mountains, the Massif Central, the Vosges, the karstic uplands of the Meuse Valley, the Upper Danube and the Carpathians. Occupation instead is powerfully associated with plains landscapes in the middle and lower reaches of drainage systems. While this might in part reflect the limited lifespan of caves in limestone uplands, this cannot fully explain the paucity of evidence for Lower Palaeolithic occupation of Europe's high-relief regions.

The answer seems to lie in the spatial grain of Pleistocene vegetation communities in these regions. Evidence from a range of proxies and from many parts of the world shows that high-amplitude temperature oscillations operating on wavelengths of two or three millennia were a pervasive feature of Pleistocene global climate (Dansgaard et al. 1993; Little et al. 1997; Oppo et al. 1998; Raymo et al. 1998; Schultz et al. 1998). From an ecological stand-point these were catastrophes repeated on ecological timescales. The compact vegetation patches typical of plains landscapes have low edge:centre ratios, a property which permits them to support both edge and centre-dwelling species and limits their reactivity with surrounding patches. In the Pleistocene this acted as a buffer against catastrophe-induced patch and species loss. By contrast, and unlike the Holocene, the elongate, altitudinally defined patches typical of hilly and mountainous landscapes displayed much higher edge:centre ratios, supported fewer centre-dwelling species, showed higher reactivity with the surrounding environment and were in consequence much less resistant to catastrophic destruction. The equilibrium spatial structure in Pleistocene plains mosaics was therefore high-diversity and fine-grained in character, with a wide range of species in close spatial proximity, whereas high-relief landscapes were coarser-grained and of lower species diversity (Hopkinson 2001). The Italian Apennine mountains, which did support Lower Palaeolithic human occupation, were exceptional in that finer-grained mosaics were present (Mussi 1995), possibly as a consequence of volcanic activity.

Taken together, the impoverished occupations of highly seasonal and of coarse-grained landscapes suggest that projects for living in the European Lower Palaeolithic were persistently directed towards high levels of resource proximity in space and time. Just as the practice of handaxe fabrication persisted with little change through glacial cycles (Roberts *et al.* 1995; Tuffreau and Antoine 1995), so too did settlement, provided that these conditions were met. The twenty-two British Acheulean sites examined in White's (1998) analysis show occupation across a wide climatic-ecological spectrum from warm temperate (Swanscombe, Elveden, Wolvercote), cool (Hoxne Upper Industry, Gaddesden Row) to cold (Furze Platt). Yet these climatic oscillations effected radical transformations in the particular character and properties of the material world in which Lower Palaeolithic peoples were immersed. In mobility and landscape use as in lithic technology, individuals equipped with a narrow but flexible repertoire of socially received, historically transmitted knowledge and skills were able to apply them creatively and appropriately to a wide range of encountered material conditions and contexts. And as with handaxe fabrication, the structuring principles of action persisted for hundreds of millennia, apparently resisting structurated transformation.

Discussion

It would appear that the persistence of the principles that structured lithic-technical and landscape use practices in the European Lower Palaeolithic contradicts the notion of the structurated project for living outlined earlier. But we do not believe that the notion should be abandoned. Instead we conclude that Acheulean practices were indeed conditioned by a structurated mutuality between individual agency and the received project for living, but that the dynamic of this mutuality was radically different from today. It seems inescapable that the power of the individual in the Acheulean to effect enduring transformations in the received project through the performance of different or innovative practices seems to have been only weakly developed.

Why should this have been so? The spatiotemporal scale on which the knowledgeability of the individual agent operated in the Acheulean appears to hold the key to this problem. The obligate occupation of environments with high levels of resource proximity in time and space makes sense only in terms of individuals whose knowledgeability was scale-limited. Agency operated within a scale domain measured in terms of days and the distances that could be covered in that time horizon. Individuals did not incorporate larger seasonal or regional scales of resource distribution into schemes of knowledgeable action.

Yet the Acheulean project for living was extraordinarily long-lived over a huge geographical range. Structure and agency were therefore separated by a scalar gulf, a fact that compromised their mutual sensitivity (Hopkinson 2001). In any system organised on multiple scales, very large-scale, very long-term processes are immune to short-lived events in very small-scale, very short-term processes even when the two are mutually dependent (O'Neill *et al.* 1986). Many species of tree depend on insects and birds for pollination and seed dispersal, but short-term oscillations in the populations of these agents do not induce the expansion or contraction of forests. Structurated practice in the Acheulean was locked into a similar scalar dynamic; the relative insensitivity of long-term structuring principles on the one hand and their short-term application by individuals on the other to mutual transformation reinforced the stability of both in time and space.

This in turn implicates the mechanism that links the two scale domains of knowledgeability – the social transmission of knowledge – as a crucial factor in limiting the liability of the Acheulean project to transformation through its own expression in practice. It is not that individuals in the Acheulean were not creative; we have seen that they were. Rather, innovation was much less readily institutionalised in new structuring principles of action than is the case today, and less so than was the case in later prehistory. It is tempting to explain this simply by appealing to innate limitations in the cognitive capacities of Middle Pleistocene European populations and the concept of the project for living, by incorporating biology in the realm of received knowledgeability, does not rule this out. However, one must also consider other factors that may have impacted upon the transmission and reproduction of knowledge in time and space, such as low population densities, a consequent rarity of encounters with individuals who did things differently, and the frequency with which local populations, with their particular cultural stores of knowledge, became extinct (Hopkinson 2001; Shennan 2001).

Conclusions

The search for the individual in the Acheulean, indeed in the Palaeolithic, is not simply a matter of identifying individual acts from archaeological evidence of appropriate resolution. Without a theoretical framework that recognises the dynamic links between such acts and received ways of life in real and changing material circumstances, this retreats either into naïve reconstructionism or into the implicit dissolution of the revealed individual into the structuring entity. By recognising that both the individual agent and constraining precedent structures are always present in any act, it is possible to understand each in terms of its relation with the other and to move towards a balanced understanding of the factors that generated behaviour in the Palaeolithic past. Furthermore, through a programme of rigorous comparison, informed as far as is possible by chronological control and environmental reconstruction, it is possible to identify *different* relations between structure and agency in the Palaeolithic, and to place the history of these relations at the centre of our investigations into the hominid evolutionary trajectory. By this means might it become possible to bring the Palaeolithic individual in from the cold.

Notes

1   Margaret Thatcher's twin proclamations that: 'There is no such thing as society, only individuals and their families', but at the same time 'You cannot buck the market', nicely sum up this contradiction.

2   'Conscious' should be understood to include habituated and intuitive, as well as calculative and reflective, aspects of minded knowledge, which itself is continuous with embodied knowledge or Leroi-Gourhan's 'visceral rhythms' (Leroi-Gourhan 1993 [1964]). Embodiedness and mindedness do not polarise, but are poles on a continuum of, knowledgeability.

3   Although human occupation at La Micoque might have commenced in Oxygen Isotope Stage (OIS) 12 (430–480,000 years ago), the location was then a gravel bar in a river terrace rather than a rock shelter at the foot of a cliff (Turq 1999).

Chapter 3

Transformations in dividuality

Personhood and palaeoliths in the Middle Pleistocene

A. S. Field

Introduction

Understanding the individual requires a discussion of how we perceive action in relation to notions of time and space, which together establish context. The current concept of the individual hominid by Palaeolithic archaeologists can be criticised because, from a contextual point of view, it renders time static and divorced from space. Consequently, Middle Pleistocene hominid identity is composed of a bipartite structure where the individual establishes a static snapshot in time, while society portrays long-term behaviour. In this chapter a new interpretative framework suggests that context is a process of active transformations and identity can be multiple. This alternate proposal for interpreting identity draws on recent approaches to corporeality (Hamilakis *et al.* 2002a) and the idea of the dividual or partible person (Strathern 1988).

The partibility of the person is particularly useful to the Palaeolithic in thinking through the fragmentation and accumulation of artefacts over time. Applying this approach allows the body to be composed of multiple identities depending on context. These identities can be used to establish the materiality of social relations across time and space. Using a revised understanding of social context (Table 3.1) three forms of materiality have been recognised:

1   The objects themselves, necessitating a discussion of the dividual.
2   Collections of objects, interpreted here as an *oeuvre*.
3   The technology and techniques of objects, analysed through praxis.

The case studies use European Middle Pleistocene archaeological examples from southern England and northern France to investigate change and explore identities through these forms of materiality. This time period has been chosen because of the current emphasis on the transition between the Lower and the Middle Palaeolithic. The first discussion explores the dividual nature of the relationship between handaxes and prepared core technology (PCT). The second part is an analysis of accumulations (groups) of bifaces and PCT from the Somme Valley, France applying the concept of the *oeuvre*. The third looks at active identity, inserting praxis within the *chaîne opératoire* of stone tool production as a culturally mediated practice that is integrated within the 'taskscape' (Ingold 1993a). My overall aim is to interpret changing social life in the European Middle Pleistocene and to demonstrate potential avenues for research that stem from an alternative theoretical argument of how identity was contextualised.

Transformation: time for change

Time, change and the individual: the problem

Time and space derive from human involvement in the world. They are not mutually exclusive but bound together through action (see Table 3.1). Their relationship is such that a particular approach to time and space affects our understanding of the individual; to explore one is to explore the other. Time and identity are usually interpreted in archaeology through artefact change and variation where,

1   Variation in artefacts creates an interpretation of time as a short-term, synchronic event, which leads to a description of hominid individuals or small hominid groups comprised of individuals.
2   Change in artefacts creates an interpretation of time as long-term, diachronic events, which leads to a description of hominid taxonomic groups.
3   Transition is the junction point at which these two types of evidence are linked. It is this missing link that is the highly sought after origin point for change.

As a result the long and short term are usually interpreted as 'change through time' and 'variation across space'. These concepts have had a significant effect on research goals which seek to locate a transition by allocating change and difference in hominid behaviour to particular points in time. I would argue differently, that change is a constant, albeit not consistent occurrence in time. This shifts the approach from categorising hominids into established boxes of behaviour along the timescale, e.g. 'Acheulean behaviour' or 'Middle Palaeolithic behaviour', to interpreting contextualised social relations.

Approaching transformations: a solution

Hominids create time and space through action (Table 3.1) and change is involved in this process. Hence, just as there is a mutuality of production of space and time, so change and variation are a part of each other. Therefore, rather than thinking about change in terms of transitions and origin points, I suggest that change should be understood as transformation. A transformation

Table 3.1 The location of identity in a socially defined context

Spatial context	Relationship to time	Process of time and time through change		Comment — Timing change in a socially defined spatial context	Location of identity		Case studies / New interpretations
1. Location of the site in relation to world	Time as past, present and future	Directional	A	Directional time is • The result of intentional action and intended consequences leading to change through **difference**. • Experience connects structure and process, emphasising the significance of human agency in making history.	**Difference** = variation via change	P	Handaxe tips and prepared core technology shaping agency and dividuals
2. Location of the site itself	Time as past, present and future	Reversible	C	Reversible time is • The result of unintentional actions and unintended consequences leading to change. • Tradition is generally the medium of reversible time supplementing daily life with institutional structures through routine and social **memory**.	**Memory** = agent via structure	R	Remaining influence of handaxes
			T				
3. Internal structure of the site	Time as a (multi-directional) channel for movement	Linear	I	Linear time is • Physical as can only be in one place at one time. • Cultural construction of positioning in time and space by agreed social referents, i.e., the **habitus**. • Establishes ontological security in the social institution.	**Habitus** = time via space	A	Raw material movements
4. Single stratigraphic levels of the site	Time as chains of action	Cumulative	O	Cumulative time is • The result of social learning of ways of action, i.e. acculturation, but at the same time, a reflexive relationship with structure evident in variation. • **Routinisation** of day-to-day life in the taskscape.	**Routinisation** = structure via agent	X	Oeuvre of handaxes and prepared cores and flakes
			N			I	
5. Materials within each level of the site	Time as movement	Circular		Circular time is • Orientated around changes in the body over the life cycle • Change in **positioning** of relationships • Biographies of peoples, objects and their relationships are constantly transformed as they gather time and movement.	**Positioning** = space via time	S	Prepared flake variability

implies something actively under change while a transition sits between two things. A transformation is part of the ongoing process of change resulting from the notion that time is constantly becoming (Gell 1992: 157). This would imply that time is never broken as the process and the event are linked and origin points are no longer a possibility. By linking these concepts the long and short term are dissolved, as is the individual, thereby creating a social context in which human action is both the medium and outcome of production, change and variation. Table 3.1 describes the five interlinking levels of research that can be used as the basis for the interpretation of change. Using this approach change and variation are not two separate processes in time, but construct each other, as variation in a part affects and changes the whole. Being and change are located in the performance of actions in time and space. Artefacts are the medium by which we can demonstrate how changing social relations are materialised in the context of action. It is at the moment of bodily performance that there is a conjuncture of structure and agency (Gosden 1994) and therefore one could argue that the body is the nexus for change.

Personhood: changing bodies

Redefining the body: defining identity

The importance of the body as a vehicle for cultural discourse has only been recently realised within archaeology as a focus of interpretation (Hamilakis et al. 2002b; Pettitt 2000). This is partly a reaction to the Cartesian mind–body dualism and the privileging of the cultural mind over the biological body, particularly in Palaeolithic archaeology (cf. Mellars and Gibson 1996; Mithen 1996b). The aim here is not, however, to privilege the body and consequently reverse the mind/body polarity, but to approach them as a single organism. Thereby 'embodiment' could just as easily be 'enmindment' (Ingold 2000a) since both incorporate each other. By grounding cultural, historical and personal difference in theories of embodied practice 'doing' is not overlain onto subjects or objects but becomes the *way* of being in and of the world. Following this approach, identity is no longer a static list of 'things' that make up a Lower Palaeolithic 'package', such as the Acheulean, but a multi-layered and shifting concept established through the different expressions of social relations.

Scales of analysis: locating identity

If the corporeal body is no longer central to social relations then how can we locate identity? In Middle Pleistocene research the 'individual' has been used as a way of injecting intentionality and personality into the hominid record as a part of a scalar model for society (e.g. family/site, group/assemblage, population/region). The application of social systems to archaeological cultures has created an antinomy between 'society' and the 'individual'. The paradox of this dualism is that the term society implies a collective but is conceptually distinct from the relations that bring them together (Strathern 1988). This Western understanding of social 'systems' is historically derived from the European Enlightenment, which produced a very particular understanding of personhood that is largely located around the concept of the individual (Thomas 2002). In this context the individual occupies the body, both 'possessing it' and being bounded by it. The individual body 'as person' is the origin point for action, carrying the mind, the soul and agency. It is regarded as the neutral template through which people live out their life/self (Fowler 2002). In contrast, ethnographic research has questioned these normative assumptions of identity. Mauss' exposition on the subject of the self demonstrated that the person might actually exceed the body in its participation with other people, artefacts, animals and places (Mauss 1985). This does not reject the notion of individuality (free will is an important aspect within agency, cf. Moore 2000: 260 and LiPuma 1998) but allows for the extension of agents and agency beyond the individual-body-subject. From this viewpoint the conceptualisation of bodies and entities is far less clearly drawn (cf. Fowler 2002). Persons can be as dividually as they are individually conceived (Marriott 1976: 111) and likewise, the collective action of 'society' often presents the image of one body/group thereby creating a singular unit (Strathern 1988: 13). Pluralising the person and singularising sociality is not intended to recreate the opposing dualism but is to be used as a way of expressing that relations involve homologies and analogies rather than hierarchy (ibid.). The body is a social microcosm of diversity and multiple identities dependent on context. This multiplicity is important as it undermines binary modes of thinking and negates the possibility of applying typological terms such as individual or group. The multiple person is produced as the object of multiple relationships and it is this plurality which allows partibility and therefore the disposition of parts in relation to others (Strathern 1988: 185). In consequence a dividual or 'person' is composed *of* rather than *has* relations, i.e. (ibid.: 268–9) '*knows* himself only by the relationships he maintains with others. He exists only insofar as he acts his role in the course of his relationships' (Leenhardt 1979: 153, my emphasis).

Therefore, if social relations construct identity we need to think about how relations are made apparent. Possibly the most appropriate analogy for the location of identity is a comparison between the onion and personhood (cf. Gell 1998: 139–40). As the onion is layered, so identity is both an accretion of biographical experience and a fractal of multi-layered relations. Hence the five locations of identity given in Table 3.1 can be accentuated separately (the text below draws them out in bold), as well as combined and recombined.

The accretion of biographical experience, visualised as onion layers, can be interpreted through an understanding of structuration theory (Giddens 1984), which considers relations to be recursive between structure/object and agency/subject. The structural elements of society only exist insofar as they are reproduced in social conduct across time and space. This allows social rules and cultural conventions to be understood, but at the same time their use can be manipulated creatively rather than followed passively. In this way the structure can be both reinforced and transformed. For the most part, knowledgeable agents continue their day-to-day lives through practical consciousness, which has little discursive expression, but is bound up in the routinisation of social contexts. Routine is the habitual actions that are repeated during the course of day-to-day life. The routinisation of social practice is vital to ontological security as social relations can only be formed in the context of social memory, which draws on 'stocks of knowledge' to understand how to interpret the actions taking place. The contexts of interaction within which social relations occur are structured by both the routinisation of the actions taking place and the 'fixity' of the setting within which they occur. This setting is structured by the positioning of the body in relation to others (cf. Goffman 1959), as well as the positioning of all other subjects/objects of material culture, i.e. it is all that concerns social relations in respect to position. Positioning, as used here, therefore expands beyond Giddens' meaning which focuses on the agent and thus overlaps with the concept of *habitus* which establishes the architecture within which positioning occurs. Bourdieu's (1977) concept of the *habitus* allows the body to be a material phenomenon that both constitutes and is constituted by society. Acquiring the techniques of the body, the *habitus*, occurs through conventions established in social relations (Mauss 1979 (1936)). Although both the terms *habitus* and positioning are used for discussing identity, they are actually very similar things. The underlying difference between them is that positioning emphasises time over space (Giddens 1984: 84) while *habitus* emphasises space over time (Bourdieu 1977: 90–1).

The multiple layers of social relations are better approached through ideas stemming from anthropology where the difference of intentional actions is emphasised over the deference to traditional actions (Yates 1990). While Giddens' (1984) focus is on the composition of social relations through a study of the constitution of society, others such as Gell (1998) and Strathern (1988), have focused more on the de-composition of social relations through the constitution of personhood. For example the Melanesian approach would view relations

> . . . through its decomposition into a series of other images. Men's body would be seen to contain the children of women, and looking at the maternal body would be looking at the transactions of men.
>
> (Strathern 1988: 343)

Both authors look at the effects of objects and how they are created and used in social relations, but how can we apply these forms of identity in the Palaeolithic? Problems have continually risen in relation to the process of analysing groups of artefacts that may range widely in age and are therefore considered to derive from a 'mixed' context. One strategy, usefully employed in Bronze Age archaeology (Jones 2001), has been to interpret disparate sets of artefacts through pairing the concepts of citation (Butler 1993) and *oeuvre* (Gell 1998). This relationship between materiality and citation can be effectively explored within the notion of *oeuvre*. Gell (ibid.: 232–51) developed the concept of *oeuvre* to investigate related works of art that are extended across time and space but possess common elements. His definition (ibid.: 236) of an *oeuvre* is a

> set of material objects; they are not a person or a set of subjective experiences (cognitive states). They comprise a set of indexes from which the artist's personhood and agency can be abducted.

In relation to this Jones (2001: 340) points out that archaeologists assume artefacts to be temporally or spatially co-extensive if they appear the same. Rather than viewing this as a concern, he utilises this assumption, linking pottery and metalwork through Gell's notion of the *oeuvre* to analyse the citations and social relations encapsulated by it. In a similar fashion, Middle Pleistocene stone tools can be viewed as a 'network of stoppages' (Gell 1998: 249) where the agency of these material forms are argued to objectify social relations. To quote Jones (2001: 340) paraphrasing Gell (1998: 250), 'each object is a place where agency stops and assumes material form'. However, stone tools in this context are not just the 'doings' of agents, nor are they the culmination/end products of action but rather the distributed extension of personhood. In this sense there is an inseparable transition between the agency in objects and the actual human agents, both stone works and working stone constitute bodies of action. In the Pleistocene this is generally represented through the *chaîne opératoire*, which can be a flexible non-linear approach when reformulated within praxis.

Contextualising the distributed person: constructing identities

Finally we must consider the important concept of praxis in binding these five locations of identity together (Table 3.1). Praxis can be defined as the practical working of relationships through engagement with materials. Applying this approach,

> there is no objectification of work apart from its performance. It is social relations that are objectified in pigs and gardens: work cannot be measured separately from relationships.
>
> (Strathern 1988: 160)

The processes underlying this knowledge of 'doing' leads us towards an understanding of agency (Gell 1998: ix), which is the link between the forms of materiality that draw together structure and agent. As Ingold (1993b: 438) says, while a general technology (e.g. handaxe production) may be indifferent to personhood, techniques of manufacture are the active ingredients of personal and social identity. Thus practising a technique is a form of 'doing' or praxis to construct and relay identity. However the activities taking place do not express a rigid identity but instead generate particular sorts of experience. It is during their performance that transitions, or more literally transformations, occur and therefore personhood is something one *does*, not something one *is* (Thomas 2002).

Where time is viewed in flux as a constant transformation, artefact interpretation is focused on 'doing'. If in 'doing' we move away from a linear approach to time, we can look at the different relationships of time through change (see Table 3.1), opening up new operational spaces of identity through praxis. When the subject and the object are divided, action is based on material and not contextualised within the matter around it. Hence it is unsurprising that stone tools are only described, as the hominid who made them cannot be seen and so social behaviours are thought to be impossible to view. But when the subject and object are connected and mutually created, i.e. embodied in and embedded in action, the performativity of personhood and thereby social relations can be interpreted. In this context, Butler's (1993) concept of performativity is an important and useful concept for an embodied archaeology that wants to move away from a linear chain of actions. The notion of performance presumes a subject whereas performativity contests this notion, while remaining focused on action (of speech/discourse in Butler's examples (1993: 223–42)) as central to social relations. Performativity draws on an understanding of production as always containing a certain element of repetition and recitation, which implies that discourse (or in my terms action) has a history. In other words skilfully constructed forms of social action draw on existing notions of correct action. Therefore production cannot be considered as one act because it contains reiterative and citational practices. This decentres the present or presence of the subject as the origin point for action.

Case study: European Middle Pleistocene stone tools

The important question to ask of this approach to identity is how can these concepts be incorporated into interpretations of Middle Pleistocene data? My focus is on the production and circulation of stone tools in the context of social relations. Three case studies illustrate ways in which objects can materialise social relations. The analysis studies the relationship between bifaces and prepared core technology (PCT) in Middle Pleistocene Europe. By investigating similar knapping practices across different time periods, I hope to show the contextual nature of change and the importance of integrating multiple approaches for investigating assemblage details when attempting to locate identity and interpret social relations. Table 3.1 shows that although time and identity can be separated into five variations their expression in the transformation of social relations is multiple and therefore these elements are combined in my interpretations.

The case studies address three forms of materiality and the production of identity:

1   From: the objects themselves
     To: investigate the dividual
     Studying: the large flake removals at Cagny La Garenne

2   From: collections of objects
     To: investigate the *oeuvre*
     Studying: bifaces and PCT from northern France

3   From: the technology and techniques of objects
     To: investigate agency and praxis
     Studying: *façonnage* and *débitage* in north-west Europe

Circling variation, product or performance? Biface production and prepared core directions

The arrival in late Middle Pleistocene Europe of PCT is currently viewed as an important moment of difference in the Acheulean archaeological record. During the transformation into the Middle Palaeolithic, the variation in production techniques of PCT and the resulting types are key to the interpretation of circular time where biographies of objects and peoples are transformed by reproduction. This section of the case study looks at change through directional and circular time using the sites from northern France and showing the relationship of dividuals in stone tool 'types' over time.

At present PCT is argued to arise from biface production (White and Pettitt 1995: 33). One of the earliest examples in Europe to demonstrate the technological link between these production methods is the OIS 12 site of Cagny La Garenne (CLG) in northern France (Tuffreau and Antoine 1995). This site has been used to stress the false nature of the classical divide between the Lower and Middle Palaeolithic (ibid.). Levallois cores have been described (Tuffreau *et al.* 1997), and a conceptual link proposed between the production of bifaces, where a large flake is preferentially removed from some of them (ibid.: 152–3), and PCT.

It is argued instead that bifaces with a large flake removal are not equal to PCT. The importance of PCT is that it demonstrates the intention of hominids to prepare and maintain core surfaces for the recurrent production of particular flake forms (Boëda 1988; Boëda *et al.* 1990; Van Peer 1992). The interpretation of stone tools as exhibiting the intention of making particular flake forms is only clearly made in the archaeological record where there is a repeated pattern.

Although at Cagny La Garenne a 'rather high percentage of bifaces' (Tuffreau *et al*. 1997: 230) is described, only 'some bifaces' demonstrate characteristics of a prepared core technique (ibid.: 231) and only one artefact of this type has been illustrated (Tuffreau and Antoine 1995: 153; Tuffreau *et al*. 1995: 418). In addition there is no clear evidence that it is the flake from the biface that these hominids were interested in. Isolated examples of large 'Levallois-like' removals on bifaces have also been found at sites such as High Lodge and Stoke Newington. These have been interpreted as a technique for thinning relatively thick biface butts (Callow 1976). Hence, although the emphasis on this interesting phenomenon is justified, its interpretation should not be based around concepts of either PCT, or the Lower to Middle Palaeolithic boundary or modernity.

I would suggest that the importance of change in this instance is not in the origin point of PCT but in its effects on social relations, as this is where we can make behavioural interpretations. It is argued here that the reported Levallois element at CLG should not be described as an early example of this form of technology or related to the Middle Palaeolithic. It is a part of its own chain of differences in social relations. The description of changes in terms of technology may be correct, in that the possibility of making Levallois may well have developed from the knowledge of biface production. However, its accidental arrival or intended innovation has to be sustained by a social process before we will find it in the archaeological record. This means that searching for origin points is futile as changes have already happened before we find them reflected as a recognisable pattern in the archaeological record. Rather, we should concentrate on interpretations of how the social process is re-orientated by the social relations of PCT. Instead we should look at Levallois as a trans-formation in the relations of production. At CLG there are no prepared cores, but the diversity in biface types suggests that perhaps it is the dividual's performance rather than the product that is at the centre of the social narrative. A comparison of handaxe sizes between CLG and Gouzeaucourt shows that although artefacts from both sites have similar lengths and widths (Figure 3.1), those from CLG demonstrate many more diverse shapes when the tip and butt ends are compared (Figure 3.2). At CLG the wide range of biface shapes suggests that performance (the actions of making an artefact/biface) is more important than the product (the biface).

The emphasis lies not in the formulation of a specific handaxe composition but in the actions of making using and perhaps exchanging them. This site can be contrasted with the later OIS 8 site of Gouzeaucourt (Tuffreau 1992; Tuffreau and Bouchet 1985), where large numbers of similar bifaces and PCT are both present.

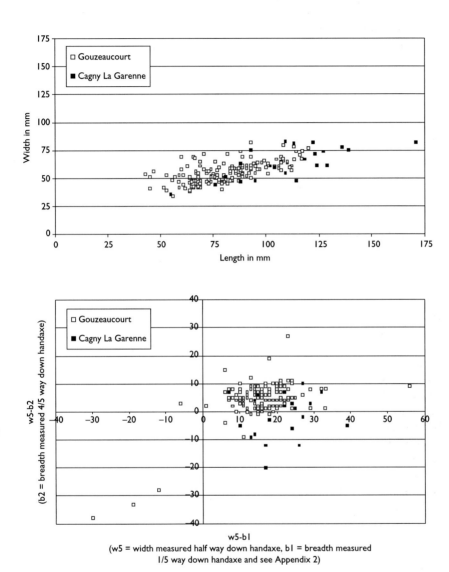

(w5 = width measured half way down handaxe, b1 = breadth measured
1/5 way down handaxe and see Appendix 2)

Figure 3.1 A comparison of handaxe size (top) between Gouzeaucourt and Cagny
La Garenne and handaxe shapes (bottom) from Gouzeaucourt and Cagny
La Garenne.

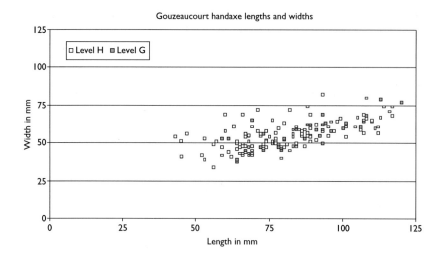

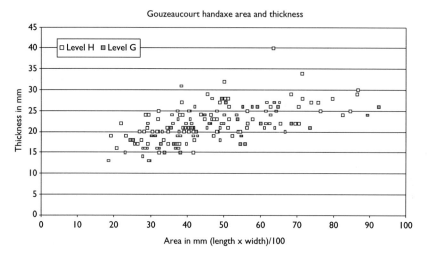

Figure 3.2 Gouzeaucourt handaxe lengths and widths (top) and Gouzeaucourt handaxe area and thickness (bottom).

Accumulating change, contextualising the oeuvre

Gouzeaucourt is a site with over 500 bifaces, retouched tools and some Levallois pieces (Lamotte 2001; Tuffreau 1992). The retouched tools are interesting in that they are particularly refined, and likewise the bifaces are all very similar in form (Figure 3.2). In contrast to the wide variation in biface types at CLG, at Gouzeaucourt the bifaces are all very similar in size and shape and are produced hundreds of times over. It is therefore suggested that at Gouzeaucourt, although biface technology has always been present, the technique of manufacture has changed as relationships between bifaces, retouched tools and PCT changed each other as they changed themselves (circular change). What is apparent is that there was directional change as hominids expressed their relationships in similar ways through both biface and retouched tool production. As the arena of social power shifts, the rigorous process of preparing cores is reflected in the standardisation in biface forms and each affects the other in a situation of increasing social connectedness. There is a similar monitoring of dividuals and their different reduction processes in a reflexive way to shape the outcome, establishing the relationship of citation and materiality within the concept of the *oeuvre*. Schlanger's work on Marjorie's Core (Schlanger 1996) concludes that we cannot separate out doing, i.e. the actions of making prepared flakes, and thinking, i.e. the mental intentions for and of action. Likewise I argue that we should not always separate out alternative methods of knapping. In dividing up production techniques it is forgotten that these processes and hominids are working together in tandem. Although bifaces, retouched flakes and prepared cores are made in both different and similar ways, their relationship is evident not in their technologies but in the form of the artefact produced as a part of a social milieu of a more organised and structured way of life. Just like artefacts, people were also being more carefully monitored and shaped into particular forms in the loose structure of social relations. The importance then, lies not in the number of technological 'steps' taken but in the representation of particular forms. This style of reproduction in both forms can be considered part of the same *oeuvre*.

The active landscape in praxis

This case study investigates the movement of things and time in the changing importance of material accumulation, particularly in relation to handaxes and Levallois flakes and cores, during the Acheulean and Middle Palaeolithic in Europe. Accumulations of artefacts have led to the interpretation of identity as a cohesive list of behaviours. Elsewhere I have problematised the universal models put forward for the Acheulean and MP (Field 2002) as these lead to the amalgamation of time into two blocks that are linked by a single transition (Figure 3.3). One manner of reformulating this is through a study of handaxes, which are present throughout Europe during the Lower and Middle Palaeolithic. Although traditions are often maintained over hundreds of years there will be gradual (and sometimes reversible) changes in meanings, techniques and technologies. It may seem unusual to investigate tradition for the purpose of analysing change, but it is often forgotten that tradition is always renegotiated in the context of the moment. Change in this instance can be investigated through reversible time, as this is the time of tradition, linking the actions guided by cultural routine with ongoing changes in daily life. Therefore time can also be extended backwards into the past, as cumulative

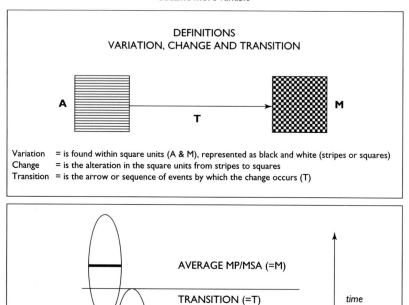

The *static* Acheulean tradition *changed* about *300 kya* into the Middle Palaeolithic/Middle Stone Age where stone tool types became more *variable*

DEFINITIONS
VARIATION, CHANGE AND TRANSITION

A   T   M

Variation   = is found within square units (A & M), represented as black and white (stripes or squares)
Change   = is the alteration in the square units from stripes to squares
Transition   = is the arrow or sequence of events by which the change occurs (T)

AVERAGE MP/MSA (=M)

TRANSITION (=T)   time

AVERAGE ACHEULEAN (=A)

Figure 3.3 Differentiating the terms variation, change and transition as currently under-stood for a Middle Pleistocene context. These terms are widely employed to explain the archaeology of this period and such generally accepted 'facts' could, as shown here, be applied to my study (Field 2002).

time. This has an effect on the interpretation of artefact accumulations as cumulative time is played out in changes through accumulation (of experience, knowledge, stone tools, etc.). If in 'doing' time we move away from a linear approach to the *chaîne opératoire* and look at the different relationships of time through change, we can open up new operational spaces of identity through praxis.

The physical actions of knapping time in the Middle Pleistocene have been approached through a model that divides the archaeological record into two reduction methods, *façonnage*, to obtain bifaces and pebble tools, and *débitage*, to produce various flake based technologies (Boëda *et al.* 1990). In Europe, the

change in emphasis from *façonnage* to *débitage* over the course of the Middle Pleistocene has been linked to altered mobility strategies as a consequence of the climatic downturn (White and Pettitt 1995). The problem is that accumulations of artefacts have been time-averaged and therefore sites are amalgamated into a network by 'connecting the dots'. This has resulted in interpretations of mobility by calculating the movements between the dots (e.g. Féblot-Augustins 1999), rather than by focusing on changing movements at particular places. As a result, little consideration is given to the differences in social relations that these two contrasting types of production (*façonnage* vs. *débitage*) may have been associated with, or the possible alterations in social relations that may be implicated in these changes.

In the Lower Palaeolithic material is transported as one block, to one place, for one result. The knapping of handaxes can be said to be associated with the process of accumulation. Production is usually orientated specifically towards the creation of a single handaxe out of a single block of raw material, as for example at the Horse Butchery Site at Boxgrove (Roberts and Parfitt 1999). These single artefacts then tend to be related to places of specific action. In the Middle Palaeolithic material is transported in stages, as several pieces for several places and artefacts travelling the greatest distances were retouched and Levallois pieces (Féblot-Augustins 1999). In contrast the knapping of retouched tools and Levallois is a process of organised fragmentation, controlling the breaking of the stone into many parts. At the same time in the Middle Palaeolithic there is evidence for the regular use of composite tools, which bring these fragmented pieces together as sets (Chapman 2000: 7). Although arguably these concepts could be (and sometimes were) reversed, the emphasis on fragmentation or accumulation is different at different times. There are many different stone tool forms, but it is the repeated patterns that we can view as archaeologists that lead us to particular interpretations of the structure of events. In the Acheulean the focus of production is on the preparation of the edge and on accumulation, while in the Middle Palaeolithic the focus of production on the preparation of the surface for controlled fragmentation.

Raw material studies have suggested that there is a shift from the provisioning of *place*, to the provisioning of *people on the move* (Féblot-Augustins 1999: 206). I would like to take this interpretation one step further to suggest that changes in the way relationships are bonded together is also reflected in stone tool knapping patterns. The processes of fragmentation and accumulation were embedded in mobility and can be used to interpret social relations (Table 3.2). To investigate this, the movement of material at two localities is considered; firstly the Acheulean site of Boxgrove and then the early Middle Palaeolithic levels at La Cotte de St Brelade.

Boxgrove is a Middle Pleistocene Acheulean site situated under a relict cliff face in southern England (Pope and Roberts this volume). The many trenches excavated at this site clearly demonstrate *in situ* knapping floors of handaxes,

Table 3.2 Predominant production techniques and raw material movement in the Acheulean and Middle Palaeolithic/MSA

Continent	Acheulean	Middle Palaeolithic / MSA
Europe	Façonnage Bifaces mostly from pebbles	Débitage Levallois pieces removed mostly from pebbles
	Raw material moved	Raw material moved
	ACCUMULATION	FRAGMENTATION
Africa	Façonnage and débitage Bifaces mostly from flakes	Débitage Levallois pieces removed mostly from pebbles
	Raw material not moved	Raw material moved

flakes and retouched pieces. From the work done at Boxgrove three parts are discussed here:

1 The refitting work and careful description of the artefacts by the excavating team has allowed for detailed interpretation of the evidence. Tables 3.3 and 3.4 give a brief description of each excavation area and the number and type of handaxes and flakes found there. Interestingly the distribution pattern of flakes indicates that the handaxes were roughed out and finished at adjacent locations (Roberts and Parfitt 1999: 349).
2 Also published is a preliminary description of the Horse Butchery Site GTP 17, which describes the import of six to seven nodules onto the site, the likely production of handaxes from these nodules and the subsequent removal and discard of the handaxes elsewhere. The site of GTP 17 is considered to be a discrete event (Roberts and Parfitt 1999: 374), where hominids brought all these nodules to the site to knap handaxes.
3 In addition to the controlled excavations, it has been noted that sharp handaxes are found in large numbers elsewhere in the quarries (Pitts and Roberts 1997: 201) and certainly, were not being discarded because they were worn out. It has been suggested that the significant number of handaxes produced could be explained as either knapping enjoyment or an act of social significance (ibid.: 287).

The land surface of Unit 4c at Boxgrove is considered to have been open for only twenty to a hundred years and Unit 4b may be even less. It is suggested here that these may have been produced by dividuals that were socially interactive, as so many of the handaxes have a tranchet tip (Table 3.3). It is unusual to find so many handaxes with such a distinctive tip form from a single site. The combination of sites at Boxgrove, including the information given

Table 3.3 Bifaces/handaxes and tranchet tips from Boxgrove

Trench	Unit	Description from Boxgrove volume	Total number of handaxes	N = handaxes with tranchet tips	N = % of handaxes with tranchet tips
QI/A	4c	*In situ* knapping scatter No discrete episodes Probably accumulated over several years	5	5	100
QI/A	4b	*In situ* knapping Isolated scatter produce by one seated knapper Handaxes present were knapped elsewhere	3	2	66
QI/B	4c	*In situ* knapping – at least three events Final 3 flakes from handaxe 95 refitted No other débitage relates to handaxes	8	4	50
Q2/A	4c	Variety of flint forms – nodules and roughouts Refitting studies indicate several finished tools were carried away.	5	3	60

Source: Data from Roberts and Parfitt 1999: 309–61.

for GTP 17, suggest that there is a repeated pattern at these sites and a model (Figure 3.4) can be formulated for the movement of materials at this location.

This model suggests that there may be a form of enchainment process where imported handaxes remain, and new ones are made and taken away to maintain the chain of relations with that place, the actions occurring there (butchery/ plant processing), and the people that they are involved with. There seems to be a consistent separation between bifaces and flakes. Evidence from GTP17 suggests that several hominids were involved in the processing of this large carcass which implies a context of social negotiation. The staged knapping of handaxes suggests that there was probably equally a procedure for the carcass. The timely removal of the tranchet flake from a handaxe may be related to a particular form of butchery time. This pattern of specific deposition is not restricted to this cliff face but is a part of ongoing movements of hominids through the landscape. Studies by Féblot-Augustins (1997, 1999) demonstrate that bifaces were rarely moved any great distance. However I would suggest that the way that hominids moved raw materials and bifaces at the local level is interesting in itself. It does not need to be understood as a sign of little social complexity or organisational skills. Instead, perhaps Acheulean materials only move short distances because the making of handaxes is part of the ritualised performance of other activities, and thereby socially tied to the locality.

Table 3.4 Bifaces/handaxes and flakes from Boxgrove

Excavation level	Handaxes (with refits)	(no refits)	Flakes Rough out %=	Thinning %=	Finishing %=	N=	% refit	No. in longest sequence	Size of bulk of scatter in m²
QI/A 4c	x	5	14.5	29.1	56.4	124	31	4	>2.00
QI/A 4b	x	3	x	27.0	73.0	59	51	24	0.25
QI/B 4c	1+	7	11.0	36.0	53.0	253	47	13	>2.00
Q2/A 4c	1*	3	52.1	27.7	20.2	213	17	10	>2.00

Source: Data from Roberts and Parfitt 1999: 309–61 and Roberts et al. 1997.

Notes
+ Three flakes refitted to this unfinished, rough-out handaxe.
* Two tranchet flakes refitted to the tip of this handaxe (total of 3 refits, 1 whole and 2 broken flakes).

Figure 3.4 Model of possible material movements at Boxgrove.

At the Middle Palaeolithic site of La Cotte de St Brelade the situation is different. The lack of refits suggests that the manufacture and deposition of artefacts was possibly occurring at very separate points in the landscape (Table 3.5). From a published study of 2,476 resharpening flakes, no refits were found (Cornford 1986). The exception is a single refit from Layer 5 (ibid.: fig. 29.3), a later level that is not included here. It would seem that those artefacts knapped on-site were taken elsewhere and those deposited here were made in a separate location.

The growing use of tranchet flakes at La Cotte is actually considered to be a response to the diminishing supplies of flint (ibid.: 337) and these unmodified edges are thought to have been deliberately manufactured for use. However, in Layer A, there is a relatively greater percentage of quartz than flint burins. In addition, although bifaces are found in many levels, it is only in Layer A that bifaces are found with tranchet tips (Table 3.5). I would like to suggest instead, that there is a particular cultural way of making, using and reusing stone tools during this time period, which demands these particular edges and this is reflected in the technique of manufacture across different tool types.

These two sites should not be considered as models for all Acheulean and Middle Palaeolithic sites, but should be regarded as different sites demonstrating the same tool types constructing completely different identities. Previous studies of the Lower Palaeolithic have emphasised the proximity of raw materials to knapping locations in a negative way, as an argument against seeing complexity in these hominid lives. Instead, perhaps the focus should be on local networks of interaction. Rather than calculating distances, what is really interesting is the interaction of hominids through investigating the detail of how material was actually moving about, not just the scale on which it was moving. This study has suggested that at least one Acheulean site, place is marked through the knapping of stone tools and remembered through their transfer across the landscape. In contrast, in the Middle Palaeolithic it is argued that greater amounts of fragmentation implies larger networking groups, which demand different tasks, as social relations also involve political separation.

Table 3.5 La Cotte de St Brelade: numbers of burins, bifaces and resharpening flakes

Type	Level									Total
	H	G	F	E	D	C	B	A	3	
32-Flint Typical burin	0	7	3	4	6	9	10	91	0	130
33-Flint Atypical burin	0	1	3	3	3	4	4	58	4	80
Relative % of burins	0	1.2	0.7	1.1	1.2	1.4	2.2	4.2	3.1	2.4
Total – Flint tools	296	685	917	650	757	948	639	3561	129	8582
Total – Quartz burins/ total tools	0 /4	0 /16	0 /20	5 /53	2 /96	3 /28	4 /45	23 /421	2 /163	39 /846
Relative % of burins	0	0	0	9.4	2.1	10.7	8.9	5.5	1.2	4.6
Long sharpening flakes (flint)			131			250		1814		2195
Transverse sharpening flakes (flint)			67			63		151		281
Burin spalls (flint)			15			17		72		104
Total			213			330		2037		2580
Bifaces with tranchet tips	0	0	0	0	0	0	0	6	0	5
Bifaces Total number	0	0	0	0	6	11	5	98	2	122

Source: Data from Callow and Cornford 1986.

Conclusion: identifying change, changing identities

To summarise, there has been an overemphasis by Middle Pleistocene researchers on the occurrence of change at particular points in time. By contrast, a stress on continual change through interaction with the world creates a new perspective both on views of the world and views of the body. In response, this chapter has aimed to interpret hominid identities through the social texture of change in material culture. Approaches to the body and interpretations of material culture can be established following the framework provided by social space and time (Table 3.1). This requires a movement away from the physical context towards an interest in how people change the world and how the effects of changes set up new conditions for social action. To orient my research goals towards this more reflexive approach an alternative theoretical proposal was assembled by putting forward three concepts for interpretation; dividual, *oeuvre* and praxis.

This chapter has demonstrated that we cannot measure change through time, we can only look at the effects of difference and transformation. Transformations and differences can not be judged on a tool type, a site, a technique or a (in)dividual but must be looked at as the product of social relations in a specific context. An understanding of objects cannot be arrived at through a description of their attributes alone, as stone tools have to be mobilised and sustained by a social process. It is the embodiment of this social process which creates identity, and identity is expressed in artefacts through praxis and its five forms of manifestation (Table 3.1); memory, routinisation, positioning, *habitus* and difference. All of these factors are thus combined through an understanding of the taskscape as comprised of places of accumulation and fragmentation. Particularly important is the connected relationship of technologies during change through time. Bifaces and Levallois change together at Gouzeaucourt, while at other sites bifaces change in other ways, such as through tranchet flaking at Boxgrove or large flake removals at CLG. Each set of actions had specific relations with place, space and time and the interpretations of these events may be linked through time, not progressively, but as alternatives. I hope I have shown that to investigate the detail of these relations a multiple approach to hominid identity is required that moves beyond individual assemblages, and groups of handaxes, towards a more thorough study of hominid identities through the body and material culture.

Chapter 4

Seeking the Palaeolithic individual in East Africa and Europe during the Lower-Middle Pleistocene

J. A. J. Gowlett

This chapter aims to look for the individual by considering and comparing data from the Acheulean, concentrating on evidence from Africa, about one million years ago, and extending themes to Europe about 0.5 million years ago. Both of these zones fall within the domain of *Homo erectus* as commonly conceived, though towards the time when more progressive hominids appear.

Both are zones of concentration of archaeological effort, because of good local preservation. Their palaeoanthropology tends to be conducted by different communities, but similarities in the basic data are evident, and present challenges to us. Both areas sometimes offer data at very high resolution. In stone technology, this comes predominantly in two forms – as refit sets that trace an individual's action through time; and as shaped artefacts which record some events in an individual's pathway towards producing the final object.

In general now refits grab the attention, with their many pieces and spatial spread – here is the appeal of visible dynamics, and the compelling perfection of jigsaws. Yet shaped artefacts may preserve much of the same information, and sometimes more, about design goals, final stages of production and use of tools.

Refits stand out as something rare in the record, as a complex of related finds. The idea of the single piece tends to be lost in our perception of a whole assemblage of similar artefacts – almost automatically we reduce the individual specimen into the averaged host. We see the mass rather than the individual hominid.

Curiously, though, when it comes to interpretation, the refit set is also often used not to show the individual, but to illustrate the general – the aim seems to be to find 'social habit' (Leroi-Gourhan 1993; Roche *et al.* 1999). Conversely, I aim here to turn things round – to use the case of the tools or end-products to illustrate the individual.

But given the similarities in the two situations, we can ask across the board 'how far do we hang onto the individual' whose actions have been illuminated? The problem is a Palaeolithic example of a more general case, in archaeology and life: where archaeology has a little data, it is hard to see or demonstrate a pattern. Where we have a lot of data (and it can be a vast amount), our strong need is to standardise, summarise or abbreviate it statistically – thus losing most of the high resolution which we have tried so hard to acquire (cf. Gowlett 1997).

In this chapter, I aim to use examples from the two areas so as to explore repertoires of behaviour, and to find modes of retaining more of the individuality which we uncover.

Issues

There are times when we can trace individual actions in the past with brilliant precision, as when a knapper strikes a single flake, and we find core and flake side by side. This evidence seems to provide historicity, in the same way as history labels an individual – for example, Q. Laberius Durus, a Roman officer who fell in Caesar's second campaign in Britain, the first named person to die in British history (Caesar, *Gallic War V, 15*).

There is a view then, given our confidence in his reality and the date, that this is 'historicity'. Perhaps archaeology, which used to be interested in classification and technology, can now similarly reach towards the individual, achieving a similar sort of historicity – Proctor (2003) cites evidence that this is the trend. Certainly history can reference the individual by name, whereas prehistory by definition cannot. Beyond that, there is far more similarity in the cases than meets the eye.

Archaeology actually shares this difficulty with history – the problem of 'averaging' data – taking the exceptional back to the median. Thus Bertrand Russell (1921), contrasts the full human 'impersonal' history with the richness and value of individual experience. James (2003) in considering conscious selves develops a similar point about the relationship between individual experience and social pattern. The relationship between individual and wider structures has also been explored over a long period (Boulding 1956; Hinde 1976), and explicated in terms of the Palaeolithic (Gamble 1998b). Here the focus is not so much on the relationship itself, as on finding time and space to discuss both individual and group or set.

The individual in early East Africa

East Africa is rich in Lower Palaeolithic assemblages, but they extend through a huge span of time, from 2.5 million years to about 250,000. East Africa is the key territory for examining the Oldowan and early Acheulean. The sampling density is nevertheless very low. Each is known from less than a dozen major studied sites, although some of the 'sites' such as Olduvai or Lake Turkana embrace many localities. Among all these, refitting evidence that allows us to see sequences of actions blow by blow comes from just a few sites:

East Turkana (e.g. FxJj50)	(Bunn *et al.* 1980; Isaac 1981a)
West Turkana (Lokalalei)	(Roche *et al.* 1999)
Chesowanja (very few)	(Gowlett 1999)
Isenya	(Roche *et al.* 1988)
Peninj	(de la Torre *et al.* 2003)

When such refits were first searched out (e.g. Isaac 1981), it was with the aim of investigating patterns in early hominid behaviour, and alongside that to help explain taphonomic contexts, charting the extent of secondary disturbance, as at FxJj50 at East Turkana (Bunn *et al.* 1980). The involvement of French scholars led to a greater emphasis on shared social practice of tool-making (Leroi-Gourhan 1993; Roche *et al.* 1999). Those at Lokalalei at West Turkana, for example, represent the earliest set of Palaeolithic refits, in more than sixty groups (Roche *et al.* 1999). They show a complexity of production routines that was largely unexpected for such an early period. They also help to document imports and exports of raw materials (Schick and Toth 1993). Similar evidence has come recently from Peninj, where de la Torre and colleagues argue for elaborate patterns of core-reduction which are socially standardised (de la Torre *et al.* 2003; Domínguez-Rodrigo *et al.* 2002).

At Chesowanja, of similar age, the very small number of refits is simply enough to give some idea of the level of disturbance on GnJi 1/6E site (Gowlett 1999). This occurrence illustrates our lack of confidence about structure, on early sites. The possible 'hut base' structure at Olduvai DK has never been corroborated by other features (Leakey 1971). The only possible structured model for examining Chesowanja is that of features surrounding a hearth. Although these are well developed by various methodologies (Binford 1978a; Stapert and Street 1997), the potential for nature to mimic a pattern cannot easily be discounted, nor can probabilities of this be calculated.

In general, although the refits demonstrate much about production, in East Africa they show very little about formal tools (Isenya being an exception illustrating modes of biface production).

In contrast to this enigmatic picture presented by refits, we have large assemblages of formal tools on land surfaces, in such numbers that they must represent most of the local repertoire of stone tools in use.

Kilombe, an Acheulean site complex in Kenya, offers a prime example of this. The site is aged about 800,000–1 million years. The bifaces are scattered across a vast area, largely on a single visible surface (Bishop 1978; Gowlett 1978, 1988, 1991, 1993; Figure 4.1). Gowlett (1996b) argued that we had scarcely begun to look at the issue of 'who made what?' in the sense of asking why each specimen deviated from the norm, and by what allowable amount.

It was argued that each time an individual makes a specimen, they are in effect moving a 'personal pointer' to a particular point within the zone of all allowable permutations made by the group. But generally, we did not (and do not) know whether one individual might move the pointer to far separate regions; or whether the individual would operate within a very restricted zone of the total. Would large individuals make the larger tools? Would it matter whether the use was by a male or a female, single-handed or double-handed?

In general, archaeologists portray such fields of variation either graphically as a scatter plot, or by the use of means and standard deviations (e.g. Isaac 1977). These 'ideal' statistical measures fit surprisingly well in many cases, although skewed distributions are likely to occur, and barcharts of frequency distributions should offer a fuller picture than summary statistics.

To look at the individual, we need to escape these standard procedures. Two attempts at providing an insight are offered here:

1   Variations of cluster analysis
    Perhaps where bifaces are clustered on surfaces, on rarest occasions it may be possible to isolate a group which is the select production of one individual in a limited area. One can ask how this output compares with the overall production, and how it compares with the modern production of an individual within a group.
2   Selection and examination of 'extreme cases' from the range of various assemblages
    How much latitude was there for an individual to stretch norms at the margins? This investigation is conducted from a set of African Acheulean assemblages (Kalambo Falls, Kilombe, Kariandusi, Sidi Abderrahman).

Cluster analysis

The purpose of the cluster analysis is to find similar specimens, or to isolate groups of artefacts which demonstrate some particular coherence. When it is applied we also have to ask why we might expect some patterning in the particular context. At Kilombe, where artefacts are strewn across an extensive surface (Figure 4.1), there is a chance that for one reason or another there may be groups that are locally distinctive. One approach – Wishart's mode analysis – was used by Gowlett (1988) at Kilombe, in order to test for Developed Oldowan-like phenomena, by seeking out 'natural' clusters of artefacts. The Mode analysis looked at the total production in two areas at Kilombe. In each area it produced two groups at the highest level (the 'large' and 'small' groups, surmised to correspond with 'Acheulean' and 'Developed Oldowan': Gowlett 1988).

The data produced another distinctive feature – a small group of highly similar bifaces which clustered within the large set at the highest level. This was a group of six handaxes distinguished by their particular thinness. They can be plotted both in figures and graphics against the 'parent' population (Table 4.1; Figure 4.2 indicates the measurements taken).

Overall, this limited set of 'thin' specimens shows half to two-thirds of the variability of the entire AC/AH main group.

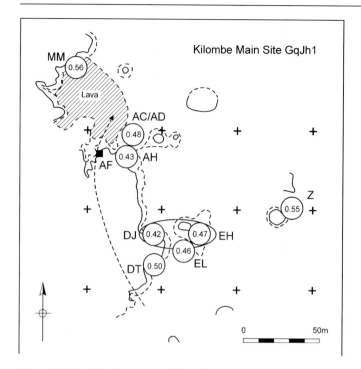

Figure 4.1 The Kilombe main surface, showing the localities of studied biface samples.

Its breadth and thickness as absolute measures vary much less than in the general assemblage, showing the tightness of the grouping. Length is also constrained. The group also stands out from both the large group and the small group in being far thinner than either (reflected in the T/B ratio), and being much more oval rather than pointed (reflected in the BA/BB ratio). As the group is intermediate in general size between the large and small group, it is the more notable that these differences buck any allometric trends along a gradient from small to large hand-axes, such as those subsequently isolated by Crompton and Gowlett (1993).

Just possibly, here is the output of one individual working through an hour or two. Or perhaps, here are the efforts of two individuals carrying in specimens together. At any rate the cluster separation itself is an objective reality: the coherence of this subgroup stood out clearly.

The 'small bifaces' also form a small cluster group – could they similarly be the output of an individual? The original analysis found corresponding 'small' groups both here, and on EH excavation at the other end of the site. On EH the small series was dispersed across the excavation, perhaps suggesting that various individuals were involved over a longer period. It will be shown below that in general there is more variation among small than larger specimens.

Table 4.1 Kilombe bifaces, measurements and mode analysis

	EH Large group (n=80)	EH Small group (n=15)
L	163 +/– 22	108 +/– 12
B	100 +/– 13	68 +/– 9
T	45 +/– 9	31 +/– 6
T/B	0.46 +/– 0.10	0.46 +/– 0.14
B/L	0.62 +/– 0.07	0.64 +/– 0.08
BA/BB	0.90 +/– 0.23	0.69 +/– 0.14
TA/L	0.15 +/– 0.03	0.16 +/– 0.04
PMB/L	0.45 +/– 0.10	0.37 +/– 0.14
	AC/AH Large group (n=70)	AC/AH Small group (n=6)
L	154 +/– 30	88 +/– 10
B	91 +/– 12	57 +/– 7
T	40 +/– 8	33 +/– 4
T/B	0.45 +/– 0.09	0.58 +/– 0.05
B/L	0.60 +/– 0.08	0.64 +/– 0.05
BA/BB	0.81 +/– 0.17	0.73 +/– 0.17
TA/L		
PMB/L	0.44 +/– 0.09	0.44 +/– 0.13
	AC/AH Thin group (n=6, subset of 'Large' group)	
L	134 +/– 19	
B	84 +/– 5	
T	24 +/– 5	
T/B	0.29 +/– 0.06	
B/L	0.63 +/– 0.06	
BA/BB	0.91 +/– 0.09	
TA/L		
PMB/L	0.45 +/– 0.08	

How do the discrete groups mentioned above compare with other clustering, such as we might see in an ethnographic record? The most useful comparative series comes from a recent study by Stout (2002) working with the Langda in New Guinea. The research is notable for concentrating on individual production, and investigating how the output of individuals relates to the group norms. Plainly the influence of master-craftsmen is such that only they can produce the best and largest specimens. Apprentices are also unable to reproduce some features of the best specimens, such as a dorsal ridge (Stout 2002: 708).

The adzes have a different plan shape from classic bifaces (relatively far narrower, although lengths are in the same range), and doubtless are produced with different considerations. But is the relation of individual to population in any way similar? Stout's set of specimens is relatively small, twenty-five

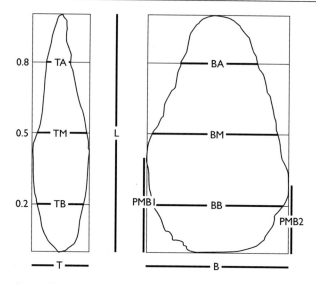

Figure 4.2 Measurements taken on bifaces, labelled following Isaac 1977.

adzes. Individuals produced up to six specimens. Most prolific were individuals 1 and 5. In terms of length and breadth their results were as follows:

Table 4.2 Langda adzes

	Number	Length	Breadth	B/L
Maker 1	5	160 +/– 14	33.5 +/– 1.5	0.18 +/– 0.012
Maker 5	6	192 +/– 40	33.9 +/– 2.1	0.18 +/– 0.033
All	25	187 +/– 40	35.9 +/– 3.2	0.20 +/– 0.042

Source: Data after Stout 2002.

There is a contrast: both Maker 1 and Maker 5 achieve a 'tighter' breadth and breadth/length ratio than the whole group of *c.* 9 knappers. But Maker 1 produces a very focused standardised group by length (160–198 mm), whereas Maker 5 samples most of the length variation in the whole assemblage (min 136–max 245 mm, compared with 122 and 272 for the whole group).

Overall, the comparison throws out these hints: that the output of a competent worker may reflect about half the shape variation in a whole assemblage, and differing percentages of the size variation according to context. Apart from Stout's work few other comparisons are available – Wiessner (1983) was working with individuals who could not always identify their own production. The Kilombe 'thin group' is certainly compatible with individual production, though we can never be certain in the distant past.

Density analysis

The next point is to ask whether such groups might be recognised by other techniques. A further cluster analysis has been used to look for natural groups in the whole Kilombe series, initially with the particular aim of 'comparing cluster centres for small and large bifaces'. This aim, though, was written down before the analysis took place.

It was carried out with Density analysis, now recommended by Wishart (1999) as a successor to the Mode analysis used in Gowlett (1988). A fascinating and completely unexpected finding was that the technique recognises a different grain of natural clustering from the earlier Mode analysis – and that each of these is in a sense relevant to its archaeological *Zeitgeist* – one to 'hominid tradition' questions of the 1980s, the other to the topical issue of 'individual interest'.

Whereas Mode analysis picked out the largest natural clusters, it was found that Density analysis tended to pick out small tight groups. These generally contained between two and ten specimens. The question naturally arises 'could these be the output of one or two individuals operating in very short periods of time?'

Exciting as that possibility is, it needs to be seen in a deeper context. A first question was 'how valid are the groups?' Different approaches to cluster analysis will yield different results, so a robust approach is needed. A particular issue is whether to standardise the raw measurements, so as to give equal mean and variance to each measured variable. This is often the best approach in multivariate analysis, as it gives equal importance to each variable. Yet, in a two-variable example, plotted as a scattergram, it is evident that 'stretching' the scale on one or other axis can alter the cluster groups (Wishart 1999). Arguably, shaped artefacts, in their geometric reality, offer the one case where it is worthwhile to preserve actual dimensional relationships (example: say, length ranges from 80 to 240 mm; breadth from 50 to 150 mm; equalising these two scales may alter some cluster relationships).

There is a further question of whether a logarithmic transformation would be useful. Possibly a 2 mm difference between two specimens about 80 mm long should be scaled to be equivalent to a 4 mm difference between two specimens about 160 mm long – but we do not know this. It happens, though, that most of the distributions conform closely with a normal distribution, and again this argues for not making transformations. A practical way to resolve these issues was to run analyses on transformed and untransformed data. The groups which emerged were very similar.

One way to test the results was to compare two similar analyses. The first was run on specimens from within a single excavation (EH). The second used specimens from several areas of the site (EH, AH, DJ, MM, Z). If groups had a highly local significance, they might tend to come from one locality. If they were randomly made-up, a group of (say) six specimens might be divided across several areas. Empirically, to have the results would be useful, but the relation to hypotheses need not be exclusive. Individuals who made six similar bifaces in one area might well have dropped one or two elsewhere, for example. In any case, the bifaces from some different parts of the Kilombe site are so similar in measured spectra that even a discriminant analysis is poor at classifying specimens back to their own 'home' area.

The density analysis is presented in Table 4.3.

Although it would be very good to apply a significance test to this distribution, the number of specimens expected in each cell is unfortunately too low to justify a chi-square test. Even when EH is compared with 'the rest' (that gives 96 EH specimens vs. 84 others, but distributed between twenty-two clusters) the expected frequencies are low. Nevertheless, it is possible to plot the ratio of bifaces between EH and other localities (Table 4.4)

Table 4.3 Kilombe bifaces: results of Density analysis

Cluster No.	EH	AH	MM	DJ	KZ
1	5		1		(1)
3	1	2	1		
4	2	1	1		
5	5	3	1	1	1
7	1		1		1
8	2	3	1		
12	4				1
16	5			1	
17	8		3		
21	2			1	1
22	6	2	1	5	2 (1)
23		3	2		
26	6	1	3	1	
29	6			1	
30	2		1		
37	2		1		(1)
58	2				1
Totals of bifaces in analysis	96	23	33	12	16 (3)

Table 4.4 Ratio of EH bifaces to all other bifaces in Density clusters

Ratio in cluster of EH bifaces to all other bifaces	<0.25	0.25 – 0.5	0.5 – 1.0	1.0 – 2.0	2.0 – 4.0	>4
Number of clusters	0	1	5	3	3	4

In seven out of the twenty-two clusters, EH specimens outnumber all others by at least 2:1; in contrast, they are outnumbered in similar proportion in only one out of twenty-two — whereas the distribution ought to be roughly symmetrical around the value 96:84 (~ 1:1).

Further inspection of the Table 4.3 shows that Cluster 22 mops up in addition to EH specimens, as many as five (50 per cent) of the DJ specimens; moreover, each of the remaining DJ specimens clusters with group dominated heavily by EH.

This tends to signal a very close relationship of similarity between DJ and EH, which makes sense in terms of the site plan (Figure 4.1). It contrasts with AH, which although a small set tends to dominate each of its own clusters.

Overall, these results can be taken to indicate that the cluster segregation is quite highly structured, and certainly non-random. From that we could proceed to look at selected clusters, to see what might be specific and individual(ised) about them.

The clusters do show some distinctive features. First, cluster 1 picks out a small, fairly thick-pointed group. This seems quite similar to the group in AC/AH isolated by Gowlett (1988) (see Table 4.1).

Then groups 12 and 16 share a very similar footprint, very close to the Kilombe mean, but they have quite different thicknesses. Cluster 12 is about the 'normal' average thickness for Kilombe, but sixteen (and clusters 22 and 29) are all about 20 per cent thinner than the average. This idea of a 'footprint' sometimes being much more stable than the associated thickness bears out previous studies, which distinguished AH from Z mainly by the latter's much greater thickness (Crompton and Gowlett 1993).

Certainly something other than allometric weight-saving is involved here, as Cluster 16 is far thinner than the similarly-sized Cluster 12. Cluster groups 22 and 29 seem to pick out larger and smaller versions of the 'fairly thin biface'.

Lastly, if the cluster groups are valid, would they stand out on the excavation surface? Figure 4.3 shows the plots of the group members within the EH excavation. This is merely preliminary work. Only 'pairs' and 'trios' are plotted. There are approximately 100 bifaces from the 25 m² excavation, yielding an expected nearest neighbour mean distance of 0.25 metres, if the pieces are randomly distributed (Clark and Evans 1954). The actual mean nearest neighbour distance for cluster pairs is 3.25 metres, and for trios, 1.85 metres. This result may indicate that very similar bifaces have a strong tendency not to occur together. On the other hand, if the whole 25 m² contained two bifaces set at random, the mean expected distance between them would be 2.25 metres; and between three specimens, 1.75 metres. The results are inconclusive, but on average the second member of a pair is more than ten times more distant than the nearest biface.

Table 4.5 Mean measurements (cluster centres) of selected Kilombe clusters

Cluster No.	T	L	B	BM	BA	BB	V7	V8	TA	T/B	TA/L	BA/BB
Cluster 1*	33	104	69	61	36	65	29	33	15	0.48	0.14	0.55
Cluster 12*	45	151	101	97	74	86	54	65	24	0.45	0.16	0.86
Cluster 16*	34	153	95	90	64	81	61	66	18	0.36	0.12	0.79
Cluster 22*	27	119	76	72	50	66	40	47	16	0.36	0.13	0.76
Cluster 29*	36	165	102	100	70	83	71	85	19	0.35	0.12	0.84

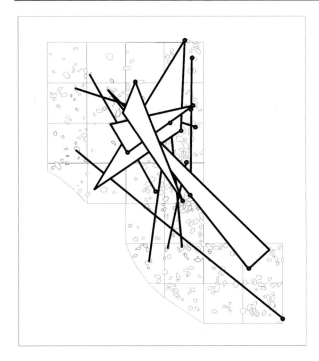

Figure 4.3 Clusters of bifaces within Area EH isolated by Density analysis: pairs and trios are shown linked.

'Extreme cases'

A separate approach to seeking the individual in these biface assemblages is to study *idiosyncracy*. Here the idea was to isolate specimens from the extremes of the range, and examine their characteristics. Which biface is the most extreme in this or that character, perhaps such as to be on the edge of usability? In this study bifaces had been measured by eight and ten variables: suppose we selected the specimens that were more than two standard deviations from the mean (plus or minus) for any variable – would they be equally far from the mean in other variables? Where there are systematic high correlations between a set of variables, this would be expected – so for Breadth and Length, the shortest might also be the narrowest. But how far would the principle hold? In bifaces, correlations range from about 0.90 to about 0.10, depending on the variable pair selected (Gowlett 1996b), so the outcome could not really be predicted.

In order to come up with a methodology which concentrates on the individual case, and rather than deal in standard deviations (and hence fractions of artefacts!) I have adopted an approach of selecting specimens representing the minimum and maximum values for each measured variable in a dataset. Thus for Length, we select the longest and the shortest cases. As this is done for an average of nine variables, roughly speaking the process would isolate from two to eighteen individual 'extreme' specimens from each dataset. If all the bifaces were geometrically identical, then as few as two specimens would emerge (smallest and largest); if the extremes are not correlated, there could be as many as 9×2 specimens, with the number increased further if two or more specimens should have the same value for some variable (e.g. two with a maximum thickness of 55 mm).

An important point about the procedure in this search for 'individuality' is that it needs to be robust, but does not have to follow formal statistical rules. The approach is empirical. At a superficial level, it does not obviously depend on sample size: any assemblage with more than twenty specimens could provide the necessary number of 'extreme values'. It could be held that only larger assemblages will provide the rare cases. But that assertion follows the assumption that we are taking random samples from some greater population, and at best we can only take the production from an area and ask if it behaves *as if* such assumptions were true.

Thus the approach can be followed across varied datasets – rather than concentrating on mean values we treat variation in the assemblage as a sort of hollow globe, and study the points on its surface. Apart from Kilombe, assemblages used here came from Kariandusi, Kalambo Falls and Sidi Abderrahman Cunette (Gowlett and Crompton 1994; Clark 2001; Gowlett *et al.* 2001; Biberson 1961; Crompton and Gowlett 1997; Raynal and Texier 1989).

The first interesting result is that in most datasets the selection tends to produce about ten to fifteen specimens. In other words, most of the extreme specimens reach their extremeness in only one or two variables. It is very rare for an individual specimen to reach its extremeness in as many as four of the nine measured variables.

This observation holds for each of these datasets (Table 4.6)

Even in the highly standardised Sidi Abderrahman Cunette series, the most 'extreme' biface is extreme in only five out of nine variables. In that particular

Table 4.6 Extreme cases among bifaces

	Extreme cases	Small extremes	Large extremes	Out of total	Max. individual extremeness
Kilombe EH	13	8	5	95	3
Kilombe AC/AD	10	5	5	121	4
Kariandusi Lava	19	11	8	73	3
Kalambo Falls A6	13	6	7	45	4
Cunette	5	3	2	122	5
Kariandusi obsidian	15	10	5	60	3

case the utter 'smallness' of a biface is so marked that it carries across numbers of variables. Generally, however, remembering that between two and twenty specimens might be marked by one or extreme or other, it is notable that in five assemblages out of six at least ten specimens are involved.

Do these extreme specimens differ from their parent group in more general respects? Here one could examine the selected specimens against their parent group. For area EH the mean values for all 'extreme' specimens are much the same as for the whole assemblage, except that they are smaller. This bears out the point that there are fewer very large specimens making a contribution.

The results give the impression that the individual making a large biface may have less possibility of choice than the individual making a short biface. To test this idea further, these results have been checked against the whole Kilombe series of about 400 specimens. The group of specimens shorter than one sd from the mean was compared with the corresponding group more than 1 sd longer than the mean (i.e. the shortest 16 per cent versus the longest 16 per cent). It is then found that the long specimens have not much more than half the shape variation of the short specimens:

57 longest bifaces Mean L = 199 mm B/L = 0.56 +/– 0.05 T/B = 0.46 +/– 0.07
56 shortest bifaces Mean L = 101 mm B/L = 0.67 +/– 0.08 T/B = 0.51 +/– 0.14

The standard deviations on the breadth/length and thickness/breadth ratios make this point clearly. The figures also demonstrate both the extraordinary symmetry of the length distribution around its mean, and the shape-shifts which prevent bifaces from becoming disproportionately heavy as they double in length from c. 10 to c. 20 cm.

Hence, the individual making a long (?impressive) biface does indeed have far less shape choice than the individual making a short biface.

Is the underlying cause of this restriction more function or appearance? The question touches on issues previously raised in allometry studies, where Crompton and Gowlett (1993) concluded that the largest bifaces were relatively narrow and relatively thin mainly through an effort to limit weight. The causes of allometric adjustment in small specimens were less plain, and it may indeed be that the allometry measures in small specimens are simply giving the average of a variable set.

Extending the search. . . .

One of the puzzles of the Acheulean is to know how far comparisons can be extended. Europe does not in general preserve extended surfaces covered in bifaces, like Africa, or India. Nevertheless, up to 1,000 bifaces can come from the various localities of important sites such as Boxgrove, or the Somme (Roberts and Parfitt 1999; Tuffreau et al. 1997). For the Acheulean, European datasets can be very like African ones, but some differences can be expected.

Here Beeches Pit offers an example, a site where the individuality of the bifaces is the first thing that impresses itself. Beeches Pit is a Middle Pleistocene site in Suffolk, England, dated to about 0.4 Ma (Andresen *et al.* 1997; Gowlett *et al.* 1998; Gowlett and Hallos 2000). Springs and the availability of flint drew humans to occupy the north bank of a watercourse. Although flint-knapping activities by a creek were obviously prolonged, relatively few bifaces were discarded. Each one therefore appears distinctive.

Nevertheless, there is also a clear difference between the two site localities at Beeches Pit. Differences between small and large biface specimens are so pronounced that one would assume different functions were envisaged.

The biface finds are summarised in Tables 4.7 and 4.8. In the upper part of AH excavation two small bifaces were found almost side by side. Nearby were pieces of flint which could have made suitable blanks for further similar specimens. These two artefacts, less than 100 g in weight, are considerably different from one another, although of similar length.

In AH, 20 metres to the east, and at a lower level, several biface specimens were found scattered in the flint concentrations that lie just to the north of a set of hearths (Figure 4.4). One biface blank is linked to these through refits. It would be hard to determine whether the others are contemporaneous or not. Each specimen, however, is distinctive – they show a set of different approaches to manufacture, and different design targets. It could be said perhaps that the seven Beeches Pit bifaces include more variation in some respects than the entire Kilombe set (Table 4.8).

The measurements do however combine to show rather similar variation to that on early African sites (compare with Table 4.1). At Kilombe, it seems natural to combine, to look at distributions and the whole pattern. At Beeches Pit it seems almost an offence to combine measurements for artefacts that are so clearly individual and distinctive (Figure 4.5).

Yet, one can argue that both approaches are valid. The rationale is summarised well in James' point (2003) of the individual and the pattern. Even among its host, each Kilombe specimen is an individual expression, as has been shown. Equally, each Beeches Pit specimen so distinctively made is made by an individual working *within* a group norm and collective cultural memory – the statistics 'ghost in' the thousands of other bifaces made by those people on that landscape and never to be found by us.

Conclusion

In this study I have tried to seek out and appreciate individuality even within the supposed sameness of the Acheulean. The approach has been exploratory – some elements or patterns are convincing; others could be artefacts of randomness, and require further testing.

Two things seem at least to be strong likelihoods. First, that modern human individuals making tools and working within group norms operate within a

Table 4.7 Beeches Pit bifaces

Ref. number	Description	Weight	Length	Breadth	Thickness	East	North	Level
BP AF5331	Small biface	55	72	49	19	52.29	96.54	28.81
BP AF6196	Small biface	85	73	60	20	52.50	96.31	28.72
BP AH229	Other biface	510	117	100	35	79.80	92.74	28.12
BP AH411	Other biface	265	99	75	42	79.19	91.79	27.7
BP AH1300	Biface	435	123	87	48	78.55	93.15	28.03
BP AH2105	Disc	45	52	48	26	78.17	90.04	27.53
BP-Ashmolean	Pointed	288	125	81	40			

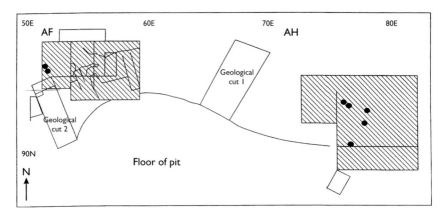

Figure 4.4 Beeches Pit: distribution of biface finds (black dots) in the excavations on the north side of the pit.

Table 4.8 Means and Standard deviations for Beeches Pit bifaces

Beeches Pit bifaces	(n=7)
L	94 +/– 29
B	71 +/– 20
T	33 +/– 11
T/B	0.46 +/– 0.10
B/L	0.77 +/– 0.10

substantial but limited part of the whole group range. A case has been put that individuals may have operated similarly in Acheulean times, and that behaviour consistent with this proposition can sometimes be picked out. Second, that the limits of group norms are somewhat, but not very, elastic. Somebody making a biface can go to the extremes of the range in one or more variables, but not all; and usually in only one or two. It is not clear whether functional or cultural constraints cut in first.

In Palaeolithic archaeology there is no difficulty in seeing the individual – the comparison with history is something of a false one. The initial assumption is that history sees the individual clearly, whereas archaeology is anonymous. This is only so if we require a name. The better comparison is rather with tombstones – in history many individuals feature as a name, not for any actions. They have historicity, but one that is then lost in any manipulation that seeks to extract more meaning from the data.

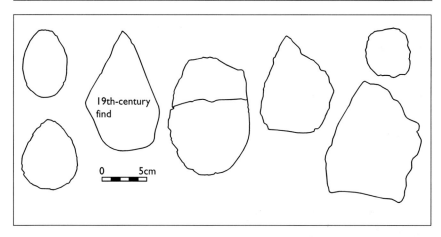

Figure 4.5 The varied form of Beeches Pit bifaces in plan view. The two small specimens
on the left come from AF. The remainder come from area AH, apart from a
nineteenth-century find now in the Ashmolean museum, exact provenance
unknown.

Archaeology must choose how sharply to focus, again with the dilemma that
the more individuals who feature, the less time for each. Indeed, this is the
human dilemma highlighted by the social brain – we all labour against the
cognitive load imposed by numbers.

Chapter 5

The making of the biface and the making of the individual

Martin Porr

The Acheulean biface, or handaxe, is possibly the most intriguing starting point for an investigation of the individual in the Lower and Middle Palaeolithic, because it signals one of the most important steps in human technical and social evolution. In particular, such bifaces provide the first indication of the use of artefacts beyond an ape-grade technology (Wynn and McGrew 1989) and they continue, as many of the chapters in this volume demonstrate, to be the focus of investigations in this distant period. The handaxe also played a crucial role in the establishment of human antiquity in the formative phase of Palaeolithic archaeology (for discussion see Grayson 1983). The importance of bifaces to these developments was the result of one visually striking characteristic that we have trained ourselves to appreciate for its taxonomic and typological advantages: similarity in style. It was their recurrent style, as revealed by their apparent similarity, which suggested to those archaeological pioneers that bifaces were recognisable human artefacts. In order to understand why the Acheulean biface is such a style icon both for our own discovery of a remote past and for the inception of such behaviour in human evolution it is necessary to gain an understanding of the role of style and how it relates to individuals and their social practices in the Lower Palaeolithic.

In this chapter I develop a model of the processes in which both style and bifacial tools were first created about 1.5 million years ago. I will begin by critically discussing a number of approaches towards style in Palaeolithic archaeology to show that a satisfactory explanation of Lower Palaeolithic bifacial tools has so far not been achieved. I will argue that the creation of style must be seen as a reflection of the incorporation of material artefacts into socially constructed power relations. The extended periods of learning and mastering the production of bifaces became an important mechanism in controlling and restricting the access to positions of power. I will make the case that bifaces materialised abstract social structures which before only existed in the dynamic interactions between individuals and in the heads and bodies of actors. At the time of *Homo ergaster* scavenged and/or hunted carcasses became the catalysts of this process because they provided the social arenas where this shift could take place (see also Porr 2000). However, the social significance of bifaces was still linked to the condition of co-presence among social actors, so that Acheulean bifaces did not become independent social symbols.

Style and Lower Palaeolithic stone tools

Style is one of the central and most important topics in archaeology and continues to create much debate and many definitions (Gamble 2001: 107–13 for some of them). Here I will follow only those developments which help us to understand why Lower Palaeolithic bifacial tools provide a significant challenge to the common understanding of style. In Palaeolithic archaeology style was at the centre of one of its most famous scientific arguments, the 'Mousterian debate' between Francois Bordes and Lewis Binford (see references in Binford 1983; Mellars 1996a). This exchange focused on a topic that has remained with the discipline ever since, the relation between function and cultural form. While the matter was obviously much more complicated, Bordes argued that the changes he observed between different Mousterian layers in rock shelters in Southern France were related to ethnic differences between groups. Binford, in contrast, stressed that these differences were rather the product of different activities (potentially, by the same group). Binford not only denied that the differences in artefact shapes and assemblage composition were a consequence of 'ethnic' differences. He also denied that such a capacity existed in the Middle Palaeolithic at all. Both authers consequently saw the relations between artefacts, hominids and their material environment in a fundamentally different way, albeit one centred on the group rather than the individual. In Binford's case the environment seems to determine the shape of stone tools, because they are a function of their actual material use. In this sense, the style of artefacts is caused by the material conditions in which they are produced and to be used. According to Bordes's interpretation the artefact (and the composition of an assemblage) is shaped by cultural traditions, irrespective of the material tasks to be executed in a particular situation. In this sense, the shape of the artefact is caused by the mental images or concepts that are stored in the heads of actors and which are transmitted between generations. The 'Mousterian debate' consequently touches upon fundamental issues of archaeological explanation: How does culture relate to nature, how does arbitrary form relate to the necessities of survival?

This latter distinction is also central in the contributions of Sackett who regards 'style' as a reflection of 'ethnicity'. Accordingly the similarity of objects relates to a social closeness of their manufacturers (Sackett 1982: 74). Style, however, is not only a matter of specific ethnic markers (e.g. decorations). Style is regarded as a part of all choices of a group in everyday life. Sackett assumes that a number of functionally equivalent material solutions exist for every possible task. Within this pool of possibilities people make their stylistic choices. The process of choice is an ongoing and mostly unconscious procedure that is implicated in every daily action. This is the core of Sackett's 'isochrestic' model.

It draws attention to the fact that every behaviour has stylistic dimensions so that the analysis cannot be limited to those objects or aspects of objects that are traditionally regarded as 'stylistically' significant (such as pots, decorations, ornaments, etc.).

The topic of style has also been examined in ethno-archaeological case studies (e.g. Hodder 1982) and among these Wiessner's (1983, 1984) examination of style in Kalahari San projectile points is of particular interest for this discussion. Her analyses draw attention to the fact that style plays an important role in the negotiation of social as well as personal identities of individuals – two inter-related aspects, which she regards 'to be necessary for identity formation' (Wiessner 1984: 225) in a psychological sense. Her fieldwork clearly shows that a model which equates stylistic similarity with affiliation and stylistic dissim-ilarity with differentiation is too simplistic. Style has not only to be analysed in relation to groups but also in relation to socially situated individuals.

Gamble (1999) has recently summarised several contributions that point in similar directions and has developed his own concept that explicitly takes the individual as a starting point of analysis. Gamble (1999: 50) proposes that the use of formal material symbols is directly related to the social distance between partners in interactions. Within their intimate networks individuals commu-nicate primarily, but not exclusively, with emotional resources (e.g. speaking, grooming, etc.), whereas communication in more extended networks has to involve material and stylistic symbols (e.g. clothing, uniforms, flags, etc.). His model points to some fundamental relations of social interactions and stylistic objects. Every individual needs to restrict the investment of emotional resources (because of limited time) but at the same time needs to be able to deal with individuals that are not personally known.

Despite the unquestionable elaboration of the models serious difficulties remain in all models mentioned in explaining the origin and persistence of Lower Palaeolithic bifacial tools. For example, within Gamble's (1999) system there is neither the need nor a justification for a stylistic tool within Lower Palaeolithic groups, because all social interactions were restricted to face-to-face relations. The shape of the biface would have to be interpreted as a reflection of 'symbolic or material' resources, which imply complex commu-nications between groups. However, there is no sign of such complexity in the Lower Palaeolithic. The distribution of bifaces across large areas of the Old World clearly cannot be interpreted as being the reflection of an ancient world-wide communication system. The Acheulean biface consequently contradicts one of the central assumptions in the context of style. In the Lower Palaeolithic stylistic similarity in objects clearly does not relate to either a social or ethnic similarity or a social closeness between their makers. Following Sackett's terminology, individuals in the Lower Palaeolithic made a very specific choice from a pool of isochrestic alternatives. However, no ethnic differentiation between groups was involved as well as no further choices for a very long time. Consequently, Sackett's isochrestic model does not provide an explanation of this phenomenon, and this is mainly due to its lack of interest in the mechanisms of style production and reproduction. In the approaches mentioned above only Wiessner (e.g. 1984: 225) has so far considered the importance of intra-group mechanisms in the creation of style. However, active creation of identity by individuals is usually disregarded in the case of the Lower Palaeolithic. Moreover, it seems as if there is hardly enough variation over time and space to assume such a dynamic process. Nevertheless, Wiessner's approach already shows that style can indeed be understood if the role of situated individuals and their interactions with respect to ways of transmission are considered.

Generally, approaches that understand style as a communication within and between social groups have so far struggled with explaining Acheulean bifaces. However, also the functional argument does not make much sense, because the Acheulean biface is not a very functional tool. In fact, it is simply unnecessary from a functional point of view. Of course, there can be little doubt that bifaces were used for a variety of tasks and definitely performed very well – but their elaboration and symmetry, especially in the later stages of the Acheulean and even the Middle Palaeolithic, cannot be explained by functional necessities (see e.g. Kohn and Mithen 1999: 520). The different possible uses of the biface can always be performed by other tools as well, which could be produced with much less effort. Schick and Toth (1993) have accidentally illustrated this in a diagram where bifaces only occur within functional categories together with other artefacts. Acheulean bifaces were not only over-designed in relation to their most commonly assumed main use, the dismemberment of large animal carcasses, but in relation to other tasks as well. Finally, the standardisation of the biface also presents serious problems for their makers, because it puts serious restrictions on the range of suitable raw material nodules (Porr 2000: 20–2). An argument that concentrates on the functional efficiency of the Acheulean biface is consequently inappropriate.

From this brief review of different approaches towards style in Palaeolithic archaeology several points can be gained. The major problem of most models is their reference to much more complex social situations than have to be assumed in the Lower Palaeolithic. This is understandable in an attempt to emphasise and access the complexities of Palaeolithic social life (especially in Gamble 1999). However, it also leads away from the micro-dynamics of social life and intra-group processes, which must have been responsible for the relevant developments that can be observed in the archaeological record. There is consequently the need for a theoretical perspective that concentrates much more closely on the actions and interactions of individuals. Furthermore, it will also be necessary to draw upon different materials to test and illustrate these ideas. While in the past most inferences were drawn from case studies of hunters and gatherers and more complex societies, I will develop the argument below with explicit references towards the social and technical behaviour of living great apes, especially the chimpanzee. While this decision certainly is not without problems, I follow Boesch and Boesch-Achermann (2000: 272) in their assertion that 'chimpanzees were more similar to our ancestors than any living human being'. The available wealth of information about chimpanzees provides the best starting point for an exploration of the life of our ancestors in the period before bifacial tools were produced. It also contains several critical elements that allows the modelling of one of the most important shifts in human history.

Pan, Oldowan and Acheulean technologies – material and dynamic style

To move beyond the problems of the approaches mentioned in the preceding section, I want to introduce an analytical distinction that addresses one important aspect that has so far not received much attention in Palaeolithic archaeology: 'style' does not only reside in finalised objects, but also in processes and practices. This is obviously a difficult subject for archaeologists, and especially for those studying the Palaeolithic. However, it needs to be stressed that human artefacts are connected to practices at every stage of their life history so that there exists a mutual relationship between them. From this follows that practices will have effects on the manipulated objects just as the latter will influence the way human beings will use and produce them. These relations will differ with the social position of the involved objects, the social occasions and individuals, and these will influence their transmission.

For the following discussion of Lower Palaeolithic technologies I therefore propose a distinction between 'material style' and 'dynamic style'. 'Material style' refers to the specific material form that objects are given by human beings. It can both refer to single artefacts or the composition of an assemblage. It can even be related to the material consequences of moving objects from one place to another (such as caching stones). Material style is usually explained in terms of group identity and group membership. Most importantly, material style is related to the demonstration of group membership of individuals in relation to other groups (Wobst 1977). While some authors accept the possibility that stylistically similar objects increase intra-group coherence, nevertheless the generally accepted social function of material style is the establishment of inter-group boundaries (e.g. Hodder 1982).

To a certain extent material style is independent of the actions of individuals. Indeed, material objects that have been given a particular style refer to something beyond the individual, they can refer social entities that sometimes can have quite an abstract existence (e.g. a flag that stands for a nation-state). Consequently, even if material stylistic objects are produced by individuals and individual practices, they usually do not depend on individual persons to be understood. In this sense, material stylistic objects have a life of their own and can play an active role in social processes. They can influence the actions of other individuals just by their material presence and can even establish power relations (e.g. a traffic sign) if the involved parties know how to read the messages.

These relations between material stylistic objects that transport certain cultural messages between individuals have been exhaustively discussed in archaeology in the past. However, much more relevant for an understanding of Lower Palaeolithic contexts is 'dynamic style', which relates to the similarities in the actions of individuals within close face-to-face social formations. Here insights from primate studies are relevant. According to Boesch and Tomasello (1998) the mechanism of 'ontogenetic ritualisation' is mainly responsible for such similarities within groups and populations in chimpanzees and other primates. In this process 'individuals essentially shape one another's behaviour over time' (Boesch and Tomasello 1998: 600; Tomasello 1994). It is important to note that these processes are not directed at other groups or even related to the existence of other groups. Ontogenetic ritualisation is automatically created within groups of individuals that live together and are in close face-to-face and body-to-body contact. Groups will consequently develop their own 'dynamic style' of doing everyday tasks. Boesch and Tomasello (1998) have examined the use of material objects in African great ape populations and found that behaviours vary independently from adaptive/ecological factors. As these behaviours are not genetically transmitted, they draw the important conclusion that these differences have to be regarded as 'culturally transmitted traditions'. For the argument here it is not important if we call this 'culture' (Foley 1991). It is only relevant that groups will habitually develop different dynamic styles, because individual group members will imitate or learn other individual's behaviours in the ongoing processes of actions and interactions (Tomasello 1994).

The material effects of dynamic style are much more subtle and more difficult to discern than those of material style. Similarities in objects are only created by the application of replicated practices. Individuals do not attempt to replicate a particular material form. The intention of the producer is not directed at the shape of the end-product but at the creation of particular material properties (e.g. sharp edges). In modern humans such a relation between practices, intentions and material artefacts is virtually non-existent, because every individual is already enmeshed in a web of pre-structured objects and practices. However, this is neither the case for the material culture of chimpanzees nor was for the technology of the Oldowan. Wynn and McGrew (1989) found that no aspect of Oldowan technology exceeds the limits of chimpanzee behaviour. This applied to both the use of specific objects for the manipulation of the environment and the spatio-temporal organisation of objects, such as transport of raw material for future use. Consequently, 'the Oldowan pushed the limits of ape grade adaptation; it did not exceed them' (Wynn and McGrew 1989: 394). The latter conclusion fits well into the general picture of the behavioural ecology of the Australopithecines and early *Homo*, which has emerged in the last ten years. These hominids were not adapted to an open savannah environment and had not developed a full bipedal locomotion (e.g. Tobias 1999 for a summary). Their behavioural ecology can therefore very well be compared to modern chimpanzees. The introduction of stone tools and their transport into the behavioural repertoire of these hominids was a new element, but it was not fundamentally different from the transport of hammer stones to nut-cracking sites by modern chimpanzees (Boesch and Boesch-Achermann 2000).

Oldowan and chimpanzee technologies are the products of pure dynamic style. The intention of hominids in the Oldowan was to produce flakes or choppers with sharp edges that enabled them to cut through the thick skin of large animal carcasses. The result of their actions was a range of transitional core and flake tools that all met certain material requirements, but are not formally shaped (Potts 1993: 60). The same can be said of chimpanzee material culture, which is flexible and differentiated, involves the use and transport of a range of raw materials, but does not include any formally designed objects (McGrew 1992, 1994). This characterisation can be related to social contexts of co-presence and different forms of direct cultural transmission between individuals (see Tomasello 1994). In these conditions the establishment of social relations depends on the co-presence of the individuals involved. The social order and the structure of power within a group needs to be constantly reinforced, because it is constantly challenged. These dynamic relations can be observed in chimpanzees in the wild (Goodall 1986) as well as in captivity (de Waal 1998). A similarly flexible social system can reasonably be assumed for hominids during the Oldowan (Boesch and Boesch-Achermann 2000: 276). In the case of chimpanzees the learning of the production and manipulation of material tools is part of the daily flow of learning, producing and reproducing the group's dynamic style. Participating in this flow contributes to the cohesion of the group and enables individuals to efficiently participate in social interactions. However, the manipulation of material objects is not a necessary requirement in any of these interactions. Even though chimpanzees sometimes use material objects in individual interactions (e.g. using a branch or a large stone to threaten opponents; see de Waal 1998: 120), objects are never integrated into relations between individuals on a regular basis and are therefore not given a lasting social significance. The structural similarities of the archaeological evidence clearly suggest that this also was the case during the Oldowan.

The beginning of the 'Acheulean stage' of the Lower Palaeolithic did not represent a fundamental change in the composition of the Oldowan tool kit, but is characterised by the inclusion of symmetrically shaped bifaces into assemblages. Wynn (1995: 10) defined them as 'bifacially trimmed core tools', which first appeared in rather crude examples in East African inventories around 1.5 million years ago. From time to time it has been suggested that the final shape of bifaces was not an intentional product at all (e.g. Weissmüller 2003; Noble and Davidson 1996), but rather an unintended consequence of highly controlled flake production. In the face of hundreds of finely shaped examples from all over the world that are carefully retouched around the edges as well as examples where the retouched edge actually mirrors a naturally shaped one, this idea can surely be rejected (see Wynn 1995: 13, Figure 3; Marshall *et al*. 2002).

Acheulean bifaces are the first artefacts in history that show an intentional imposition of arbitrary form. 'Shared knowledge of arbitrary design' and 'rudimentary ideas of spatial measurement and symmetry', which are expressed in the Acheulean biface, both signal capabilities beyond the 'ape grade adaptation' (Wynn and McGrew 1989: 394–5). They consequently represent a quality that is neither present in chimpanzee technologies nor the Oldowan. In the context of this chapter they relate to the creation of material style within contexts of dynamic style. Just as Oldowan technology does not disappear with Acheulean tools, material style is now added into the dynamics of social life. Structured sets of practices were now also aimed at replicating a recognisable material form. In the next section I will draw attention away from the finished objects and stress instead the consequences of the replication of a material style for the practices of their makers. I will argue that it was not the end-product itself that was important and of social significance, but the demonstration of the ability to replicate the intended and predefined form in specific social contexts. Acheulean bifaces are products of the interdependence of material and dynamic style as well as the context of dominance and power in which they were first created.

Bifacial tools and the behavioural ecology of *Homo ergaster/erectus*

The earliest Acheulean bifaces coincide with a new hominid species, *Homo ergaster*, which is most prominently represented by the 'Nariokotome boy' (KMN-WT 15000) from Lake Turkana (Walker and Leakey 1993) and several specimens from Dmanisi in Georgia (Gabunia *et al*. 2000). *Homo ergaster* is the first hominid with a post-cranial anatomy that is very similar to modern humans and a full bipedal locomotion (Henke and Rothe 1999: 229). The various physical characteristics of this species, which can be related to an adaptation to a life in open environments, have been described elsewhere (e.g. Cachel and Harris 1999; Foley 1987, 1999; Henke and Rothe 1999). The savannah is mainly characterised by a limited supply of water, an abundant and diverse large mammal fauna and a marked seasonality. Hominids apparently responded to these conditions either by specialising in the processing of low-quality plants (*Paranthropus*) or by incorporating meat into their feeding habits on a regular basis (*Homo ergaster*). *Homo ergaster* began to exploit 'a range of mammal species . . . to an extent unknown in modern non-human primates' (Foley 1987: 215). The inclusion of meat into the diet is 'likely to have developed in the context of seasonal stress among early African hominids' (Foley 1987: 214). Ultimately, this behaviour not only helped hominids to cope with the difficulties of life in a savannah environment, but as a result of the extension of home range sizes it can also be linked to the extraordinary dispersal of *Homo ergaster* out of Africa (Gamble and Steele 1999: 397; Aiello and Wheeler 1995). However, the question that needs to be examined here is how these changes affected the (re)structuring of social relations.

As a high-quality source of protein and fat, scavenged or hunted animals have an irregular and patchy distribution in the landscape. Because animals are mobile they need to be hunted and because carnivores are competitors their kills need to be found before everything has been eaten. Both strategies are uncertain and unpredictable. However, if either strategy is successful then a carcass provides a large quantity of high-quality food. The higher nutritional value and in most cases its availability in large quantities meant that animal carcasses had important and significant consequences for the relations between hominids.

This is certainly the case with chimpanzees where the acquisition and distribution of meat is always of particular social importance. In the Taï forest the animals follow complex and co-ordinated strategies in hunting the arboreal red colobus monkeys. The hunt is therefore a social activity whose structure is also reflected in the way the kill is distributed. The animals do not hide the prey from the other members of the group, but form feeding groups within which meat is distributed. On these occasions the chimpanzees apparently acknowledge the contributions that different individuals made to the success of the hunt. Male chimpanzees that arrive after the hunt has finished are not included in the distribution – irrespective of their formal rank (Boesch and Boesch 1989; Boesch and Boesch-Achermann 2000). The hunt and the distribution of meat is consequently a very tense social occasion that can influence the power structure of a group, especially the relations between adult males. Nishida and his colleagues (1992) were even able to observe a case in which a male chimpanzee in the Mahale Mountains tried to strengthen his position by differentially sharing meat with males and females according to their social rank. These examples emphasise more than the possible social importance of meat for forest chimpanzees and, by analogy, early hominids in open savannahs. The chimpanzees provide an example of the problems that a highly desired resource can present for a social system without formal rules but with alliances based on grooming and other face-to-face interaction. The tensions for such limited social actors can become very strong indeed, as de Waal (1998: 10) also found among captive chimpanzees where fights over food stemmed from similar pressures.

Because of their large package size and high nutritional quality animal carcasses must have presented similar social tensions for *Homo ergaster*. But at the same time they also provided more than any other form of food the possibility for extraordinary political and social action. The importance of meat for the development of social relations in human evolution has, of course, been recognised before, for example, in Isaac's (1978b) seminal food-sharing hypothesis which emphasised the establishment of home bases and closer ties between group members within the landscape. Hill (1982) argued that the habitual hunting of male hominids enabled them to fulfil their nutritional needs in the savannah environment much more efficiently and resulted in the distribution of surplus meat to females. Hill's approach does not ignore the differential interests of individual hominids and illustrates that regardless of its actual importance for survival, a large animal carcass can indeed be a powerful political arena, and one that goes beyond any other social occasion available to living primates.

For an understanding of the origins of bifaces it is necessary to integrate the changing roles of stone tools in these contexts. During the Oldowan hominids already transported suitable lithic raw materials short distances (Stiles 1998). The tools that were produced only had to meet a few requirements, mainly sharp edges, and a high degree of flexibility in form existed. Oldowan hominids were only beginning to get involved in hunting or competitive scavenging that resulted in regular social arenas surrounding large carcasses. Stone tools in the Oldowan were still of little importance for the structuring of power relations at social occasions which involved the consumption of food. *Homo ergaster* continued the integration of the acquisition of stone raw materials and the production of tools in the rhythms of daily lives, but during this time hunting and the acquisition of meat gained much more importance. Consequently, if either a carcass or meat in general was simultaneously an economic as well as a political resource, then we can assume that both the tools and the skills that were used to gain access to this important resource acquired 'political' significance as well as conferring functional advantage.

This is an important point as it helps to understand why style developed even in the apparently limited Lower Palaeolithic social contexts of co-presence. The need to create a formalised object, to replicate a particular material form, indeed affects all aspects of the production sequence from raw material acquisition to the actual acts of stone-knapping. If a material style is to be replicated then this project significantly constrains the actions that are acceptable in order to reach the desired result. Bifaces were consequently not important as isolated objects; their creation was more likely a consequence of an increased level of social control that was associated with the whole set of practices that was connected with the acquisition and distribution of animal carcasses.

The production of bifaces forced hominids into a much more complicated chain of operations, which necessitated the investment of more time and effort. This investment not only included the actual time an individual needed to find a suitable nodule and the increased effort of production. It also included the mastery of these skills over a considerable period of time. This latter aspect has largely been ignored in the discussion of the origins of bifaces. The appearance and continuing production of these objects necessitated not only cognitive and manipulative abilities, but also ways of transmission and the time in which learning could take place. In short, hominids needed to learn how to make bifaces and these activities needed to be integrated into the rhythms of every day life. Judging from observations in ethnographic contexts and in wild chimpanzee populations as well as from experiments this is not a trivial aspect.

Observations in the Taï Forest have shown that it takes up to eight years for a chimpanzee to master all aspects of nut-cracking, even though this time involves intense learning relations (mostly between mothers and infants; Boesch and Boesch-Achermann 2000; Hedwige Boesch, personal communication). In modern humans it can take even longer to become an effective stone adze-maker (Stout 2002) or become a skilled craftsman in other fields (Roux 1999).

The introduction of bifacial tools consequently reflects the development of an area in which the actions of the involved individuals were much more constrained than before. Learning the ability to make a bifacial tool did not take place in isolation. It must have been a communal undertaking, because it involved the constant monitoring and correcting of the achieved results, which finally had to be replications of already existing objects. These processes of learning are obviously processes of domination and control. In contrast to the acquisition of the dynamic style of the group that mostly involves the unconscious imitation of bodily practices in face-to-face situations, this cannot be assumed for a complex task such as the making of a biface, which requires a high degree of attention and manual skills. In contrast to Oldowan tools the production and use of bifaces held a special position in early hominid society – a position that was special enough to motivate hominids to subject themselves to long periods of apprenticeship.

Power, apprenticeship and the biface

The development and establishment of a savannah adaptation in hominid evolution has often been described as a time of stress and in terms of the difficulties that hominids needed to overcome. However, looking at the biface from an energetic point of view this seems highly unlikely. The costs of making such a tool can hardly be justified by its contribution to survival if 'cheaper' alternatives were available and could have been produced much more efficiently. These costs are even multiplied if the efforts of individual learning are taken into account. The production of bifaces in fact rather seems to suggest that the activities associated with them were actually not central for survival, simply because the pressure for effectiveness was obviously not particularly strong.

In this context, Kohn and Mithen (1999) have proposed that the elaboration of bifaces is in fact related to processes of sexual selection. As products of specifically male actions they enabled females to monitor several dimensions of fitness at once (e.g. resource location abilities, planning, good health, etc.). Given the complexities of primate societies I think that already in the Lower Palaeolithic the links between male behaviour and female choices were much more complicated. But the main problem of Kohn and Mithen's model is the assumption that bifaces were produced within contexts of intense competition and essentially as individual projects. In this scenario, every individual would have to achieve the best (biggest, most symmetrical, etc.) result with minimised co-operation and maximised deception. In the light of the long periods of apprenticeship that have to be assumed and the persistence of the form of the biface with only minor changes over long periods of time this can hardly have been the case. In fact, bifaces seem to exclude individual and innovative influences.

In the context of the Middle Palaeolithic occupation of Europe Roebroeks (2001) has made the point that human hunting cannot be understood as an individual task, but only as a highly communal and social one. Already at the time of *Homo ergaster* individuals needed to learn how to hunt, how to find prey or carcasses and they needed to learn how to process them. The acquisition of these skills must have been subject to significant processes of interaction and ways of transmission of knowledge between individuals. These processes involved the learning of a specific dynamic style. But at the time of *Home ergaster* this alone was not enough anymore. Hunting, accessing and processing meat ceased to be unproblematic tasks in which a high degree of flexibility was allowed. It necessitated the introduction of a new level of social control that connected the mastery of technical and mechanical aspects with the mastery of social and political aspects.

The biface is a reaction to the social tensions that originated from the integration of large carcasses into *Homo ergaster* society. The hunter needs to learn from others, but needs to make the kill alone. He or she can bring down an animal, but needs to co-operate with others as soon as the carcass can be butchered and utilised. For a hominid there is no way to escape the social, it is implicated in every act. But hominids or humans actually do not want to escape the social, they want to create and manipulate it. It is possible, by analogy to chimpanzees, but difficult to test further that these new social mechanisms were largely restricted to the male domain. However, one of the fundamental characteristics of chimpanzees, and most likely of early hominids, is a highly formalised male dominance system (Boesch and Boesch-Achermann 2000; de Waal 1998) that favours the ability of individual actors to apply and manipulate specific rules during social interaction. When combined with the larger group size that have to be assumed for *Homo ergaster* (Foley 1987: 173–4) then the conditions for the development of a new level of formalisation can be understood. It is therefore probable, but not yet proven, that it was predominantly male individuals that were involved in hunting and carcass exploitation – and consequently created bifaces.

The biface is both individual and communal; it is both utilitarian and non-utilitarian. It was made by single individuals but slavishly reproduced a socially defined form. It can be used very efficiently in various tasks, but its elaboration is unnecessary. The biface is the material effect of a certain power structure, which is reproduced by and within a system of learning processes and apprenticeship The biface is not just about competition. It is about competition within structures of learning and control. It is about social competition within communal structures. Within these structures individuals can only gain control by learning the rules, by learning the structures. It is very likely that only the mastery of the biface allowed individuals to use meat as a political resource or to control this resource at all in any form. The biface must be understood as a sign of authority, but it was not detached from its maker. A curious phenomenon of the Acheulean is the large number of similar (and still 'functional') bifaces that can be found at some sites (e.g. at Olorgesaille or the Somme gravels). At other sites bifaces were produced and discarded in the same location (e.g. Boxgrove) without any traces of use (Roberts *et al.* 1997). These observations clearly show that *Homo ergaster/erectus* and later *Homo heidelbergensis* society were still tied to co-presence and social integration (Gamble 1999). During the Acheulean it was the sequence of acts and the practical mastery of production that was powerful and not the finalised object alone. For these hominids the 'release from proximity' in their social lives had not yet taken place (Rodseth *et al.* 1991). The implication is that if bifaces became detached from their maker they lost their social significance.

Conclusion

The biface continued to remain the only formally shaped stone tool for a long period of time, and it continued to stand in contrast to the basic structuration of Lower Palaeolithic social relations within close and intimate networks. By including aspects of power and the socially situated individual the model proposed in this chapter aimed at exploring the links between bifaces and their makers in a different way. It is not intended to explain all cases of the occurrence of bifaces. It also does not predict that *Home ergaster/erectus* everywhere produced bifaces. During the million years of their existence bifaces were certainly made and used in a variety of contexts and these need to be critically examined in every case study. The biface cannot be understood as an isolated object with a single meaning. It is certainly wrong to see it as a status symbol or as an object of power in itself. It has to be seen as a part of a social dynamic and its makers demonstrated their power and ability because they controlled and mastered this dynamic. Face-to-face interactions between individuals in the contexts in which bifaces were used were socially more important than the objects that were implicated. More innovations and more variations between and within populations would have occurred if this would not have been the case. The only pieces of evidence that seem to point into this direction are the 'giant bifaces' that have been found at several sites (e.g. Isimila, Tanzania – Henke and Rothe 1999: 153; Furze Platt, England – Roe 1981; Olduvai Gorge, Tanzania – Roe 1994). However, even these exceptional examples demonstrate that hominids did not really innovate in this context. They concentrated on refining and expanding already existing features. Their aim was not the creation of an individual project but the elaboration of a communally defined one. The mastery of the biface consequently reflects the mastery of a particular set of social relations. In the long period of apprenticeship the learning of social rules and the successful acquisition of the group's dynamic style was always more important than the material object itself.

Chapter 6

Observations on the relationship between Palaeolithic individuals and artefact scatters at the Middle Pleistocene site of Boxgrove, UK

Matt Pope and Mark Roberts

Introduction

Twenty years of research, focused on the Boxgrove palaeolandscape in Southern England, has made us very aware of the immediacy of evidence recovered from this fine-grained Palaeolithic record. This immediacy stems in part from the perfect preservation of knapping scatters and the spatial arrangement of activity areas at the site. These affordances allow us to occupy the same geographical space as the Boxgrove hominins and, during the process of fieldwork, re-inhabit the vacant spaces their physical forms left behind. We can pass clusters of unproductive test pits at the site and effectively cross the empty areas of grassland which witnessed only the passing movement of hominin groups. We can circle a waterhole where tools and butchery activity were concentrated in a few minutes, or squat beside a knapping scatter at an excavated kill site and view the constellations and clusters of stone debris left in a state of preservation which betrays their remote antiquity. Boxgrove is a rare example of a record in which the processes of burial and preservation have left large tracts of a half-million-year-old landscape, with associated scatters of stone artefacts and butchered faunal remains, virtually undisturbed: a record which we feel holds the potential to bridge the gap between individuality as expressed by Archaic *Homo sapiens* and our own direct experience as individuals within modern social and environmental contexts. During the process of excavating these exceptional sites, our most effective analytical tool has been our ability as individuals to occupy the same physical spaces, and to directly interact with parts of the same natural, technological and social environments as those who created the record (Figure 6.1).

It is therefore frustrating, given such an exceptional data set, that the individuals who formed these signatures remain so elusive in our final analyses. Despite detailed fieldwork, and exhaustive study, they often emerge as purely technological agents or else become submerged in wider discussions of group behaviour, large-scale colonisations or typological variation (Bradley and

Figure 6.1 Scatters under excavations from the landsurface at GTP17 (GTP = Geological Test Pit).

Sampson 1986; Mithen 1994; Gamble 1998b). Part of the problem may stem from the fact that we are too ready to see scatters of stone and bone as merely a static by-product of the indisputably dynamic rhythms of Palaeolithic life. As archaeologists we are prepared to accept that this evolutionary jetsam can be interrogated, through increasingly detailed analysis, to yield meaningful information about our remote prehistory. We are perhaps less equipped to examine the extent to which Palaeolithic individuals interacted with such scatters, in both physical and cognitive ways, and to what extent such scatters helped to structure the patterns of land use, social interaction and palaeoecology.

In this contribution we explore the possibility that Palaeolithic individuals were not simply passive, disengaged agents in the formation of the Middle Pleistocene archaeological record. We will argue that the Boxgrove evidence provides some indicators that hominin individuals actively engaged with their own archaeological traces: that they had 'history' in the sense explored by Bradley (2002) for much later prehistoric societies. On a physical level these hominins selectively relocated, reused and discarded material in remarkably structured ways. These strongly patterned signatures may have allowed individuals to cognitively infer much about their own ecological and social reality. At a time when we are focused on our abilities to access the individual from scatters of flaked stone and butchered bone in a meaningful way, it may be fruitful to consider the abilities of Archaic *Homo* to do the same.

Background to Boxgrove

The site of Boxgrove is located in the county of West Sussex, Southern England (Figure 6.2). Topographically it occupies a position at the intersection between a chalk escarpment and a low-lying coastal plain fringing the English Channel. The coastal plain has been formed over the past 500,000 years by marine erosion during high sea-level events in warm interglacial stages which, due to gradual tectonic uplift, has formed a staircase sequence of wave-cut platforms. A suite of marine, lagoonal and terrestrial sediments comprising the Boxgrove geological sequence is preserved on the highest and oldest of these wave-cut platforms at an altitude of 40 m above sea level. The deposits themselves have now been mapped over 26 km (Roberts and Pope in preparation) and have been dated on the grounds of mammalian biostratigraphy to around 480,000 years ago (Roberts and Parfitt 1999).

Excavations began at the quarry in 1982 and have continued since then in a series of large-scale multidisciplinary research projects. The results of these have been published in a series of papers (Roberts 1986; Bergman and Roberts 1988; Bergman et al. 1990; Austin 1994; Roberts et al. 1997) and monographs (Roberts and Parfitt 1999; Roberts et al. in preparation) documenting the geological, palaeoecological and behavioural context of the archaeological material. The artefacts from the site form an industry with Acheulean affinities characterised by finely made ovate bifaces which are found in association with a wide range of butchered mammalian fauna. Evidence from these faunal remains, in the form of butchery marks underlying carnivore gnaw marks and

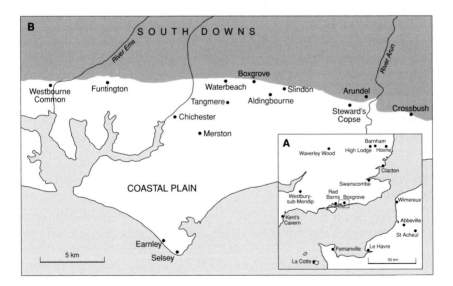

Figure 6.2 Location map for the site of Boxgrove.

impact damage, suggest primary access to carcasses and the possible use of wooden projectiles also seen at Schöningen (Thieme 1996).

However, the overall importance of the site comes from the association of these exceptionally preserved *in situ* signatures with a temporally discrete and spatially extensive palaeolandscape. These factors allow the examination of variability in hominid behaviour across kilometres of conformable fine-grained sediments for which we have a detailed knowledge of environmental conditions and the duration and nature of formation processes. This remarkable record of hominid activity within an entire landscape, relating to perhaps occupation by a single hominin generation, offers a level of interpretive precision usually dismissed as impossible in Lower Palaeolithic open-air contexts (Stern 1993, 1994). A selection of this evidence, which now follows, will show how this exceptional dataset might begin to be translated into a description of the routinised patterns of individual behaviour for Archaic *Homo sapiens*.

Isolating individual actions from the fine-grained record at Boxgrove

More than ninety separate areas have been investigated within the Boxgrove Quarries. Over half of these produced artefact assemblages, some associated with butchered faunal assemblages. This sample provides us with an exceptional record of variation in hominin behaviour across a spatially extensive palaeosol (Unit 4c) and within underlying well-preserved but originally short-lived land surfaces associated with inter-tidal silts (Unit 4b). The analysis of these stone tool assemblages has therefore provided an opportunity to look at hominin individuals operating within entire landscapes and in contexts that are well defined in terms of both environmental and spatial parameters. The evidence varies from the fine-grained, short-term record of the lower land surfaces, through spatially extensive *in situ* signatures of the palaeosol to localised concentrations of material associated with freshwater deposition. However, detailed study of assemblages across this preservational gradient has produced a remarkably consistent picture of tool-using behaviour. By exploring these patterns we have been able to begin framing variation in terms of individual rhythms of movement and land use routines at Boxgrove.

The individual and the chaîne opératoire of biface manufacture

The starting point in the Boxgrove palaeolandscape for understanding all Middle Pleistocene tool-using behaviour at the site is the ancient cliff line. This was an imposing but progressively degraded chalk landform that ran for some 20 km along the northern edge of the Boxgrove palaeolandscape (Roberts and Parfitt 1999). Fresh nodular flint would have been abundantly available within the talus slopes at the cliff base (Bergman and Roberts 1988) and nearly all the bifaces are manufactured on this material. As a result the individual can be approached at Boxgrove through the specific operational choices they made. Blocks of tested raw material litter the cliff-scree along with partially finished bifaces and both types of artefact were abandoned during the process of manufacture because of internal flaws or unworkability due to overall shape. We know from the refitting of nodules at the butchery sites that large blocks were transported away from the talus slopes after only a couple of flake removals (Pope 2002). This was just enough to test, through the sound of percussion and flaking properties, that the material was suitable. From the reconstruction of these few primary flake removals alone we can place the individual at the centre of both patterns of landscape movement and competing operational priorities. These priorities included decisions about whether an individual should leave a carcass vs. maintaining a defensive presence, the degree of confidence an individual had in assessing the suitability of raw material, and weighing up when to return to the kill site. These decisions required the individual to negotiate operational tensions between the functional need for butchery tools, effort in transporting unmodified raw material to a kill site, risks to the individual in leaving a large group, and keeping a carcass secure from other scavengers. The evidence from the talus slopes alone therefore points to hominins operating in space at short-term timescales within a personal geography in which their attention might be divided simultaneously between a number of different locations and competing priorities.

Individual choices and behaviour are brought into sharper focus when we turn to the fine-grained record of the lower land surfaces. These best preserve the signatures of short-term butchery and tool manufacture and extend our knowledge of the *chaîne opératoire* beyond the initial selection, preparation and transport of raw material. Within these levels, short-lived discontinuous landsurfaces perfectly preserve knapping scatters, sometimes as isolated occurrences (e.g. Site Q1/A), or as more complex groupings of scatters associated with butchery (e.g. GTP17). The assemblage from Q1/A consisted of a single discrete scatter of material some 25 cm across (Austin 1994; Roberts and Parfitt 1999). The scatter was so well defined that it preserved the outline of the individual's lower body and the accumulation of flakes which had rested against the inside of his or her right thigh (Figure 6.3). Austin managed to refit 65 per cent of the material from this scatter into two major groups. Both of these refitting groups related to the thinning of a break surface on a previously prepared rough-out/core. Numerous smaller refit groups seem to relate to the same reduction sequence and appear to have resulted from the thinning of the artefact's opposite end (Austin 1994).

While immediate, these details, however, do nothing to define the individual beyond being an agent of manufacture, matching entirely the procedural observations we record in the modern experimental manufacture of bifaces. As such they fail to help us define the distinct nature of Middle Pleistocene individuality, either in relation to his/her environment and society, or as distinct

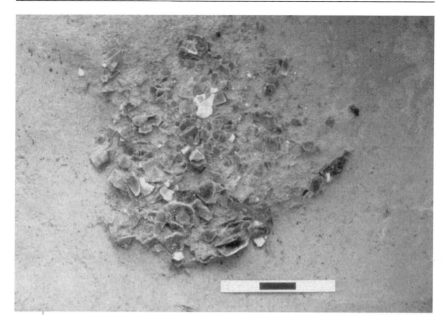

Figure 6.3 Individuals in isolation. Perfectly preserved individual knapping scatter from
QI/A (Q = Quarry).

from ourselves. In order to do this we have to infer beyond the scatter and
view it in relation to the wider record, utilising the fine-grained record as a
calibration tool to unpick coarser, more complex signatures. Once we begin
to do this, however, we immediately start to lose sight of the individual in
isolation. The personal choices underpinning the *chaîne opératoire* are still
identifiable but they become overprinted by social interaction and interpersonal
negotiation.

Contrasting signatures and discard rules: the GTP17(Geological Test Pit) and QI/B (Quarry I) assemblages

At GTP17, lithic artefacts associated with a fine-grained intra-Unit 4b horizon
were traced over a 68m^2 area. During the excavation of this surface a series of
eight visible scatters of debitage were identified associated with the butchered
remains of a single horse. The taphonomy of the horse carcass has been
described previously by Parfitt (Roberts and Parfitt 1999) while the taphonomy
and technology of flint artefact assemblage from the same site was discussed
by Pope (2002). Analysis of the faunal remains showed damage from both
carnivore gnawing and flint tool cutmarks, although where superimposed the
primacy of the latter is demonstrable (Roberts and Parfitt 1999). The site
therefore appears to conform to the expected configuration of a short-term

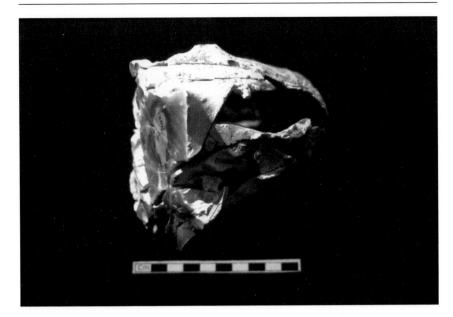

Figure 6.4 Refitted biface reduction sequence from GTP17.

butchery locality, with all the stone artefacts contextually associated with the processing of a single horse carcass. Analysis of debitage and refitted artefacts indicate that biface manufacture predominated at the site. Material from all stages of the biface reduction sequence is represented within the assemblage (Figure 6.4). Yet, apart from two flake-derived bifacial tools, no bifaces were recovered. This evidence appears to match that from site Q2/D indicating that at some activity areas, despite the demonstrable manufacture of several bifaces, these tools were subsequently removed from the area. It also reinforces the evidence from other Boxgrove locales which shows that hominins routinely moved these tools within the landscape and manufactured and modified them at more than one location.

It is at this point that we can begin to think of the individual beyond the accessible but unremarkable behaviours associated with tool procurement, manufacture or discard and start to view these behaviours in a social context. Pivotal to this is the evidence, at GTP17 and Q2/D, to suggest that the individual patterns of tool use and landscape movement were embedded in routine social actions. The data shows the consistent removal, by several individuals, of bifaces away from a single butchery event. This suggests behavioural uniformity despite the fact that we know, from the refitting evidence , that hominin individuals were introducing bifaces in various stages of completion. The pattern of tool transport was not therefore controlled by functional constraints upon the individual but was instead subject to other, possibly social, factors governing the use and transport of artefacts. For

Figure 6.5 Palimpsest signatures from the Q1/B waterhole site.

whatever reason, individuals were conforming to an embedded rule, a technique of the body as described by Leroi-Gourhan (1993: 231–2) and which embodies social practice in a largely unthinking, routine way (Gamble 1999: 80–4).

The presence of such socially embedded rules can also be clearly seen in area Q1/B. Here freshwater sediments preserved 20,000 lithic artifacts alongside butchered fauna and fragmentary hominin remains (Stringer *et al.* 1998) (Figure 6.5). While the investigation of this material is still ongoing, preliminary results suggest that the sediments here were formed through a series of erosive fluvial events, associated with variations in discharge from springs at the base of the cliffline and periods of soil formation and channel infilling. Ostracod species indicate that, for a substantial part of the sequence of infill, a stable freshwater body was present at the site (Roberts *et al.* in preparation). The atypical freshwater sediments appear to have been deposited during a time-span broadly coeval with the formation of the Unit 4c palaeosol. Thus the site appears to represent a seasonally wet waterhole throughout the 20–100-year lifespan of Unit 4c.

The artefacts were recovered alongside the butchered remains of numerous mammal species including red deer, rhinoceros, bovids and horse. Dense concentrations of artefacts and fauna were found throughout the freshwater deposits, but notable spreads of material were recovered from the truncated surface of the marine sand on the edge of small channels. The stone tool assemblages appeared to contain a large proportion of bifaces. This fact, combined with evidence for butchery from the faunal remains, suggests that the site formed a focus for hominin activity on numerous occasions, perhaps representing a favoured locality. The artefact assemblage stands out as atypical because in addition to the bifaces there is an abundance of flake tools, percussors and the presence of at least three antler soft hammers, the latter not previously recovered from a Middle Pleistocene context. When compared to single episode sites, characterised at Q2/D and GTP17 by low tool counts, the Q1/B assemblage appears to represent a distinctive archaeological signature.

Our taphonomic analysis (Pope 2002; Roberts *et al.* in preparation) determined that the high biface numbers were a result of behaviour and not simply a product of fluvial modification through size-sorting or winnowing. The evidence suggests that hominin individuals were routinely discarding bifaces at this point in the landscape. When taken in association with the GTP17 evidence, this emphasised that contextual controls were underpinning discard behaviour. Individuals at the site were more likely to drop bifaces at locations that had proved themselves productive and had been routinely visited than at single episode butchery sites. There is also another possibility, which remains to be explored further, that the very presence of large quantities of tool in a restricted area created a feedback mechanism, either by triggering occupation activity or increased tool discard rates.

In Figure 6.6 the proportion of bifaces within each of the major assemblages are shown as a percentage of the minimum numbers of flake removals (MND), as documented through debitage analysis, and plotted against their distance from the cliff. The plot indicates that bifaces become proportionally

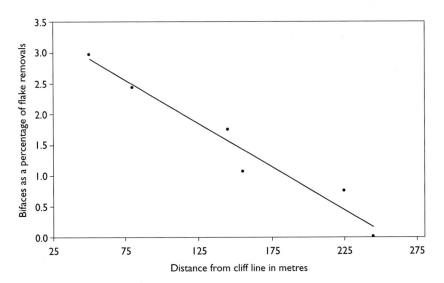

Figure 6.6 Variation in biface discard across the 4c palaeosol showing higher discard rates in reoccupied areas close to springline at the cliff base.

less common with increasing distance from the cliff, a finding confirmed by regression analysis ($r^2 = 0.95$). The strong statistical relationship implies that hominins operating 130 metres or more from the cliff were more likely to transport their tools off-site when abandoning a locality than when leaving a site closer to the cliff.

By establishing that hominins at Boxgrove were discarding bifaces more readily in areas close to freshwater at the base of the cliff indicates that the distinctive assemblages characteristics at GTP17 and Q1/B are not simply anomalies, but form part of a range of variation in biface transport and discard behaviour. As an extremely short-term, single-episode butchery site, the GTP17 assemblage has a clear contextual basis from which its distinctive characteristics can be translated into a behavioural model of assemblage formation. Since the removal of all classic bifaces at GTP17 appears to be a group behaviour directly associated with the abandonment of a single-episode butchery site, we can begin to infer some of the controls underpinning the wider landscape patterns. When applied to the observed spatial variation in biface discard within the palaeolandscape of the Unit 4c palaeosol this contextual association indicates that assemblages recovered away from the cliff with fewer bifaces might also arise from short-term occupation episodes. Conversely, sites closer to the cliff with assemblages containing higher proportions of bifaces may have been more routinely occupied. An alternative explanation of resource tethering can be ruled out due to the small transport distances (maximum 250 metres) within the study area.

Summary of the Boxgrove evidence

It was recognised from an early stage in the Boxgrove excavations that the overall character of technology at the site was very consistent with most assemblages relating to the manufacture and use of ovate bifaces (Roberts 1986; Bergman and Roberts 1988). In accounting for the relatively minor differences observed in assemblage variability prior to the discovery of the Q1/B locality in the late 1980s, a fairly restricted series of explanations have been repeatedly employed. Central to these accounts is the recognition that assemblages formed as a result of the interplay between patterns of artefact transport and discard. Each of the assemblages we have studied provided detailed evidence, sometimes directly documented through refitting, for individuals moving bifaces and biface rough-outs. Bifaces, in varying stages of completion, were routinely transported within the Boxgrove landscape, with assemblage composition reflecting the net product of variation in tool discard and transport behaviour over real functional differences. Taken at face value the GTP17 assemblage indicates a contextual association between hominin behaviour involving the removal of bifaces and a single-episode, short-term butchery event. Conversely, at Q1/B a possible association between high biface discard rates and reoccupation of the site is indicated.

These patterns point to the conclusion that the archaeological record at Boxgrove is structured as the result of self-organising action rather than conscious, planned decisions. This structure developed over time, crystallising out of hundreds of individual actions but conforming to embedded principles of hominin involvement with artefacts, principles which governed to a considerable extent transport and discard behaviour. Hominin individuals can therefore be seen as organising agents imprinting and modifying the archaeological signature through time from a series of isolated, undifferentiated knapping clusters into an emerging 'scatter and patches' signature where assemblage content and quantitative on-site/off-site asymmetries are closely linked. There is, therefore, an underlying paradox here between the apparent freedom of movement and adaptability shown in the reconstruction of individual knapping sequences contrasted with the overall conformity of long-term transport and discard behaviours. Patterning in the archaeological record of Pleistocene landscapes may therefore be a product of these tensions, expressing the duality between increasingly flexible and complex individual behaviour structured through emergent complexity in the guiding social and cultural frameworks (Giddens 1984; Gamble 1999).

Discussion: individuals and structured discard in the Palaeolithic record

Within the Lower Palaeolithic record there is evidence that individual discard patterns, comparable to those we have traced at Boxgrove, are a widespread behavioural characteristic of early *Homo*. Furthermore, these patterns could help to explain aspects of Acheulean assemblage variability.

The appearance of bifaces in Oldowan assemblages began around 1.7 Ma. Jones (1994) studied the smaller bifaces of the Developed Oldowan from Olduvai Gorge, Tanzania, and interpreted their size and more intensive retouch as indicating worked-out tools with obtuse edges and failed flake detachments. As at GTP17, it is possible that individuals were selectively discarding redundant, failed or non-classic biface forms at certain locations, and thereby defining the Developed Oldowan through personal choices that conformed to long-term, embedded patterns of behaviour. According to this model, more classic, symmetrical and larger forms would have been transported off-site. They were then more likely to be discarded by individuals at locales associated with wider patterns of land use embedded in routine action.

At Gadeb, in Ethiopia, assemblages characterised as Developed Oldowan by Clark (1987) are found from 1.5 Ma. Clark isolated similar contexts amongst the assemblages of Gadeb to those identified by Hay (1976) at Olduvai. At both locales assemblages were recovered from streamside contexts exhibiting multi-occupation, multi-episode signatures, and in which bifaces comprised >25 per cent of all tools. This contrasted with single-episode butchery sites with assemblages containing much lower proportions of bifaces. Clark did not resort to any elaborate explanations invoking competing technological traditions or species. Instead, he viewed the variation as simply stemming from different aspects of land use by a single population using the environment and tools in new, more organised ways. 'The two kinds of activity can be seen as complementary and suggest a more structured pattern of behaviour' (Clark 1987: 809).

The Gadeb evidence, mirrored also in the Ethiopian sites of Melka Kunturé (Chavaillon *et al.* 1979) and the Middle Awash (Clark 1987), matches the pattern of assemblage variability established at Boxgrove in showing a direct link between biface discard patterns and land use. It is therefore possible to apply our explanation of the Boxgrove data to Gadeb and propose that the relative absence of bifaces at single-episode butchery sites was due to the off-site transport and suppressed discard of these tools by hominin individuals. If this is the case then it is plausible that the biface-using hominins at Gadeb were already beginning to develop structured patterns of land use and tool transport/discard remarkably similar to those still in operation within Northern Europe one million years later. Moreover, from the time bifaces first appear in the Palaeolithic record, the discard of these tools seems contextually tied. Small bifaces are discarded at different locations to larger more classic forms, and a clear dichotomy between biface-rich and biface-poor sites is so marked that it suggests to some (Leakey 1971) either overlapping between species or competing technological traditions. Structured biface discard by individuals, which we would argue had a strong role in the formation of all biface-rich sites, is therefore a fundamental and defining part of the hominin land use patterns which gave rise to the Developed Oldowan assemblages. The evidence for the Developed Oldowan and early Acheulean sites discussed here matches the Boxgrove data extremely well and echoes observations for apparent differential discard of artefact types in Oldowan assemblages (Potts 1988; Blumenchine and Masao 1991). The data suggests that increasingly structured land use patterns were inseparable from technological development during the Early Pleistocene.

The patterns of assemblage variability become easy to understand once broad frameworks of ecology, raw material distribution and the behaviour of transport and discard processes are modeled (Potts 1988, 1994; Hay 1976). These patterns, as at Boxgrove, also become more apparent when studied within sedimentary sequences which preserve evidence for successive palaeolandscape occupation within well-defined spatial/temporal contexts. For example, through the work of, successively, Isaac (1967, 1977), Potts (1989, 1994) and Potts *et al.* (1999), the Early Pleistocene site of Olorgesailie in Kenya has become one of the most intensively studied and informative Pleistocene palaeolandscapes. Isaac drew attention to the main features of inter-assemblage variation by demonstrating an inverse correlation between the presence of scrapers and bifaces (Isaac 1977). The bimodality of scraper-dominated vs. biface-dominated assemblages was contextually underpinned by a clear association of biface-rich assemblages with sandy channel areas. Potts focused on localities in Member 7 which had produced dense concentrations of Acheulean bifaces; these included sites DE/89, H9, Mid and Meng (Potts *et al.* 1999). The investigations revealed that the bifaces were almost exclusively limited to the sandy channels, but no direct evidence could be found to suggest that these assemblages were formed by hydraulic action as usually envisaged (Schick 1987, 1992). Potts *et al.* (1999) suggested that large biface-rich assemblages formed at the junction between the higher plateau with its abundant lava outcrops and food-rich lake basin environments. The sandy channels may have formed route ways between the two areas. Bifaces were discarded at these sites because they were carried around as useful sources of raw material, even as flake dispensers in the lower areas (Potts 1989), and then discarded as hominins re-entered locales where they could easily reprovision themselves with stone tools. The Boxgrove bifaces may have been used in a similar way. Here the evidence comes from the frequent and distinctive removal of tranchet, or resharpening, flakes (Figure 6.7) from bifaces (Roberts *et al.* in preparation). We regard Boxgrove's tranchet-sharpened bifaces as an elegant, flexible solution to reconciling increased mobility and range required

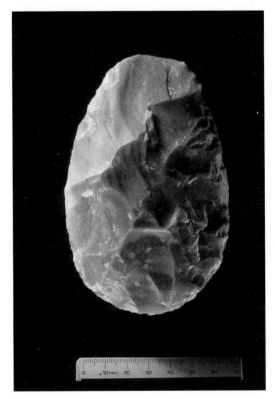

Figure 6.7 Adaptable and mobile. Tranchet-sharpened bifaces allowed hominin individuals greater flexibility in hunting strategy.

by hunting (Gamble and Steele 1998) with the constraints of raw material transport.

By contrast, Potts also identified assemblages that appeared to relate to single episodes of butchery and generally lacking even moderate quantities of bifaces. At Site I5 the skeleton of a single *Elephas recki* was discovered alongside a localised artefact scatter with low biface counts. Some parts of the carcass were still anatomically joined and exhibited cuts marks marking this out as a butchery site and, given the lack of primary carnivore gnawing, a possible kill site. The nature of the site exactly parallels the GTP17 horse butchery locality with a discrete concentration of 2,322 lithic artefacts over $64\,m^2$ but containing only two bifacial tools. These occurred beside the remains of a single animal carcass. In addition, the UMP1 palaeosol at Olorgesailie was dominated by assemblages with low biface counts and represented a relatively undifferentiated grassland environment (Potts *et al.* 1999). At Boxgrove, low biface counts were similarly observed for sites on grassland areas away from the cliff base at the palaeosol level and for the rapidly formed land surfaces of the lower silts.

At the Middle Pleistocene site of Aridos in Central Spain (Santonja and Villa 1990) there are further examples of assemblages with distinctive GTP17 type signatures. Aridos 1 and 2 (Villa 1990) both provide evidence for the butchery of a single elephant carcass. They are associated with stone tool assemblages which relate to the manufacture and off-site transport of finished bifaces and the on-site resharpening of existing tools. As at GTP17, finished tool forms at Aridos were often selectively transported off-site. The similarity also extends to the overall taphonomic condition of the faunal and lithic assemblages at the sites. Both lines of evidence suggest single short episodes of occupation during which hominins gained primary access to a carcass and then systematically butchered it. The Aridos and *Elephas recki* assemblages can be viewed alongside the Mwanganda elephant butchery site (Clark and Haynes 1970), the hippo carcass at Isimilia, Gadeb 8F (Clark 1987) and the elephant at Lehringen (Thieme and Veil 1985), since all of them confirm the negative association between bifaces and single carcasses. The lack of a clear association between bifaces and unequivocal butchery sites might be taken to indicate that bifaces were not used in animal-processing activities at all. This follows Binford's (1972) proposition that 'light artefact arrays' were the signature butchery kit of Early and Middle Pleistocene hominins, with scrapers and flake tools used to assist in the marginal scavenging of carcass elements. Similarly, Clark and Haynes (1970: 409) suggested that bifaces were not used in butchery on the reasonable assumption that if they had been, 'it would be expected that they would occur in large numbers on the sites . . .'. Yet this assumption only remains reasonable as long as one accepts a direct relationship between tools used at a given locale and the artefacts discarded at that place; the evidence from Boxgrove suggests that such simple relationships should be treated with caution.

For example, if the larger stone tool accumulations were simply repetitive, compound signatures of the same behaviour exhibited at single kill sites, we would be left with an archaeological record differentiated only in terms of the spatial distribution and size of assemblages. Instead, faunal and lithic assemblages throughout the Lower and Middle Pleistocene are characterised by qualitative as well as quantitative variability. Neither, as Isaac (1972) once described with his random walk model of technological and typological development, was this a simple linear process. As such, assemblage variability should be explained in terms of context-specific behaviour and it also has to be accepted that assemblage composition changed over time. Therefore we must recognise that assemblages had mutable, evolving characteristics that were controlled in part by the selective transport and discard behaviour of individuals. For example, any attempt to infer significance from the dominate shape of biface types in assemblages (White 1998; McPherron 1996; Gamble *et al.* 2000) must consider the possibility that hominin individuals may have selectively removed preferred artefact forms from the assemblage under consideration. The data from Boxgrove and other Acheulean localities show that classic Acheulean sites are more clearly defined by contextual relationships rather than by quantitative measures of assemblage composition and tool morphology alone. In this light we may be able to understand the Acheulean in terms of the individual choices of hominins within the framework of social dynamics, ecology and land use patterns of hominin groups. At this level hominin individuals were actively creating a structured record.

Conclusions: structured discard, land use and the individual in the Palaeolithic record

In attempting to model the relationship between biface-rich assemblages and those lacking bifaces, we draw attention to Ashton's useful distinction between 'fixed' and 'mobile' resource sites (Ashton 1998 *et al.*). This relationship is robust and demonstrated repeatedly across the Old World during the Lower Palaeolithic. GTP17-type assemblages are apparently associated with the exploitation of single animals in largely open, undifferentiated grassland habitats. Q1/B-type assemblages are repeatedly associated with particular locales, usually channel contexts which provided combinations of fresh water, game concentrations, raw materials, vegetable resources and access routes between or through habitats. The different ways in which mobile and static resources were exploited would have required a flexible role for individuals within group social dynamics. Increasing reliance on hunting may have necessitated a shift in land use and social behaviour (O'Connell 1997). While 'fixed' areas where game might be intercepted can be remembered and incorporated into fundamental patterns of routed land use, the hunted animal, once intercepted, becomes a 'mobile' and unpredictable resource. We would argue from the Boxgrove data that changes in land use, partly brought about by the spatial scale, unpredictability and danger of game pursuits, stretched patterns of land use even further in the Middle Pleistocene. Although large groups are advantageous in competitive scavenging situations, to drive off competitors and prevent the reacquisition of carcasses by other carnivores, family groups, which would have included nursing mothers, infants and the elderly, could not have participated in long-distance hunting pursuits. The Acheulean and its associated structured signatures may be one such manifestation of this change: a product of the adaptive behavioural responses required to maintain group cohesion as increasingly wider resources and areas of landscape were exploited.

The ways in which hominins used space has undergone enormous changes since stone tools first appeared some 2.7 million years ago. While shifts in the scale of land-use behaviour can be documented in the archaeological record of specific sedimentary basins, the bigger picture of global colonisation in the more recent past points to enormous changes in the spatial context of human social life. While Gamble (1996a) sees a fundamental shift in the nature of social land use occurring during the past 100,000 years or less, structured patterns of land use and artefact discard may have allowed more complicated patterns of social land use to develop earlier in the Pleistocene. Large, stable populations engaging in active predation would have had to disperse on a daily basis at scales which would have rendered primate mechanisms for individuals to maintain group cohesion obsolete, e.g. sight-lines and sound attenuation (Wrangham 1979). Structured artefact discard would have marked areas of regular re-aggregation with large accumulations of bifacial tools. Just as these areas signal specific patterns of group behaviour to the archaeologist, so too would basic associative reinforcement have marked such sites as socially significant to hominin individuals. Without the presence of structured discard, set within a 'scatters and patches' (Isaac 1977, 1981a; Roebroeks et al. 1992b; Pope 2002) distribution framework, hominin individuals would have inhabited undifferentiated social landscapes characterised by simple, repetitive and dispersed signatures. Structured discard would mark out not only ecological affordances but also would have helped to maintain group cohesion, marking areas of demonstrated aggregation from other identical stretches of landscape. Such landscapes, which would have developed over time under favourable conditions, would have been unconsciously, although actively, formed by hominin individuals following routines and contextually reinforced patterns of social behaviour.

We would suggest that structured discard provides a mechanism whereby the routinised hominin behaviour patterns foreshadow the ability in modern humans of habit-plus (Gamble 1996). Archaic *Homo sapiens* individuals may not have been consciously manipulating symbolic environments in the modern sense, but the very presence of structured cultural landscapes would have fed back into the complexity of social land use. Through such habitual rhythms, hominin discard patterns would have created an Acheulean landscape rich with valuable and usefully contextualised ecological and social information. Once set in motion, evolutionary processes would have started to select for structured discard and the necessary symbolic, abstract and inferential thought processes required for individuals to make use of the information stored within such signatures. Such processes would have been a necessary precondition to establishing the first true social landscapes and routine use of symbolic information in the Late Pleistocene.

The model of structured land use put forward here suggests how modern human land use and cultural environments may have developed during the course of the Pleistocene. In structured landscapes artefacts may have stood as proxies for the hominin individuals themselves, providing a mechanism through which groups could go beyond the limitation of direct perception to effect a 'release from proximity' (Rodseth *et al.* 1991: 240). Yet the durability of stone tools would have allowed the contextual triggers implicit in such distribution patterns to be made available across far wider temporal scales than those of day-to-day foraging. With wide territories and seasonal movement patterns, the persistence of structured landscapes, especially with large concentrations of highly visible tools, would have provided in effect a trigger for groups to recommence the successful land use patterns of an earlier season. The presence of such signatures would also have allowed a hominin individual entering an area for the first time to track on to previously successful patterns of earlier, group land use. Where environmental conditions remained stable, biface-rich signatures would have marked optimal locales for resource exploitation, allowing basic information to be transmitted across time and space without either the use of language or deliberate symbolic behaviour. We can place the hominin individual within such landscapes as rudimentary archaeological beings, capable of making inferences from the arrangement and content of discarded material. Once *Homo* began to litter the landscape with a durable record of behaviour an inevitable process of enculturation was set in train, enmeshing individuals into patterns and rhythms of movement reinforced in part by their own contextually guided discard patterns. Structured patterns of discard could have been one mechanism by which individual actions contributed to increased group cohesion and flexibility. They provide one possible adaptive mechanism by which modern social behaviour, so heavily dependent upon the verbal and symbolic exchange of information, was engendered.

Chapter 7

The natural and socio-cultural environment of *Homo erectus* at Bilzingsleben, Germany

Dietrich Mania and Ursula Mania

Introduction

The site on the 'Steinrinne' in the Triassic landscape of Bilzingsleben has produced rich material of a Lower Palaeolithic culture and the natural environment in which it was embedded. It originates from a find horizon of a travertine complex and relates to a camp site of early hominids (Mania and Mania 2002). With these remains it is possible to reconstruct important elements of the culture of early man, especially their social and economic behaviour. The extensive geological, palaeontological and geomorphologic evidence allows the detailed reconstruction of the former environment in which these humans were living (Mania 1995c, 1997). The study of the remains of two skulls, one mandible and eight teeth clearly demonstrated that these hominids belong to a species of late *Homo erectus* (Vlček 1978, 2002). The geological situation of the site allows a precise stratigraphic location of the travertine containing the archaeological materials into an interglacial between the Elster and the Saale glaciation (Mania 1997). Radiometric dating methods have so far produced an average value of 370,000 BP so that it is possible to place the finds into OIS 11 (Schwarcz *et al.* 1988; Mallik *et al.* 2001).

The local situation and site formation

The camp site was originally situated on a peninsular-like terrace at the shore of a shallow lake. Not very far away was a source of fresh water rising through the karst rock. Its calcareous water flowed into the lake next to the terrace. Here a wide fan of sandy travertine sediment was deposited, which contained a substantial number of cultural remains. After a longer period of use the camp site was eventually flooded by the rising water level and abandoned. The lake terrace was covered with chalk. Apart from stone objects this situation also led to the preservation of a number of artificially manipulated objects made from bone, antler and teeth. The chalk even conserved calcified wooden objects. The accumulation of chalk among the local plants (moss, grass, etc.) finally produced a solid travertine cover that protected the find horizon until the present day.

The natural environment

The numerous plant remains that were preserved in the travertine sediments contained a number of exotic species that point to a sub-Mediterranean and sub-continental influence. They allow the reconstruction of specific plant communities such as the open and dry box-tree and mixed-oak-tree forests (*Buxo-Quercetum*) and bush communities containing box-tree and lilac (*Buxo-Syringetum*) and other similar species (*Berberidion, Juniperus-Cotoneaster, Corylus-Pyracantha*). This vegetation was mixed with heath areas (*Potentilla fruticosa*) and open steppe environments (*Astragalo-Stipion*) (Mai 1983). These different plant communities provided the habitats for large herds of herbivores and the ecology is confirmed by the study of the molluscs (*Helicigona banatica*-community) (Mania 1983; Mania and Mai 2001) and the ostracod fauna (Diebel and Pietrzeniuk 1980).

The vertebrates provide a very diverse picture with a large number of species. These remains are partly of natural origin but can also be related to human activities such as hunting, gathering and raw material procurement. The vertebrate remains include a large number of fish (e.g. *Esox lucius, Silurus glanis, Tinca tinca, Phoxinus phoxinus, Lota lota* and *Cottus gobio*; Hebig 1983; Böhme 1998), amphibians and reptiles (e.g. *Triturus triturus, Pelobates* sp., *Bufo bufo, Rana temporaria, Natrix natrix, Angius fragilis, Lacerta* sp., *Emys orbicularis*; Böhme 1998) and birds (*Anas platyrhynchos, Bucephala clangula, Cygnus olor, Haliaeetus albicilla, Strix aluco, Turdus* sp.; Fischer 1997). Among the small mammals the presence of *Spermophilus (Urocitellus)* sp. and *Lagurus lagurus* is remarkable, because both species are distributed today in the south-east European and western Asian steppe environments (Heinrich 1997a, 1997b, 1998). This observation emphasises the strong influence of a continental climate. *Castor fiber* and *Trogontherium cuvieri* were also present.

The large mammals can all be related to a *Palaeoloxodon antiquus*-faunal community and are all the products of human activities. The species represented include the herbivores *Stephanorhinus kirchbergensis, Stephanorhinus hemitoechus, Equus mosbachensis-taubachensis, Bison priscus, Cervus elaphus, Dama clactoniana, Capreolus suessenbornensis, Sus scrofa* and the carnivores *Panthera (Leo) spelaea, Ursus deningeri-spelaeus, Canis lupus, Crocuta crocuta, Vulpes vulpes, Meles meles, Martes* sp. (Fischer 1991; Heinrich 1997a; van der Made 1998, 2000; Musil 1991; Toepfer 1983). The remains of one primate species (*Macaca florentina*) have also been identified. The complete faunal evidence presents a detailed picture of the diverse ecological situation around the former camp site with lakes and rivers, open and forested areas within the landscape. The climate was warm and temperate (Cfa-climate after Köppen, see Mai 1983). On average the temperature was about 3–4°C warmer than today. Summers were particularly warm and dry, which favoured open forest communities with areas of bush and grass land.

Preservation of the find horizon

A substantial number of the cultural objects, especially the larger and heavier ones, were still in their original positions, where they were discarded by humans. This, however, can only be assumed for about 20 per cent of the total material. The smaller objects, mostly stone and bone debris, were moved during the flooding process of the camp site and eventually deposited in the sandy chalk that today covers the archaeological horizon. Carnivore activities apparently played no substantial role in these processes as almost no gnaw marks were found on the faunal remains. From the primary deposited objects it is possible to infer settlement structures as well as different artefact concentrations. Both observations make it possible to reconstruct activity zones on the site. The partial reworking of the archaeological materials during the flooding of the site necessitates an approach that is different from a 'ring-and-sector-model', which is only applicable to undisturbed contexts.

The cultural behaviour of *Homo erectus* at Bilzingsleben

The artificial micro-environment

The evidence from Bilzingsleben demonstrates that early man was fully capable of creating his own artificial environment. This was the open-air camp site on the shore terrace next to the freshwater source and the small lake. Despite the relatively warm climatic conditions winters could still be cold with temperatures below 0°C. It was therefore necessary for humans to adapt culturally to these conditions. The primary means in this context were simple living structures, the use of fire and the establishment of a base camp. The latter had a diameter between 35 and 40 metres as determined by the natural boundaries on three sides. Since carnivores were absent it can be concluded that humans were always present. Bilzingsleben consequently was a settlement that was used for a longer period of time, a true base camp.

It was possible to recognise three settlement structures (Figure 7.1). They had a circular to oval layout with diameters between 3 and 4 metres. Their entrances were pointing in a south-eastern direction, away from the predominant direction of the wind. It was here that the hearths were located. These were evidenced by concentrations of charcoal and burned stones. In the same area two working places were also recognisable by the presence of stone anvils, discarded debris, flint tools and choppers. The position of large tools made from stone, bone and antler and even some preserved wooden objects also allows us to infer the position of the huts. It seems as if these were mostly placed on the outside of the walls so that their position finally reflected the outlines of the living structures.

At a distance between 3 and 5 metres in front of the living structures a general activity zone was found. It was about 6 metres wide and approximately

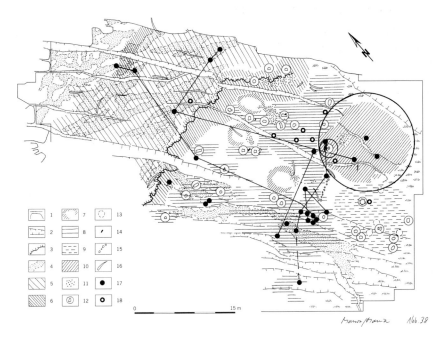

Figure 7.1 Plan of the structuration of the camp at Bilzingsleben.

Key: 1. Limits of excavated area; 2. Geological fault lines; 3. Shore line; 4. Sandy travertine sediment; 5. Alluvial fan; 6. Activity area at the lake shore; 7. Outlines of living structures; 8. Workshop areas; 9. Special workshop area with traces of fire use; 10. Circular paved area; 11. Charcoal; 12. Bone anvils; 13. Stone with traces of heat; 14. Bones with intentional markings; 15. Linear arrangement of stones; 16. Elephant tusk. 17. Human skull fragments; 18. Human tooth.

30 metres long. This activity zone was characterised by the presence of material that can be expected in the context of working places: large amounts of debris of stone, bone, antler and ivory, choppers made from quartzite, Muschelkalk, travertine and other raw materials, numerous small flint tools, large bone and antler tools, anvils and pebbles. Within this area it was possible to distinguish working places where predominantly wood, bone/antler or flint was processed. A different activity zone was found in the south of the site. It extended for about 100 m² and was formed by a pavement made of pebbles of a different travertine. These pebbles had to be carried to the site from a distance of *c.* 250 metres. The same applies to large blocks of travertine with weights around 75 kg that were utilised as working supports. These were often found together with similar large stones of unknown function that show traces of intense heat. Flint artefacts are generally rare in this area. Tools are mostly hammer stones and large bone scrapers.

To the north of the huts a different activity area stretched along the shore of the small lake. It contained a number of specific tools such as club- or hoe-like instruments made from red deer antlers and very large scrapers with retouched edges made from the long bones of elephants. A large anvil of quartzite marks another special work place in this area. The anvil contained small particles of bone in its fissures, which points to the processing of animal bones in this context. This conclusion is also supported by the occurrence of articulated skeletal remains in this area. The alluvial fan in the immediate vicinity contained at least 3,500 kg of small debris together with some larger objects. The composition seems to show that the dry patches were also visited from time to time by the inhabitants of the camp.

The most peculiar activity zone, however, is an almost circular pavement with a diameter of *c.* 9 metres in the eastern section of the settlement. This area was apparently not affected by the rich workshop area that surrounded it. It is paved with flat non-local travertine and Muschelkalk stones as well as small pieces of bone and teeth. All of these objects were pressed into the soft surface and form only one layer. These pieces of evidence point to an artificial arrangement. In contrast to the rest of settlement area the pavement contained almost no pebble, bone or antler tools. However, outlines and remains of elongated wooden objects were quite frequent. Near the centre of the pavement a temporary hearth was situated. At the eastern periphery a large boulder of travertine rose above the surface with a size of *c.* 80 × 60 × 40 cm. A very intense fire must have burned here, because the travertine block was broken into a number of pieces and its surface is heavily affected by heat. A boulder of quartzite was found in the western section of the pavement. It was embraced by the horns of the skull of a large aurochs (Figure 7.2). The space around this anvil is free of any tools or production debris; it appears as if it was intentionally cleaned. Next to the anvil and in the wider area around the pavement, fragments of two hominid skulls have been found, which therefore seem to be in some relation to the circular paved structure. In the natural crevices of the anvil small fragments of bones can be observed that prove that on this anvil bones were intentionally smashed. A histological analysis has so far not produced clear results. However, the whole spatial arrangement of the paved area, the anvil and the human remains lead us to suggest that the circular area at Bilzingsleben was used for 'special cultural activities'. This interpretation is also suggested by a linear structure of larger pebbles, which seems to run towards the circular area and which ends appear to have been marked by 1.8-m long elephant tusks.

Altogether, the complete evidence suggests that Bilzingsleben was a camp site that was used over a considerable period of time and reflects the creation of a specific artificial micro-environment with living structures and hearths at the centre surrounded by different activity zones and an area that apparently had a special cultural significance. This spatial differentiation most likely reflects a social differentiation within the group of early humans. Together with the sophisticated acquisition of different types of food that also involved organised big game hunting the site shows the level of cultural adaptation that

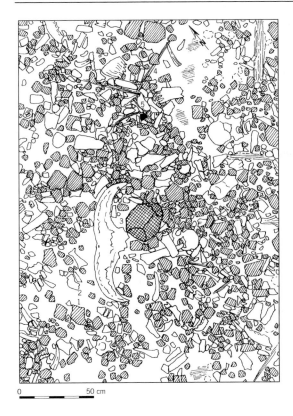

Figure 7.2 Section of the circular paved area: 1. Travertine or Muschelkalk stones; 2. Bones; 3. Aurochs skull with quartzite anvil; 4. Fragments of wooden objects; 5. Human skull fragment.

0   50 cm

was necessary to survive in the temperate climatic regions of Central Europe. We can consequently safely assume that *Homo erectus* did not come as a naked savage into these regions, although the motives for this move are much more difficult to infer. Maybe curiosity, the developing self-consciousness and cultural capacity were already enough to facilitate a distribution out of the tropical climatic zones. Certainly, also *Homo erectus* needed to protect himself from unfavourable environmental conditions. The evidence clearly shows that he was able to achieve this by cultural means, by the creation of clothing and the use of fire – reflected by the presence of fine flint borers and charcoal.

The almost permanent settlement of the base camp at Bilzingsleben almost certainly had consequences for the structuring of the social groups here. Within each of the relatively small living structures there was only enough space for up to six persons. This structure points to the existence of certain social units among the inhabitants of Bilzingsleben. A separation of activities based on biological differences seems to be likely, and these were emphasised by the permanent use of the camp. Here, mothers and small children could safely stay together with the elderly and ill persons. Other members of the group were therefore able to move more freely within the landscape to hunt, gather and even to stay away for longer periods of time. They were able to follow more specialised activities as is, for example, represented by the contemporary site of Schöningen II-4 (see Thieme 1997, 1998, this volume).

The establishment of a permanent camp facilitated the development of practices that required more time and effort, such as the intense processing of different raw materials. Processes of cultural learning and the transmission of knowledge became more intense as well. It is possible that the circular structure also has to be seen in this context. In societies without a tradition of writing rituals are often important in the transmission of socially vital information.

Artefacts and systematic behaviour

In the ongoing process of cultural adaptation tools made from different raw materials acquired an ever-increasing importance. The hominids at Bilzingsleben produced a large number of different tools for different purposes. From the inventory a number of characteristics of the behaviour of these early humans can be inferred.

Choice of raw materials

The choice of raw materials for the production of different tools, which were in turn intended for specific purposes, clearly reflects a high level of sophistication. Quartzite, hard pieces of limestone and travertine were used as choppers and for various heavy-duty functions while flint was utilised for the production of small tools such as scrapers, knives and borers. If larger tools were needed they were made from large splinters of elephant bones. They simply could not have been realised in any type of rock or stone. The change in raw material was therefore the logical solution to this kind of problem.

Functional differentiations

We can identify tools that had simple functions and which were used and produced on the spot for an immediate purpose. No effort needed to be invested in the production of hammer stones and even the costs for the production of choppers are almost negligible. Even the special flint tools were produced with minimum costs and were used for simple and specified tasks. This very cost-effective strategy was especially applied to those tools that were used to produce other tools. These latter objects, however, already received more care. Some knives were carefully retouched and were backed. The same can be assumed for wooden objects like the spears from Schöningen (see Thieme, this volume), but probably included a whole range of other wooden implements. Because of the extra amount of care that was invested, these tools were also more effective and probably more valuable to their users. This might be a reason why they are so rarely found in an undamaged condition. At Bilzingsleben a number of pointed and partially ground fragments of elephant tusks with a length between *c.* 60 and 80 cm possibly represent such a class of object.

Small specialised flint tools were produced with small quartzite hammer stones and different retouchers. Their working edges show that they were intentionally produced to meet a number of different functions: cutting, scraping, boring, etc. They were consequently made to work different organic materials, especially wood. In the case of the backed knives, they were used in the dismemberment of carcasses. The relatively small size of these tools did not depend on the available raw material. All flint tools were made so that they could be used without hafting and handles (Mania 1994). Most of them are between 4 and 5 cm, the tools for wood shaving were between 2 and 3 cm and some special scrapers had a diameter of only 8 mm.

Maybe the most specialized tool is the borer. These objects are quite frequent in the Bilzingsleben inventory. Some of them can have long and carefully prepared tips of up to 15 mm length. Their working edges sometimes show a characteristic use-wear, which implies that they were used by right-handed individuals. Most likely, these tools were used in the production of clothing and simple containers. This indirectly implies some knowledge of tanning technique to make leather. In any case, the flint tools clearly point to the use of a range of other raw materials that are not preserved. This is also implied by little notches that can be found on numerous working edges. Their small size and their particular fine damages can only be explained by their use in the processing of plants, fibres and grass.

At the other end of the spectrum we can observe rather large tools that were not made from flint. Hominids instead used the thick outer parts of elephant long bones. This raw material was acquired in macerated condition from the dying grounds of elephants. Tools were made by deliberately producing large flakes, which were frequently retouched to produce scraper-like working edges. These scrapers occur in different sizes between *c.* 15 and 78 cm (Mania and Mania 1997), which certainly reflects some kind of functional differentiation. They frequently carry scratches and are sometimes polished. Others are damaged, suggesting that they were used as chisels or wedges, while some pieces are bifacially retouched. A dagger-like tool also occurs, which was purposely made from a rhinoceros ulna. Finally, apart from large stones and pebbles, a number of large bones were used as anvils or working supports and were sometimes intentionally fixed to the ground.

Formal characteristics of tools

The formal shape of the tools or at least the working edges at Bilzingsleben mostly depends on the intended function. However, in the case of the small flint tools a certain degree of shaping is done beyond simple functional necessities. In some cases the pieces almost seem to reflect some form of aesthetic sense. In any case, the flint tools follow a certain degree of standardisation that allows their grouping to certain formal groups. For example, thin flint points with uni- or bifacial retouch occur, which are reminiscent of bifaces. Furthermore, triangular points also occur far too regularly to regard them as simply accidental. Often these tools are only minimally retouched as they apparently already had their desired form. In other cases they were carefully modified with lateral retouches so it is possible to recognise Tayac-, Quinson- und Chalosienne-points (Laurat 2000).

Production techniques and intentional behaviour

Apart from simple techniques that were described above, artefacts at Bilzingsleben also exhibit chains of production that were much more complicated and let us infer a high level of forward planning. One example is the production of bone tools. As a first step the joints were smashed away with large choppers. The remaining shaft was then split with stone wedges to acquire longitudinal pieces of the compact parts of the bone. By retouching these working pieces they were subsequently turned into a number of different tools.

In the production of flint tools specific designs were also followed. The prepared core technology was already known, but it was rarely used because the available raw material did not favour this technique. Furthermore, bifacially retouched knives as well as different points were made according to a pre-conceptionalised image, which was realised in different stages. Different working supports of pebbles and large splinters of bones were intentionally fixed to the ground to make them more stable. In one case the tibia bone of an elephant was supported by a fragment of a pelvic bone of a rhinoceros (Figure 7.3). On the one side the former bone was fixed by the acetabulum of the pelvic bone, on the other side a slate of stone was driven through the *Foramen obturatum* to stabilise the whole construction. In the southern part of the workshop zone a large block of travertine ($60 \times 60 \times 35$ cm) with a weight of more than 75 kg was used as a working support, which can be concluded from the scratches and polish on its surface. Under this large stone a smaller block of travertine was found (*c.* $25 \times 25 \times 25$ cm) that had crudely been worked and was subsequently exposed to intense heat (Figure 7.4). As its underside also shows traces of heat the block was apparently placed into the small pit while it was still hot. This was done intentionally, although we cannot infer the function of this behaviour.

All of these examples demonstrate the ability to execute complex and planned actions, the cognitive mastery of the properties of different raw materials and the ability to put them to adequate use in the production of various tools. This goal-oriented behaviour, the intentional application of different techniques, the deliberate choice of specific raw materials for different tasks and the reproduction of preconceived material forms lead us to suggest that abstract thought was well developed in *Homo erectus* at Bilzingsleben.

Figure 7.3 Plan of an intentionally fixed elephant bone that was used as an anvil.

Methods of food acquisition

Apart from the economic-technical aspects we also need to consider the economic-productive aspects in the behaviour of *Homo erectus*, which are mostly related to the acquisition of food. Without doubt both animals as well as plants were utilised as food. Plant remains, however, are rarely preserved. An exception is the remains of cherry stones that were found at Bilzingsleben. We can only infer the most likely use of plants from the calcified plant remains in the travertine deposits, which give us a detailed picture of the floral communities in the vicinity of the former camp site, and even without the firm evidence of fossilised remains we indeed need to assume that plant food played an important part in the nutrition of the Bilzingsleben hominids. People most likely also took advantage of gathering opportunities provided by resources such as mussels or birds' eggs. In general, however, in adaptation to the temperate zones of Eurasia early man reacted by actively hunting big game. The

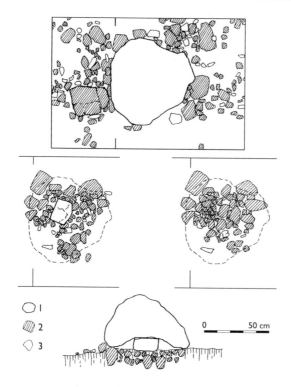

Figure 7.4 Plan of a large travertine anvil under which a heated block of travertine was intentionally placed: 1. Travertine; 2. Muschelkalk stones; 3. Bone.

finds of wooden spears at Schöningen – in our opinion – clearly refute any scavenging hypothesis.

We can therefore assume that most of the faunal remains in the find horizon of Bilzingsleben are the product of hunting behaviour. Preliminary examinations of these remains show the following composition of the available material: 60 per cent consists of the remains of large animals; rhinoceros is represented with 27 per cent alone, the remaining animals in this class being young elephants, aurochs, horses and bears. Medium-sized game, mostly red and fallow deer, is represented with 20 per cent In the remaining part we find small mammals, such as beavers with 19 per cent (*Castor fiber* and *Trogontherium cuvierii*), and various species of fish. It is interesting that in each class of animals one particular species is predominantly represented (rhinoceros, red and fallow deer, and beavers). We interpret this as a result of intentional choice. The other animal species were only hunted occasionally, either because it was simply inefficient (in the case of roe deer) or too dangerous (wild pig or felids). Consequently, these latter species occur only in very small numbers among the faunal remains from the site. Altogether, the observed pattern is very difficult to interpret because of the extensive period of use of the camp site. We would expect that hunting behaviour varied considerably during and between years. However, these variations cannot be inferred with any certainty.

Big game hunting certainly was a communally planned and executed activity. This probably involved disabling prey in their various aggressive or flight capabilities. To be able to do so, humans needed to have an exact knowledge of the different aspects of the behaviour of the hunted species, of the peculiarities of the landscape and the influences of the seasons over the course of the year. In particular, the latter aspect became much more important in the process of adaptation to the temperate climate zone.

With reference to the evidence from Schöningen, Rieder (2000) has argued that the use of spears and throwing sticks facilitated the development of co-ordinated and conditional characteristics in early hominids, which are today regarded as especially important in the context of competitive sports: dexterity, physical strength, responsiveness, speed and stamina. To what extent were these characteristics developed in *Homo erectus*? Certainly, *Homo erectus* required not only physical capabilities, but also needed to master them cognitively. Successful hunting and the use of long-distance weapons consequently implicated a much more efficient way of linking decisions with actions. A more complex level of information processing and the anticipation of situations is therefore implicated involving attacking and flight, tracking and killing wounded prey and the support of fellow hunters in critical situations. Rieder (2000) concludes that we can use these relations very well to speculate about the level of cognitive capabilities in *Homo erectus*. He believes that it implicates a highly developed level of consciousness, memory and reflexive thinking. As today, a lot of the fast and complex actions during a hunting operation were probably made instinctively, but were subsequently reflected upon and communicated. We agree with Rieder (2000) in his analysis. It is important that the perspective of sports science allows us to infer a number of cognitive and physical characteristics of *Homo erectus* about 400,000 years ago from the presence of hunting spears and their extraordinary features (see Thieme, this volume). Consequently, it supports our conviction that hominids at Bilzingsleben were fully capable of abstract thought, language and complex goal-oriented actions.

We have already discussed above the advantages of a base camp, which enabled the group of hunter-gatherers at Bilzingsleben to operate in a specific home range. This home range probably was covered by a day's walk. We suggest that it had a diameter between 15 and 20 km, *c.* 350 km². This area had to be carefully used if the base camp was to be occupied for a long period of time. Possibly, humans at Bilzingsleben purposely used different ecological zones on a seasonal basis to achieve this. The ecological differentiation of the landscape around Bilzingsleben clearly allows such a structured behaviour. To the north more mountainous areas could be found, while the south was largely flat with wet and marshy river beds. Even further to the north a number of saltwater springs occurred, which must have been attractive for humans and animals alike.

The establishment of a base camp also enabled smaller groups to operate more independently in their quests for food or raw materials beyond the home range. This larger territory of the group at Bilzingsleben we call the group's district. It was mainly defined by natural boundaries, which were potentially difficult to cross. In our case these were the Central German mountain ranges to the south, which were covered by almost impenetrable forests, and the extensive marshy river valleys of the Elbe and Saale rivers to the north. This district extended for about 10,000 km². Within this district humans probably used similar habitats to the ones known around Bilzingsleben itself. In the north the plains of the dry centre of present-day Germany were especially favourable for large herds of grazing herbivores. Perhaps hominids targeted this area and brought back meat that they had already conserved with simple techniques.

The site of Schöningen II-4 fits very well into such a model of behaviour outside of the home range (see Thieme, this volume), even though it is slightly younger than Bilzingsleben and already shows an adaptation to a cooler, boreal climate with pine and birch forests. Specialised hunting locales of the humans at Bilzingsleben probably looked similar. It was a favourable site for an ambush at the shore of a lake with closed reed vegetation and a nearby forest. The hunters remained at this location for some time as is suggested by the presence of several hearths. The hunting weapons were probably left behind because they could no longer be used. It seems unlikely to us that sophisticated tools that represent such a considerable amount of effort were simply forgotten.

Special cultural and cognitive aspects

Comparable to some structures at Bilzingsleben a number of distinctive artefacts suggest non-utilitarian behaviours and are connected to reflexive thinking. These objects carry regularly executed series of cut marks, which cannot be the accidental product of some form of working process. They were deliberately made and obviously had specific meanings, which were materially and visually fixed (Mania and Mania 1988). The following objects have to be considered in this context:

Object 1
This is a long splinter (39.5 × 12 × 6.5 cm) probably made from a tibia of a straight-tusked elephant (Figure 7.5).

It was found between two workshop areas in front of the central living structure. This piece of bone was used as a tool and it exhibits clear fracture marks, which suggest that it was some form of chisel. The breaking of the piece led to the loss of some of the markings at one end. The other end is pointed and rounded. One side of the object is a flat and regular surface with a breadth between 5 and 6 cm. It is marked with a regular set of parallel lines that were carefully cut with a flint knife. Next to the pointed end these lines form a set of seven diverging lines. After a short distance a set of fourteen parallel cuts is

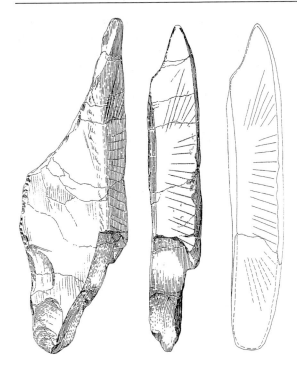

Figure 7.5 Object 1: a large splinter from a long bone of an elephant with regular cut marks.

set on the central part of the surface. The cuts are between 3 and 4 cm long and diverge slightly and symmetrically towards the outer edge of the bone. The remaining part of the cut marks are apparently destroyed when the piece was broken. Here, another set of seven lines possibly existed to form a symmetrical arrangement.

Object 2

This piece is a fragment of a flat rib of a large mammal (28.6 × 3.6 × 0.5–0.9 cm) (Figure 7.6).

It was found on the surface between the working places of the northern living structure. The surface of the rib seems to be intentionally polished on both sides. The outer side carries parallel and regularly spaced incisions that are arranged diagonally across the piece. The first cut is 6 cm long. It starts as a slightly curved incision, which is extended by two others. Three centimetres away the next line follows, which is made in a similar fashion. The next set of incisions is placed 1 centimetre away and is again arranged in a linear way. The final incision is only extended once and has a length of 1.3 cm.

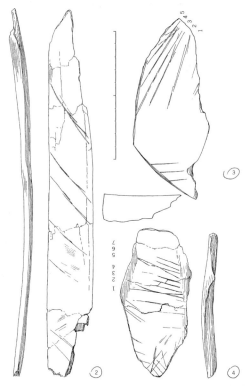

Figure 7.6 Objects 2, 3 and 4: bone fragments with intentional cut marks.

Object 3

This piece is a triangular artefact that was made from a thick splinter of an elephant long bone (14.1 × 6.1 × 2.0 cm) (Figure 7.6). On its surface a set of five diverging cuts are visible. They are up to 8.5 cm long and each consists of two incisions that are cut very close to each other.

Object 4

This thin piece of bone (11.4 × 5.5 × 0.9 cm) was found in direct contact on a large travertine anvil that possibly involved in the processing of wood (Figure 7.6). On the smooth, flat upper side was engraved a set of parallel lines. The arrangement starts with two thin lines with a length of *c*. 3.5 cm. These two lines run across each other in the middle and recreate a cross-like form. This is followed by seven parallel lines (1.5 cm each). The fourth and fifth line converge slightly towards the centre of this piece.

Object 5

In contrast to the other objects this one is a slab of quartzite (15.0 × 11.0 × 3.9 cm). It was lying to the west of the central living structure and functioned as a chopper. It carries numerous scratch marks but also an arch-like motive that is finished at its bottom by a straight line.

Object 6
This object is a tarsal joint bone of a straight-tusked elephant (17 × 10.5 × 5 cm), which was found in the central part of the alluvial fan. On its concave surface it carries a number of rectangles that were placed into and on top of each other.

In none of these cases is it possible to see the series of cut marks or patterns as accidental products. In this regard it is especially the set of lines on object 1 that is of particular importance. It certainly has to be interpreted as a visual representation of an abstract thought. From this piece alone we can infer that its producer was fully capable of this cognitive capability, abstract and symbolic thinking as well as the ability to transform this thinking into communication. This is also the case if we are actually dealing with some form of calculation or even a calendrical observation. For us this pattern on the bone is proof for the existence of language as a means of communication is some kind of form in *Homo erectus* 400,000 years ago. We can assume that this way of communicating abstract meanings was possibly much more common but was realised in perishable materials that have not survived.

Early ritual behaviour

In the discussion of the peculiar paved area above we already suggested that this structure probably played a role in some kind of ritual behaviour, possibly in relation to the transmission of socially vital knowledge and in the development of habits and practices beyond actions aimed at securing the subsistence of the group. The particular treatment of the human skull fragments – smashed in macerated condition – also points in this direction. In this form they provide a link to the quartzite anvil in the western part of the paved area. Both human skulls can be reconstructed from fragments that were either found to the northwest of the circular structure in the alluvial fan (Individual I) or to the south of it in small rivulets (Individual II). The distribution of both groups seems to be related to the circular structure and its anvil, where both skulls were possibly smashed, because here fragments of both skulls were found. A right fragment of a human mandible (Individual III) was also lying on the paved area. In both individual groups there were two large pieces of the skulls that appear to be intentionally deposited. An *Os occipitale* of Individual I was found together with a number of antler artefacts in a fissure, a large frontal piece of Individual II was located in a small pit that was closed with a large slab of travertine.

On language

Culture and complex social structures cannot be imagined without the presence of language. The development of a memory structure that is based on abstract notions is a further development of structure that is just based on experiences. It can be inferred from numerous pieces of evidence, especially from the presence of complex manipulative skills and techniques in the production of tools. An abstract notion memory structure, however, is a requirement for the development of a memory system involving words and, hence, of the development of language. The latter is clearly implied by the intentional cut marks on the various objects mentioned above, evidence for the ability of abstract thinking.

Cultural adaptation

All cultural aspects that have been developed in this chapter from the archaeological remains from the site of Bilzingsleben clearly demonstrate the complex level of cultural adaptation that *Homo erectus* had reached when he settled in the temperate climatic zones of Europe. This form of adaptation further made it possible for *Homo erectus* to survive in even less favourable environments, as can be seen in the case of the site of Schöningen, which has to be placed in the boreal period at the end of the interglacial period. *Homo erectus* consequently did not disappear after the climatic optimal phase of the interglacial from the Elbe-Saale region and retreated to warmer areas to the south. Rather, he adjusted his behaviour according to the changing ecological conditions, and specialised by hunting the most common large game animal in these environment, the wild horse (see Thieme, this volume). Four hundred thousand years ago, *Homo erectus* was therefore a human being that had a fully developed mind and culture, capable in creating his own socio-cultural environment with living structures, the use of fire and special activity areas. As an active hunter he was able to use long-distance weapons and complex technologies; he was capable of abstract thinking and possessed a fully developed language. This is the level of development we, at least, have to assume for archaic *Homo sapiens* and the Neanderthals as well.

Chapter 8

The Lower Palaeolithic art of hunting

The case of Schöningen 13 II-4, Lower Saxony, Germany

Hartmut Thieme

Introduction

In the reconstruction of the long, varied and multi-layered development of humans and human society, which encompasses more than two million years, the history of work processes and the development of human activities is of particular significance. In the early periods our knowledge of these processes has almost exclusively to be inferred from the durable tools made from lithic raw materials while those that were made from organic components are almost never preserved. In this context it has been an important topic of research to examine human hunting as part of the general subsistence activities of early man as well as a key aspect of the organisation of work processes. Most significantly, one needs to find firm evidence to show when and under what circumstances the hunting of big mammals became a significant factor in human subsistence.

Very ancient evidence of the dismembering of big game animals and the eating of meat are of course known from the Early Pleistocene from East Africa and from Middle Pleistocene sites in Europe. In most cases, however, the available evidence does not allow us to distinguish if the animal died of natural causes, was killed by carnivores or actively hunted by humans. In fact, the hunting of big game animals can only be demonstrated if the respective weapons are present as well, e.g. in the form of wooden lances. These reservations are further complicated by the possibility of other forms of hunting that are almost impossible to detect archaeologically, such as the use of poison, traps, nets, pits or natural obstacles that were used to disable animals.

For a long time the evidence of hunting weapons from the earlier periods of the Palaeolithic was restricted to two finds. The first is the Early Palaeolithic lance of Clacton-on-Sea (Essex, United Kingdom), discovered in 1911. This was made from yew wood (*Taxus*) and dated to the Holsteinian Interglacial (Middle Pleistocene) (Oakley *et al*. 1977). The second object is the lance, excavated in 1948, from the site of Lehringen (Lower Saxony, Germany). This was also made from yew wood (Adam 1951; Thieme and Veil 1985) and is dated to the last interglacial (Eemian) period.

This is the background to the discovery since 1995 of the wooden spears of Schöningen. These have been excavated together with stone artefacts and the remains of big mammals, predominantly horse. These extraordinary objects are dated to the time of the late *Homo erectus* and are of paramount importance for the reconstruction of human history because they represent the oldest completely preserved hunting weapons of mankind (Thieme 1996, 1997, 1999a). Together with the adjacent complex hunting camp this series of sophisticated wooden implements allows a completely new insight into the developmental stage and the culture of early humans *c.* 400,000 years ago.

The discoveries at Schöningen took place during a large-scale project that was initiated in 1983 and has been directed by the author since then for the Bodendenkmalpflege, Hannover. This project involved the examination of an area of *c.* 6 km^2 within the area of an open-cast brown-coal mine. Over twenty years an area of *c.* 400,000 m^2 has been excavated and materials recovered from the early Neolithic to the time of the birth of Christ (Thieme and Maier 1995: 108ff.). From 1992 a new focus led to the discovery and excavation of several Lower Palaeolithic sites in the southern section of the mine (Baufeld Süd). These were located 8–15 m below the present ground surface (Thieme *et al.* 1993; Thieme and Maier 1995: 57 ff.).

Location, stratigraphy and Lower Palaeolithic sites

The Schöningen open-cast mine is located in northern Germany, about 100 km east of Hannover, north of the Harz mountains (1.142 m above sea level) and at the south-eastern edge of the Triassic limestone ridge called the Elm (323 m above sea level). This area is part of the northern region of the 70-km long sub-herzynic basin between Helmstedt and Staßfurt. In addition to the long-term archaeological excavations the massive exposed sediment layers of the Pleistocene (with a thickness of up to 30 m) were constantly monitored and analysed (Mania 1995a; Urban 1993, 1995; Urban *et al.* 1988; Urban *et al.* 1991a, b).

The oldest Pleistocene deposits exposed in the mine are the sediments of the Elster glaciation (Figure 8.1). Above these sediments a series of six major erosional channels has been documented since 1992 in the southern part of

---

Key to Figure 8.1

Key: 1. Denudation horizon; 2. Gravel sands; 3. Sands; 4. Lacustrine deposits; 5. Limnic organogenic sediments; 6. Peat; 7. Travertine; 8. Loess; 9. Soils (Lessivé, Pseudogley) and humic zones; 10. Ground moraines; 11. Laminated clay deposits; 12. Periglacial structures; 13. Lower Palaeolithic find horizons (the spears are from level 4 within the Schöningen II sequence and date from the end of the Reinsdorf Interglacial). Lg: Late glacial. Plg: Pleniglacial. Eg: Early glacial. Igl: Interglacial. 1–5: sequence within the Reinsdorf Interglacial. a: arctic; w: warm-temperate (after D. Mania).

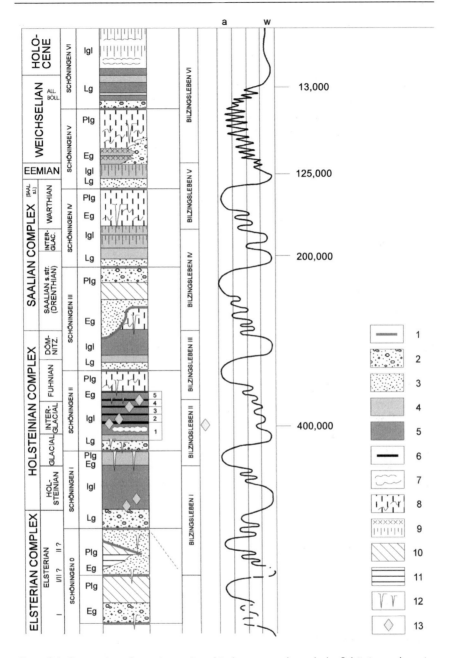

Figure 8.1 Composite schematic stratigraphical sequence through the Schöningen deposits, which cover the period from the Middle Pleistocene to the Holocene. The sequence (Schöningen 0–VI) is correlated with the climatic cycles (terrace-travertine series) of Bilzingsleben.

the Schöningen open-cast mine (Figure 8.2; Thieme and Mania 1993). The channels and their associated sediments represent a series of interglacial/glacial cycles that have been named Schöningen I–VI (Figures 8.1 and 8.2). These range from the Holsteinian to the Holocene (Mania 1995a). Channels I–III, which contain limnic sediments, can be placed into the period between the Elster and Saale glaciation *sensu stricto*.

The oldest interglacial sediments (Schöningen I) probably date to the Holsteinian (Figure 8.1). The Schöningen II channel is filled with sediments of the Reinsdorf Interglacial (Thieme *et al.* 1993) and the following Fuhne cold stage. The depositional sequence contains five levels of organic muds and peats (Figure 8.1, Schöningen II, 1–5). Level 1 represents both the early and inter- glacial maximum of the Reinsdorf Interglacial; the upper levels represent cool temperate phases and exhibit frost structures between Levels 4 and 5 (Figure 8.1). The Reinsdorf Interglacial is a new biostratigraphical unit between the Elster and Saale *sensu stricto*. Palynological analyses by B. Urban (1995) indicate that its vegetational history differs from both the preceeding Holsteinian and the succeeding Schöningen III Interglacial. The latter can be identified as the Dömnitz Interglacial (Urban 1997). The molluscs of Level 1 of the Reinsdorf Interglacial represent a species-rich thermophilous fauna; they include Mediterranean and SE-European elements (*Helicigona banatica*-fauna), which indicate temperatures that were two to three degrees warmer than today (Thieme and Mania 1993; Mania 1995b). The Schöningen IV channel is younger than the Saale glacial *sensu stricto* (Drenthe) and consists of an extensive double soil complex (Figure 8.1). The infill of channel V can be correlated with the Eemian Interglacial, while the sixth channel infill is of Holocene age. Work by D. Mania has established a correlation between the Schöningen sequence and the terrace-travertine series at Bilzingsleben in Thuringia, Germany (Mania 1993, 1995a, b).

However, recent palaeo-carpological investigations of the Reinsdorf Interglacial (Jechorek 2000) have demonstrated the presence of a forest steppe with the element *Acer tataricum* L. within the climatic optimum, which makes it difficult to link Schöningen II to Bilzingsleben II. A similar situation emerges after the first investigations of the horse remains from level 4 (the 'spear site') of the Reinsdorf Interglacial by R. Musil (2002). According to this analysis the equids from Bilzingsleben II are phylogenetically older than the equid population from the end of the Reinsdorf Interglacial (Schöningen II), which generally seems to point to the existence of an additional Interglacial period within the Holsteinian complex (Figure 8.1).

The Lower Palaeolithic sites at Schöningen (Thieme and Maier 1995: 57 ff.) have been discovered and excavated in interglacial sediments, dating to the Holsteinian complex: the oldest, a lakeshore site (Schöningen 13 I; Figure 8.2, B), discovered and partially excavated (120 m²) in 1994, is from the earliest part of the Holsteinian complex (Figure 8.1, channel Schöningen I). Its material comprises flint artefacts, mostly small flakes, numerous pieces of burnt flint

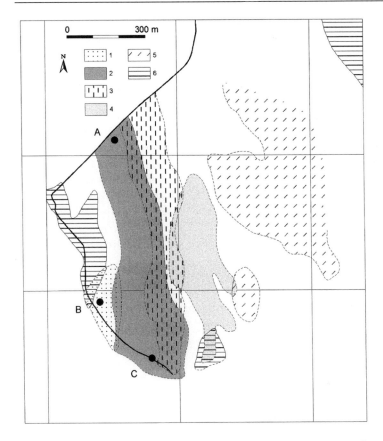

Figure 8.2 Course of the six Pleistocene/Holocene channels in an area of one km² in the southern part of the Schöningen open-cast mine.

Key: 1. Schöningen I; 2. Schöningen II; 3. Schöningen III; 4. Schöningen IV; 5. Schöningen V; 6. Schöningen VI. The Elsterian glacial deposits lie beneath all the channels; between the channels of Schöningen III and IV lies the glacial series of the Saalian glaciation *sensu stricto* (Drenthe). The channel of Schöningen VI contains Holocene deposits. The solid line in the North and Southwest is the border of the open-cast mine in the area.

Lower Palaeolithic sites mentioned in the text: A: Schöningen 12 (excavated in 1992) with two archaeological find horizons. B: Schöningen 13 I (excavated in 1994). C: Schöningen 13 II (excavations in progress since autumn 1994) with the 'spear site' (Schöningen 13 II-4) (geol. map: D. Mania).

and a fossil fauna with *Mammuthus trogontherii*, bovids, horse and red deer (Thieme 1995a). On the surface of an overlying organic mud the remains of a *Bison* sp. skull and several tracks of large mammals were observed.

The Schöningen 12 site, another lake-shore locale excavated over 150 m² in 1992 (Thieme 1995b, 1999a; Thieme *et al.* 1993), dates to the following

Reinsdorf Interglacial (Figure 8.1, channel Schöningen II, Level 1). It contained flint artefacts, a *Palaeoloxodon antiquus*-fauna with more than a thousand bones, including maxillae and mandibles, and teeth of more than ten taxa (van Kolfschoten 1993, 1995) as well as remains of birds, fish and reptiles (Böhme 2000) (Figure 8.2, A). The most important finds from this site are four worked branches of the common silver fir, *Abies alba* (Schoch 1995). These wooden tools have a diagonal groove cut into one end, probably for holding flint tools or sharp flakes to create a more efficient tool (Thieme 1999a). If this supposition is correct, these implements were cleft hafts, and represent parts of the oldest composite tools in the world. The specially selected material for these Lower Palaeolithic cleft hafts consists of the hard intact roots of the boughs of rotten trunks of the common silver fir (Schoch 1995: Figure 70). A second archaeological horizon was discovered 2–3 m higher up and excavated over 30 m² in peat sediments of the Reinsdorf Interglacial (Figure 8.1, Level 2). It contained some flint artefacts and the butchered remains of large mammals (Schöningen 12, find layer 2).

Because of the rapid pace of brown-coal mining since 1992, rescuing the evidence has had absolute priority. Because of this situation most analyses of the Lower Palaeolithic sites are currently preliminary and this applies to Schöningen 13 II-4 site (Figure 8.1, channel Schöningen II, Level 4 = end of the Reinsdorf Interglacial).

The horse hunting site of Schöningen 13 II-4

The archaeological context

The Schöningen 13 II-4 site, the 'spear site', was discovered in the autumn of 1994 (Thieme 1995c) about 10 m below the present ground surface. The site is situated on the shore of a shallow water course with ravines that were created when the falling water level exposed the chalky mud sediment of the periphery of the lake (Figure 8.2, C). The archaeological materials lie in an organic mud (layer 'b'), which underlies a peat horizon (layer 'a') (Figure 8.1) und have a vertical distribution between 30 and 40 cm. To date, an area of c. 3,200 m² has been intensively examined (Figure 8.3). Analyses of the molluscan fauna by D. Mania and the pollen spectra by B. Urban suggest a boreal, cool temperate climate. The vegetation was a mix of meadow and forest steppe. All finds were three-dimensionally recorded and documented with photographs and drawings. Geological profiles were recorded every metre along the x-axis and every 5 metres along the y-axis to make a detailed reconstruction of the development of the find layer (Figure 8.3).

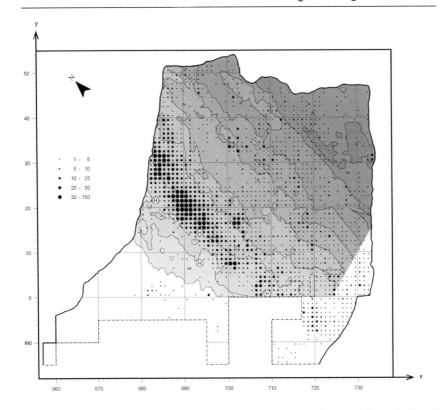

Figure 8.3 The site of Schöningen 13 II-4: map of the excavated area at the end of 2003
(c. 3,200 m²). The palaeorelief shows the surface of the chalky mud (layer 'c'),
which underlies the find bearing humic mud (layer 'b'). The relief is shown in
steps of 0.5 m, from 103.00 m to 98.50 m NN. The mapping of the densities of
finds ('1–150') includes all three-dimensionally and individually recorded objects
per m² (smaller fragments of bone [< 5 cm] are not included). The main find
scatter is located on the upper banks of the lake and is more than 50 m long and
about 10 m wide. H = Hearths (under investigation). Scale in metres.

Artefacts and archaeological structures

The excavation has yielded more than 25,000 well-preserved faunal remains.
Most of the fossil fauna (much more than 90 per cent) is horse (*Equus
mosbachensis*). Many of the bones display traces of butchery in the form of cut
marks and intentional fracturing. The assemblage of stone artefacts are all made
of flint. It includes many carefully retouched scrapers, some points (Figure 8.4)
and about 1,200 pieces of debris from retouching. The lack of waste materials
from blank production indicates that the flint tools were brought to this
location and were then resharpened or reworked. A soft hammer technique was
used and bone retouchers have been found.

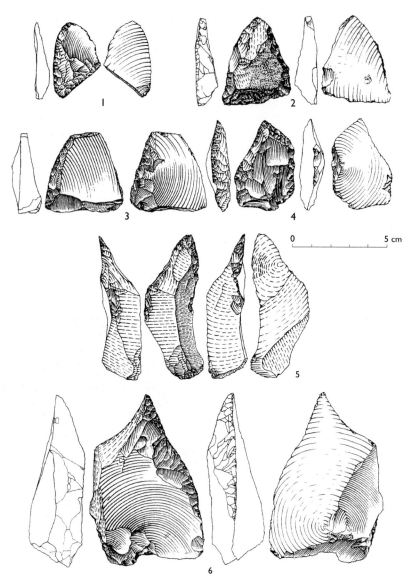

Figure 8.4 Schöningen 13 II-4: flint tools: 1 and 2. Convex side scrapers. 3. Alternate retouched side scraper. 4. Déjeté scraper. 5 and 6. Pointed tools.

The first wooden tool from this site, discovered on 20 October 1994, was situated only *c.* 1 metre away from the edge of the mine (x 684, y 31; see Figure 8.3). It has a length of 0.78 m with a maximum diameter of 30 mm and is made of spruce (*Picea* sp.). It was made from the stem of a small tree from which all side branches had been accurately removed (Thieme 1995c). Both ends were very carefully sharpened to a point (Figure 8.5). This excellently preserved implement most probably functioned as a throwing stick, resembling in shape and size the throwing sticks used by Australian aborigines (Cooper *et al.* 1981: 95) to hunt birds in flight. This tool could have been used to hunt flocks of geese that lived in the reed belt around the lake. Goose bones have already been identified among the faunal remains (T. van Kolfschoten, pers. comm.).

The three spectacular wooden spears (Figure 8.6) came to light in autumn 1995 (Thieme 1996, 1997, 1999a). Since then a large collection of more than half a dozen exceptionally well-preserved spears with lengths between 1.82 m (Spear III) and 2.5 m (Spear VI) and maximum diameters between 29 mm and 50 mm have been excavated. These hunting weapons were found in association with abundant faunal remains next to the main find concentration, approximately between co-ordinates x 690 and x 710, scattered along *c.* 25 m (see Figure 8.3). In early 1999 a 60-cm long fragment of the tip of another spear (VIII) was finally discovered further to the south of the main distribution.

Figure 8.5 Schöningen 13 II-4: view of the Lower Palaeolithic throwing stick (length: 0.78 m; *Picea* sp.) excavated in October 1994. Next to the stick is a larger bone fragment with a flint scraper to its left.

Figure 8.6 Schöningen 13 II-4: spear II discovered in November 1995. Its elongated point is in the front of the picture, the base is broken and incomplete (L: at least 2.30 m). To the right of the spear is a skull of a horse and other skeletal remains.

The spears are made of spruce (*Picea* sp.), with the exception of Spear IV which is made of pine (*Pinus* sp.). The wood selected exhibits a dense concentration of growth rings indicating slow growing conditions in a cool environment with some warmer elements. The spears are made from individual trees, which were felled and the branches and bark stripped off; the tip/distal ends (up to 60 cm long) are made from the hardest part of the wood at the base of the tree. Although the points are symmetrical, they are cut to avoid the pith ray. The tails are long and taper towards the pointed, proximal end. The surfaces of the spears are very carefully worked and intentionally polished and cleaned. With the maximum thickness and weight situated a third of the way from the tip, the spears resemble modern (competitive) javelins and were used by late *H. erectus* to hunt horses at the shoreline of the elongated shallow lake (Figure 8.2, channel Schöningen II).

Apart from these hunting weapons numerous other worked wooden objects, and fragments, have been excavated. Most of these await detailed analysis. Among them we have identified a charred stick (Thieme 1999b), which I will now describe in order to reconstruct its original form, use and function.

The wooden stick was manufactured from a spruce tree (*Picea* sp.) and has a length of 0.88 m with a maximum diameter of 36 mm (Figure 8.7.1). The bark was stripped off and all branches (more than fifteen) were carefully removed, with the exception of one branch near the tip/upper end. The latter now forms an extension of about 7 mm (Figure 8.7.2a, c). The distal and proximal ends of the stick are also worked (along lengths of 24 cm and 28 cm). Especially at its base the surface of this stick gives the impression of extensive use as if it was polished by long manual handling. The other end of the stick is completely carbonised over a length of about 8 cm (Figure 8.7.2a–d). The carbonisation, however, did not reach the inner sections of the wood but only covers the surface in a thick layer. This evidence suggests that the wood was apparently quite fresh at the time of use.

The use of this charred wooden stick as a tool is therefore suggested by several lines of evidence. Some effort was clearly invested in the choice, acquisition and preparation of the raw material as well as the basic shaping procedures. The same applies to the intensive and intentional manipulation of both ends of the stick. The effort that went into making this object makes it unlikely that we are dealing with a piece of wood that accidentally came into contact with fire or that it represents a broken fragment of a former tool that found its final use as fuel. If wood played a significant role as fuel the hearths at Schöningen, which is far from clear at present, then it had to be introduced into the site, as no natural remains of trees or bushes, apart from small traces of the reed vegetation, have so far been identified in the excavated area.

The carbonisation traces on the wooden stick clearly suggest a direct functional connection with the hearths that are situated along the western edge of the main find distribution. The position of the charred stick lies 6–7 m from two of these fire-places (Figure 8.3, H = hearths), and this wooden tool could

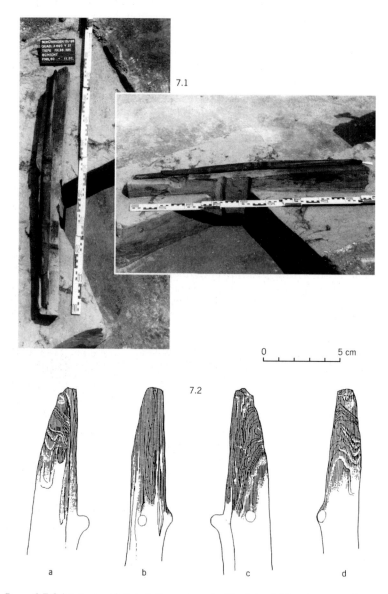

Figure 8.7 Schöningen 13 II-4: 1. Two views (a, b) of the 0.88 m long wooden stick (*Picea* sp.) that is carbonised at one end. 2. Details (a–d) of the upper part of the wooden stick, showing the extent of the carbonisation.

have functioned as a firehook to feed the fire as well as a spit to roast, and also smoke, strips or pieces of meat. For the latter activities, the protruding, and not altogether carefully worked, branch, which lies right at the end of the charred part (about 85 mm below the distal end), could indeed be interpreted as an intentional, functional element of this tool (Figure 8.7.2a, c). This protruding branch may have prevented chunks or strips of meat slipping off. Even the surviving length makes sense if this stick is interpreted as a spit (*Bratspieß*) as it would enable any user to remain at an almost ideal distance of about 1 m from the hot centre of the hearth.

The hearths themselves have characteristically changed the chalky mud sediment that is situated just below the find layer. In the affected areas the heat has turned this sediment red, which now also displays fossil drying cracks (Figure 8.8) (Thieme 1995c: Figure 99). At least four of these structures have now been identified. They are all located at the western border of the dense find distribution and are separated from each other by several metres and have diameters of approximately 1 m (Figure 8.3, H).

Figure 8.8 Schöningen 13 II-4: hearth 1 (Ø c. 1 m). In the area of the former fire the light-grey chalky mud (layer 'c'), directly below the find-bearing humic mud (layer 'b'), has turned red (dotted line) and shows ancient shrinking and drying cracks (arrow). The position of Hearth 1 is c. x 683 and y 23 on Figure 8.3. Scale in cm.

The significance of the discoveries of Schöningen and a preliminary interpretation

Organisation and division of labour, individual and collective behaviour, reconstruction of hunting behaviour, estimation of the season of occupation and evidence of storage

For the first time in the Middle Pleistocene we have access to a wide spectrum of well-preserved wooden tools from two very closely related sites (Schöningen 12, Fundschicht 1 and Schöningen 13 II-4). Apart from the two wooden lances of Clacton-on-Sea and Lehringen almost no other wooden remains have been found in Palaeolithic contexts since Smolla's (1953) summary. One of the lesser known examples was a long stick (*c*. 2.2 m × 40 mm) discovered in 1987 at the Middle Pleistocene travertine site of Stuttgart-Bad Cannstatt (Baden-Württemberg, Germany). This object apparently had a clearly identifiable pointed end but was unfortunately so badly preserved so that all attempts of recovery and preservation failed (Wagner 1995: 54ff., Anm. 101). At the site of Bilzingsleben a larger number of calcified remains of wooden objects in different shapes and sizes have also been found. Some of these could indeed have been spears or lances (Mania and Mania 1998; see Mania and Mania this volume).

The excellently preserved collection of wooden tools at Schöningen, in contrast, not only includes the earliest secure evidence of the standard-ised use of composite tools (Schöningen 12), but also a whole series of the earliest completely preserved wooden spears (*c*. 400,000 years old). These were unequivocal hunting tools – throwing spears and a throwing stick (Figures 8.5 and 8.6). They were highly sophisticated long-distance throwing weapons, which reflect an extraordinary skill in wood-working, to produce well-balanced ballistic characteristics. A test reconstruction indicates a range of up to 60 m with good penetrative power (Rieder 2000). These characteristics clearly reflect a long tradition in the production and use of such weapons. This conclusion emphasises the importance of the Schöningen finds in relation to the question of the significance and emergence of big-game hunting in human history. Before the discoveries at Schöningen the wooden lance of Lehringen was the only completely preserved Palaeolithic hunting weapon and it was apparently used to kill a straight-tusked elephant during the Eemian-Interglacial 120,000 years ago (Thieme and Veil 1985).

Furthermore, the throwing spears were found in the context of a large hunting camp and in immediate association with the remains of at least twenty horses. These were most likely killed with these weapons. The spears conse-quently point to a new understanding of early big-game hunting because they were specifically used to hunt a very mobile and fast animal species from a distance – a technique and specialisation that was previously unknown for the Lower Palaeolithic. Moreover, 'mono-specific accumulations of faunal remains', which in Palaeolithic contexts were used as evidence for 'intentional human hunting behaviour' were thought to appear 'regularly only after the Eemian-Interglacial' (Gaudzinski 1996: 222). Therefore, it was assumed that this kind of hunting behaviour was restricted to the Middle and Upper Palaeolithic (Musil 1993).

The throwing spears also put to rest one view (Dennell 1997) in the Anglo-American literature that did gain the status of a Palaeolithic doctrine (Binford 1981a). According to these ideas early hominids and Neanderthals were portrayed mainly as scavangers and as opportunistic hunters of small game animals. Only anatomically modern humans, it was claimed, were capable of the systematic hunting of big game animals. However, the hunting spears and horse carcasses from Schöningen dramatically show that *Homo erectus*, and by extension Neanderthals as well, did not depend on scavenged meat (Nitecki 1987; Gamble 1987), but were instead sophisticated hunters. This is also reflected in the differences in the dimensions of the spears, which certainly relate to the individual abilities of the respective hunters and therefore further stress the level of efficiency that characterised this communal hunting occasion. *Homo erectus* in the Middle Pleistocene was fully capable of organising, co-ordinating and successfully executing the hunting of big game animals in a group using long-distance weapons. They therefore possessed some of the key intellectual capacities that have previously only been ascribed to anatomically modern humans.

These complex abilities are also demonstrated by the other wooden tools. These are clearly the result of the mastery of complicated technical operations that involved a precise knowledge of different raw materials and required subtle decisions from their acquisition to the actual use of the tool. Altogether, these lines of evidence certainly reflect the existence of sophisticated operational chains of actions and a similarly complex abstract thinking that must have been complemented by verbal communication. If the interpretation of the apparently insignificant charred wooden stick as a spit is correct, then we have discovered another, so far unknown, Lower Palaeolithic tool, which demonstrates the complexity of the operational chains that involved the use and maintenance of the 'natural power' of fire. This tool also gives us new insights into the activities that were connected with an effective use and preparation of food resources, with all the implications for our understanding of the dialectical relations between humans, their social behaviour and the natural environment. It is also quite significant that all of these behavioural patterns can be observed well after the climatic optimum of the Reinsdorf-Interglacial, under boreal and cool temperate climatic conditions within a relatively open wooded steppe and grass-land environment: another piece of evidence which confirms the highly developed adaptive strategies of these early humans.

It is possible to make further inferences in this direction from the structure of the complete excavated area (3,200 m²; see Figure 8.3) as well as several additional pieces of evidence. The hunt took place on the western shore of a shallow elongated lake with a length of about 800 m (Figure 8.2, channel Schöningen II). This area must have been dry and was covered by a belt of reed vegetation without trees or bushes and therefore provided unimpeded views for the hunters. Over a length of about 50 m and a width of *c.* 10 m we excavated a continuous concentration of finds that is not separated by clear empty spaces and which includes up to 150 objects per m² (see Figure 8.3). According to the number of the complete skulls (Figure 8.6), many with the mandibles preserved, the find concentration contains the remains of at least twenty horses (MNI: 20). As it seems to be the case that the events of hunting and subsequent butchering are spatially identical we need to ask the question if this structure was the product of a single event, where a single group of horses was targeted, or the result of repeated hunting operations over a longer period of time. From preliminary studies it is already clear that the horses at Schöningen contain adult males and females as well as juvenile individuals. The evidence including the structure of the site and the excellent preservation of all organic materials suggests that Schöningen II is indeed the product of a single event, a successful interception of a complete herd of wild horses that moved along the shoreline of the lake (Figures 8.2, 8.3).

Such a sophisticated hunting strategy and co-operative endeavour is so far unique in the Lower Palaeolithic. It needs to be understood in relation to the need for meat, hides, etc. and an ability to process these resources quickly and efficiently. While the hides and skins could have been used for tent covers or clothing the enormous amounts of meat would have caused strategic problems because it was too much to be consumed on the spot by a relatively small group of Lower Palaeolithic hominids.

Is it therefore feasible to conclude that even in the Lower Palaeolithic meat was possibly cut into small strips and then dried in the open air or smoked so that a system of food storage was already in existence? These kind of abilities have so far only been ascribed to anatomically modern *Homo sapiens sapiens* after 40,000 BP. However, at Schöningen 13 II-4 there is further evidence to support a dramatic re-interpretation of the cultural development of *Homo erectus* in this respect. To the west of the main distribution of finds the hearths are arranged in a single line (Figures 8.3 H, 8.8). In these positions they could have played a central role in the activities surrounding the preservation of food and the creation of food reserves. In addition, the material also contains a number of working 'anvils' (Mania this volume), mostly radius bones of bison (*Bison* sp.) the flat dorsal surfaces of which were covered with a series of intense and similarly oriented cutmarks (10 cm long, 4 cm across) – clear evidence of the repeated cutting of organic materials with sharp edges of flints.

Further information on the season of the hunt can be inferred from the archaeological materials. The position of the hearths (Figure 8.3 H), within a dry zone of peat and mud around the edge of the lake, shows that it did not hold much water at the time of the occupation. This situation was most likely the case in late summer or autumn, a time with low precipitation and low water levels. Furthermore, almost all of the bones and skeletal elements carry thin brown to black stripes of humidic acid mostly on their upper surfaces, which can be related to the decay of organic plant materials of the reed belt. These processes obviously happened shortly after the butchering and processing activities so that we have to assume that shortly after the human activities a thick protective layer of decaying plant materials covered the whole site (including the wooden tools). The earliest this happened was probably late autumn when snow cover pushed down the reed vegetation. Until this time the whole site was apparently still controlled by humans who were living in the immediate vicinity, because on the thousands of animal bones only a few traces of gnawing by carnivores have been found. It is even possible that the occupation of this locale extended well into the winter or beyond – which would make sense in the light of the preceeding interpretation that stored food resources were produced. In the following spring, with the melting of the snow and the rising of the water level of the lake the find materials would have been rapidly covered by sediment and new vegetation and the wooden implements would have been perfectly preserved in the fine mud.

Finally, I would like to address one more question concerning the Lower Palaeolithic horse-hunting camp of Schöningen 13 II-4 that may not be easy to answer even by future research: why did we not only find a single spear at the site, but a whole collection of at least eight wooden spears and possibly the larger part of the weapons that were used in this hunting event? Is it possible that these spears were simply forgotten in this intensely utilised and limited area of butchering and processing activities? Or did the hominids at Schöningen always have enough access to weapons, not only to hunt but also as a protection against carnivores, and the necessary raw materials, so that the loss of such an object did not cause much of a problem? The obvious explanation would of course be the damage the spears suffered in the course of the hunt, so that they could not have been used again – an interpretation that is difficult to support because of the different post-depositional damages the spears have suffered. In any case, one needs to ask why these weapons, which have been produced according to individual needs and abilities and with a considerable amount of effort, were not reworked and used for other purposes, e.g. digging or throwing sticks. Is the act of leaving behind these important tools maybe a reflection of differentiated hunting rituals, which we have to assume for the time of *Homo erectus* and which prohibited further use of the tools used for killing? Was a taboo placed on them, to secure the success of future hunting activities? And does this stand in connection with the skulls of the killed horses that were not smashed or used in any form so that one gets the impression that they were treated with respect, to ask the animals for forgiveness after the act of violence?

In the light of these questions I would like to add one example from an ethnographic case, a statement of an Eskimo hunter:

The greatest danger for life comes from the fact that every food of man is made of souls. All the animals we are killing and eating have souls just as we have; souls, which do not perish with the bodies but need to be appeased, so that they do not take revenge because we once took their bodies away.

(Quoted after Haeckel 1966: 412)

Conclusion

The focus of future work at Schöningen will be to examine the artefacts and structures in more detail to gain a better understanding of the individual capabilities, the social behaviour and the general level of cultural development of the early humans who once lived at this site. For example, the exact reconstruction of the hunting event and the economic behaviour connected with it will be of major importance. It needs to be deciphered with the help of taxonomic and taphonomic studies as well as analyses of the numerous very well-preserved cutmarks, which should give us a very good picture of the butchering and processing strategies at this site – possibly even insights into storage behaviours and the production of leather and clothing. Because of its extraordinary preservation the site also holds the potential to link these activities to a whole range of tool types, which can furthermore be placed in relation to spatial structures, most importantly to workshop zones that can most likely be related to the hearths. The prospects for the study of the individual at Schöningen are only just being realised.

Acknowledgements

We are grateful to the Braunschweigische Kohlen-Bergwerke AG (BKB), Helmstedt, for the technical and organisational support of the long-term archaeological excavations in the Schöningen mine, especially for their efforts and their courtesy in enabling us to excavate and analyse the complete sedimentary sequence of the new Reinsdorf Interglacial. I would also like to thank the Deutsche Stiftung Denkmalschutz for a grant in 1996 that supported the rescue excavations at the 'spear site'. Thanks are due to A. Pastoors (Cologne) for the drawings of Figures 8.1–8.2, U. Böhner (Hannover) for the drawing of Figure 8.3 based on extensive investigations of the data, B. Kaletsch (Marburg) for the drawing of Figure 8.4, A. Bojahr (Hannover) for the drawing of Figure 8.7.2a–d, P. Pfarr (Hannover) for the photographs of Figures 8.5, 8.6 and 8.8 and M. Porr (Halle/Saale) for translating larger sections of this paper.

Chapter 9

Tracking hominins during the last interglacial complex in the Rhineland

D. S. Adler and N. J. Conard

Introduction

Over the last decade issues relating to the technological, organisational and cognitive capacities of hominins have come to dominate research agendas on the Middle Palaeolithic throughout Eurasia (e.g. Gibson and Ingold 1993; Kuhn 1995; Steele and Shennan 1996; Gamble 1999; Roebroeks and Gamble 1999; Bar-Yosef and Pilbeam 2000; Conard 2001b). As scholars continue to analyse the spatial relationships between different artefact categories and sites, and begin to apply these data to new research questions, they increasingly obtain important insights into the social realm of Palaeolithic lifeways. Elsewhere (Conard 2001a), we have addressed some of the fundamental issues relating to studying individuals in the Palaeolithic and have advocated using shifting scales of temporal, spatial, demographic and behavioural analysis (Figure 9.1). In our view the study of individual action is a valid goal, and an ethnography of extinct hominins is partially obtainable in Palaeolithic settings (Conard 1994, 2001a). Unfortunately, from a practical point of view, the main problem often faced by prehistorians is the lack of data derived from primary archaeological contexts. Studies are further hindered by a lack of well-preserved open-air sites that can be used to test models of hominin behaviour that are often based on the deep, time-averaged sequences from caves and rock shelters. 'High resolution' open-air sites can provide detailed observations on the day-to-day activities of extinct hominins that complement the long-term and coarse-grained behavioural histories that dominate the literature.

Another important issue, as the editors of this volume point out, stems from the reluctance of many prehistorians to frame their research and interpretations within the paradigm of the individual, instead opting for collective summaries that stress artefacts, their distributions, and the methods of their production, use and discard. As stated by Gamble and Porr (this volume, page 4) ' . . . we all know that individuals were responsible [for the archaeological record], but we prefer a collective summary of the evidence'. It is understandable, in a science-based, inference-driven discipline such as twenty-first century archaeology, why many researchers shun what might otherwise be considered

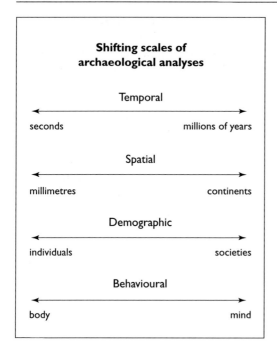

Figure 9.1 Schematic diagram showing the interrelated and shifting scales of archaeological inquiry (after Conard 2001a).

subjective speculation. Like many archaeologists, we recognise the potential importance of a research paradigm based on the action of individuals, but see no reason to abandon collective summaries. The key point is the need to combine inferences made using different scales of analysis. This having been said, there is a growing sense among many archaeologists that consideration of the less tangible, less obvious aspects of prehistoric societies and individual action is of importance, especially given the growing body of high-quality data from the Palaeolithic.

Such data are currently available from a growing list of high-resolution, open-air Middle Palaeolithic sites located throughout north-west Europe. Work at Maastricht-Belvédère (Roebroeks 1988), Rheindahlen (Thissen 1986), Tönchesberg (Conard 1992), Molinons/Le Grand Chanteloup, Bettencourt-Saint-Ouen, and Beauvais (Deloze *et al.* 1994; Depaepe 1997, 2001; Locht 2002) has focused on the excavation of large horizontal surfaces in an attempt not only to document individual sites, but also to reconstruct the surrounding landscapes traversed and experienced by hominins, including the scatters, patches and empty areas, and the interplay between different site types and their occupants. Integration of 'landscape', 'off-site' or 'siteless' archaeology (cf. Ashmore and Knapp 1999) with traditional site-based studies allows researchers the opportunity to consider the principal archaeological components of a site or sites and integrate them into larger systems of mobility, land use and individual action. Using this approach, researchers can reconstruct what Gamble refers to as the 'landscape of habit', that is 'The wider region, traversed by the individual and all those with whom he or she interacts, [that] forms a spatial network of intersecting paths' (1999: 87).

In this chapter, we discuss specific hominin behaviours and actions at Wallertheim, a Middle Palaeolithic open-air locality in the Rhinehessen region of Germany. We have chosen to showcase this site since it provides episodic, high-resolution data with which to track hominin actions and movements across the landscape and through time, allowing us to piece together the larger environmental and social contexts within which they operated and how these landscapes of habit may have evolved in response to changing environmental conditions. We do not attempt to reconstruct individual lived lives, as it is our opinion that Wallertheim, like certain other Palaeolithic sites, provides mainly episodic, situational data on individual actions that represent specific behaviours by specific hominins at specific points in time. We do not believe that such data are suitable for the construction of individual hominin biographies. Since we cannot provide a detailed outline of our research in the space provided, we would like to draw the readers' attention to several recent publications (Conard et al. 1995a, 1995b; Conard and Adler 1997; Conard et al. 1998; Conard and Prindiville 2000; Adler et al. 2003).

Background considerations to the last interglacial complex

Within the context of the Eemian Middle Palaeolithic of Western Europe, as defined by Conard and Fischer (2000), sites are relatively rare and few are well preserved. Taphonomic forces such as the erosion of Eemian deposits in association with the climatic decline that followed the interglacial, as well as the paucity of exposed terrestrial sediments, may help explain the general lack of Eemian sites outside sediment traps and travertines (Roebroeks et al. 1992a), but it is unlikely that such forces were capable of erasing or obscuring the entire slate of Eemian occupations across the continent. Other factors such as habitat preference, environmental circumscription and population density may also affect the frequency of sites on the landscape and their archaeological visibility. Gamble (1986, 1999) proposes that the low visibility of Eemian sites in Europe is due in part to environmental preference by hominins. He argues that, because of a relative decline in edible and accessible biomass, hominins were not capable of subsisting in the densely wooded environments that dominated the Eemian landscape. The growth and spread of dense deciduous forests and the concomitant disappearance of mosaic environments limited the sizes of animal populations and their distributions, thus making animals less numerous and less predictable on the landscape. Faced with such potential dietary shortfalls, individuals had to choose between intensifying their exploitative efforts or moving to more productive, less densely forested regions (Gamble 1999: 229–30).

While foraging in dense forests without sophisticated technological and social aids is a difficult proposition, could such conditions really have precluded the occupation of large expanses of Europe during OIS 5e? Based on the current and growing body of evidence, it appears that the answer is no. Many of the best-known European Eemian sites are intimately associated with sources of water such as rivers, lakes and springs (Roebroeks and Tuffreau 1999; Adler *et al.* 2003), locales that were attractive to numerous animal species and that, in many instances, became foci of hominin occupation and activity within the larger forested landscape. Many of these sites preserve what are often interpreted as single-animal kill and butchery events, such as Neumark-Nord (Mania *et al.* 1990; Mania 1991; but see Gamble 1999), and Gröbern (Mania *et al.* 1990), or time-averaged accumulations from sediment traps or travertines, such as those around Weimar (e.g. Behm-Blancke 1960).

While sites deposited in such environments may experience rapid burial via alluviation and calcite precipitation, and thus be more likely to survive later post-depositional destruction, it is unlikely that this factor alone determined relative site visibility and preservation during OIS 5e. Although few in number, cave sites such as Grotte Vaufrey (Level IV; Rigaud 1988) and Scladina Cave (Level 5b; Bocherens *et al.* 1999) also contain occupations dated to the Eemian, but such deposits are generally rare, perhaps reflecting hominin habitat preference. These data suggest that Middle Palaeolithic hominins were not excluded from Eemian Europe, but rather were capable of exploiting particular elements of the Eemian landscape, specifically locales where a suite of key resources were concentrated and where mobility was perhaps facilitated by more open terrain (Roebroeks and Tuffreau 1999; Adler *et al.* 2003). The excavation of Wallertheim Layer A (Wal A) provides a case in point, and allows us the unique opportunity to address the issue of Eemian settlement as well as to investigate the organisation of space and individual action in an open-air setting.

The context of Wallertheim

The history of research at Wallertheim has been outlined in several publications (Conard *et al.* 1995a, 1995b, 1998; Conard and Adler 1997; Adler *et al.* 2003) but a few introductory comments are warranted. Wallertheim is situated in the Rhinehessen region of Germany in alluvial sediments deposited by the Wiesbach River, a tertiary drainage of the River Rhine (Figure 9.2). Our work at the site ran from 1991 to 1994 and was conducted by the University of Connecticut in co-operation with the Römisch-Germanisches Zentralmuseum, and the Landesamt für Bodendenkmalpflege, Mainz. Six Middle Palaeolithic find horizons (Wal A–F) dating to the period between the Eemian Interglacial and the accumulation of the main early Weichselian humic deposits were identified during excavations (Figure 9.3). Wal A is comprised of fine-grained, yellow-brown silts and is correlated with Oxygen Isotope Stage 5e (OIS 5e) via thermoluminescence, sedimentology, biostratigraphy and correlations with the Milankovitch Cycle. In total, $176\,m^2$ were excavated and archaeological materials were recovered from sediments deposited on the aggrading floodplain of the Wiesbach.

Analysis of these sediments indicates that a stable, grassy surface existed on this portion of the floodplain and that this low-lying position in the landscape experienced mainly alluvial deposition on a seasonal basis. Palaeoenvironmental data indicate the presence of various thermophylic, forest and open-habitat elements, suggesting that the surrounding environment was composed of a generally open, warm, meadow landscape with significant bush and tree cover in the lower lying areas near the Wiesbach.

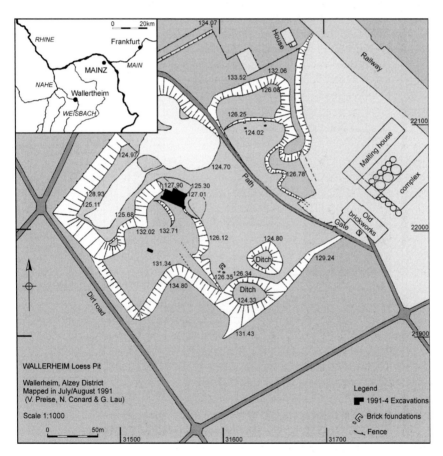

Figure 9.2 The location of Wallertheim with the excavations indicated in black (after Adler *et al.* 2003).

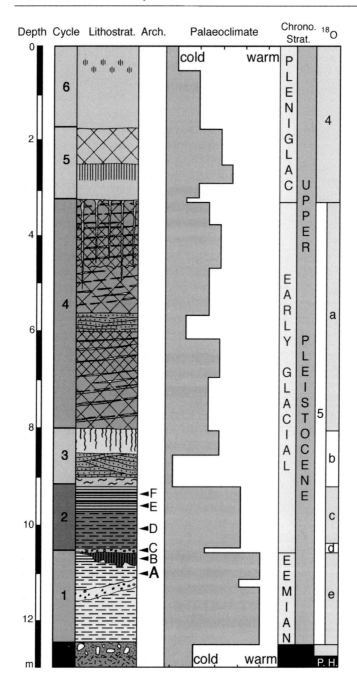

Figure 9.3 The chronostratigraphy of Wallertheim, with climate, temperature and chronological correlations (after Adler *et al.* 2003).

The constructed space at Wallertheim A

We decided to discuss Wal A in the present context due to the high-resolution nature of its archaeological deposits and the detailed information found at the site regarding land use and individual action. In a recent paper (Adler *et al.* 2003) we provided a detailed accounting of the site's taphonomical, sedimentological and archaeological history. The faunal and lithic remains recovered in situ from Wal A (these were distributed 5–10 cm in the vertical dimension) were found in direct association with a hearth and several large stone manuports. Research at the site provides clear evidence for intentional burning by hominins, particularly within Wal A where a minimum of thirty-three small fragments of calcined bone (3–19 mm in size), most likely attributable to fallow deer based on cortical thickness, were found concentrated within a single square metre area (Figure 9.4). The colour and condition of these remains are correlated with burning stages II–IV (Shipman *et al.* 1984), suggesting a fire that burned at temperatures of 285–940°C. Also found

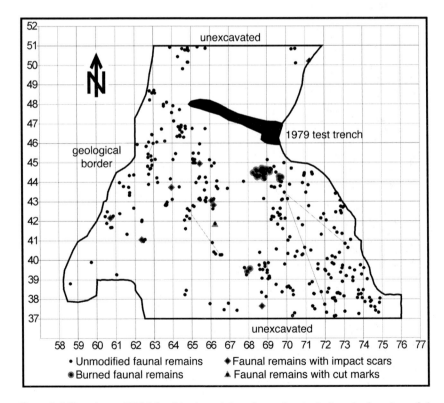

Figure 9.4 Plan view of Wal A with plotted faunal remains, including the location of the hearth and modified faunal remains; scale in metres.

associated with these calcined bones were seventy-three charred/burned bone fragments exhibiting a black, brown or white colour and a chalky texture. Although these finds were too small (<3 mm) and friable to study, based on their distribution we believe that most if not all of them belong to the neighbouring hearth.

Analysis of sediment samples from the hearth indicates that the area is enriched with the opal-phytoliths of woody plants compared to surrounding areas (Schiegl in press). Based on preliminary comparison with a modern reference collection, these phytoliths show strong similarities with *Fagus sylvatica* (common beech). This discovery is noteworthy given that the soil characteristics of Wal A are otherwise indicative of a grassland environment. Damblon's (in press) recent analysis of wood charcoal from Wal A allowed the identification of 194 specimens to three taxa: *Prunus* sp. (wild cherry/ blackthorn), *Populus* sp. (poplar), and *Populus/Salix* (poplar/willow), with the latter most clearly associated with the area of intense burning. Damblon interprets these data as indicators of riparian woodland, with a deciduous forest environment near the site.

Associated lithic scatters are concentrated around but not within the hearth. Moreover, the waterscreening of sediments comprising and surrounding the hearth did not yield any burned lithics. The clear spatial segregation between areas of lithic reduction and burning suggests that these features are strictly contemporaneous, reflecting a single short-term occupation during which particular spaces were designated for different yet associated activities (Stevenson 1991; Jones 1993). Given these observations it appears that this was a rather small open hearth built directly atop the occupation surface that burned for a relatively short period of time but at high temperatures, and in which wood was the main fuel.

Seven large, unburned, silicified limestone blocks (n=6 after refitting) were also found distributed among the lithic and faunal remains in the eastern portion of the site. Given their individual and combined size and weight, and their location within the fine-grained, low energy silts of Wal A, we believe that they were transported to the site intentionally by hominins; it is likely that these blocks originated from neighbouring deposits located at the edge of the floodplain. Although there are few clues as to their function, it is possible that they served as anvils for bone-processing and marrow extraction or as weights designed to anchor or otherwise stabilise elements of a windbreak or other structure (see Kolen 1999).

Faunal processing and consumption zones

Detailed zooarchaeological analyses indicate that the remains of adult *Dama dama* (fallow deer), *Bos/Bison* (aurochs/bison), and *Equus ferus* (wild horse) are most numerous, followed by lower frequencies of *Cervus elaphus* (red deer), *Canis lupus* (wolf), and *Castor fiber* (beaver) (Table 9.1) (Adler *et al.* 2003). The vast majority, but not all of the identified specimens represent high-survival, low-cost elements, suggesting that taphonomic forces have had an important impact on the assemblage. The presence of high utility elements and a relative paucity of toe bones suggest that entire carcasses were not transported to the site or that post-depositional forces such as carnivore ravaging or trampling led to the preferential destruction of more delicate elements. Unfortunately, the small sample size (n=382) limits our ability to conduct more rigorous taphonomic analyses.

Various modifications to the fauna have been identified including cutmarks and impact fractures on long-bone fragments of large bovids and cervids and carnivore damage at the extremities and along the shafts of the equid remains, suggesting that the large bovids and cervids are likely of anthropogenic origin while the equids appear to result from carnivore activity. Analysis of *cementum annuli* from prime age specimens of fallow deer and large bovid suggests that Wal A was occupied during the summer (Pike-Tay 1997; but see Stutz 2002). If that is accurate, this pattern of seasonal floodplain exploitation is mirrored in Wal D–F (Burke 1997; Pike-Tay 1997). Aside from severe drought or catastrophic events, the most common cause of death among prime age individuals during summer is hunting by hominins (Stiner 2002). This pattern has been documented at several sites within Germany (Gaudzinski 1995a, 1995b; Gaudzinski and Roebroeks 2000; Conard 1992; Conard and Prindiville 2000) and elsewhere (e.g. Bar-Oz *et al.* 2002), and appears to have been an important aspect of Middle Palaeolithic hunting behaviours.

Finally, faunal remains are distributed across the entire excavation area but specimens appear to cluster in two main areas, perhaps indicating functional zones within the site (Figure 9.4). The hearth and the hearth-based lithic scatters located in the eastern portion of the site (east of the 67 Line) retain much of their spatial integrity, suggesting that post-depositional disturbances were minimal. The fauna recovered from this portion of the site bear few overt traces of hominin modification save for those located within or adjacent to the hearth. The second major concentration of fauna is located several metres to the west (west of the 67 Line) (Figure 9.4) and exhibits the highest frequencies of hominin modifications other than burning. These data suggest that different areas of the site may have been designated for different stages of faunal processing, consumption and/or discard.

Lithic procurement and reduction zones

Analysis of the lithic assemblage from Wal A (n=6686) (Table 9.2) was conducted following the *châine opératoire* approach and was greatly facilitated by the diversity of raw materials present, a detailed raw material sourcing study of the surrounding landscape, and the refitting of hundreds of artefacts. In a previous paper (Conard and Adler 1997) we framed our discussion of raw material economy and lithic reduction in a generalised classificatory system for

Table 9.1 Wallertheim A fauna, with NISP, MNI, and weight

	Bos/Bison	Cervus elaphus	Dama dama	Cervidae sp.	Equus ferus	Equus sp.	Castor fiber	Canis lupus	Total
HEAD									
Horn/antler	1			1					2
Skull frag.	4				2				6
Mand. cond. and frag.		1	1						2
Teeth	15		8		6	2		1	32
BODY									
Vert: Cervical	2		1						3
Vert: Thoracic									
Vert: Lumbar									
Vert: Caudal									
Sacrum									
Sternum									
Rib frag.	1								1
FORELIMB									
Scapula	1	1	1		1	1			5
Humerus: prox									
Humerus: dist									
Humerus: shaft									
Radius: prox									
Radius: dist									
Radius: shaft	3	1	4		1				9
Ulna: prox	1				1				2
Ulna: dist									
Ulna: shaft	1								1
Metacarpus: prox	1							2	3
Metacarpus: dist									1
Metacarpus: shaft									
Carpal	1								1

Table: Hindlimb and toe skeletal element representation

									Total
H Acetabulum									
I Femur: prox					1				1
N Femur: dist	1		3						4
D Femur: shaft									
L Tibia: prox									
I Tibia: dist	2								2
M Tibia: shaft	5								8
B Patella				1					
Astragalus									
Calcaneum									
Coboid									
Metatarsus: prox	1				1				2
Metatarsus: dist	1								1
Metatarsus: shaft	3				1				5
Tarsal	1				1				1
T Phalanx 1									
O Phalanx 2	2								2
E Phalanx 3									
Seasamoid									
Metapod: cond									
Metapod: shaft	2		2						2
NISP	46	5	23	1	13	3	1	3	95
% NISP	48.4	5.3	24.2	1.0	13.7	3.2	1.0	3.2	100
MNI	4	1	5	—	3	3	—	3	15
Grams	257.0	96.3	191.7	61.6	511.9	143.9	2.0	9.0	1273.4

Size-class 2 N=31, grams=152.4 (e.g., boar, fallow deer, reindeer, wild ass)
Size-class 3 N=99, grams=1617.7 (e.g., red deer, horse, aurochs, bison)
Indeterminate N=157, grams=180.3
Total N=382, grams=3223.8

Note
See Adler et al. (2003) for detailed taphonomic and zooarchaeological analyses.

Table 9.2 Wallertheim A lithics

	Core	Wt	Tool	Wt	AD	Wt	Flake	Wt	SD	Wt	MD	Wt	Total	Weight
Agate	–	–	**1**	4.11	**1**	3.31	**2**	4.94	**7**	0.43	**10**	0.035	**21**	12.82
			(5.9)	(2.5)	(1.3)	(1.1)	(0.36)	(0.32)	(0.4)	(0.3)	(0.25)	(0.2)	(0.31)	(0.5)
Andesite	**1**	71.3	–	–	**3**	23.68	**1**	1.45	**2**	0.07	–	–	**7**	96.5
	(12.5)	(13.92)			(3.7)	(8)	(0.18)	(0.09)	(0.01)	(0.05)			(0.1)	(3.6)
Quartz	–	–	**1**	26.01	**2**	10.25	**2**	4.65	**19**	1.7	**9**	0.1	**33**	42.71
			(5.9)	(15.9)	(2.5)	(3.5)	(0.36)	(0.3)	(0.9)	(1.2)	(0.22)	(0.5)	(0.5)	(1.6)
Quartzite	**1**	91.67	**2**	18.74	**1**	0.93	**11**	33.25	**13**	1.54	**7**	0.07	**35**	146.20
	(12.5)	(17.90)	(11.8)	(11.4)	(1.3)	(0.3)	(1.97)	(2.15)	(0.6)	(1.1)	(0.2)	(0.4)	(0.52)	(5.46)
Red Rhyolite	**3**	77.03	**5**	18.45	**21**	62.4	**86**	207.97	**183**	16.11	**190**	1.32	**488**	383.28
	(37.5)	(15.04)	(29.4)	(11.3)	(26.3)	(21.1)	(15.41)	(13.45)	(9)	(11.3)	(4.8)	(7.2)	(7.3)	(14.3)
Tuffaceous Rhyolite	**3**	272.13	**7**	84.46	**52**	194.84	**454**	1288.96	**1798**	122.26	**3780**	16.8	**6094**	1979.45
	(37.5)	(53.14)	(41.2)	(51.6)	(65)	(66)	(81.36)	(83.38)	(88.7)	(85.6)	(94.6)	(91.7)	(91.1)	(73.9)
Volcanic Materials	–	–	**1**	11.93	–	–	**2**	4.7	**5**	0.68	–	–	**8**	17.31
			(5.9)	(7.3)			(0.36)	(0.3)	(0.2)	(0.5)			(0.12)	(0.6)
Total	**8**	512.13	**17**	163.7	**80**	295.41	**558**	1545.92	**2027**	142.79	**3996**	18.32	**6686**	2678.27
	(0.12)	(19.12)	(0.2)	(6.1)	(1.2)	(11)	(8.35)	(57.72)	(30.3)	(5.3)	(59.8)	(0.7)		

Note

Wt=weight, AD=angular debris, SD=small debris (<15–5mm), MD = microdebitage (<5mm). Counts are in boldface, weight is in grams, and (%) is calculated by vertical category. The total row at the bottom reflects the total counts (%) of the entire assemblage (N=6686; weight=2678.27g).

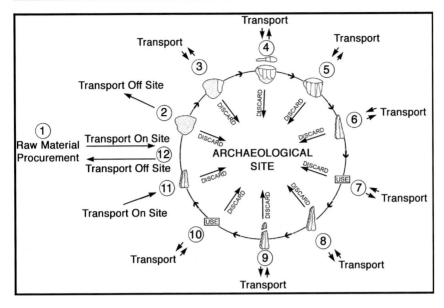

Figure 9.5 Schematic illustration of generalised reduction sequence, with numbers 1–12 referring to various phases of a reduction sequence (after Conard and Adler 1997).

the various phases of an idealised lithic reduction sequence, which we employ here (Figure 9.5).

The raw material survey determined that the lithics found at Wal A were derived from two distinct source areas, one, located less than 100 m from the site, comprised gravel deposits (e.g. quartz, quartzite, agate, andesite and a variety of volcanic materials). These river cobbles occur in a variety of shapes, sizes and textures, and were immediately available to hominins in the exposed gravels in the Wiesbach. The other, located no closer than 6 km, was comprised of primary source material (e.g. rhyolite) situated in elevated positions beyond the floodplain, in wooded areas drained by the Wiesbach (Haneke and Weidenfeller in press). The distinctive lithological characteristics of the raw materials allowed the identification of specific raw material units (RMUs), the attribution of each find to one of these RMUs, and the reconstruction of knapping episodes on a cobble-by-cobble basis.

Lithic refitting led to the conjoining of over six hundred artefacts (Figure 9.6) and the identification of 111 refit groups (RGs). Based on several of the RGs, it was possible to reconstruct two different systems of reduction: (a) the flexible, primary reduction of low-quality raw materials transported from primary sources (tuffaceous rhyolite and red rhyolite), and (b) the ephemeral, poorly defined use of locally available river cobbles from the Wiesbach. Although both systems of reduction are represented within the same, thin

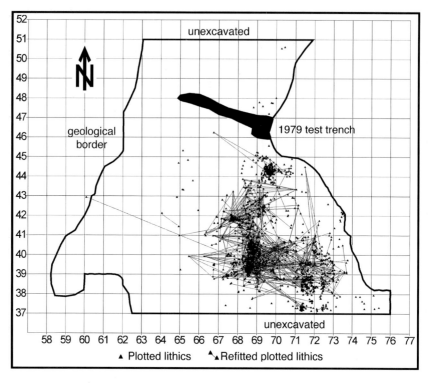

Figure 9.6 Plan view of Wal A with plotted lithic finds and refitted finds; scale in metres.

archaeological deposit, their technological differences are related primarily to: (a) fracture mechanics; (b) the proximity of the two raw material sources to the site; and (c) the specific land-use practices of the site's occupants.

The rhyolite (n=6582) artefacts document the on-site reduction of two to three blocks of material from primary sources located more than 6 km to the south. This is a production-oriented reduction system, with larger blanks being chosen for retouch and transport off site (Figure 9.7), and small debitage and microdebitage dominating the assemblage. Overall these rhyolites are internally heterogeneous and structural irregularities can cause them to fracture in unpredictable manners, rendering technological interpretations problematic; it is this feature that leads us to classify these materials as low quality. However, 59 per cent of the finds larger than 15 mm could be refitted, and in several instances the general sequence of reduction could be established (Figure 9.8). This illustrates a flexible approach to lithic reduction that maximises the flaking potential of poor-quality materials by frequent rotation of the core. It is clear that the efficient reduction of this material was by no means a straightforward task. Successful knapping required a keen understanding of the material's fracture properties as well as a preconceived plan for its

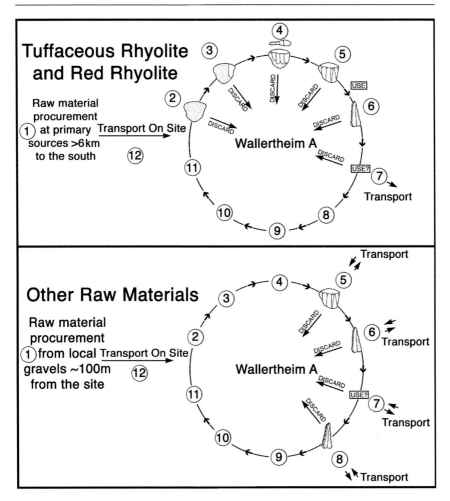

Figure 9.7 Generalised reduction sequence for the tuffaceous rhyolite, red rhyolite and other diverse materials (after Adler *et al.* 2003).

exploitation. Without this prior knowledge and forethought it seems unlikely that a raw material of this kind would have been transported such a distance when more homogeneous materials of greater flaking potential were available in the local gravels. Therefore, it seems likely that the occupants of Wal A were well acquainted with this raw material and its peculiarities and/or they were provisioning themselves in the uplands with a fresh supply of raw material prior to venturing on to the Wiesbach floodplain.

Associated horizontally and vertically with the concentration of rhyolite is an assemblage of artefacts (n=104) produced on diverse raw materials, which, based on a range of characteristics, are derived from at least twenty-two river

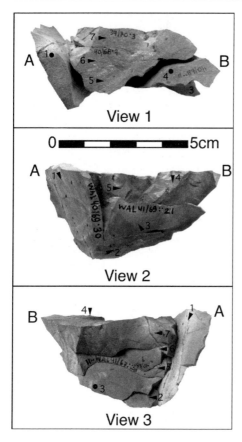

Figure 9.8 Refit Group 76, tuffaceous rhyolite. Numbers 1–7 indicate the reconstructed sequence of detachments. Dots indicate impact locations and arrows indicate direction of detachment (after Adler *et al.* 2003).

cobbles (Table 9.2). The clear association of these finds with the rhyolites suggests that they were all buried together rapidly. However, many of these finds were likely not part of the main occupation as they are distributed over a larger area of the site and do not appear in any clear clusters. Instead these finds document the repeated, ephemeral use of this portion of the floodplain and can be considered analogous to Isaac's Type A sites (Isaac 1981, 1984; Roebroeks *et al.* 1992b) or, employing our taxonomy, geologically contemporaneous finds (Conard and Adler 1997; Conard 1998). Thus it appears that these finds represent items that were lost or discarded on this portion of the landscape, perhaps over the course of a single season or year, rather than items produced and discarded during a single event or occupation (Adler *et al.* 2003). In contrast, the dense accumulations of rhyolite and a portion of the fauna at the site represent a single, short-term occupation (Stevenson 1991; Jones 1993) within a landscape that hominins traversed and littered regularly.

Intra-site spatial patterning and site use

Within the scatter of rhyolite several related areas of reduction are visible. These areas are most clearly visible in Figure 9.9, where the highest density of finds cluster in three distinct yet related areas. This pattern is mirrored among the distribution of both the measured and water-screened finds, indicating individual yet overlapping reduction areas that are strictly contemporaneous. One of these is located immediately adjacent to the hearth while the other areas are dispersed south of this feature. The distributions of particular refit groups and the refitted artefacts as a whole suggest a degree of interplay between the various reduction areas, probably in relation to the movement of cores and/or individuals about the site. The overall impression given by these combined archaeological elements is of a semi-circular or crescent-shaped distribution of material similar to that documented ethnographically (Binford 1978a).

It appears, however, that something other than the hearth, perhaps a shade tree or an archaeologically ephemeral activity, 'anchored' these short-term activities to this portion of the landscape. If space and activities were organised

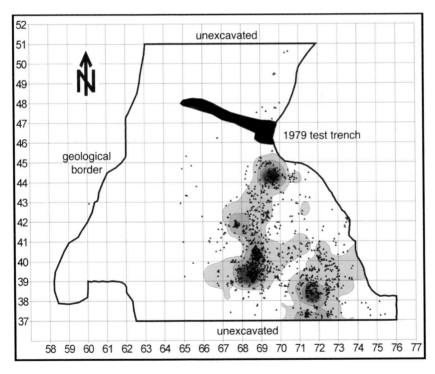

Figure 9.9 Plan view of Wal A with plotted lithic finds and water-screened find densities. Fifteen finds per contour interval, with a maximum of 260 finds per quarter metre.

around the hearth, we might expect to see a pattern similar to that predicted by Binford (1983) and reported at Middle Palaeolithic sites such as Tor Faraj (Henry 1998), Les Canalettes (Meignen 1993) and the Abric Romaní (Vaquero and Pastó 2001). Instead, the hearth at Wal A appears to be peripheral to the major areas of lithic reduction. Based on analogies with modern and historical hunter-gatherer (e.g. Yellen 1977; Kelly 1983, 1992, 1995; O'Connell 1987; Fisher and Strickland 1991; Jones 1993), some researchers believe that such a spatial pattern can be used to estimate group social structure or the number of individuals that originally occupied a site (e.g. Yellen 1996). While the application of such analogies is tempting, it is difficult to assess whether or not these ethnographic patterns accurately reflect Eemian Middle Palaeolithic lifeways and social structures. We also do not know the full spatial extent of the site, therefore we make no attempt to estimate the original number of site occupants other than to say that, based on current evidence, there were likely not many.

Our spatial analyses indicate that the distribution of the fauna is also not random, with larger specimens preferentially distributed to the west and smaller specimens to the east (Adler et al. 2003). If we assume that all of the fauna and the assemblage of rhyolite stem from the same occupation, then this analysis suggests the possible deposition of larger faunal specimens away from the central portion of the site where most of the domestic activities occurred. Further analyses reveal that the distribution of the three main taxa is also not random, with large bovids and fallow deer distributed rather evenly across the site, while all of the equid remains are restricted to the west.

If we accept that the large bovids and fallow deer were deposited on site during the same period of occupation (combined MNI=9), the obvious discrepancy between the large amount of meat that would have been available and the ephemeral, short-term character of the main areas of lithic reduction and burning must be explained. If all of these animal resources were procured, processed and consumed over the course of a single occupation, we would expect to see evidence for a larger, more diverse, more heavily consumed and more dispersed lithic assemblage, and perhaps the use of multiple hearths. Such evidence is lacking in the area of excavation. We believe that it is very unlikely that a small group of hominins could have taken full advantage of such abundant resources over the short span of time suggested by the ephemeral archaeological features preserved at the site. Our analyses lead us to conclude that an undefined component of the fauna is representative of a background assemblage related in part to repeated, low-level hominin activity on the landscape prior to and/or following the main occupation associated with the rhyolites and the hearth. We also believe that natural deaths and/or carnivore activity may have played an important role in the ultimate composition and distribution of this background assemblage. For example, due to the mode and frequency of faunal modification we believe that the equids identified at Wal A, in particular wild horse, likely resulted from carnivore activity and/or natural attrition. At least in this case the data suggest that more solitary, forest-dwelling species may have been preferentially targeted for exploitation rather than taxa that congregate in larger herds. In a mosaic environment such as that within which Wal A was situated, we feel that these are the most parsimonious, albeit conservative interpretations that the present data can support.

Discussion

On the basis of the data presented here we interpret the main component of Wal A as a short-term occupation on the Wiesbach floodplain, perhaps in the summer, during which hominins processed, roasted and consumed the remains of at least one fallow deer in association with a hearth and the reduction of primary source lithic material (Figures 9.4, 9.6, 9.9). While group size and the duration of the occupation are difficult to assess, the presence of an *in situ* knapping scatter, a moderate amount of processed animal remains from at least one individual, and a lack of lithic material from other knapping episodes suggest a single short-term occupation by a relatively small group of hominins lasting perhaps a day or two. Although all of the lithic material, save that comprising the background assemblage, can be linked to this occupation, it is difficult to say how much, if any, of the fauna in the western portion of the site is related to this short-term occupation.

There is clear evidence for several ephemeral, unrelated visits to this portion of the landscape prior to and/or following the main occupation outlined above, but the intensity and duration of these 'occupations' appear rather limited. These visits likely included the butchering and processing of several large bovid and fallow deer carcasses (or portions thereof) accompanied by phases of tool use and discard but not sequences of intensive lithic reduction or tool production. The presence of a background lithic scatter points to the repeated passage of hominins across this stretch of the floodplain and can, in a sense, allow us to track hominins across the landscape. In an unconstrained floodplain setting such as this it is not surprising to find patches of intense activity distributed amidst the more ephemeral, generalised signature of hominin activity (Isaac 1989a; Conard 1998). In fact an analogous situation has already been identified in Wal D (Figure 9.3) where an occupation broadly similar to that discussed here has been discovered in close association with other background assemblages of lithics and fauna (Conard and Adler 1997). At the opposite end of the spectrum, Wal E and Wal F contain only background lithic and faunal assemblages, with no clear evidence for distinct occupations (Conard 1998; Conard *et al.* 1998).

Another intriguing aspect of Wal A is the lack of evidence for the exploitation of distant resources and habitats. Although archaeological data sensitive to patterns of land use and mobility are difficult to derive from many Palaeolithic contexts, lithic raw material procurement, reduction and consumption behaviours can be used to gauge territory size or the frequency and scale of prehistoric mobility (Kuhn 1992, 1994, 1995; Gamble 1999). Several important studies of European Middle Palaeolithic raw material transfers illustrate the movement of materials over substantial distances and their intensive reduction (e.g. Gamble 1986; Geneste 1988a, 1988b; Roebroeks *et al.* 1988; Conard 1992; Kuhn 1992; Floss 1994; Conard and Adler 1997; Adler 2002); however, such cases are exceptional (Féblot-Augustins 1997, 1999). In the present case it appears that the hominins who occupied Wal A routinely procured materials from local sources, whether they be the ubiquitous Wiesbach gravels or nearby primary source materials.

Taken as a whole, the available data regarding raw material diversity, frequency and distribution at Wal A suggest that hominins within the surrounding region may have structured their activities and social relations within relatively small territories that could be covered in a single day's trek. According to Gamble (1999), a reliance on local commodities (e.g. primary or secondary lithic sources, key ambush or habitation sites, animal and plant resources, or mating and exchange networks) appears to characterise much of the European Middle Palaeolithic. However, the ephemeral, short-term nature of the occupations at Wal A suggests that local groups may not have always stayed in one place very long and may instead have been highly mobile, perhaps seasonally, within these small territories. The faunal data suggest that they may have relied more heavily on forest species than those commonly associated with more open environments.

Conclusions

If we assume that the archaeological occurrences and behavioural patterns documented at Wal A are generally representative of their time, an assumption not without its dangers, then we can attempt to compare particular aspects of hominin behaviour (e.g. mobility, land use and social network size) over time. The landscape of habit created and experienced by hominins within the local Eemian environment appears to have been rather limited in extent and diversity. In a recent study (Adler *et al.* 2003) we suggested that the social networks prevailing in the region during OIS 5c (Wal D) appear to have grown to include more distant regions, resources (e.g. raw material from >25 km), and individuals, although in keeping with Gamble's (1999) observations, the overall pattern still retained a very local flavour. Maintaining the assumption made above, these data suggest that hominins adapted to the more open OIS 5c environment by exploiting larger territories and provisioning individuals with portable implements, perhaps as a seasonally oriented strategy (Conard and Adler 1997). It is also possible that the disappearance of the dense Eemian forests allowed, or perhaps even forced, hominins to traverse and exploit a wider array of habitats and thus extend their social network, as well as reorganise their subsistence strategies, at least in part, around the exploitation of equid herds that now occupied the open grasslands of the post-Eemian landscape

(Conard and Adler 1997). Evidence for such reorganisation can be seen in the increased numbers of sites from this period (Gamble 1999), the exploitation of more distant lithic resources (Floss 1994; Féblot-Augustins 1999; Gamble 1999), and the development of specialised blade technologies (Conard 1990; Révillion and Tuffreau 1994; Conard and Adler 1997; Bar-Yosef and Kuhn 1999). Based on a handful of artefact clusters from a single site, with no other contemporaneous archaeological points of reference, we are unable to determine the precise nature of Middle Palaeolithic mobility and land use in this region during the last interglacial complex. Thus the ideas presented here should be viewed as working hypotheses that can be tested through the excavation and analysis of additional archaeological sites situated in similar environmental and chronological contexts.

At Wal A, we are able to trace the actions of individual knappers and tool-users, and, where the data permit, we are able to link these hominins to patterns of butchery, fire-making and seasonal mobility. Contrary to the common perception that the individual is archaeologically invisible, our work in well-preserved archaeological settings allows the individual to be documented through the material remains of his or her actions. When we move to a more general level of analysis it becomes increasingly difficult to correlate the behavioural patterns attributed to a small number of individuals with larger scales of demographic analysis. Despite these limitations, recent research, including contributions to this volume, demonstrates that relevant observations of human behaviour can be made at multiple scales of spatial, temporal and demographic analysis, and that by shifting between different scales of analysis a more complete and multidimensional view of the Palaeolithic past is possible.

Chapter 10

Bones and powerful individuals

Faunal case studies from the Arctic and the European Middle Palaeolithic

Clive Gamble and Sabine Gaudzinski

Introduction

It is not difficult to find individual action preserved in the Palaeolithic record. Neither is it hard to insist on the importance of the individual in the creation of variability in that record, either as idiosyncratic features or submerged in repetitive patterns. But an insistence on methodological individualism does not advance our understanding of the Palaeolithic any more than a belief in culture did forty years ago when, in Flannery's famous description, the Indian holding the artefact was the cultural source of any variation. That explanation, he argued, should be replaced by the organisational system that stood behind the Indian.

> Obviously individuals do make decisions, but evidence of these individual decisions cannot be recovered by archaeologists. Accordingly it is more useful for the archaeologist to study and understand the system, whose behaviour is detectable over and over again.
>
> (Flannery 1967: 119)

Since then the organisational system has been criticised as strongly as the culture history of the artefact-toting Indian (Johnson 1999). However, in the Palaeolithic tradition dies hard and mention of the individual elicits an instant rebuke (Clark 1992).

Our aim in this chapter is to consider the Palaeolithic individual in relation to the second major source of Palaeolithic evidence, faunal remains. We will ask how a consideration of individual action can change our understanding of the relationship between a hominid and his/her landscapes. In particular we concentrate upon the social dimension of Palaeolithic life that has been little discussed by archaeologists studying the period. Elsewhere, one of us (Gamble 1999) has argued for a focus on the individual in the construction of Palaeolithic society. Without such a focus it seems there can be no social archaeology for this period since it lacks monuments, rich burials, agriculture and the other landmarks which have fuelled both processual (Johnson and Earle 1987; Kirch

1984; Renfrew 1972) and post-processual (Barrett 1994; Thomas 1991; Tilley 1996) accounts of social life in later prehistory.

Viewed against the complex records of these later periods the Palaeolithic seems simple indeed. We will use this common appreciation to our advantage to explore the networks by which individuals rather than groups are manifest. We will argue that the perspective the individual brings to the study of resources such as animal carcasses is relational rather than rational. These resources are one of the common currencies by which we can measure the use of space and time by individual hominids within the framework provided by archaeological evidence.

With this perspective we will first re-visit Binford's (1978b, 1981a) classic ethnoarchaeological studies of Arctic hunters that have shaped the endeavours of a generation of faunal studies. Then we will examine the use of animal carcasses at one late Middle Palaeolithic site in Germany, Salzgitter-Lebenstedt (Gaudzinski and Roebroeks 2000; Pastoors 2001; Tode 1953, 1982), and consider these using the methods of fragmentation analysis (Chapman 2000).

A rational approach to carcasses

The organisational system has been the most potent framework for understanding Palaeolithic data. So much so that Binford's claim from his groundbreaking ethnoarchaeological study of the Nunamiut remains largely unchallenged.

> Without exception, all the documented variability in faunal assemblages is directly referable to functional variability.
>
> (Binford 1978b: 455)

By championing the system and the group as units of analysis Binford has produced a frame of reference that is scientific and rational (Binford 2001). Human behaviour and organisation are best understood as the attainment and maintenance of security (Binford 1991: 127). He is therefore equally unconvinced that patterning and variation arise either from individual free-will or the goal of maximising reproductive success (ibid.). Security provides a rational account of individual action within a group context.

However, this position sits uneasily with his influential accounts (Binford 1978b, 1981a) of carcass butchery by modern hunters and gatherers. The unease is not the usual and easily countered one associated with the appropriate use of analogies from the present to understand the past. Rather the issue is the way that knowledge about the system was acquired. This depended, as it must, on individual biographies. The Nunamiut hunters provided personal pragmatism based on local knowledge while Binford supplied the rational, systemic argument that apparently has universal application.

While Binford analysed Nunamiut butchery and storage decisions as outcomes of group behaviour the many photographs and descriptions in his books are of acts by individuals (e.g. Binford 1978b: Figures 4.3–4.5, 1981a: Figures 4.02 and 4.03, 1983: Figure 45). In particular, Simon Paneack, Billy Morry, Zacharias Hugo, Johnny and Jane Rulland as well as members of the field crew from Albuquerque, Dan Witter, Charles Amsden and many others (Binford 1983: Figures 47 and 48) are presented as personalities with an impact on the intellectual outcomes of the project. For example, read Dan Witter's own account of learning marrow-cracking from the Rullands (Binford 1978b: 153–5), the memorable sled rides that Binford took with several hunters (1978b: 55–9), or Simon Paneack's object lesson in pragmatism, the tale of the baby grayling (1978b: 454), and from which Binford admits he learnt much about Eskimo attitudes to knowledge.

But of course knowledge about how people live their everyday lives comes down to individuals. The point is not that the personalities of either the Eskimo hunters or the Albuquerque archaeologists make *Nunamiut Ethnoarchaeology* a study of the individual through the analysis of faunal remains. It is instead that a study presented as a *rational* appreciation of how decisions are made as part of a wider adaptive strategy is instead a product of *relational* behaviour.

A good example of this perspective is provided by the 'butchery school' which Dan Witter attended (Figure 10.1).

Here the pupil imitates as precisely as possible the master butcher in order to learn how to disarticulate the foot of a caribou using a knife and leverage. This vignette shows two things. First, knowledge is being transferred as part of the relationship between master and pupil, hunter and archaeologist. Second, the photos show clearly that what is being transmitted is a set of body techniques. But because Binford's is a rational enquiry into dismemberment rather than a relational study of how knowledge is transferred, the photograph crops the men's heads, obscuring one aspect of their individuality, showing instead only what is considered relevant: their bodies and the caribou legs (see also Dobres 2000: Figure 1.2 for the disembodied hand which represents stone technology). However, the close mimicry in the body positions of the two men is itself evidence of an understanding, a relation governed by attention and the intention to instruct and learn. Furthermore, becoming a master butcher, a knowledgeable actor, is about mastering the appropriate body techniques. In the absence of a figure caption it is the body language that tells us who is master and pupil. In Figure 10.1 the master wields the knife with a light precision grip, while the pupil holds it in a powerful, 'uneducated' fist grip. Their bodies express the skills they have, the knowledge that is being acquired and the relational manner in which it is being learnt and applied.

Such body techniques are best known to archaeologists as examples of *chaînes opératoires*. These involve learned techniques of bodily movement that incorporate technology and resources. In a *chaîne opératoire*, as Graves-Brown (1996: 89) has argued, 'the "artefact" is subsumed within a series of gestures or actions

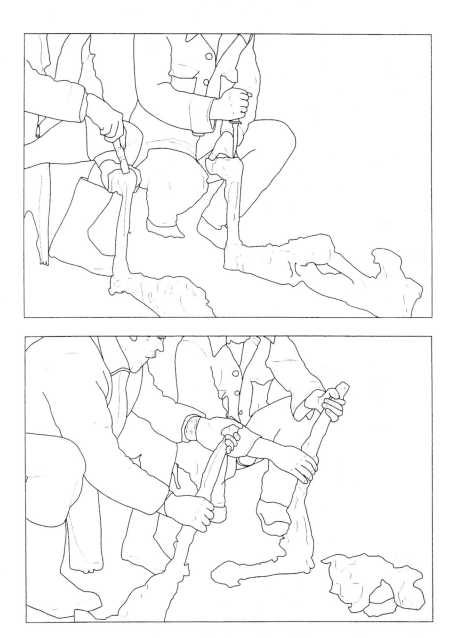

Figure 10.1 Butchery school with the Nunamiut (Binford 1981b: Figures 4.12 and 4.13).

and hence we are not simply concerned with final form, but with the modality of which the artefact is the outcome'. The modality derives from the relationship between the artefact and the individual and between them and the activities they are involved in. It just happens in the Nunamiut example to be butchery and decisions about food. But if the links are to be understood then they are relational rather than rational.

Elsewhere, Binford (1991) has presented a more explicitly relational appreciation of his Nunamiut learning experiences. His account of settlement dynamics is predicated upon an understanding of the individual and their relationship to places in the landscape. He presents detailed site histories and draws heavily upon the diary of one man, Homer Mekiana, for the period 1950–1 (Binford 1991: 102–7). Here the individual is the route to learning about the group. However, when it comes to settlements the individual has primacy, 'There is a personal relationship between a person and a place (ibid.: 66)' such that 'places own men' (ibid.). It is the relationship between place and person which produces power. This is most clearly seen when bestowed on *umialiks* 'the men who are followed when the going gets tough'. The power of their social position is based on their reputation to do the right thing in the context of the landscape they know well (ibid.: 55).

Furthermore,

> a person can have the same special relationship with animals or any other dynamic manifestation of 'power'. Thus a 'powerful man' is commonly 'owned' by certain places that are marked by substantial investments of labour by male relatives of previous generations. He is linked to these places and the previous generations they represent by his knowledge of the folklore – his ability to relate stories about the activities of persons who were 'owned' by the same place.
>
> (Ibid.: 66)

Games against nature

But despite these statements the 'doing' of Nunamiut ethnoarchaeology is principally presented as a rational account of variation among one class of data, bones, and towards a single topic, food management. Decisions which lead to variation are part of a basic knowledge of what to do. But the decisions which have to be made change as a result of the ongoing character of man–environment interaction (Binford 1978b: 455) and where the attainment and maintenance of security is the dominant principle.

The environment the Nunamiut live in today is the Anaktuvuk Pass, Alaska, and they rely on the caribou herds it supports. Most importantly the main herds migrate through the pass for only a short period of time in the spring and autumn. Storage is therefore essential if a residential base such as Anaktuvuk village is to be provisioned. There may be strong selection in such a tundra setting to conform to the behavioural norm of security because the penalties for failure are severe and swift.

In Binford's study these environmental constraints which contribute to repetitive, patterned behaviour are complemented by the biological givens of the caribou skeleton. The energy humans can obtain from a caribou may not be uniformly distributed across the carcass but at least this pattern has remained constant whenever hominids have hunted them. For example, some parts have higher values than others as measured by the Modified General Utility Index (MGUI). Furthermore, the joint structure of their skeleton presents opportunities and challenges for access to this nutritional resource. From these constraints Binford presents a complex picture of decisions that are conditioned by the properties of the wider adaptive system with its immediate and future needs for energy, as well as the local circumstances at the butchery site such as distance from the village, the presence of dogs to carry, carnivores to scavenge, temperature and season.

The result is a rational logic to the patterned outcomes in faunal assemblages, exactly what Binford would require from a scientific approach to the past. What comes out of carcasses in this approach is meat, marrow and grease as well as hides, antlers, bone and sinews. The result is rational and hence open to scientific analysis because humans are extracting these resources out of the environment to solve problems presented by those same environments. Despite Binford's discussions of place and power (see above) and his reference to individual experience and biography, the Nunamiut, like the ignored individuals of the Palaeolithic are locked into a 'game *against* nature' (Jochim 1976: 6).

Applied Nunamiut ethnoarchaeology: hunting vs. scavenging

The initial impetus for the Nunamiut study was Binford's long-term interest in Mousterian variability (1983: 108) and later the comparative question of how Neanderthals differed from Cro-Magnon people (Binford 1989). In summary, if assemblage-by-assemblage or site-by-site variation among archaeological faunas is as great as that documented for the Nunamiut then we are dealing with complex logistic organisation that merits the description, on an archaeological timescale, of modern behaviour (Stiner 1993, 1994). Alternatively there may be either less inter-site variation or changes in carcass treatment over time, suggesting improved ways of managing these essential resources. Such differences led to the opposition of scavenging to hunting between hominids at either end of the Pleistocene (Binford 1984, 1985; Binford and Stone 1986). However, the systematic application of Binford's economic anatomy to Middle and Lower Palaeolithic assemblages has not supported such a simple evolutionary story. Even allowing for taphonomic blurring it is increasingly the case that the 'Nunamiuts' seem to be original rather than recent (Gaudzinski and Roebroeks 2000; Gaudzinski and Turner 1999). The discovery of a Lower Palaeolithic hand-held wooden technology at Schöningen (this volume and Thieme 1997) drove a further stake into the coffin of hunting as a recent development. Stable isotope analysis (Richards *et al.* 2000) has demonstrated the prominent role of meat in Neanderthal diet and pointed to their position as top carnivores. Roebroeks (2001) interprets their dependence on megafauna as a strong evolutionary selection towards social co-operation over extensive areas. In his opinion, such co-operation would have involved the exchange of information between individuals of different groups as well as the complex transmission of information, probably involving language, between older and younger individuals.

It therefore appears that in those northern Eurasian latitudes occupied by Middle Pleistocene hominids, acquiring and processing animal protein was not left to chance. Gaudzinski (1999a: Figure 10) has shown their preference for prime aged animals as revealed by mortality patterns and the close comparison with monospecific bison assemblages from the Holocene of North America. There were differences, as a comparison by David and Farizy (1994) between the utilisation of bison at Middle Palaeolithic Mauran and the Clovis bison jumps of North America has shown, but no one is doubting that in both cases the animals were hunted.

Relational rather than rational carcasses

The scientific approach exemplified by economic anatomy has resulted in making a hunter of everyone, hominids and humans.

So what more is there to say? The position we adopt here is to expand the rational view of why and how hominids used animals. Of course, hominids needed to eat and obtain hides to make clothes. To these ends gourmet and bulk-processing strategies (Binford 1978b: 81; Boyle 1997) reflect the imme-diate and future circumstances in which hominids found themselves. It is also the case that animal protein offered nutritional advantages over other foods that can be measured (Aiello and Wheeler 1995; Speth and Spielmann 1983) and which had evolutionary consequences (Foley 2001a). Hunting is therefore regarded as a complicated package of rational decisions, challenges and outcomes, summed up by Binford (1989) as the ability to plan, and plan deep.

But hunting is more intricate than simply meeting biological needs in the most direct way. If, as we saw above, it is a complex activity with an old rather than recent ancestry then there must be profound consequences for our understanding of hominid, rather than just human, social life. One result is that the featureless cultural landscapes where hominids dwelt are no better or worse for investigating their social lives than those later ones studded with cave art, tombs, monuments and villages. When the focus has been on the system organising the group, its works and institutions, then hominids and their use of animal resources have seemed biological rather than cultural, natural instead of social. If we shift the perspective to the individual and therefore to a different appreciation of what constitutes social life (Gamble 1998b) then faunal remains become a new currency for fresh investigations. The question is why?

In answer, we would argue that a rational approach needs to be augmented by a relational one. The shift in approach is fundamental. Instead of hunters acting on the environment to satisfy their own perceived requirements they work with it and through it. The difference is summed up by Brody from his experience of Athabaskan hunters

> To make a good, wise sensible hunting choice is to accept the inter-connection of all possible factors, and avoids the mistake of seeking rationally to focus on any one consideration that is held as primary. What is more, the decision is taken in the doing: there is no step or pause between theory and practice . . . Planning as other cultures understand the notion, is at odds with this kind of sensitivity and would confound such flexibility. The hunter, alive to constant movements of nature, spirits, and human moods, maintains a way of doing things that repudiates a firm plan and any precise or specified understanding with others of what he is going to do.
>
> (Brody 1981: 37)

Brody's relational standpoint is in marked contrast to Binford's rational view of survival and adaptation:

> Humans seek to solve both individually and collectively the problems presented to them that appear to threaten the security of life in all its organizational dimensions.
>
> (Binford 1991: 127)

A relational approach seeks connections rather than following plans. People are related to the world and to everything in that world. They are not detached from it and playing games against it. Lienhardt (1985), for example, has strongly criticised the value of a rational model founded on a separation of mind and body, culture and nature, to provide a universal description of the individual, because it

> is achieved at the price of severing all the traditional bonds by which man has been joined to other men and the world around them, but also of splitting in two the personal union of mind and body and expelling the instincts of the latter.
>
> (Ibid.: 152)

But the outcome is not a simple choice between two opposing principles. As LiPuma (1998) shows, the traditional bonds are always relational as well as rational. A rational approach characterises the individual as a physical presence bounded by skin and separate from other such individuals, as well as their material culture and the natural world. By contrast a relational view looks to the networks which link people to characterise human social life. The individual is therefore constituted by relationships and rather than stopping at the skin their presence extends in time and space. Such distributed persons, or dividuals (Bird-David 1999; Strathern 1988), are not separated from the world of things and objects in the manner bemoaned by Lienhardt. They are instead enchained through *hybrid* networks which are constructed from elements that cannot be easily separated for analytical purposes. Artefacts and animals, for example, are equivalent in relational terms to other flesh and blood hominids. Since individuals are not separated from the landscapes they dwell in they cannot play a game against their natural environment. Instead, their landscapes surround them and provide mutual references of who and what they are in a continuous act of self-creation (Toren 1999).

With this perspective an animal carcass is not simply a source for calories but also the resource which mediates the relationship that is being negotiated by the individual (see Lienhardt 1961 for further examples in a different social context). Similarly, the decision to store or share meat with others is not just a response to systemic properties of either minimising the risk of dietary failure or securing the future. Such actions constitute individuals as persons. What differs historically is the degree of authority that either relational or rational bonds exerted over the construction of personhood (Bird-David 1999). What we get out of carcasses are relationships and memories which support the habitual actions and rhythms of the body as much as marrow, grease, fat and meat satisfy our energy requirements.

Fragmentation: a basic social act

But how are we to examine animal carcasses as part of these relational, hybrid networks? A start has been made by Chapman (2000) in his study of how material culture was actively involved in the construction of personhood and identity during the Neolithic and Bronze Age of Eastern Europe. He follows the relational concept of the distributed person, the dividual, where items in circulation are aspects of that extended identity. He refers to this as the social practice of enchainment and contrasts it with accumulation as two ways of constructing relationships. Material culture enters this process in several ways. First, there is the part standing for the whole. The first phalange of a caribou stands for the entire animal. The flint flake stands for the original stone nodule. Second, a web of connections is implicated through the act of fragmentation. Stone and carcasses are deliberately fragmented, moved around and altered. They are brought into relation with other people and objects in the hybrid

Table 10.1 An archaeological model of social practice

Social practice	Accumulation (relations achieved by production and reproduction)	Enchainment (a chain of social relations achieved through exchange)
Material life	Sets (place)	Nets (landscape)
Examples of material and social outcomes	Caches, stores 'family'	Stone and bone transfers 'friends and relations'
Social action	Consumption	Fragmentation

Source: Adapted from Chapman 2000.

network from which we derive our identity. Fragmentation is part of the process of distributing personhood through enchainment, or what here we would call nets (Table 10.1). However, items are also brought together to form sets (Gamble in press).

These accumulations are also about the construction of identity. The rational approach would be to call the bones in a pit a store, the clutch of flakes in a cave a cache and relate them to future planning even though they were never retrieved. The relational approach would see the same evidence as indicative of the construction of individual identities at different places in an individual's landscape.

Moreover fragmentation is original.

> Ever since the butchering of dead animals, whether killed by humans or by animal predators, became a common Palaeolithic practice, it is possible to argue that the fragmentation of a carcass could have acted as an analogy for enchained human relations at an early stage of human development. The division of a carcass of a hunted animal provides an archetypal instance of a fractal resource, where each portion carries its own value as well as the symbolic value of the whole animal and the successful hunt.
>
> (Chapman 2000: 40)

What needs to be added to this insight is the action of consumption which also relates people and which in the example of animal carcasses also involves embodiment (Hamilakis *et al.* 2002b). In both actions the individual is implicated as the agent creating symbolic force (Gamble in press) and which we identify through the material examples of *sets* and *nets* (Table 10.1). With this model we can return to the butchering of carcasses and the food management strategies of both the Nunamiut and the Neanderthals of Salzgitter-Lebenstedt and revisit the question of social life and the relationship between hominids and their environment.

The spring system revisited

Nunamiut Ethnoarchaeology is archaeology's *Moby Dick*. Endless descriptions of cutting up caribou and whales are how the authors of both books explore the relationship between humans and nature and the forces, systemic or spiritual, which drive people. And both accounts depend on the individual to move the story along so that we learn about the world through the experiences of a small, tightly knit crew.

It is possible, thanks to Binford's thoroughness, to consider his book in a relational as well as rational manner. One example will suffice here, Billy Morry's camp (Figure 10.2) where eleven caribou were killed during the spring of 1972 and from which at least six separate archaeological assemblages were created (Binford 1978b: Figure 5.2 for locations).

Morry killed and butchered the caribou alone but was later joined by his wife and oldest daughter. Over the following summer food was moved from the drying racks to other camps in the valley. Single decisions led to the initial

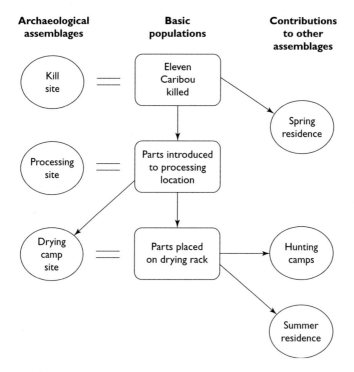

Figure 10.2 Billy Morry's lone activities at his spring hunting sites where killing, processing and drying took place between 17 and 21 May 1972. The sites were five miles from Anaktuvuk village and two miles from his anticipated summer camp (Binford 1978b: Figure 5.2). In Binford's analysis these three sites formed a logistical rather than maintenance location (Binford 1978b: Figure 5.33).

hunting and processing. But by the time the meat was being moved to other locations a complex web of social relationships governed what went where.

The complexities as described by Binford are immense and potentially overwhelming for the archaeologist. However, as they stem primarily from local contingencies of mobility (ibid.: 234) they can, he argues, be understood. He does this by using these data to examine the relationship between the number of animals, the number of people and the length of occupation (ibid.: 421–2). He presents the impact of storage on the dismemberment and distribution of bones within social and spatial networks governed by time. The big difference is killing for the future or killing for now. At the centre of this network is Billy Morry himself: the individual meeting his network requirements and obligations both today and in the future. In that sense he is linked to others, enchained, and concurrently engaged in the social practice of accumulation (Table 10.1). Like everyone today, and probably all hominids before us, his social actions simultaneously assist fragmentation and consumption.

Morry's activities form an important example in Binford's (1978b: Chapter 5) wider study of spring activities among the Nunamiut (Figure 10.3). These activities are presented as a logistical system which conditions their behaviour. Two examples will serve to show how caribou act as a currency to measure the use of space and time and provide pointers to patterning in archaeological data. First, Binford documents a decrease in marrow bones and an increase in meat-bearing bones between procurement and consumption sites (Table 10.2): in his terms, from logistical procurement to residential maintenance.

Second, dismemberment ratios confirm this spatial/temporal relationship (Table 10.3). These ratios are calculated because butchery is about dismembering rather than breaking bones. 'Butchering generally involves the disorganisation of the anatomy into various *sets*; rarely does butchering result in the complete disorganisation of the anatomy into discrete or individual bones' (Binford 1978b: 64, italics original). Binford reported (ibid.) that a greater degree of anatomical organisation is found at kill sites and that 'conversely, the longer the time that parts of animals are subjected to extended decision-making sequences, the less anatomical organization observed'.

Table 10.2 Proportions of marrow bones at different site types in the Nunamiut spring logistical system

Site name	Site type	% marrow yielding parts
Anavik	Major hunting stand	63
Mask site	Observation post	59
	Dispersed hunting stands	40
Village	Residential base	29

Source: After Binford 1978: Table 5.20.

Table 10.3 Dismemberment ratios for spring and autumn assemblages

Site type	Spring		Autumn	
	Front limb	*Rear limb*	*Front limb*	*Rear limb*
Kill and processing (Logistical)	0.94	0.81	0.93	0.71
Hunting stands and camps (Maintenance)	0.3	0.34	0.34	0.21

Source: After Binford 1978: Tables 5.21 and 7.27.

Note
The similarities reflect the importance of short-season migration hunting at these two times of the year.

Dismemberment therefore increases as time passes. The question is whether the clock is running to either a spatial rationale or social relations? The former is the geographical principle of the 'attrition of distance', what Binford refers to as the entropy of dismemberment (Binford 1978b: 64). The latter is indicated by the 'maze of pathways' (Figure 10.3) along which bones can move (ibid.: 248), supplied by individuals such as Billy Morry and consumed by a variety of people in different spatial locations. At first sight the situation as described seems infinitely varied. This is simplified by Binford's claim that

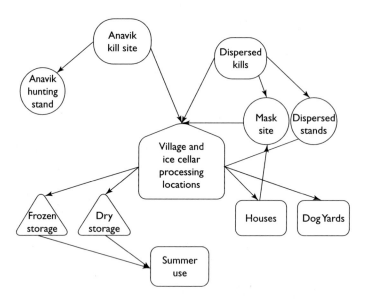

Figure 10.3 Logistics in the contemporary spring system (Binford 1978b: Figure 5.57). The sites are an outcome of interlinked networks – intimate, effective and extended (Gamble 1998) – based on the individual although they are invisible.

it is of course the reality of the pathways with differences and variability in the organized use of the anatomical knowledge that we seek to understand and through our understanding provide a behavioural window to the past.

(Binford 1978b: 248)

The basic pattern is a flow of materials along networks which delay consumption (Figure 10.3). People are enchained through the fragmentation of caribou. There can be a temporal punctuation before accumulation occurs in the form of storage. Among the Nunamiut accumulation often precedes consumption. Networks are created and sets of material, as in Figure 10.2, produced. Social practice and action are mediated through material culture, in this case caribou. However, if, as Binford claims, the knowledge of caribou anatomy creates the paths in the system, where are the people? The answer is that they are not needed as individuals since his is a rational rather than relational study. Our point is that the shift to a relational viewpoint which foregrounds those individuals neither requires a distortion of the evidence nor a retreat into methodological individualism. We only need to accord them a standpoint to see their importance to the analysis.

Social life at Salzgitter-Lebenstedt: a faunal approach

But is a relational standpoint accessible among the bones and stones of the Palaeolithic? Roebroeks (2001) has recently restated the view that large-mammal hunting in the Middle Pleistocene of Europe must have been a co-operative activity only made possible by verbal communication and social interaction between individuals from different groups. Since a relational standpoint (co-operating individuals) is therefore expected in order to exploit large animals by killing them, why cannot it be extended to their subsequent dismemberment and distribution?

And this is the conceptual problem. Roebroeks' conclusion, predicated on the demands of efficient killing, is a rational not a relational concept of the group. Co-operation benefits the group and so the individual vanishes. In the same way the individual remains invisible even though the many cut- and fracture-marks on the bones attest to their activities. The evidence for highly standardised carcass-processing was guided not by individual intention but, as Binford argued, by animal anatomy. Accordingly, odd and idiosyncratic departures from either the dictates of the MGUI or the outcome of applying levers and fulcrums to the task of dismemberment are not glimpses of someone intentionally bucking the trend. They are instead variance in an organised process of behaviour. To dwell on them as significant would be regarded by supporters of this approach as an example of misplaced methodological individualism.

We would agree that the individual is not to be found in such variance. However, what we question is the rational approach as the only way to understand such repeated patterning in faunal assemblages. What follows is therefore an attempt to carry through the relational standpoint from the bonds of co-operative hunting to the network ties of sharing and consumption. We will argue that co-operation is predicated on the social practices of enchainment and accumulation and can be applied to all stages of people's involvement with animals; alive, dead, fragmented and consumed (Table 10.1).

Our example comes from the late Middle Palaeolithic open locale of Salzgitter-Lebenstedt, 50 km south-east of Hannover in Germany. The fauna is dominated by at least eighty-six reindeer (*Rangifer tarandus*), NISP = 2130. The assemblage is dominated by adult males which were killed during a short period of time in autumn. The bones were found in association with Middle Palaeolithic stone tools, including distinctive plano-convex bifaces, and twenty-eight bone tools (Gaudzinski 1999b). Five hominid remains were recovered (Hublin 1984) and a background fauna dominated by mammoth, horse and bison identified (Gaudzinski 1998). The reindeer bones display unambiguous traces of meat and marrow-processing by Neanderthals. The best explanation for this evidence seems to be that we are dealing with ambush hunting of herds by Neanderthals (Gaudzinski and Roebroeks 2000).

Fragmentation in action: cut and fracture patterns

The reindeer remains display numerous traces of hominid modification in the form of cut-marks. Almost 40 per cent of all reindeer specimens carry these traces (Gaudzinski and Roebroeks 2000: Table 2). The majority of cut-marks were observed on the trunk which is underrepresented among the surviving skeletal elements (ibid.). Nearly one-quarter of all cut-marks occurred on ribs and a further 15 per cent were observed on vertebrae. Long-bones were less cut-marked. The shafts of metatarsals were the most modified of the axial elements with 8 per cent cut-marked (Gaudzinski and Roebroeks 2003). Most cut-marks relate to carcass de-fleshing. Only rarely do they occur on proximal and/or distal long-bone epiphyses. This indicates that systematic dismemberment of entire carcasses was not undertaken at Salzgitter-Lebenstedt.

Table 10.4 compares the meat utility indices for caribou with the Salzgitter-Lebenstedt cut-mark data. With the exception of the femur, where cut-marks are considerably underrepresented, the proportion of cut-marks corresponds directly to the distribution of meat on the reindeer skeleton. If we assume that the quantitative occurrence of these traces is a measure of the intensity of processing it appears that elements rich in meat such as the trunk were more intensively de-fleshed than skeletal parts with lower meat utility.

In addition to cut-marks the reindeer assemblage is characterised by conchoidal impact fractures which are due to marrow-processing (Table 10.5). The position of these fractures on the bones, as well as the morphology of discarded

Table 10.4 Standardised meat utility indices and percentages of cut-marks (n=895) on skeletal elements of reindeer at Salzgitter-Lebenstedt

	Meat utility index	*N cut-marks*	*Cut-marks %*
Skull	18.1	64	7.1
Mandible	31.1	76	8.4
Vertebrae	47.2	131	14.6
Ribs	51.6	211	23.5
Scapula	44.7	50	5.5
Humerus	28.9	45	5
Radius	14.7	34	3.9
Metacarpus	5.2	20	2.2
Femur	100	28	3.1
Tibia	25.5	53	5.9
Metatarsus	11.2	74	8.2
Foot	1.7	34	3.7

Source: MUI after Binford 1978.

Note
Compare also Gaudzinski and Roebroeks 2003. Sternum, pelvis, calcaneus, astragalus and cubo-naviculars are not included.

Table 10.5 Bone marrow cavity volumes for caribou and percentages of conchoidal fractures on skeletal elements of reindeer at Salzgitter-Lebenstedt

	Marrow-cavity volume	*N conchoidal fractures*	*Conchoidal fractures %*
Mandible	11	0	0
Pelvis	6	0	0
Scapula	5	0	0
Humerus	38	15	6.8
Radius	36	27	12.2
Metacarpus	21	6	2.7
Phalange 1	4	0	0
Phalange 2	2	0	0
Femur	52	25	11.3
Tibia	64	62	28.1
Metatarsus	51	85	38.5

Source: After Irving 1972. Gaudzinski and Roebroeks 2003.

bones in the archaeological assemblage, underlines the conclusion that dismemberment of entire carcasses was not undertaken. Proximal and distal epiphyses of bones were always intact and major parts of the bone shaft are still attached. Bone-marrow fracture followed a standardised and very systematic pattern, especially with the metatarsals. Here the anterior face of the bone was removed to open the bone cavity for marrow extraction. In almost all cases the marrow cavity was opened by blows to the proximal area of the lateral and medial face of the metatarsals.

More than one-third of all long-bones display conchoidal impact fractures. Furthermore, almost two-thirds of the instances were on metatarsals and tibia shafts (Gaudzinski and Roebroeks 2003: Table 2).

Most of the metacarpals were intact and only 2 per cent showed impact fractures. By contrast only eleven metatarsals were complete with a further 163 fragments. The ratio of complete to fragmented bones shows that skeletal elements with low marrow contents were ignored for marrow processing (Table 10.6). This is well illustrated by a correlation analysis of the occurrence of impact fractures and values for marrow bones ($r = 0.83$).

Age and condition

The age of the animals, as well as the marrow content of particular bones, played a significant role in carcass exploitation. The mandibles, metacarpals and phalanges of adults remained intact while bones from sub-adult individuals were also subject to intentional selection during marrow exploitation. This selection is illustrated by the proportions of complete bones among the total NISP from adult and juvenile individuals (Table 10.6). Among adults the front leg was more intact than the hind leg. The same applies for juveniles, though the overall amount of complete bones is considerably higher than for adults (Table 10.6).

The Neanderthals at Salzgitter-Lebenstedt: a rational assessment

The evidence from Salzgitter-Lebenstedt reveals a mass kill encounter of a reindeer herd or herds with a focus on adult males, which might imply ambush techniques. Following the intercept, parts of the carcass which we know are rich in meat and marrow were intensively de-fleshed and broken, while other poorer elements were processed to a lesser degree. Carcasses were not entirely dismembered before processing. Furthermore, prime adults rather than sub-adults and juveniles were selected and limb bones were systematically exploited

Table 10.6 Proportions of complete bones with proximal and distally fused and proximal and/or distally unfused bones at Salzgitter-Lebenstedt

	NISP adult	NISP sub-adult	N complete adult	% complete adult	N complete sub-adult	% complete sub-adult
Humerus	64	9	5	7.8	5	55.5
Radius	106	14	9	8.4	9	64.2
Metacarpus	38	8	34	89.4	7	87.5
Femur	74	22	0	0	14	63.6
Tibia	174	18	0	0	7	38.8
Metatarsus	117	24	4	3.4	7	29.1

according to marrow quantity. Bones with little marrow were left intact. The Salzgitter-Lebenstedt evidence shows that Neanderthal subsistence was directed towards the exploitation of only high food-value parts of the carcass.

Butchery was also co-operative. The goal was to maximise the food management strategy within a behavioural framework where time and available labour drove the outcome. This produced an archaeological signature dominated by the 'gourmet' curve of high food skeletal elements as measured by their meat and marrow potential (Binford 1978b: 81).

A relational addition

What can a relational approach add to this analysis and in particular to our stated objective of better understanding hominids in their landscapes? Let us start by placing Salzgitter-Lebenstedt within the hierarchy of settlement that Binford determined from his ethnoarchaeological work (Table 10.2) and where at autumn sites a single species also formed the hunting focus.

In Table 10.7 we assess the relative contribution of marrow and meat among the reindeer bones. These proportions compare well with the major hunting stand and observation post (Table 10.2). Therefore Salzgitter-Lebenstedt stands at the start of the chain of relationships, that 'maze of pathways' (Binford 1978b: 248) which initiates the movement and distribution of food.

Table 10.7 Salzgitter-Lebenstedt marrow and meat proportions

	MNI
Marrow	
Humerus	27
Radius	27
Femur	25
Tibia	42
Metatarsal	44
%	*62*
Meat	
Mandible	41
Scapula	25
Femur	25
Ribs	11
%	*38*

Source: Method based on Binford 1978: Table 5.19.

Note
Calculated using those anatomical elements with a marrow cavity >30 cm^3 and a Meat Utility Index >30 (after Gaudzinski and Roebroeks 2000: Table 2)

Table 10.8 A measure of dismemberment in the Salzgitter-Lebenstedt reindeer bone
assemblage

	MNI	Marrow cavity volume	Ratio
Front leg			
Scapula	25	5	2.7
P Humerus	9	38	1
D Humerus	27		3
P Radius	27	36	3
D Radius	20		2.2
P Metacarpal	19	21	2.1
D Metacarpal	17		1.9
Rear leg			
Pelvis	26	6	1.9
P Femur	14	52	1
D Femur	25		1.8
P Tibia	34	64	2.4
D Tibia	42		3
Calcaneus	32		2.3
Astragalus	23		1.6
P Metatarsal	44	51	3.1
D Metatarsal	38		2.7

Source: Method after Binford 1978: 64–9.

Note
(MNI from Gaudzinski and Roebroeks 2000: Table 2). The small number of phalanges have been
omitted as they have been subject to size bias recovery. The lowest values in both the front (proximal
humerus) and rear (proximal femur) legs can in part be explained by their small bone density values
which has affected their survival (Gaudzinski and Roebroeks 2000: Table 3).

This position in the network is further confirmed by an analysis of the
dismemberment ratios of the front and rear legs of the reindeer remains (Table
10.8). We interpret these data as low dismemberment. This measure of skeletal
completeness accords with Binford's expectations for a logistical location where
the anatomy is relatively complete rather than disorganised. The highest values
in the front leg are for the humerus/radius articulation that is also high in
marrow volume. In the rear leg the highest values are lower down at the tibia/
metatarsal articulation, once again a site of significant marrow volume. The
incidence of conchoidal fractures (Table 10.5) further supports the importance
of bone breakage for marrow extraction while Table 10.4 which records 895
cut-marks shows a different pattern where ribs, vertebra and mandible have
the highest values. Only the metatarsus has comparable values.

Salzgitter-Lebenstedt therefore follows the much wider faunal pattern
identified by Boyle (1990: 269–70 and Table 9.3) in her study of hunted faunas
from the Upper Palaeolithic of south-west France. She discovered that the
major species in the assemblage normally produce a gourmet curve of high

food-value anatomical elements while secondary species are generally represented by lower utility parts in a bulk curve. Her conclusion (ibid.) is that gourmet assemblages are found at 'base camps' such as Abri Pataud and that processing sites, where most anatomical elements have MGUI values of less than 38 (Binford 1978b: Table 2.7), are comparatively rare.

Hominids in landscapes

Our analysis suggests a rather different reading of the data and returns us to our individual hominid in their landscapes. Conard and Prindiville (2000: 304) have pointed out that true base camps, comparable to the substantial Late Glacial settlements of Gönnersdorf and Andernach, have yet to be found in the Middle Palaeolithic of the Rhineland, and their conclusion also applies to the Salzgitter-Lebenstedt landscape. Moreover, on the basis of the faunal evidence their conclusion could also be extended to many of the Upper Palaeolithic rock shelters from south-west France analysed by Boyle. Therefore rather than conceiving of these rationally as 'base camps' in an adaptive landscape such locales are the start of relational networks in a landscape of habit where resources are accumulated so that enchainment is possible. Moreover, at both Salzgitter-Lebenstedt and the Dordogne rock shelters the economic anatomy of the major species consistently shows evidence, on-site, for both consumption and fragmentation. However, the secondary species point to other positions in the networks that individuals negotiated and created across their social landscapes and where identities were primarily defined through enchainment involving animal parts.

At issue is not the definition of site types but rather what kind of landscape we conduct our analysis in. As we saw above a strictly rational analysis places hominids in a game against nature. Solutions are inevitably group-based since their continuation is the measure of organisational success. Alternatively the layered social landscape with its components of habit and scale (Gamble 1999: 87–91) focuses on the individual as he/she lived their lives. The relationship is therefore mutual rather than competitive. We agree with Binford (1978b: 81) that what produces the differences between bulk and gourmet curves 'derive from the actors' evaluations of differing contingencies in different situations'. But what is required is an interactional as well as an adaptive understanding of how those decisions were made. And to do that we need to situate the assemblages within the two landscapes which constructed and were constructed by hominids through practice, action and material life (Table 10.1).

Following the descriptions of the faunal assemblage given above it is accumulation rather than enchainment that characterises the social practices undertaken in the Salzgitter-Lebenstedt locale/landscape. For example, some eighty-six reindeer have been accumulated in one place either as one hunt or more probably over time. Evidence for enchainment is low as shown by dismemberment. At the level of social action (Table 10.1) consumption rather than fragmentation is more common as demonstrated by the variety of material sets that were created. The intention of individuals at this locale was to bring together and accumulate the resources of social life. The first set comprised the hunters themselves using their effective networks (Gamble 1999) to constitute a co-operative hunting party. A second set was created by the selection of adult reindeer, predominantly males, as opposed to juveniles and females. A third set was made up of anatomical element recognised by food utility and age. And finally there are the material sets derived from fragmenting the animals and accumulating at this locale from a wider social landscape. Such sets include the 156 antlers from 82 individuals, an MNI that far exceeds the highest estimate based on the bones (proximal metatarsal = 44 MNI). Another set was formed by the shaping of mammoth ribs (n=8) and fibulae (n=3) into regular tools by selecting from the bones in the background fauna (Gaudzinski 1999b: 138) and creating a uniform set of materials for the locale. Finally there are the stone tools made on local stone. Among these are the distinctive asymmetrical plano-convex bifaces and Levallois *chaînes opératoires* (Pastoors 2001: Table 24 and Figures 15–19) that Bosinski (1967) used to define his Upper Acheulean group in the German Middle Palaeolithic.

The evidence for social action at Salzgitter-Lebenstedt is very clearly pointing towards consumption rather than fragmentation (Table 10.1) while the social practice favoured accumulation over enchainment. The evidence for this interpretation consists of the cut-marks, marrow-cracking and the rarity of materials being taken away for distribution elsewhere through extended networks (Gamble 1999). The extent to which other material was carried into the locale or transferred through extended networks is difficult to determine in the absence of distant shells, ochres or lithics (Féblot-Augustins 1997).

One exception might be the five Neanderthal remains comprising two femurs and three skull fragments and among which an adult and sub-adult can be distinguished. Although carnivore gnawing can be seen on the adult femur (Gaudzinski 1998: 169) it is possible that hominid remains were intentionally fragmented and transferred within the landscape of habit surrounding Salzgitter-Lebenstedt. This was the case in Lateglacial France (Gambier 1992; Le Mort and Gambier 1992) and Germany (Orschiedt 1999). Complete bodies are very rare and it is common to find body parts, often cut-marked, that were clearly once circulating between persons and places.

The distinction is one of scale in the relations which these material embodied. While Boyle's (1990) Upper Palaeolithic base camps in south-west France reveal a similar structure to the creation of reindeer sets there would be increased evidence for enchainment in the ornaments, art and the presence of raw materials from much greater distances (Féblot-Augustins 1997; Taborin 1992). To complement this greater social extension sets were also more varied as the social practice of accumulation responded to individuals creating nets through enchainment. For example, we find accumulations of stones to create hearths as well as sets, or caches, of ochre, stone blades and ornaments (Gamble 1986).

Conclusion

In previous analyses of Salzgitter-Lebenstedt the results have been directed towards the debate over hunting and the implications for modern behaviour (Gaudzinski and Roebroeks 2000). In this chapter we have asked a different set of questions and placed hominid individuals in their landscapes rather than their evolutionary stage. The latter will probably always require a unit of analysis that recognises the primacy of the group. The former, however, opens up another perspective on Palaeolithic data that all too often are regarded as too meagre to answer social questions. We have resisted identifying either individuals or the places which own them (Binford 1991: 66) through speculative site biographies (e.g. Isaac 1976: 484–5). Instead we have used the concept of the individual as a knowledgeable actor able to influence outcomes and involved in the self-creation of social life. We have shown how bones carry more information than just calories and dietary specialisation. We conclude that a different debate about the significance of patterning is possible with Palaeolithic data. The rational accounts of human beings which have dominated for twenty years can be augmented by a relational framework that leads us to fresh enquiry and a re-unification of the Palaeolithic, and all its hominids, with a common, but variable, expression of identity in the rest of the human past.

Acknowledgements

The chapter has benefited from the comments of Yannis Hamilakis, Andy Jones, Kristin Oma, Yvonne Marshall, Martin Porr and Jo Sofaer. The illustrations were expertly redrawn by Penny Copeland.

Chapter 11

All in a day's work

Middle Pleistocene individuals, materiality and the lifespace at Makapansgat, South Africa

Anthony Sinclair and John McNabb

Once we might have imagined our hominid forebears living a simple and somewhat impoverished life in comparison to the complexities of later pre-historic and historic times. But our perceptions have changed. No longer do earlier hunters and gatherers live at the mercy of their environments, biting their nails in fear of having missed the last meal, whilst later prehistoric humans make lasting field monuments and create enduring and complex social relations. Instead we have come to see that for early hominids, their brains and bodies were made for gossip (Dunbar 1996a and b), tactical deception (Byrne and Whiten 1988; Byrne 1995) and all the complex inter-personal relation-ships that make up a primate's full and demanding social life (Humphrey 1976; de Waal 1982). And that is before we even consider the sophisticated physical thinking and procedural schemes with which they repeatedly created their material engagements with the world (Schlanger 1996); or the astonishing sense of intimacy with huge tracts of landscape that hominids made themselves familiar with since birth. It is this new breadth of perspective that makes Palaeolithic archaeology so fascinating and rewarding. It still remains, however, a real challenge to get to grips with the individual hominin in the context of her Palaeolithic life.

We place the Palaeolithic individual at the centre of a complex series of relationships that affect all aspects of life and the consequent archaeological record (Sinclair 2000). For example the individual exists in the context of other members of her hominin society in social relationships that may be constructed according to gender, kin relations with or between generations, and also alliances of short or long duration. At any moment she may be acting in contexts of subsistence activities such as hunting, gathering, raw material procurement, and so forth. There is the bodily context related to sexuality, maturity or sense of age; or the place in a landscape defined by the tasks that she may be engaged in, the settlement history and pattern of her society. Furthermore, each of these contexts has a dimension in time, from the moment to the day, season, year, lifetime and onwards. And, while the archaeological record of the Palaeolithic can provide us with that rare glimpse of a moment in time, via the refitted lithic assemblage and its manifest interplay of thought, technique and purpose (Schlanger 1996), for the most part these are glimpses of simple sequences of actions. We cannot as yet place these actions within distinct contexts that would allow the application of the contextual approaches to archaeology used for later periods (for example: Thomas 1991; Edmonds 1999). Rather we have disjointed contexts and sequences, of which the fullest is most clearly the lithic record with its evidence for deliberate action, even if the individual hominin concerned may have been acting in a quotidian and practical sense. It is this lithic record, therefore, and its relationship with individual hominins that forms the basis of this study.

Individuals, material culture and lithic technology

Any contemporary knapper will be able to tell you that the products of individual stone knappers are easily recognisable in the prehistoric record. The reason is simple. Each and every biface, core, flake and flake tool is the product of individual action. They are the results of individuals making and using things. In that sense then it is relatively easy to see individuals. But the question becomes much more difficult, and more interesting, when we narrow the focus. Is it possible to see individuality (or put another way personality or personhood) in the Stone Age archaeological record? It is especially difficult when that record consists almost entirely of the results of working stone, most of which is debitage.

But first let us define in a simple and heuristic way what we think it means to be an individual or a person. The concept of the individual person has a very specific usage in western industrial/capitalist societies. It refers to the self-conscious recognition of an individual's life experience as being separate from those around her. She is self-aware and recognises that state in others. But she is also conscious that self-awareness in others around her will be constituted differently to her own. This notion of self-conscious, distinctive separateness is at the heart of being a person as we understand the western European tradition to mean it. It also underlies common approaches to agency in archaeology that rely on being able to identify the individual since they have the power to act in a particular and unique way (Gero 2000). But this perspective of being a person entails the fusion, on an unequal basis, of three different elements: individuality, personality, personhood. They can of course mean different things to different people, and their meaning has changed for 'individuals' with time and place. There is consequently a vast anthropological literature on the nature of individuality and personhood (Carrithers 1996). This is not the place, however, to review this research, and we shall continue with common sense heuristic interpretations of these labels that will allow us to peruse our goal – the study of the relationship between hominins and their material culture in the Stone Age of Africa. The definitions that we shall use for this study are as follows:

- *Individuality* is the self-conscious recognition of that sense of separateness.
- *Personality* can be taken as the outward manifestation of how that individual comports herself.
- *Personhood* is the state of belonging to a commune ('any small group of people having common interests or responsibilities' *The Collins Paperback English Dictionary*). To have personhood implies that you are a member of a group, to lack it makes you a non-person, you are outside of some perceived and imposed boundary. Personhood is, therefore, a cultural construct.

The definitions stated above are of course a very simplified western perception of these concepts and terms. An excellent exploration of the different ways individuality and personhood is constructed outside of the western discourse is presented by Carrithers (1985). Of importance here is the way that many gatherer-hunting peoples perceive the relationship between hunters and their prey as this highlights just how deeply socially constructed these three concepts can be. In many such societies hunted animals are also seen to possess an individuality and personhood, in every way the equal of the person who is hunting them (Bodenhorn 1988). Personality (and agency), in the sense we describe it above, is also often attributed to animals and to inanimate objects. Prey and hunter can even merge to become part of the same life experience. Some detailed and fascinating examples are given by Ingold (2000b).

It is at present impossible to infer a detailed understanding of the complexities of individuality, personality and personhood from the Stone Age archaeological record, but the 'common sense' interpretations described above give us an opportunity to explore at least one way of inferring individuality and personhood as expressed through material culture. If there is one thing that modern humans do it is make things in a regular or standardised way. This regularity expresses itself in three ways: (1) the idea or concept (the design) is standardised, (2) the method of manufacture is standardised through a series of fixed stages that are followed through to the final product, (3) the final product itself is standardised and will be very similar (though not necessarily exactly the same) when comparing one example to others. It follows that in a society in which material culture is standardised, 'personhood' may be expressed by the reproduction of the expected designs and techniques of manufacture, whilst individuals may express their distinctiveness (i.e. their own sense of individuality or personality) by 'departing' from the norm (see Dobres 2000: 187–201 for an effective demonstration of this method). The key to recognising this in the archaeological record is to identify the normal procedures and designs by which any item of material culture is made, so as to be able to identify any departure from these norms.

Standardisation in the material culture of modern humans engages all three traits. From the earliest European Upper Palaeolithic regularity is present in both what is made and how it is made (Davies 2001), though rarely in terms of a strict control on the absolute dimensions of finished artefacts (Marks *et al.* 2001). In Africa this regularity is present earlier in time because modern humans are evolving in Africa from earlier species of *Homo* (McBrearty and Brooks 2000; Bräuer 2001), and appear there possibly a hundred thousand years before they do in Europe (Grün and Beaumont 2001). Traditionally archaeologists of the Earlier Stone Age (ESA) confine the search for such information to the handaxe/cleaver or large cutting tool (LCT) element of a stone tool assemblage. This is because these tools are deliberately thinned and shaped to a pre-conceived intentional design. The *assumption* is that this intentionality is a product of learned behaviour reflecting group norms in practice and acceptability. So for the hominins of the African ESA regularity in practice and form is a reflection of standardised practice. Put more simply it is assumed to be cultural. In this chapter we shall argue that in the ESA only one of the three operating criteria described in the last paragraph is present, that of the standardised idea or concept (and even this is limited). The absence of the other two implies that the imposition of cultural norms, presumably emplaced by social learning, is either absent or very weak. From this we infer that culture as a mutually and self-consciously recognised system of linking persons together is weakly developed, if present at all. Consequently we should not look for individuality or personality in the ESA. We suggest that while hominins may well have had the conscious recognition that they lived in a group, there was no sense of conscious identity to that group. Consequently there was no sense of personhood as defined above, and therefore no individuals with personality to subvert the norm. As will be shown there was no norm. In the Middle Stone Age (MSA), we shall see that the archaeological record reveals a slightly different pattern. In the earlier part of the record, there is little evidence for standardisation of the final form of pieces, though there is evidence that hominins had a concern with the demonstration of technical expertise and thus personality. In the latter part of the MSA, though, the situation is different. Hominins are making a number of retouched tools, that possess the attributes of hafted projectile points, that are much more standardised in size, though still quite variable in terms of the amount and placing of retouch. We interpret this to mean that in the early MSA hominins desire to express their sense of individuality in material performance through elaborate technical expertise. In the later MSA, hominins are using elements of material culture to express a sense of personhood.

Technological contexts in Southern Africa

The South African ESA and MSA represents a period of time when profound changes occured in the hominin behavioural record as explored through archaeology and hominin palaeontology. The ESA in South Africa begins about 2.0 mya at Sterkfontein (Kuman 2003) with the Oldowan, and continues with the Acheulean, from about 1.7 mya also at Sterkfontein. The MSA, whose earliest manifestations are difficult to define, may begin about 0.27 mya at Florisbad (Kuman *et al.* 1999) and continue until *c.* 28 kya at least at Rose Cottage Cave (Clark 1997) where sediments preserve the transition to the Later Stone Age (LSA) at about this time. The MSA sees the widespread introduction of Levallois (PCT), though this may pre-date the earliest MSA by some unknown period of time. Spanning the gap between ESA and MSA is the Fauresmith (van Riet Lowe 1945; Sampson 1974). This assemblage type is a mixture of elements and appears to represent a people who used both bifaces as well as laminar and convergent (point) Levallois technology (Beaumont 1999). Southern Africa in the ESA potentially shows the incipient development of tool behaviours that are regionally specific. Inland on the interior plateau (highveld) a number of Acheulean sites possess the enigmatic Victoria West technology (van Riet Lowe 1945), a distinctive ESA form of prepared core technology that appears to produce blanks for bifaces and cleavers. It is not present at Acheulean sites on the coastal plain (lowveld) (Volman 1984).

Current interpretations of the South African Middle Stone Age are remarkably perplexing. Before radiometric dates were commonplace, interpretations of the South African Middle Stone Age suggested that there was clear chronological and regional patterning (Sampson 1974) with the result that a number of local variants were named according to their region, such as the Pietersburg, Stillbay and Mossel Bay industries. These variants, however, are now thought to be chronological not geographical variants (Deacon and Deacon 1999). Yet, while there are some clear chronological variations through the MSA sequences in South Africa, with the Howiesons Poort and Stillbay industries the most recognisable and temporally contained, studies of MSA technology repeatedly note the striking technological continuity that seems to run through the entire length of the MSA sequence (Singer and Wymer 1982; Volman 1984; Thackeray and Kelly 1988; Thackeray 1989; Thackeray 1992; Avery *et al.* 1997). It has been noted that MSA artefacts are generally not retouched, and even when they are, that retouch is non-standardised and minimal, usually precluding the assignment of retouched pieces to distinct types (Avery *et al.* 1997). Indeed Wymer, in his analysis of the Klasies River Mouth sequence, noted how little difference there was between the uppermost and lowest MSA assemblages from a technological and typological perspective (Singer and Wymer 1982: 107). The large mammal faunal assemblage from Klasies River Mouth suggests that MSA populations focused selectively on the eland, yet their lack of success in hunting the more abundant Cape buffalo has suggested to some that such 'specialisation' reflects an inability to hunt more aggressive animals (Klein and Cruz-Uribe 1996, 2000). The absence of flighted birds among the faunal remains, the wide spread of ages for hunted seals and the constant large size of tortoise bones at both Klasies River Mouth and Die Kelders Cave further convince Klein and Cruz-Uribe (2000: 191–3) that Middle Stone Age hominins lacked the essential characteristics of modern human behaviour: an ability to organise themselves and exploit their resources to the maximum.

Technologically, the ESA to MSA is a shift from a hand-held, on-the-ground, processing technology to a technology that included a clear weapon-based, projectile component. This shift implies a profound change in the nature of acquiring meat; material culture shifts from being an important adjunct to the processing of carcasses and other foodstuffs in the Acheulean, to playing a crucial role in the acquisition of food. MSA technology anticipates and mitigates events in the hunting of animals. Levallois points, whether retouched or not, and other variations on the theme of deliberately made points, are elements of composite tools: they are hafted in some way. Many laminar products, whether Levallois or from prismatic cores, are also composite tool elements, either as blanks for other tools such as crescents, or as insertions into armatures (among other uses). These are elements within broader strategies that place hominins in a powerful and relatively safe place in relation to their prey and smooth out the uncertainties of the future. In one sense, therefore, MSA assemblages express the more routinised invariability of the MSA noted above. They are assemblages whose makers look forward to and prepare for 'the coming day'. It is perhaps no surprise, therefore, that with the appearance of the MSA we also see an expansion of the hominin range as hominins acquire the ability to overcome the need to remain close to water sources as did their Acheulean predecessors (Deacon and Deacon 1999).

But then what of the ESA/Acheulean? If the later gatherer-hunters of the MSA can be said to 'anticipate the day', some of the data from the South African ESA suggests that Acheulean hominins did little else other than reproduce yesterday tomorrow – a sort of primitive 'Groundhog Day'. In the following section we shall describe data from the Cave of Hearths, Makapansgat, and utilise it to explore the nature of differences between ESA and MSA material culture and what that might mean in terms of identifying the individual in the archaeological record.

The local context: the Cave of Hearths

The Cave of Hearths (CoH) is to be found in the Makapansgat Valley some 15 km to the north-east of Mokopane (formerly called Potgietersrus) in the north of the Limpopo province – formerly the Transvaal or Northern Province. The cave itself is located on the southern slopes of the small valley of the Mwaridzi stream (Figure 11.1). It is approximately 500 m away from the better-known Limeworks Site, celebrated for its Pliocene fauna and fossil remains of *Australopithicus africanus*. A full history of the site is given in Mason (1988), and a useful summary of the broader local context of CoH is given in (Mason 1962; Sampson 1974). Recent reinvestigation of the CoH has suggested a substantially different picture of the formation of the cave and of its infill than that presented by Mason (1988). Figure 11.2 shows the cave as

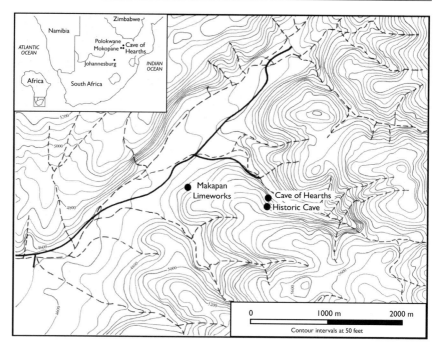

Figure 11.1 Map showing the position of the Cave of Hearths (Limpopo Province, South Africa, on the left bank of the valley of the seasonal Mwaridzi stream, in relation to the other major sites in the locality.

it is today with the sediments removed by archaeological excavation and by the earlier activities of lime miners.

Mason's conception of the cave in the Pleistocene was very much as it appears in the photograph, although the now vanished roof would have extended out further. The cave is a wide but not very deep/long cavity, whose entrance is the collapsed side of the hill slope on the left of the image. Sediments entered through this wide entrance and built up over time. Alf Latham and Andy Herries (pers. comm.) have suggested an alternative interpretation. The entrance was a smaller opening confined to an area a few metres beyond the small witness section hut seen in Figure 11.2. It opened into a large cavity of which the CoH as we know it today was only the right-hand side. The left-hand side is represented by what is now the adjacent and much larger Historic Cave. Sediment entered into both the left and the right areas down a single talus cone. In effect the sediments of the CoH are the right-hand side of the talus cone. The open and airy cavity that is the CoH today is a result of the gradual collapse of the original entrance, each episode of collapse taking more of the hillside with it. Acheulean biface-making hominins occupied the entrance of the cave and probably the daylight zone within, which would have gradually expanded with each phase of collapse toward the back wall of the

Figure 11.2 The Cave of Hearths looking along the cave from west to east. The huge Historic Cave is behind the unexcavated and cemented boulder heap.

cave (Mason 1988; on the right of Figure 11.2) and toward the position of the camera. Although some doubt exists as to whether the hearths in the cave are genuine (Herries pers. comm.), it seems more than likely that occupation did occur within the cave, as the agents of sediment input (primarily water) would not have been strong enough to move artefacts of the sizes of bifaces and cores down the uneven and rubble strewn surface of the talus cone (Latham pers. comm.). Faunal evidence supports this revision. The cave as reconstructed by Latham would be one much more attractive to denning carnivores. Recent work on the ESA faunal assemblage by Christine Ogola (pers. comm.) suggests that while a small number of cut-marked bones are present, the nature of the faunal assemblage is more like that of a carnivore accumulation. Clearly Acheulean hominins had to compete with other carnivores for living space at CoH. This fact, along with the limited area of the cave reached by daylight, may help explain why the actual frequency of stone tools is relatively small compared to the apparent area of the cave. The excavated area of the cave occupied by MSA hominins was smaller still, localised to the back wall of the cave close to the present painted legend.

On the basis of our current understanding of the technology and stratigraphy at CoH, following the Acheulean there was a long period of abandonment. Then hominins making and using a prepared core technology (PCT), for convergent flakes and some radial flakes, as well as flake-blades occupied the cave (Beds 4 and 5). At some point broadly contemporary (or perhaps earlier) with the occupation of the cave by the MSA people of Bed 6, a portion of the cave floor with sediments containing archaeology collapsed into a swallow hole at the back of the cave (located on the right-hand side of Figure 11.2). Eventually the swallow hole stabilised because of a boulder choke. Gradually the floor level built up until it reached the former level of Bed 3. At this point a huge slab of roof fell onto the former living area in the cave. From this point on occupation was only possible in the space between this boulder and the cave wall. In this cavity Mason found the MSA, LSA, Iron Age and Historic period remains of Beds 6–10

So, the MSA occupation of the CoH covers six beds of deposit (Beds 4–9), following the excavations of Mason (1988). Mason classified the MSA deposits when excavated as Pietersburg in character, with the final beds as Still Bay. It has been suggested more recently that the final MSA assemblages are possibly better described as Howiesons Poort (Thackeray 1992). Whatever names are assigned, in highly simplified terms, the earliest MSA occupants of the cave manufactured long flake-blades and convergent points, the intermediate MSA occupants produced an extensive Levallois industry of blades, radial flakes and especially convergent points, whilst the last of the MSA occupants produced a microlithic industry with small backed crescents and delicately made unifacial points. This is similar to the lower part of the MSA sequence at Klasies River Mouth (Singer and Wymer 1982).

The cave and its contained archaeology lack any of the 'moment-in-time' detail that in-situ, single event locations offer. However we believe that palimpsests of the type found in the CoH can still be entrained in the search for individuality in the Stone Age because of the potential inherent in the study of technology and patterns of manufacture.

Hominin contexts

Whichever hominin is responsible for the Acheulean at the Cave of Hearths depends on the dating of the site and on the interpretation of the two fragments of hominin remains recovered from Bed 3. The site is undated by radiometric methods. Mason (1988) dated the ESA levels at the site to approximately 250–200 kya on the basis of archaeological comparisons with other sites already established in the South African Acheulean sequence. Recent attempts at dating have suggested a date of possibly 300 kya for Bed 3. Herries (pers. comm.), suggests a date of between 400 kya and 300 kya on the basis of palaeomagnetism. Philip Tobias (1971) attributed the hominin mandible to *Homo rhodesiensis*. Cautiously a date of about 300 kya for the final ESA would appear appropriate, but this must be considered provisional. For the Middle Stone Age, there were no hominin remains found at the CoH and hominin remains in Southern Africa dated to the Middle Stone Age in general are rare (Klein 1999: 401). The few remains that are present reveal individuals that were anatomically modern in form, and quite robust in their post-cranial skeleton (ibid.: 394–401). Whilst the apparent absence of resource stress experienced by fauna during MSA times, in comparison with post-40 kya Later Stone Age times, has suggested that MSA populations were small in number and possibly quite dispersed (ibid.: 470–1).

Biface manufacture and the marking of individuality in the Early Stone Age

As noted above, in our opinion the study of the material culture of the Acheulean gather-hunters at the CoH does not really support the presence of standardised practice in the thinning and shaping, or finishing of LCTs at all. If standardisation can be taken as a proxy for group norms, and all that implies in terms of learning patterns and parameters of cultural acceptability, then it is quite possible to construct the data from the ESA levels at the site to infer a very low level of culturally standardised common practice.

This can be demonstrated by a study of symmetry (as a proxy for imposed intentional design) among the LCT element from the CoH, and a fuller description of the methodology can be found in the Appendix to this chapter. Our analysis quantifies the degree of symmetry present in an assemblage and allows us to identify any patterns in the process of regularising the outline of an LCT. The results are presented in Figure 11.3. Only a very small proportion of the LCT assemblage shows the imposition of symmetry onto the whole of the artefact. Those LCTs which can show at least two-thirds of their outline shape are symmetrical represent only about 14 per cent of the biface assemblage.

As the diagram makes quite clear the strongest signal coming from the data is the complete lack of symmetry imposed by thinning and shaping, and this holds good for bifaces as well as cleavers, irrespective of raw material. Nor could it be said that artisans were focusing on shaping the tips carefully and ignoring the rest of the piece. The data for cleavers are almost the same. Since the sample of LCTs used in this analysis is drawn from all three beds excavated (Mason 1988), and from both the disturbed and undisturbed areas of the cave, these data can be taken as a representative selection of the whole of the Acheulean LCT behaviour at the site.

In addition to a simple measure of symmetry our methodology also investigates the nature and extent of secondary thinning and shaping on LCTs, and how such flaking is applied to both faces of an artefact. This is also described in Appendix 2. Five categories are recognised, and the data for these have been grouped together in Figure 11.4. The result is the same.

The majority of both bifaces and cleavers receive only a limited amount of thinning and shaping, confined to selected portions of the margins of both faces. For bifaces this represents just over 58 per cent of the total, while for cleavers the pattern is much more robust, just over 82 per cent of the total. In other words, there is the minimum of lateral trimming on both faces. For bifaces the next most commonly occurring pattern is one face worked by

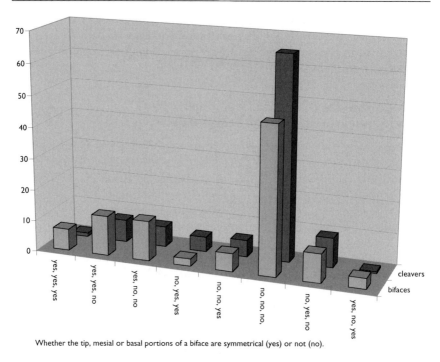

Whether the tip, mesial or basal portions of a biface are symmetrical (yes) or not (no).

Figure 11.3 Patterns of symmetry present in Large Cutting Tools (LCTs) (bifaces [n=87] and cleavers [n=169]) from the Cave of Hearths, Makapansgat. For description of method see Appendix 1.

sporadic marginal trimming while the other face has been completely thinned/ worked by secondary flaking (11 per cent). For cleavers the pattern is quite the reverse, one face worked by sporadic marginal trimming while the other has no secondary working at all (9.5 per cent). Only 6.9 per cent of the bifaces, and 0.6 per cent of the cleavers have either both faces wholly worked by secondary flaking or have a substantial portion of both faces so worked.

In effect secondary thinning and shaping on bifaces and cleavers appears to represent the minimum possible amount of work needed to render an edge suitable for use. Secondary working, apart from in a few cases, does not impose symmetry, standardise an outline or result in what we might regard as a well-finished appearance. It is difficult to escape the conclusion that this 'non-pattern' implies no strong group or 'cultural' norms were present throughout the time Acheulean gather-hunters occupied the cave. This has important consequences for the search for individuality as seen through material culture in the ESA. From a lack of culturally imposed norms we infer that for the ESA at the CoH the concept of cultural identity did not exist. You could belong to a commune of other hominins with shared goals, but there was no sense of shared identity imposed by the unique 'personality' of the group. So there could

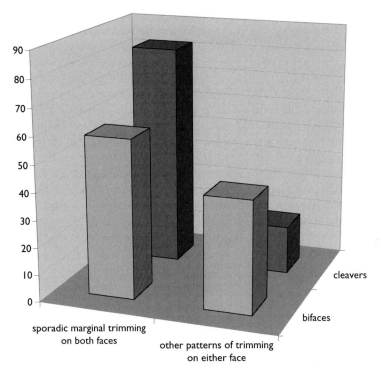

Figure 11.4 Application of patterns of flaking to LCTs (bifaces [n=87] and cleavers [n=169]) from the Cave of Hearths. For description of method see Appendix 2.

be no culturally constructed personhood, nor could there be individuals who self-consciously recognised themselves as different from the other people in their group and who then expressed that by subverting normal group practice. We suggest the notion of individuality whether at the level of one hominin or of a group with shared goals simply did not exist. So what are we to make of the LCTs? Hominins grow up in social groups where material culture is being made and used all around them. The idea of an LCT and how it is made is all around them from their earliest conscious memories. The most parsimonious way to explain the lack of standardisation in outline form, appearance, and manufacture is that no direct socially structured learning occurs. Individuals observe and copy and produce to their own satisfaction the idea of the tool. Abilities and standards of acceptability vary from hominin to hominin; individuals make tools but there is no self-conscious individuality expressed in their making.

What about the size of LCTs in terms of the expression of individuality? It has been argued (Kohn and Mithen 1999) that individuality can be seen in the manufacture of large and impressive pieces whose function is to declare the genetic fitness of the maker. This argument could also apply to those artefacts which to modern eyes appear to be superior in appearance or finish. A good proxy length for distinguishing between 'larger' and 'smaller' bifaces and cleavers at CoH appears to be a length of 150 mm. Two questions can be asked of these size data. Are the bigger LCTs more intensively worked? Are the bigger LCTs inclined to show a greater propensity toward symmetry? The answer to both is no. The mean number of scars on an LCT of 149 mm or less in length is 19.44 (SD=9.10; n=168), for one 150 mm or longer the mean number of scars is 22.55 (SD=9.37; n=105). While there are clearly more scars there are not *appreciably* more, and the *small* increase in frequency can easily be accounted for by the larger size of the artefacts. Certainly the pattern of application for secondary flaking to impose symmetry does not change from Figure 11.3. A Chi-square test supports the similarity between the two data sets ($X^2=9.541$, df=5, null hypothesis can not be rejected at 5 per cent for a two-tailed test). In conclusion then, apart from the fact that bigger LCTs are made, they do not appear to be treated differently from the smaller ones in terms of appearance or finish.

The Middle Stone Age lithic assemblages

In some aspects of tool behaviour there seems little difference in character between the ESA and the MSA at least for the earlier beds (4 and 5). MSA hominins expressed their technological skills in the making of convergent flakes, essentially Levallois points, and prepared-flake-blades from either unipolar or bipolar cores. For this purpose, locally available raw materials (quartzites, andesites and sometimes cherts) were almost exclusively used. Retouch, when present, is minimal and usually takes the form of no more than an episode of continuous retouching along a small portion of one edge of an otherwise unmodified blank. For these implements, there is simply no question of symmetry across any axis. It is not until Bed 6 that this 'minimalist' approach to using stone changes, with the appearance of distinctly retouched point forms that are of a regular size and are retouched unifacially, or sometimes bifacially. These points are made from a variety of raw materials, including hornfels, felsites and fine grey cherts that do not seem to be present in the local valleys. Beyond these clearly shaped pieces, however, the remaining stone tool assemblage from Bed 6 onwards is as minimally modified as that of the earlier MSA beds.

In comparison to the earlier bifaces and cleavers, the retouched points from Bed 6 onwards are clearly made to a pattern: they possess both a regular plan form and a repeated process of retouching from the mid-point of the flake towards the distal end. In some examples, the retouching on one face is supplemented by further retouching at either the distal or the proximal end on the other face. Therefore the pattern also allows for some form of individual judgement during manufacture. We might see in this pattern of manufacture and in the variability in the degree of retouching (from unifacial to bifacial) possible evidence for the expression of group identity or personhood in material terms, as well as, possibly, some degree of expression of personality. The point forms are seemingly more carefully and individually made, and their raw materials suggest a longer use-life or biography for each piece.

Taking a critical perspective, it might be difficult to disentangle this evidence for the material expression of personhood from the practical requirements necessary to the making of an effective point form. There is no question that these points are projectile points. In some cases, there is clear evidence for hafting, in the form of retouching at the proximal ends of the piece to thin away the bulb of percussion. Other pieces have a broken tip, indicative of fracture on impact, whilst others have a modified tip profile, indicating that they were retrimmed from a previously broken point ready for later reuse. But the record of the Palaeolithic reveals that projectile points can be made in any number of ways, though perhaps not from a convergent point technology.

The archaeological evidence from the MSA beds at the Cave of Hearths, therefore, suggests that MSA hominins, despite their anatomical modernity, are in fact more like their ESA ancestors. They are not accustomed to negotiating their identity in the context of and through the material expression of their lithic technology.

But we should perhaps not overlook the lightly retouched pieces from Beds 4 and 5 so quickly. Prepared-flake blades and convergent flakes, as noted above, were made using locally available quartzites and andesites. These materials are available both from primary contexts within 1 km of the cave, and in the case of the quartzites also in the form of rolled boulders from the local river channels. The preparation of the prepared cores requires both the creation of a flat platform, and the removal of large flakes orthogonally to the platform, but from different faces, so as to leave two large negative scars that meet in a long ridge (see Singer and Wymer 1982: 74–6 for a discussion of this process at Klasies River Mouth). Once this ridge has been produced, convergent flakes may then be struck in sequence from the same direction as the initial flake removals, whilst flake-blades might be struck either from one direction or from opposed directions along this ridge if a second platform is created at the bottom of this ridge. Flake blade cores can be rejuvenated through the striking of small core tablets (sometimes looking like steeply backed knives) that remove the platform edge and the negative scar of the proximal ends of previous removals, and in so doing refresh the platform angle. At Makapansgat, the tabular blocks of the local quartzites are especially well suited to this technique of working, since the geometric relationship between the platform(s), the primary negative flake scars and the first ridge that must be set up on a rounded boulder often pre-exists on naturally eroding quartzite blocks. But the large rounded boulders of the locally available black andesite may well have proven to be quite a challenge.

Despite the fact that there are no refitted assemblages from the Cave of Hearths, there is still enough evidence in the frequency of certain debitage pieces and the use of raw materials to reconstruct some of the processes in the production chain for the making of the prepared flakes, and any changes in these processes through time. The range of debitage (the non-retouched products, waste and non-waste, that arise from stone working) present in Beds 4 and 5 reveals that the complete reduction process was not undertaken at the Cave of Hearths. For both beds, there is a general absence of cortical and semi-cortical flakes that indicates that the first stages of working happened outside the cave. However, there are plenty of discarded prepared-core flakes, both convergent and flake-blade, as well as a consistent number of platform rejuvenation flakes. There are also very few discarded convergent flake cores or flake-blade cores at the site. This debitage evidence, therefore, indicates that the cores were prepared outside of the cave, and brought inside for a sequence of prepared flake removals and associated episodes of core rejuvenation. The cores themselves were then either taken to another site, or reworked into smaller irregular formed cores. In this pattern, the MSA is similar to the ESA where we saw that bifaces were made outside the cave and brought in (Mason 1988), though in our opinion they were brought in substantially finished (*contra* Mason).

It would be possible to account for this debitage pattern in practical terms: the preparation of cores outside the cave would ensure that little effort is wasted by hominins in transporting potentially non-useful raw materials (either whole blocks or waste cortical or semi-cortical flakes) to the cave, whilst the absence of prepared flake cores results from the reworking of the exhausted prepared flake cores into other forms, such as discoid cores, so as to maximise the exploitation of the available raw material or minimise the costs of resource extraction. It would, of course, be possible to argue that further savings of energy might be made by completing the full process of prepared flake and blade removals close to the raw material source and only transporting useable convergent flakes, flake-blades and true blades back to the cave. But this is not what appears to occur.

Furthermore, the size of the flake-blade removals is less easy to explain pragmatically. When Mason first examined the nature of technological change through the MSA assemblages he noted that the mean length of the prepared flakes decreased from Bed 4 to Bed 5 and Beds 6 to 9 (Mason 1957). Whilst this is correct, it does not tell the whole story. As noted by Kerrich (1957), in a statistical addendum to Mason's piece, the size distribution of flake-blades is in fact skewed. The distribution of lengths for flake-blades in Beds 4 and 5 and also in Beds 6 to 9 reveals a peak in frequency of flake-blades at approximately 100 mm for the quartzite blades and approximately 120 mm for those made of andesite (Figure 11.5).

In Bed 4, however, there are a number of much longer pieces up to 220 mm in length in andesite and 175 mm in quartzite. These long blades in Beds 4 and 5 are exaggerations, standing clear from the norm (Figure 11.6), and we might see them as exemplars of the expression of a considerable degree of

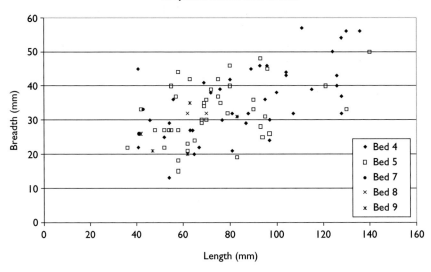

**Cave of Hearths Middle Stone Age
Prepared Core Flake-Blades**

Figure 11.5 The length and breadth measurement for flake-blades made using prepared-core techniques from Beds 4 to 9 at the Cave of Hearths, Makapansgat, South Africa.

achieved skill. Yet, as noted above, there are no retouched tools made on such long blanks, and there are no truncated flake-blade segments to suggest that such long flake-blades were more commonly produced and then snapped into smaller more useable forms. Where retouch is present, or use fractures are visible on the longer blade blanks, these retouched or used pieces are no longer than the normal size of the smaller flake-blades or convergent flakes.

It is tempting to suggest, therefore, that the makers of these exaggerated pieces were visibly and deliberately displaying their skill at a technical level beyond what was necessary. In relation to the definitions noted above, this could be clearly described as evidence for individuality. The spatial context of this activity at the cave is also interesting, since the raw material sources for both quartzite and andesite are so close to the Cave of Hearths itself, one wonders why all knapping was not undertaken either at the source or in the cave. Instead it is the performance of the removal of the largest predetermined pieces that took place in front of all members of the social group. We might suggest that the exaggerated size of the flake-blades should have been very obvious to all those present, since these pieces, and their cores would have been considerably greater than the size of a hand. From handling these pieces and listening to the ringing sound of the longest andesite flake-blades, we can also suggest that the sounds of the making and use would also have been quite different to the 'duller' sound of the smaller pieces. Therefore the context of expression of

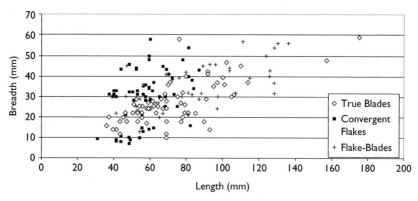

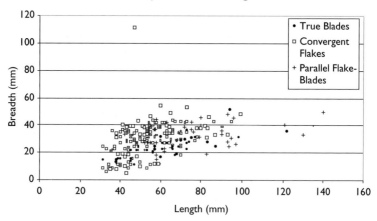

Figure 11.6 The range of length and breadth measures for debitage types produced using prepared-core techniques for Bed 4 and Bed 5 at the Cave of Hearths, Makapansgat, South Africa. (Note the small number of much larger pieces that stand out from the mass of normally sized pieces, in Both bed 4 and Bed 5).

individuality in technical skill has visible and audible components. From Bed 5 and especially Bed 6 onwards, these exaggerated pieces are no longer being made, even though the same basic technology is still in use, and the same minimally retouched pieces are still the most commonly produced. We infer from this that the nature of individual technological performance changed during the Middle Stone Age at the Cave of Hearths, from a time (Bed 4) when the material expression of individuality was important, through to a time when the expression of personhood is more significant. Importantly, the exaggerated flake-blades from Beds 4 and 5, and their evidence for manufacture in the cave itself, implies a particular social context for the expression of personality, a context in the hominin lifespace in which all members of a social group may have been present.

A shifting context for individual identity?

Recent approaches to the interpretation of material culture in the prehistoric past focus on the interplay between the individual as active agent, and their context whether in terms of gender, age or socio-politics. Individuals are portrayed as creating and representing their identity through material culture, while the physical and mental processes of making and using material things quite literally makes the individual. In this sense technological action is inseparable from all other social activities at the time (Dobres and Hoffman 1994). This approach derives from ethnographic observations made amongst living societies (for example: Hodder 1982; Miller 1985), and is, needless to say, an observation of modern humans and modern human behaviour. For the study of earlier periods, and modern humans who may not have acted in the same ways as ourselves today, the key problem is to tease apart the potentially shifting relationship between individual hominins, material culture and context through time and in space, using an archaeological record that is often an accumulation of the residues from activities over a long period of time. i.e the CoH as Palaeolithic *poubelle* palimpsest.

The nature and contexts of the expression of personality and personhood in the ESA and MSA artefacts from the Cave of Hearths are similar and yet different, technologically and typologically. The ESA assemblages suggest a process of working that is in a sense completely individual but not about individuality. No marked patterns can be observed, and little evidence exists to suggest that ESA hominins at Makapansgat used material culture as a medium of communication, at an individual or group level. For the Middle Stone Age, the lack of strongly imposed typological form, that has been noted so often for Middle Stone Age assemblages throughout Southern Africa, is also apparent, especially in the earlier Beds 4 and 5. Until the advent of unifacial projectile points in Beds 6–9, MSA hominins like their ESA forebears do not seem to be manipulating the final form of their stone tools to communicate some aspect of individual or even corporate/group identity through standardised forms. Typology, however, only tells part of the story. Technologically we can suggest that a different biography was being written. The technological skills for making prepared flake-blades facilitate the expression of individual technological expertise. Individuals are able to express a personal identity through their successful and visible manipulation of the techniques for the making of material items. In the differential preparation, working and discard of flake-blades and flake-blade cores between the assemblages from Bed 4 and

Beds 5 and later, we might perhaps see the various contexts in which individual identities may have been negotiated through the technological processes of making and use. So while Middle Stone Age hominins are likely to have been anatomically modern or very close to that form (Klein 1999: 401), their engagement with material culture seems quite different to the overt symbolism and structure that characterises the more recent modern humans of the African Later Stone Age or the Eurasian Upper Palaeolithic.

The broader context for individual action in the ESA and MSA in Southern Africa was likely to have been that of small and possibly widely dispersed social groups if site numbers and studies of faunal exploitation patterns are an accurate guide. ESA and MSA populations were able to exploit these resources without endangering their abundance in any way (Klein and Cruz-Uribe 1996, 2000). If we were to follow the implications of Dunbar's grooming model (Dunbar 1996a), we might surmise that in such small social groups the shifting relationships between individuals may well have been largely negotiated through their own bodily resources without active reinforcement by material culture. Hence the patterns that we have observed at the Cave of Hearths are essentially local and fleeting and not steps on a developmental trajectory leading to our contemporary relationships between societies, individuals, techniques and material things.

Acknowledgements

We would like to acknowledge the assistance of the British Academy and the Arts and Humanities Research Board for financial support to undertake the research reported on here, and to the Department of Archaeology, School of Geography, Archaeology and Earth Sciences at the University of the Witwatersrand, and especially, Tom Huffman, Kathy Kuman, and Lyn Wadley for their continuous support during the course of the project. We would also like to thank Gemma Hudgell, Jason Hall, Susan Andresson and Annabel Field for their assistance in the recording of some of the ESA and MSA lithic collections from the Cave of Hearths.

Appendix I

Eyeball test for symmetry in large cutting tools (LCT)

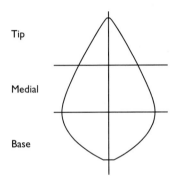

Tip

Medial

Base

Eyeball symmetry	1	2	3	4	5	6	7	8
Tip	Yes	Yes	Yes	No	No	No	No	Yes
Medial	Yes	Yes	No	Yes	No	No	Yes	No
Base	Yes	No	No	Yes	Yes	No	No	Yes

A longitudinal bisector is fixed down the length of the artefact. For pointed handaxes and other LCTs with clearly convergent tips the bisector passes through the tip. For cleavers the bisector passes through 0.5 of the width of the cleaver tip or blade. The artefact is then divided horizontally into three equal sections, and the presence of symmetry noted for each section. Symmetry was scored on a yes or no scale for each section, and the artefact placed in one of eight categories depending on the combination observed.

Appendix 2

Extent and pattern of thinning and shaping on an LCT

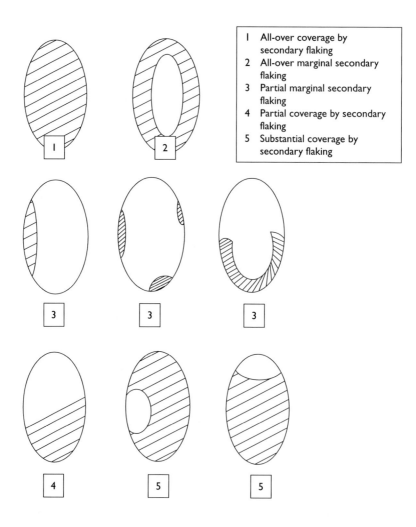

Chapter 12

Life and mind in the Acheulean

A case study from India

Michael D. Petraglia, Ceri Shipton and K. Paddayya

Introduction

Archaeologists have traditionally been sceptical about, if not downright hostile towards, the notion that individual activities and episodes in time constitute useful objects of research (e.g. Bordes 1975; Binford 1981b). The lack of interest in individual activities and 'ethnographic' time slices is, in part, due to the perceived limits of the archaeological record itself, but it is also the product of a particular theoretical orientation that views high-resolution information as an inappropriate scale for understanding long-term trends and the organisation of behaviour. Yet, those who wish to study the development of behavioural innovations and social novelty have made the point that adaptive processes must be understood at the smallest scales, such as the interaction between individuals and groups, in order to comprehend large-scale evolutionary patterns in time and space (e.g. Foley 1999, 2001b). In addition, a certain corps of archaeologists who wish to examine human choices and actions have concerned themselves with agency, or the active strategies of individuals and groups in manipulating their social environment (e.g. Dobres and Robb 2000). Although both sets of researchers pay attention to small-scale processes, those interested in evolutionary processes tend to draw on concepts from neo-Darwinian models and socio-ecological approaches given substantive changes in Plio-Pleistocene environments, human species and technology, whereas those interested in social agency and human intentions tend to concentrate on modern humans and more familiar aspects of the material record. Although there is currently little communication between evolutionary and social theorists, there is, in fact, some common ground to explore, as researchers in the two camps are concerned with small-scale practices and context-specific behaviours. Archaeologists have argued that analysis of specific details of Palaeolithic artefacts and close inspection of the material properties of high-integrity Pleistocene sites enables inferences about individual choices, social interactions and the relative 'intelligence' of hominins, i.e. the ability of individuals to solve problems and manipulate their social and natural environment (e.g. Gamble 1999; Gowlett 1996a; Wynn 1999; Sinclair 2000; Wobst 2000). A finer-grained view of archaeological phenomena also potentially provides palaeoanthropologists with an enhanced level of awareness about how hominin social structure may vary within and between groups, allowing us to evaluate whether broad trends in the Palaeolithic are, in fact, shared cultural traits across populations or whether gross patterns are more heterogeneous than previously imagined. Such information can provide insights concerning the ability of hominins to exercise choice in certain situations and the degree to which members of the group were creative agents or were influenced and conditioned by social rules.

To further an understanding of the working of the early human mind and the nature of social interactions in the Acheulean, archaeological information from a single basin in southern India are examined in this chapter. Inter-site studies and close examination of a high-resolution stone tool quarry allow us to pose questions about individual actions, collective behaviours and Acheulean society.

An Acheulean context in India

Although global patterning and a deep-time perspective remain relevant research issues for understanding the Acheulean, it can be argued that more information needs to be collected about the short term and the small scale if we wish to know more about the forces which operated to produce evolutionary changes. In this light, archaeological evidence from the Hunsgi and Baichbal Valleys in southern India is examined to understand hominin choices and small-group behaviours. In addition, stone tool evidence from the Isampur Quarry (Hunsgi Valley) is closely examined to ascertain particular hominin actions and the social context in which they occurred. The basin-wide and intra-site evidence provides the basis for interpreting aspects of local hominin cognition and sociality and ultimately its relationship to a global Acheulean.

The Hunsgi and Baichbal Valleys

The Hunsgi and Baichbal Valleys are located in south-central India (16°30' N 76°33' E) and together constitute a single Tertiary basin. The 500 km² area contains shallow but perennial water bodies fed by seep springs emanating from the junction of shales and limestones. Samples of travertine and teeth date the Acheulean occurrences from the middle to late stages of the Middle Pleistocene (Szabo *et al.* 1990). Occupations are likely much older, as indicated by a maximum uranium series date of >350 kyr and preliminary ESR dates of *c.* 1.2 myr (Blackwell *et al.* 2001). Hence the Acheulean sites under analysis here have a temporal span that may extend for more than a million years.

Archaeological surveys have been carried out in the Hunsgi and Baichbal Valleys, revealing the presence of more than 200 Acheulean occurrences (Paddayya 1982, 2001). Hominins selected for a wide variety of raw materials for tool use (Table 12.1) (Paddayya and Petraglia 1993; Noll and Petraglia 2003).

Table 12.1 Selected artefact types (A) and their raw materials (B) for selected Hunsgi-Baichbal sites

(A)	Total	Handaxes	Cleavers	Misc. bifaces	Broken bifaces	Unfinished bifaces	Hammerstones	Cores	Natural slabs
Hunsgi Valley									
Isampur Q.	244	39 (16%)	20 (8.2%)	26 (10.7%)	15 (6.2%)	16 (6.6%)	20 (8.2%)	85 (34.8%)	23 (9.4%)
Gulbal II	22	12 (54.6%)	2 (9.1%)	3 (13.6%)	–	–	–	5 (22.7%)	–
Hunsgi II	38	18 (47.4%)	13 (34.2%)	3 (7.9%)	–	–	–	4 (10.5%)	–
Hunsgi V	198	43 (21.7%)	53 (26.8%)	55 (27.8%)	–	2 (1%)	7 (3.5%)	38 (19.2%)	–
Baichbal Valley									
Yediyapur I	21	10 (47.6%)	6 (28.6%)	5 (23.8%)	–	–	–	–	–
Yediyapur IV	20	11 (55%)	6 (30%)	3 (15%)	–	–	–	–	–
Yediyapur VI	90	21 (23.3%)	17 (18.9%)	28 (31.1%)	–	–	7 (7.8%)	17 (18.8%)	–
Fatephur V	39	11 (28.2%)	11 (28.2%)	9 (23.1%)	–	–	5 (12.8%)	3 (7.7%)	–
Mudnur VIII	9	9 (100%)	–	–	–	–	–	–	–
Mudnur X	7	2 (28.6%)	–	2 (28.6%)	–	–	1 (14.3%)	2 (28.6%)	–
Grand total	688	176 (25.6%)	128 (18.6%)	134 (19.5%)	15 (2.2%)	18 (2.6%)	40 (5.8%)	154 (22.4%)	23 (3.3%)

continued

Table 12.1 continued

(B)

	Total	Limestone	Quartzite	Quartz	Chert	Sandstone	Granite	Dolerite	Schist	Basalt	Unknown
Hunsgi Valley											
Isampur Q.	244	225 (92.2%)	2 (0.8%)	–	15 (6.2%)	–	–	–	–	2 (0.8%)	–
Gulbal II	22	16 (72.7%)	–	–	6 (27.3%)	–	–	–	–	–	–
Hunsgi II	38	34 (89.5%)	2 (5.3%)	–	1 (2.6%)	–	1 (2.6%)	–	–	–	–
Hunsgi V	198	176 (88.9%)	4 (2%)	–	13 (6.6%)	1 (0.5%)	1 (0.5%)	–	–	–	3 (1.5%)
Baichbal Valley											
Yediyapur I	21	5 (23.8%)	–	–	1 (4.8%)	–	5 (23.8%)	7 (33.3%)	3 (14.3%)	–	–
Yediyapur IV	20	8 (40%)	–	–	–	–	5 (25%)	5 (25%)	2 (10%)	–	–
Yediyapur VI	90	5 (5.6%)	3 (3.3%)	1 (1.1%)	7 (7.8%)	–	35 (38.9%)	34 (37.8%)	3 (3.3%)	–	2 (2.2%)
Fatephur V	39	1 (2.6%)	–	3 (7.7%)	4 (10.3%)	–	23 (59%)	6 (15.4%)	2 (5.1%)	–	–
Mudnur VIII	9	9 (100%)	–	–	–	–	–	–	–	–	–
Mudnur X	7	4 (57.1%)	2 (28.6%)	–	–	–	1 (14.3%)	–	–	–	–
Grand total	688	483 (70.2%)	13 (1.9%)	4 (0.6%)	47 (6.8%)	1 (0.2%)	71 (10.3%)	52 (7.6%)	10 (1.5%)	2 (0.3%)	5 (0.7%)

Bifaces in the Hunsgi Valley are predominately made on limestone, whereas in the Baichbal Valley bifaces are made on limestone, granite, dolerite and schist. Limestone and granite are ubiquitous raw materials that outcrop in particular areas across the valley floor and plateaus. Schist is spatially confined to the Baichbal Valley and dolerites occur in restricted areas in the two valleys. Hammerstones are made from a variety of raw materials (chert, granite, limestone, sandstone, quartzite, quartz, basalt and schist) that occur in outcrops or as cobbles and pebbles in conglomerates and gravel beds.

Isampur Quarry and use of space

The Isampur Quarry represents a locality where hominins manufactured stone tool tools from a siliceous limestone source (Paddayya and Petraglia 1997; Petraglia *et al.* 1999; Paddayya *et al.* 2000, 2002) (Figure 12.1). More than 15,000 artefacts have been recovered in the excavations, including a wide range of chipped stone artefacts and hammerstones. Hominins were apparently attracted to an area where vital resources overlapped. At Isampur, this included high-grade limestone for stone tool manufacture, freshwater springs and animals, including wild cattle (*Bos* sp.) and pond turtle (*Clemmys* sp.) (Paddayya *et al.* 2000).

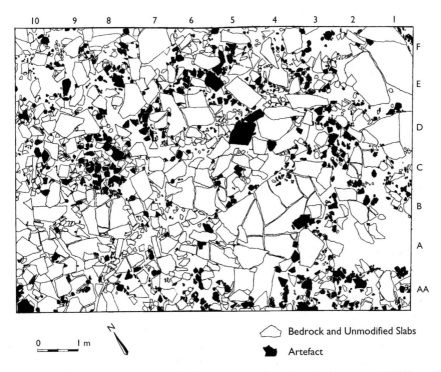

Figure 12.1 Isampur site plan from the lowermost surface (after Paddayya *et al.* 2002).

Certain material remains at Isampur have been interpreted to be the direct consequence of early human activity (Petraglia *et al.* 1999; Paddayya *et al.* 2000). Disjointed and vertically inclined slabs at the site are thought to reflect the levering actions of hominins to procure the bedrock for stone tool manufacture. The range of on-site flaking debris indicates that stone tool manufacturing steps can be discerned, including material procurement, initial stages of slab reduction and biface thinning. In some instances, particular actions of individuals could be identified; in one case a conjugate joint surface with signs of hammer battering was interpreted as the product of slab procurement (see Petraglia 2001: Figure 15.8). In another case, the overturned position of a massive and heavy core (in Unit D5) shows that the slab was flipped over by hominins by applying several vertically oriented strikes.

Preliminary spatial analysis has been conducted on the artefact distributions in Trench 1 at Isampur, providing information about Acheulean activities (Shipton 2003). Nine concentrations of artefactual material could be discerned over a 70 m^2 area (Figure 12.2a). Analysis of the concentrations shows that some consisted of cores, likely representing areas where slabs were struck and where exhausted pieces were abandoned (Figure 12.2b).

A plot of large flakes and large hammers show some degree of correspondence (Clusters 2a, 2c, 4a, 4b, 6, 8 and 1a) (Figure 12.3a). The proximity of the large cores and hammers is likely tied to biface manufacture, particularly spots where cleavers were produced, as they entail the production of large flakes. In contrast, a plot of bifaces, small hammers and small flaking debris shows a different pattern, suggesting the spots where secondary biface flaking may have occurred (Figure 12.3b). Taken together, the preliminary spatial plots suggest the specific locations where hominins procured and manufactured different tool types.

Isampur Quarry technology

Technological analysis of the Isampur Quarry materials shows that there were two main strategies for making bifaces: the manufacture of bifaces from medium-thickness units and the production of bifaces from large side-struck flakes from thick beds (Petraglia *et al.* 1999).

The manufacture of bifaces from medium-thickness slabs required the application of alternate flaking along their perimeters. Slabs of small dimension could be directly chosen for flaking and biface manufacture, or alternatively, as learned from our stone tool experimentation, a horizontally wide slab could be broken down into smaller pieces. Some bifaces showed primary stage flaking and abandonment soon after initial flaking (Figure 12.4a). Others showed initial bilateral trimming to produce bifaces of different size and shape, implying that target forms were of variable dimensions (Figure 12.4b).

Production of large side-struck flakes involved a preparatory core strategy (Figure 12.5). In an idealised trajectory, a series of steps would be applied, from

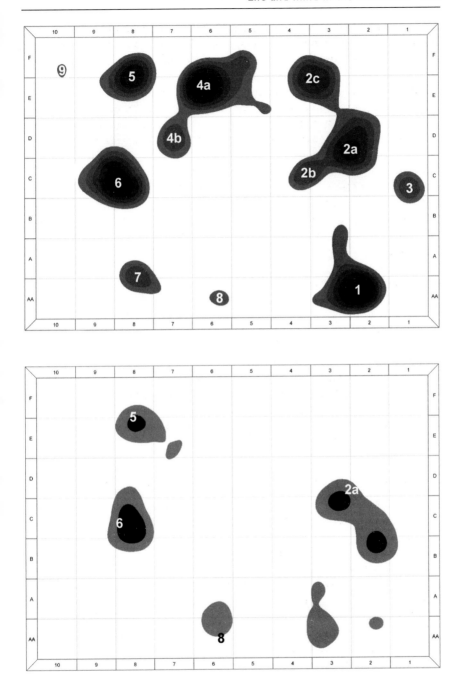

Figure 12.2 Spatial plot showing artefacts (a, top) and cores (b) in Trench 1, Isampur.

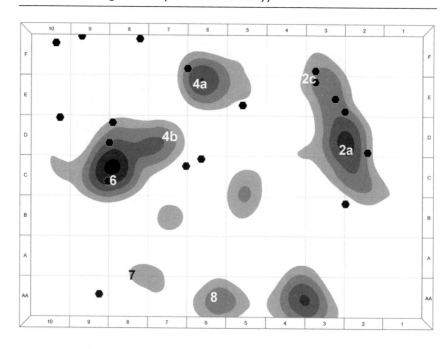

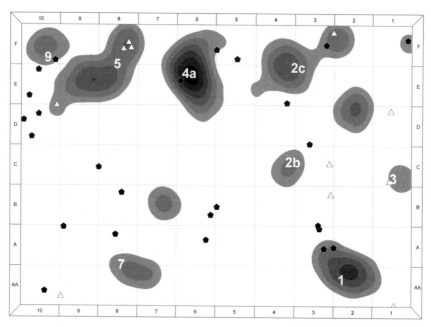

Figure 12.3 Spatial plot showing large flakes and large hammers (a, top) and bifaces, hammerstones and small flaking debris (b), Trench 1, Isampur.

Figure 12.4 Isampur Quarry artefacts showing the manufacture of bifaces from slabs. (a, top) Biface and hammerstones. It is probable that hammerstones of these sizes were selected to alternately flake bifaces. Note that the handaxe is made from a slab. (b) Bifaces showing that objects of different size and shape were made at the quarry.

Figure 12.5 Core reduction and large flake removal at Isampur Quarry. (a, top) Experiments showing the initial stage of the working of thick slabs. Large hammers were used to remove flakes in a vertically oriented direction. (b) Exhausted cores from Isampur Quarry showing that flakes were obliquely struck into the core after dressing of the core was complete. These large, obliquely struck flakes were often made into cleavers.

procurement to final manufacture of large, side-struck flakes. The first step was the procurement and identification of a thick limestone unit. In the first manufacturing stage, flakes were driven off in a vertically oriented direction, from the corners and the sides of the slabs. Initial flaking was followed by a series of obliquely oriented flake removals into a flat face of the core. In some cases, the core was more systematically flaked in order to assist in the production of a large side-struck flake.

The side-struck flake had predicted features, often including a flat edged transverse bit and long bilateral edges. The side-struck flakes were minimally flaked along their butts and their lower bilateral edges, creating the distinct cleaver form. The production of side-struck flakes involved some degree of anticipation on the part of early humans. The flaking strategy was a skilled procedure, requiring the application of dexterity and heavy force, as clearly demonstrated in our experiments. Preparatory steps in cleaver manufacture were considerably more ordered in the nearby Kolihal Quarry, which is thought to date to the Late Acheulean (Paddayya and Jhaldiyal 1999).

Collective and individual behaviour in the Acheulean

Analysis of sites in the Hunsgi-Baichbal Valley and examination of hominin actions at Isampur Quarry provide a context in which to evaluate how the Acheulean mind worked and the social and ecological context of the interactions. Certain information drawn from the investigations suggest a level of conservative behaviour across generations, consistent with interpretations about general technological trends in the Acheulean. On the other hand, the Hunsgi-Baichbal evidence suggests a greater level of flexibility in thought and actions than is normally accorded to individuals living in the Acheulean.

Tool technology and designs

The Hunsgi-Baichbal assemblages are characterised by manufacturing methods and tool types that are shared with other Acheulean industries in the Indian subcontinent (Paddayya 1982, 2001; Petraglia 1998, 2001). Based on comparative study of size attributes, the biface size parameters from the Hunsgi and Baichbal Valleys accord well with those from the Middle Pleistocene site of Olorgesailie, in East Africa (Noll and Petraglia 2003). Although a range of sizes could be found in the Hunsgi-Baichbal assemblages, with variation due to quarrying behaviours and raw materials, there appears to be an overall trend in biface standardisation (Table 12.2).

The Isampur Quarry information, together with examination of other Hunsgi-Baichbal assemblages, showed that the limestone bifaces were made using relatively consistent procedures. The dual strategy for biface production, employing slab and flake techniques, was a manufacturing strategy that was

Table 12.2 Summary of metric variables for Hunsgi-Baichbal bifaces

	Length (cm)	Breadth (cm)	Thickness (cm)	Weight (gm)
Mean	14.5	8.96	4.53	608
Median	14	9	4	525
Standard deviation	3.95	2.04	1.23	388
Minimum	6	4	2	60
Maximum	31	19	9	3000

used at a number of sites and a technology that was maintained for a long period of time. Analysis of the Hunsgi-Baichbal assemblages indicates that there was relatively low tool-type diversity, mainly concentrating on large, bifacial pieces of a few types (i.e. handaxes, cleavers, picks). The only significant metric difference in handaxes and cleavers was tip width, which is one of the basic distinctions between biface types (Shipton 2003).

On the whole, the routine flaking procedures, the repeated manufacture of a low diversity of tools and the limits on elaborate shaping show that there is maintenance of a standardised bifacial technology. The assemblage uniformity in technology and artefact style is consistent with a pattern of strong conventions held across Acheulean society in all its vast temporal and geographical range (e.g. Schick and Clark 2003). Such technological behaviour appear to be truly imitative, i.e. the end-product and the means used to achieve it are faithfully reproduced (Meltzoff 1995). The standardisation of both bifaces and manufacturing techniques suggests that Acheulean hominins had a capacity for imitation above and beyond that observed in extant non-human primates (Tomasello 1994). Yet, while early humans living in the Hunsgi and Baichbal Valleys practised imitative behaviours, indicating a relatively high level of intelligence, the consistency of the technological patterns over a long period of time indicates a relatively slow pace of innovation and change over hundreds, if not thousands, of generations.

Material transport

African studies indicate that hominins typically transported bifaces within 5 km of sources (e.g. Hay 1976; Clark and Kurishina 1979; Noll 2000; Noll and Petraglia 2003). Although most transport distances were low in Africa, after 1.2 myr maximum raw material transfer distances increase to between 15 and 100 km, which has been related to the emergence of a 'protolanguage', allowing members of a group to pool information about the landscape (Marwick 2003). On the whole, the Hunsgi-Baichbal data support the African evidence for relatively low transport distances (Figure 12.6). In an analysis of ten Acheulean sites, nine have transport distances no greater than 3.5 km, whereas the Late Acheulean site of Mudnur X shows a maximum distance of

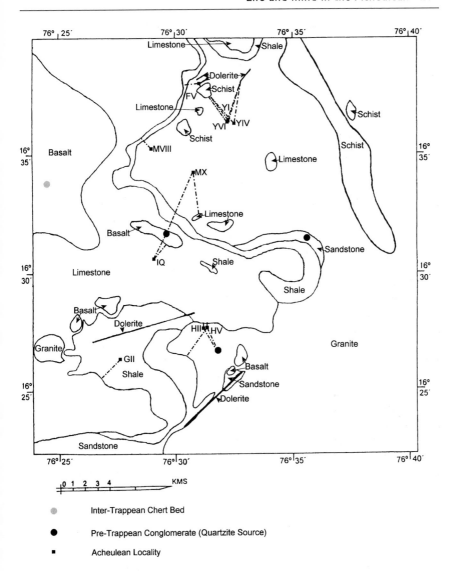

Figure 12.6 Raw material distances by site. Note that the majority of raw materials are
transported 1–2 km and usually no more than 5 km.

5 km (with a mean distance of 3.5 km). The large majority of objects occur to
within 1–2 km of available raw materials. Interestingly, there is variation in
mean average distance from the Isampur Quarry according to artefact type;
cores are 0.25 km, hammers are 0.3 km, and bifaces are 0.7 km from raw
material sources. This pattern indicates that cores were procured and reduced
on site, with little transport, hammers were found in close proximity to sites,
and bifaces were carried the furthest distance away.

An argument has been made that the Hunsgi-Baichbal bifaces were not significantly resharpened as they were carried over the landscape (Petraglia 2001; Noll and Petraglia 2003). Although long-distance raw material transfers increase over the course of the Lower Palaeolithic, the great majority of artefacts are discarded in close proximity to their source areas (e.g. see Féblot-Augustins 1997). In support of this trend, hominins in the Hunsgi-Baichbal Valleys appear to have transported and discarded large bifaces over relatively short distances from raw material sources. The recovery of Acheulean bifaces of a restricted size range and shape, and the observation of similar patterns in biface manufacture, transport and discard among sites of different ages imply temporal continuity in hominin design choices and behaviours. The manufacture and discard practices, together with the low transport distances, imply a relatively short-term planning depth.

Planning and flexibility

Aspects of landscape use and tool manufacture support an argument for some level of anticipatory planning and flexible behaviours in the Acheulean. Early hominins in the Hunsgi and Baichbal Valleys appear to have had a good working knowledge of their landscape as revealed by the use of a wide range of ecological zones across the basin and the selection of various stone tool resources. A range of raw material types and the use of hammerstones of different sizes and materials illustrate the ability of hominins to adjust to a diverse resource base to accommodate their technological needs. The broad use of raw materials suggests that hominins were able to produce bifaces from clasts of various sizes and shapes. Some degree of anticipation and planning was likely involved in procurement and selection of materials for specific uses. In one case, a 'cache' of nine large bifaces without accompanying material was identified at Mudnur VIII (Paddayya and Petraglia 1993). Although these limestone bifaces were not further than 1.2 km from the nearest source, their large size and clustering suggests that, at times, the Hunsgi-Baichbal hominins were deliberately gathering tools at particular locales in the landscape.

High-resolution information from the Isampur Quarry offers the best potential for generating interpretations about forethought and decision-making. As hammerstones were not available locally, hominins had to access materials from outcrops that were 1–2 km away. The selected hammers were of various sizes (125 gm to 4 kg), probably indicating that cobbles and small boulders were purposefully selected for different stages of stone tool reduction. Our stone tool experiments showed that large hammers were needed for major percussive force, often to strike off large flakes from cores, whereas smaller hammers were suited for alternate flaking to manufacture bifaces. Although quarrying efforts at Isampur may have taken advantage of naturally weathered slabs, it is also apparent that hominins sought geological beds that were still in place. Slabs were extracted from the geological outcrop through percussive flaking at natural joint surfaces, followed by prying up the detached slabs. Moreover, hominins targeted limestone beds of particular thickness for biface manufacture (Figure 12.7). The thinnest units (>40 mm) were virtually ignored, whereas medium thickness beds (40–88 mm) were heavily targeted for handaxe manufacture. The thicker units were used exclusively to obtain large side-struck flakes, typically to manufacture cleavers. Evidence indicates that the natural slabs greater than 120 mm in thickness were completely exhausted from Trench 1. Remnant and exhausted cores in Trench 1 showed that units up to 165 mm were used.

The different steps involved in the production of handaxes and cleavers suggest that two distinct biface forms were desired. The production of large flakes through an anticipatory core strategy at Isampur Quarry shows a depth of intelligence that is not often accorded to Acheulean hominins. Comparison of the Isampur evidence with the later Acheulean sites such as Kolihal Quarry and Mudnur X shows that there were shifts in manufacturing technology, which may in turn be related to cognitive changes occurring in the Acheulean. The Mudnur X bifaces show finer shaping and symmetry and the Kolihal Quarry site shows the production of carefully prepared cores for making handaxes and cleavers from flakes. The greater level of technological planning and the identification of bifaces with three-dimensional symmetry supports an

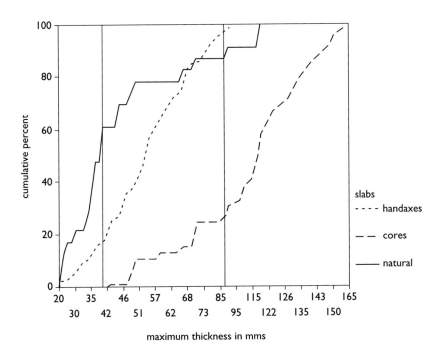

Figure 12.7 Cumulative percentages of the thickness of natural slabs and artefacts.

interpretation of evolutionary changes in spatial cognition and planning depth within the Acheulean (Wynn 1999).

Analysis of Hunsgi-Baichbal bifaces, combined with information derived from stone tool experiments, suggests that some individuals in Acheulean society probably had a proficient working knowledge of raw material attributes. Stone tool experiments indicated that some limestone beds were more difficult to work on account of their hardness and some slabs showed more natural flaws than others. Although this was the case, certain individuals skilfully produced bifaces from all units. Certain tested slabs at the Isampur Quarry were not worked any further, implying that hominins were familiar with their undesirable material properties. The experimental use of different-sized hammers to produce slab-based handaxes and side-struck flakes indicated that Hunsgi-Baichbal hominins were probably familiar with the appropriate level of force needed to successfully manufacture different tools. However, as demonstrated by the presence of broken bifaces at the quarry, hominins occasionally made mistakes, applying too much force during manufacture. In our experiments, unintentional breakage of bifaces was the result of heavy hammer blows, leading to end-shock and transverse breaks at the biface tip. In some cases, hominins appear to have rejected bifaces that were not shaped according to desired forms. Bifaces with low thickness to width ratios were apparently discarded due to the difficulty of applying alternate flaking along their edges. Observations such as these suggest a good knowledge of raw material properties, and are perhaps further indicative of a learning process in hominin biface manufacture.

Landscapes, social interactions and learning

The Acheulean record of the Hunsgi and Baichbal Valleys provides information about individual actions and small population histories that may be used to evaluate the working of the mind and social interactions. Recent studies that argue for culture in our closest living relatives (e.g. Whiten et al. 1999; van Schaik et al. 2003) are particularly relevant to the interpretation of Acheulean societies. While investigators have noted that Acheulean biface manufacture is beyond the mental abilities of apes (Wynn 1999), little information about the mind and social interactions of early hominins are offered from tool-based studies. The Acheulean evidence from the Hunsgi and Baichbal Valleys provides fertile ground to address a number of questions, including how hominins perceived each other and the material world, how individuals learned from one another, and how groups used their surroundings.

Knowing the landscape

Certain lines of evidence from the Hunsgi and Baichbal Valleys suggest that Acheulean hominins had a complex spatial memory and practised anticipatory landscape use strategies. This may not be altogether surprising given that chimpanzees show an ability to cognitively map their environment, learning about where certain food resources are located and using that knowledge to make travel decisions (e.g. Boesch and Boesch 1984; Tomasello and Call 1997). A similar knowledge of, and familiarity with, resource distributions led the Hunsgi-Baichbal hominins to visit spatially confined outcrops to procure hammerstones and then transport these tools to quarry settings at least 1–2 km away. Importing of hammers of various raw materials and sizes shows that multiple sources, in different places on the landscape, were accessed. Once tools were manufactured, they were carried short distances and discarded in specific locales, typically within 3.5 km of raw material outcrops. The concentration of sites in some places and the repeated use of particular resources, such as limestone for biface manufacture, suggests preferences on the part of Hunsgi-Baichbal hominins for established locales. Yet, these hominins did not just conform to set patterns of raw material use and travel, as witnessed by some very small transient sites and the occasional use of rarer raw materials for tool manufacture. The overall implications are that the Hunsgi-Baichbal hominins share a general mammalian ability for spatial mapping, although the anticipatory strategies and their relative flexibility demonstrate an amplification of spatial skills beyond those of living primates.

Interestingly, the short-distance raw material transfers from southern India contrasts with the post-cranial anatomy of Early and Middle Pleistocene hominins, which indicates adaptation for long-distance, high-endurance locomotion (e.g. Ruff 1991; Walker and Leakey 1993). Taken together, the lithic and anatomical sources of evidence imply either that Acheulean hominins in southern India had small home ranges and only used locally available raw materials, or that they had larger home ranges but did not transport bifaces long distances. If small home ranges were a common behavioural pattern, then the anatomy of Acheulean hominins contradicts the artefact distribution evidence. While maximum raw material transfers in the Lower Palaeolithic was 15 km between 1.6 and 1.2 myr ago, and perhaps up to 100 km after 1.2 myr, these are rare events, with the large majority (up to 98 per cent) of the artefacts falling to within 4 km of sources (e.g. Féblot-Augustins 1997). It appears that, at times, individuals carried some artefacts across the landscape as part of territorial wanderings, or that particular objects were discarded and picked up and transported more than once. On the whole, artefact transport ranges indicate that social life and bonds were typically group-oriented and local, i.e. that the great majority of social activities and resource tasks took place in a relatively small area.

Two is company

The evidence for stone tool clusters in Trench 1 of the Isampur Quarry implies that reduction activities were to some degree structured. The production of dense accumulations of tool debris in Trench 1 is unlikely to be the product of the actions of a single individual due to the energetic demands involved in making so many tools and the length of time that would have been required to produce such a high artefact density. Rather, the artefact distributions suggest that tool manufacture was carried out by different individuals, allowing for the personal space of others. The discrimination of clusters reveals that hominins spatially partitioned their labour into primary reduction areas where heavy percussive force was used and secondary reduction areas where bifaces were manufactured.

The Hunsgi-Baichbal evidence also suggests that co-operative behaviours were involved in producing Acheulean technology. As demonstrated through stone tool experiments and observations of modern limestone quarrying practices, the lifting and breaking of large bedrock slabs in the Isampur Quarry was more probably achieved through the efforts of two or more individuals working together. Indeed, the flaking process of repeatedly turning over large slabs (sometimes <1 m in size) for alternate flaking is best achieved (and less energy demanding) when two individuals are engaged in the activity. During stone tool experiments, it was found that two individuals were usually needed to hold large slabs in place to steady the pieces prior to heavy striking for production of large side-struck flakes. Moreover, the import of numerous and/or a few heavy hammerstones to quarries may be most efficient when more than one individual is engaged in this behaviour. These various lines of evidence demonstrate that individuals may have been working together to attain specific goals, suggesting that Acheulean hominins co-operated with others in carrying out tasks. Various lines of evidence suggest that individuals were able to communicate and co-ordinate their activities.

Learning from others

The Isampur Quarry provides a context for modelling how individual learning was achieved in the Acheulean. Although valuable insights are offered by examining chimpanzee tool use and modern human quarrying behaviour, the mental, social and ontological development of tool use in these populations does not provide a suitable analogy for understanding Acheulean contexts. Anatomical and metabolic studies suggest that members of the genus *Homo* probably possessed their own life-cycle patterns and physical capacities (e.g. McHenry 1994; Bogin 1997). A preliminary model that considers learning, tool manufacture and use, and life history in later *Homo erectus* populations is shown in Table 12.3.

The common manufacture of certain tool forms in the Acheulean argues for a learned and socially transmitted strategy. Learned information was apparently repeatedly transmitted by hominins as shown by the application of distinct procedural rules in Acheulean tool making, from the procurement of raw material to the achievement of an end-product (Belfer-Cohen and Goren-Inbar

Table 12.3 Preliminary model of stone tool manufacture and the life history of early humans

Life stage (age)	Stone tool behaviour	Tool use and approximate age (in years)
Infancy (birth to 3)	Stone handling stimulus	Begins 1 to 2 years
Childhood (4–6)	Stone handling stimulus, banging, throwing of small clasts	Throughout period
Juvenile (7–11)	Mimicking of stone tool manufacture	7 to 9 years
	Imitation of biface manufacture	10 to 11 years
Adolescent (12–14)	Proficient manufacture of bifaces on slabs	Throughout period, dexterity fully developed
Adult (15 onwards)	Full proficiency in the range of biface manufacture including production of side-struck flakes	By 15 years full range of dexterity and strength
	Teaching (?)	Particular adults most skilled and proficient
Mean age of death		~35 years

Source: Bogin 1997: Figure 12.

Note
Life history stages based on later *Homo erectus*, with adult brain sizes up to 1000 cm^3.

1994; Schick 1994). The Hunsgi-Baichbal evidence is in agreement with such studies, showing a series of manufacturing procedures, without much evidence for innovation in tool forms. Various lines of evidence from Isampur Quarry converge to suggest that tool-making was a learned strategy that required imitation of tool-making procedures.

In considering social learning transmission in Pleistocene hominins, life history estimates in early human populations (Bogin and Smith 1996; Bogin 1997) are important to assess since demographic aspects of social learning would differ from those of modern humans. The appearance of *Homo erectus* is marked by anatomical shifts that suggest increased longevity and delayed maturity. Given that offspring learn from their mothers in chimpanzee societies (McGrew 1992; Boesch and Boesch-Achermann 2000), it is possible that the first tool-handling and use experiences in Acheulean society occurred in the context of mother–infant and mother–juvenile care. As male hominins were larger (60 kg) and presumably somewhat stronger than smaller females (55 kg) in late *Homo erectus* populations (McHenry 1994), sexual dimorphism may have played a role in structuring tool-making practices. Male and female hominins accessing the Isampur Quarry were probably equally capable of manufacturing bifaces from slabs and retouching large flakes after they were struck from cores. Yet, certain types of stone tool reduction were likely to have been carried out mostly by adult males, as males likely possessed the *combined* manual strength, co-ordination and dexterity to consistently and commonly produce large side-struck flakes. The presence of some longer-living individuals in *Homo erectus* society, and the provisioning of children by other care-givers within the group (see, e.g., O'Connell *et al.* 1999; Key 2000), may have led to increased co-operation between individuals and contributed to longer-term transmission of learning between adults and apprentices. In taking a longer lifespan into account, the full range of proficient stone tool manufacturing abilities would probably not have taken place until adulthood, when full strength and dexterity were achieved. Although it cannot be inferred whether elder members of the population were actively teaching tool manufacture, juveniles and adolescents were probably observing and learning these skills as stone tool procedures were passed down through the generations. Study of modern stone-knappers (e.g. Roux *et al.* 1995; Stout 2002), and our own informal study of children in present-day stone quarries and groundstone tool workshops, shows that interpersonal observation in quarries is common, and that learning takes place by watching skilled workers. Juveniles imitate adults in making groundstone tools, but proficiency in tool manufacture does not occur until sub-adulthood to adulthood stages, when adequate skill, strength and dexterity have been developed. In light of the life history characteristics of Pleistocene hominins, generic technologies would be likely to offer a selective advantage, as any change in technology would be a risky strategy to undertake in the context of shorter lifespans and faster social group turnover. Such generic technology in Acheulean society certainly leaves room for differences between individuals in their tool-making abilities, and it is probable that certain individuals had superior talent in successfully manufacturing tool forms and in producing more symmetrical forms.

The archaeological evidence from the Hunsgi and Baichbal Valleys implies that hominins probably used various means of communication to conduct tasks. Previous studies have inferred that Pleistocene hominins communicated through vocalisations and not by verbal language (Aiello 1996; Mithen 1996a), implying that hominins may have passed learned technology via demonstration (e.g. Schick 1994; Toth and Schick 1993). In engaging in stone tool reduction experiments at Isampur it was found that demonstrative gestures are adequate to co-operatively perform certain task behaviours, including the procurement of appropriate-sized slabs and assistance in bedrock reduction. Yet, as suggested earlier, if Acheulean hominins acted on the landscape in ways that entailed group fission and fusion, some level of communication beyond long-distance calling to nearby individuals would seem to be required. The procurement of hammerstones was likely a task-oriented sequence that would have required only a few individuals to split from a main group. The 1–2 km distance between contemporaneously visited sites is out of reach of acoustic calls, hence some pre-planned group arrangements would likely have been needed. Group fission and delayed group coalescence would be most efficiently performed with the aid of vocalised strategies, and perhaps even some form of rudimentary verbalisation.

Discussion

The Acheulean may best be described as a technology that shows variation on a prevailing theme. After hominins dispersed from Africa, and into Europe and western Asia, the Acheulean technology did not disappear quickly, implying that social transmission and learning of skills were strongly maintained (Toth and Schick 1993). The South Asian evidence supports this view, indicating a widespread Acheulean technology with no break in social transmission and learning. It is proposed that a propensity for imitation was the basis for homogeneity in technological practices. The maintenance of this technology over long time periods demonstrates that hominins were quite successful in adapting to ecological diversity and pressures. Yet, as demonstrated in the Hunsgi and Baichbal Valleys, the behaviour of hominins creating Acheulean tools was also flexible enough to adapt to areas with different ecological settings and resource bases. The nature of this long-term but flexible technology is enigmatic, contrasting with both the significant divergences in technology that are witnessed in Late Pleistocene populations and the tool-using behaviours evidenced in modern primates, which have more idiosyncratic population differences. In contemplating the lives of Early and Middle Pleistocene hominins, we are of course investigating humans that are unlike current peoples and primates, hence we are dealing with an animal whose biological and cultural make-up is without any modern parallels.

The hominins manufacturing Acheulean technology in the Hunsgi and Baichbal Valleys presumably have encephalisation quotients that are half to three-quarters the size of those of modern humans. It may be assumed that some of the interpreted behaviours, particularly the regularised stone tool manufacturing techniques and the high discard rates of bifaces over short distances, were in some way conditioned by mental processes, particularly the reduced (relative to modern humans) ability to engage in long-term, future planning. Yet, the degree to which hominins in the Hunsgi and Baichbal Valleys could plan their technological requirements, producing particular forms including those from prepared cores, suggests a degree of forethought and decision-making that is usually only accorded to Middle Palaeolithic hominins. The Hunsgi-Baichbal evidence supports the use of prepared core technologies by the middle to late stages of the Acheulean, as also documented in other areas of India and in other regions (e.g. Rolland 1995; DeBono and Goren-Inbar 2001; White and Ashton 2003; Petraglia et al. 2003). If the date of 1.2 myr at Isampur is validated, greater cognitive depth must be accorded to early hominins than is normally the case.

The behavioural flexibility and enhanced cognitive skills of Hunsgi-Baichbal hominins suggest that there is more plasticity in the cognitive domains of early humans than has been accorded by some researchers (e.g. Mithen 1996b). Although cognitive domains may be present in early humans as part of the selection for larger brains in human evolution, the Hunsgi-Baichbal evidence suggests that the mind was advanced enough to allow an increased level of flexibility in technology and landscape use by the Middle Pleistocene. A greater time depth in forethought abilities would support a more gradual assembly in cognition and behaviour, in opposition to models that argue for an Upper Pleistocene 'explosion' of neurobiology and culture (e.g. Mithen 1996b; Klein 1999). While we would argue for a higher level of cognitive skills and more complex social behaviours in Acheulean populations than are typically argued for, our evidence leads us to believe that individuals often conformed to cultural rules and they did not actively creative and manipulate their social world in new and different ways. Although social and ecological factors have been implicated in explaining brain expansion and increasing intelligence in primates (e.g. Reader and Laland 2002; Dunbar 2003), the Hunsgi-Baichbal analysis shows that such processes may be interwoven and intimately related, both acting as a basis for learning and problem solving.

Although we have had some success at teasing out individual actions, our impression is that we can not readily or easily discern individual creativity from the Hunsgi-Baichbal evidence. This may be because the symbolic capacity of these hominins is too weak to signify the mind of a particular individual or a particular group of individuals. However, what the Hunsgi-Baichbal evidence does show us is that the individual mind must be viewed in a social context. As mental representations, bifaces were constructed through imitative social interactions. The evidence for a learning process in biface manufacture implies that the individual mind is inadequate as the smallest heritable unit of mental variation, as the individual mind changes within a lifetime. We would therefore argue that the most productive method of analysis would be to consider the social interaction as the smallest unit of analysis if we are interested in changes in mental developments over time.

Even though much of the Hunsgi-Baichbal evidence is relatively coarse-grained from a depositional and temporal perspective, we believe that the record has shed light on the nature of social interactions in the Acheulean. It is possible to say with some confidence that there was a propensity for imitation among Acheulean hominins, unknown among extant non-human primates. In true imitation, it is recognised by the observer that the observed has chosen a particular course of action to achieve a particular goal; therefore, the motives of the observed are understood by the observer (Meltzoff 1995). In order to co-ordinate co-operative manufacturing efforts and the fission-fusion use of the landscape over distances beyond audible range, it must have been possible for Acheulean hominins to convey specific information that could be reliably understood in their social interactions. At a minimum, mimetic communication, i.e. using the whole body including the vocal apparatus, would have been sufficient to accomplish the observed degree of mutual comprehension (e.g. Donald 1993). Without more complex syntax early humans may have lacked the ability to invent relational vocabulary for constructing complex sentences that allow humans to conceptualise a temporal depth to their activities and plan their movements. Lacking syntactical language, early humans were not able to share their knowledge in such a way that they could co-ordinate their activities in a more 'modern' time-oriented sense. The comprehension of the observed subject's motives in true imitation and the reliable prediction of response in a mimetic communication system suggest that Acheulean hominins possessed a rudimentary theory of mind.

Our effort to study individual actions and small-group behaviours has provided us with a better understanding of the lives and minds of Acheulean hominins. Most interestingly, our analysis, which was geared to study high-resolution and small-scale processes, did not lead us to reject the utility of the Acheulean as an analytical device; rather, our study reaffirmed what we know about the Acheulean, i.e. that there is similarity in biface technology that transcends time and space. Given that there is broad uniformity in technological patterns, we would argue that there is merit in the sustained use and study of the Acheulean, i.e. that this classification scheme is capturing some meaningful information about hominin cognition, socialisation and learning. At the same time, a sharpened focus on the individual and the small scale provided us with novel information sources that have not been retrieved in our previous studies. A change in perspective helped us to realise that there is more situational variability and choices being exercised in the Acheulean than is usually recognised. We therefore believe that a more sensitive reading of Acheulean technological practices and adaptations in different settings across the globe may reveal a greater range of localised responses. Perhaps the most significant outcome of our focused attention on the individual knapper and their skills was that there appears to be a greater depth of intelligence in Acheulean hominins than has heretofore been realised.

Acknowledgements

Our joint field research has been supported by grants from the Leakey Foundation, the Smithsonian Institution, the University Grants Commission (New Delhi), and Deccan College (Pune). We thank Richa Jhaldiyal for assisting us during our field and museum work, Mike Noll for carrying out the Isampur stone tool experiments, and David Redhouse for assisting us with producing Figures 12.2 and 12.3. We are grateful to Nicole Boivin, Adam Brumm, Clive Gamble and William McGrew for critically reading an earlier draft of this chapter.

Chapter 13

Individuals among palimpsest data

Fluvial landscapes in Southern England

Robert Hosfield

One important lesson is that one should be extremely wary on any generalization concerning the conduct of individuals.

(A. Beevor, *Berlin: The Downfall 1945*, 2002: xxxv)

Introduction

This chapter seeks to address a critical question: can Palaeolithic archaeologists consider the role of individual hominins in the Pleistocene, through the examination of palimpsest data sets? I will not concern myself with the question of whether individual hominins can be detected in palimpsest data sets, since in my opinion the answer here is a simple one: no, save for the odd fossil. The answer to the question of their role however, is not so simple. In addressing it, it is necessary to consider how individuals influence and contribute to wider hominin society and long-term behavioural evolution. At the same time, we also need to demonstrate which elements of evolving hominin behaviour are evident in a palimpsest record, and the different chronological scales associated with that type of archaeological data.

Mithen (1993: 393) provides a valuable distinction between specific and generic individuals. Mithen's specific individual is viewed here as a person whose presence and actions, whether tool-making or walking, can be demonstrated to have occurred at a specific time and place in the past. Following Mithen, it is proposed here that archaeology is predominantly unable to refer to or trace specific past individuals in the Palaeolithic record, although the physical residues of individual actions are occasionally recorded, as with the Boxgrove knapping scatters (Roberts and Parfitt 1999) and the Laetoli footprints (Leakey and Harris 1987). By way of contrast, Mithen also proposes that past, generic individuals may be referred to in terms of people of particular age and sex, in a range of social, economic and historic contexts. The behaviour of these generic individuals in particular situations can then be suggested on the basis of evolutionary theory and psychology. This approach therefore stresses the concept and the idea of individual action and behaviour, rather than its physical demonstration. From the perspective of the Palaeolithic and palimpsest data sets, I suggest that it is the behaviour of generic individuals with which we should be concerned, in particular their contributions to social processes (e.g. food-getting, learning, behavioural changes) that occur at a range of different timescales. Yet such approaches clash markedly with the majority of extant research. Numerous authors (e.g. Clark 1992; Mithen 1996a; White and Schreve 2000; Binford 2001; Ashton and Lewis 2002) have emphasised the group when discussing behavioural evolution and cultural change. As Mithen (1993) observed ten years ago, the focus upon groups has provided valuable models for Palaeolithic society, stressing adaptation at different time intervals. However, these models have only made limited contributions to our understanding of adaptation and change through time. Mithen concluded that our ability to identify and monitor groups and group actions is arguably worse than when the focus is placed upon individuals. He therefore stressed the extremely rare 'moments in time' and the very long timescales of millennia – the latter of which are the focus of this chapter. However, the exploration of individuals through palimpsest data requires frameworks that draw links and connections between individual action and coarse-grained patterning in the archaeological record.

This chapter presents recent research inspired by Shennan (2001) as an example of the type of connecting framework outlined above. Shennan emphasised the role of group size with respect to the processes of knowledge transmission and cultural change. His model of cultural evolution focuses upon the mechanisms involved in the transmission and change of craft traditions (e.g. stone tool production). He suggests that rates of successful technological innovation may have been correlated with population sizes and densities, from the earliest periods of hominin culture to the present:

> When cultural innovation processes take place and the results are passed on by a combination of vertical and oblique transmission, larger populations have a very major advantage over smaller ones. Quite simply, members of larger populations are on average both biologically fitter and more attractive as models for imitation, by virtue of the fact that the deleterious sampling effects present in small populations decline as population sizes increase. When populations are small, innovations which are less beneficial reproductively and less attractive to imitate are more likely to be maintained within them.
>
> (Shennan 2001: 12)

By stressing the roles of parent/offspring and child/adult links within the processes of knowledge transmission, Shennan's model highlights the premise that individual actions (in this case technological innovations and their subsequent transmission through social learning) can be detected in the archaeological record. He subsequently presents the Middle to Upper Palaeolithic transition and aspects of the accompanying changes in material culture as a supporting case study (2001: 12–15). However, the chronological resolution of the assemblages associated with the Middle to Upper Palaeolithic transition are in marked contrast to the palimpsest assemblages of the earlier Palaeolithic. The remainder of this chapter therefore presents two case studies which explore patterns in technological innovation and hominin demography (two fundamental elements of the Shennan model), and analyse the variable chronological resolution of these patterns within archaeological palimpsests. These palimpsest archaeological assemblages occur within fragmented Middle Pleistocene fluvial landscapes from Southern Britain: the Solent River (Hampshire, West Sussex and East Dorset) and the River Axe (West Dorset and East Devon).

Palimpsest archaeology

In the introduction to this volume, Gamble and Porr emphasise the frequent presence of well-preserved, high-resolution sites in the Palaeolithic archaeological record. Yet the data that form the basis of my contribution could hardly lie further away from those types of sites.

Palimpsest archaeological deposits (Isaac 1981a, 1989b; Foley 1981a, b; Stern 1993, 1994) can be described as forming through the deposition over time of artefacts and ecofacts within an episodically accreting sedimentary context. While the period of time associated with the formation of a palimpsest deposit may be known, the internal chronology of the sedimentary deposit remains unknown. Stern (1993) has usefully described the Lower Okote Member (LOM) of the Koobi Fora Formation (north-western Kenya) as the minimum archaeological-stratigraphic unit in her study area. The LOM consists of a wedge of sands, silts and tuffs that represent interlocking channel and floodplain deposits, up to 8 m in thickness, and comprises a set of time-transgressive fluvial subfacies (ibid.: 205). Although single flood-event tuffs punctuate the LOM, they outcrop over too small an area and/or contain a too negligible quantity of material remains to be used to document the differential distribution of archaeological debris across the ancient landscape. Instead, the LOM is defined by the presence of widespread, datable tuffs at its lower and upper boundaries:

> Thus the LOM is the smallest wedge of sediment, and hence the smallest unit of time, that can be used to study the distribution of archaeological debris across the ancient landscape in this portion of the Koobi Fora Formation.
>
> (Stern 1993: 205)

To continue with Stern's example, within the LOM it is impossible to demonstrate whether all the archaeology originates from a single behavioural event and/or accumulated during a single depositional episode, or whether it was produced over a time period of n years duration and/or deposited throughout the sedimentary history of the LOM. It can only be assumed therefore that the archaeology is a palimpsest which accumulated at different times, resulting in the mixing and overprinting of unassociated artefacts and ecofacts:

> Archaeological debris occurs at a number of stratigraphic levels within the LOM and in most but not all of the depositional environments represented in it. The distribution of this debris, both through the sequence and across depositional environments, is non-random. Most of it occurs in sediments representing proximal floodplain settings and lies towards the base of the LOM. This does not mean, however, that most of it was deposited at about the same time or over a relatively short span of time. The archaeological materials can only be considered contemporaneous within the boundaries of the LOM itself.
>
> (Stern 1993: 207)

Stern's discussion of the Lower Okote Member and its chronological structure provides a valuable parallel with the fragmented fluvial landscapes of Southern Britain. These landscapes consist of a series of terrace landforms, associated with major and minor river valleys, both extant (e.g. the post diversion Thames, the Wash drainage (including the Welland, Nene, Ouse and Cam and the Worcestershire/Warwickshire Avon) and extinct (e.g. the Solent River, the pre-diversion Thames, and the Bytham) (Figure 13.1)). The fluvial deposits associated with these terrace landforms (primarily coarse-grained gravels, but also including finer-grained sands, silts, clays and loams) have yielded the majority of the Middle and Lower Palaeolithic core and flake stone tools recovered in Britain.[1] These deposits accumulated through fluvial processes, including high-energy flooding and lower-energy sedimentation events, and are therefore secondary archaeological contexts. The key concern however regards the issue of absolute dating for fluvial sediments, which has resulted in considerable difficulties for the establishment of both high- and low-resolution geochronologies.

Numerous attempts have been made to establish the geochronology of fluvial terrace landforms and their associated deposits, primarily through the links between terrace formation and climatic variations (e.g. Zeuner 1958; Wymer 1968; Clayton 1977; Rose 1979; Green and McGregor 1980, 1987; Gibbard 1985; Bridgland 1994, 1995, 1996, 1998, 2000, 2001). These models have stressed climatic factors (e.g. Green and McGregor 1980, 1987; Gibbard 1985; Bridgland 1994, 1995, 1996, 1998, 2000, 2001), sea-levels and the differential response of rivers in their lower and upper reaches (e.g. Zeuner 1958). These attempts have been facilitated by the widespread acceptance of the marine isotope curve in the late 1980s (Shackleton 1987), which resulted in a major re-evaluation of the number of glacials and interglacials in the late Middle

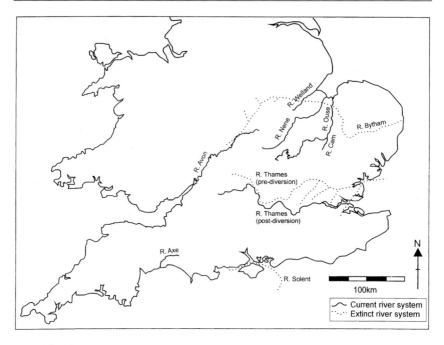

Figure 13.1 Selected river systems of Southern Britain (after Bridgland and Schreve 2001: Figure 1; Roberts *et al.* 1995: Figure 1).

Pleistocene. However, despite the archaeological value of Bridgland's climatically driven, cyclical model of terrace formation (Bridgland 1994, 1995, 1996, 1998, 2000, 2001; and Bridgland and Allen 1996), it is clear that this model only provides a coarse-resolution geochronology – in other words, terrace deposits can only be dated at the level of individual marine isotope stages, which may be greater than the Lower Okote Member in duration. Even where an aggradation event is linked to a cold/warm stage transition, the geochronological resolution is limited to tens of millennia. This coarse level of geochronological resolution also applies to models grounded in biological data, including mammal assemblage zones (Schreve 1997, 2001a, 2001b), shell amino-acid ratios (Bowen *et al.* 1989), molluscs (e.g. Keen 2001; Preece 2001) and coleoptera (e.g. Coope 2001), although Schreve (2001a) has recently suggested that mammal assemblage zones can be used to detect isotopic sub-stages.

Recent research has also highlighted the link between phases of fluvial activity (erosion and aggradation) and periods of climatic instability and transition (e.g. Rose *et al.* 1980; Vandenberghe 1993, 1995, 2002; Collins *et al.* 1996). However, all of this research has focused upon the Devensian and Lateglacial periods, for which higher-resolution geochronological and climatic data is available. Moreover, despite the high-resolution climatic records now becoming available through ice-core research (e.g. Anklin *et al*. 1993; Petit *et al*. 1999), the typically partial preservation of fluvial sequences severely restricts the potential for linking individual terrace sedimentary sequences with portions of the high-resolution, ice-core climatic record.

The partial preservation and localised erosion and reworking of fluvial terrace sequences also mirrors Stern's (1993) LOM situation in that sediments representing high-resolution events (e.g. fine-grained channel deposits) are typically not continuously preserved over large enough areas to support regional-scale sub-divisions of the terrace sediments into finer geo-chronological units. Finally, the errors of magnitude associated with optically stimulated luminescence do not enable correlation of spatially distinct sediments with either each other or the high-resolution climatic record.

In other words, and comparable to Stern's (1993) minimum archaeological-stratigraphic unit, each of the artefact-bearing fluvial terrace deposits of Southern Britain represent the smallest time unit that can be employed for analytical comparisons *between* individual sedimentary exposures. Yet within these deposits (whether coarse or fine-grained), archaeological debris (both reworked and *in situ*) can occur at a number of stratigraphic heights, and therefore cannot be assumed to have been deposited at the same time or even over a short period of time. These deposits are therefore clearly archaeological palimpsests, with the inherent problems of time-averaging and the over-printing and blurring of patterns in material culture. The following case studies investigate whether the archaeological content of these palimpsests permit the discussion of individuals and individual actions, through demographic patterns and technological change.

Fluvial landscapes and hominin demography: the Solent River

The sedimentary relics of the Solent River and its tributaries have been studied for over 150 years. Pleistocene gravels and sands occur extensively throughout the Solent Basin, overlying the bedrock at a wide range of altitudes and distributed both on- and off-shore. The first integrated interpretation of the deposits was made by Darwin-Fox (1862), who suggested the existence of a Solent River system. Darwin-Fox viewed the rivers Frome, Piddle, Stour and Avon as parts of a single river system draining west Dorset and east Hampshire. The Solent River was argued to have flowed eastwards across the land now occupied by Christchurch Bay and the East and West Solent, entering the sea at Spithead. A chalk ridge of high ground connected the Isle of Wight and the Isle of Purbeck, and formed the southern side of the ancient river valley. The Solent River was therefore seen as the major axial stream of the Hampshire Basin and the partial or complete existence of the system was recognised by the majority of subsequent workers (e.g. Evans 1864; Codrington 1870; Bury 1926; Hooley 1922). Since Darwin-Fox, various modified models have been

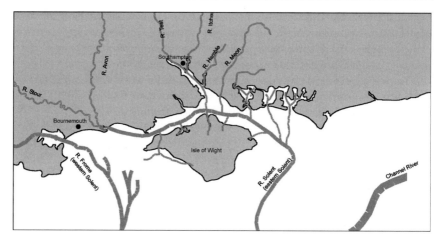

Figure 13.2 Current model of the Solent River (after Bridgland 2001: Figure 1).

proposed for a Solent River system (see Hosfield 1999 for a summary; also Velegrakis *et al*. 1999; Bridgland 2001; Dix 2001). Recently however, the view of the Solent River as a single system has been challenged, most notably by Velegrakis (1994; Velegrakis *et al*. 1999), whose work in Christchurch Bay and Poole Harbour has suggested that separate 'eastern' and 'western' Solent Rivers may have existed, following contrasting drainage routes to the Channel River (Figure 13.2).

Early interpretations of the Solent system sands and gravels tended to agree upon their fluviatile origin (Reid 1893; White 1915; Bury 1923). Contemporary with, and following, this debate came a series of classifications for the coarse-grained deposits: plateau and valley gravels (Reid 1898, 1902a, 1902b; White 1912, 1915, 1917, 1921); numbered gravel terraces, based upon the morphology and altitude of the deposit surfaces (e.g. Chatwin 1936; Green 1946; Everard 1954; Swanson 1970); and the twenty-five terrace levels identified by the British Geological Survey during the 1970s and 1980s in the areas between Bournemouth and Southampton (sixteen terraces) and Dorchester and Wareham (nine terraces).

The most widely currently accepted classification was undertaken by Allen and Gibbard (1993), which established a series of aggradation units on the basis of lithological characteristics, sedimentary structures and altitude from a type section. While acknowledging the limitations of this work (the problem of the Poole Harbour gap and the presence of just two pre-Flandrian organic deposits, both currently argued to be younger than 200,000 years BP), it has provided the basis for recent attempts at establishing the geochronology of the fluvial deposits (Bridgland 1996, 2001; Hosfield 1999). The most recent model proposed by Bridgland (2001) is supported here as a framework for the archaeological interpretation of these data.

Table 13.1 Proposed chronology for selected fluvial terrace units associated with the
Solent River complex

Terrace	Terrace pair	Downcutting event	MIS-assignment	Ages (kya BP)
Setley Plain	Setley Plain/		13?	478–524
	Mount Pleasant	Cooling limb	13/12 transition?	
Mount Pleasant			12?	423–478
		Warming limb	12/11 transition	
Old Milton	Old Milton/		11	362–423
	Tom's Down	Cooling limb	11/10 transition	
Tom's Down			10	339–362
		Warming limb	10/9 transition	
Taddiford Farm	Taddiford Farm/		9	303–339
	Stanswood Bay	Cooling limb	9/8 transition	
Stanswood Bay			8	245–303

Source: Bridgland 2001.

Note
MIS = marine isotope stage. 'Limb' = the cooling and warming limbs represent the cold–warm and warm–cold climatic transitions within the glacial/interglacial climatic cycles.

Although the Pennington and Lepe deposits consist of 'upper' and 'lower' gravels encompassing fine-grained organic sediments (following Bridgland's (1996) 'sandwich' model of fluvial terrace deposits), the majority of fluvial deposits associated with the Solent River complex consist of undifferentiated coarse-grained gravels. These deposits can only be classified as archaeological palimpsests (as described above), since they cannot be sub-divided on the basis of current stratigraphic understanding and absolute dating resolution, although it is likely that that fluvial sedimentation occurred episodically, in response to short-lived phases of climatic change (Rose *et al.* 1980; Vandenberghe 1993, 1995, 2002; Collins *et al.* 1996; Maddy *et al.* 2001). The minimum archaeo-logical-stratigraphic unit therefore ranges in duration between *c.* 20,000 years (the Tom's Down gravel, assigned to MIS [marine isotope stage] 10) and *c.* 60,000 years (the Stanswood Bay gravel, assigned to MIS-8), following the Bridgland model (2001; Table 13.1).

The archaeology within these palimpsest sand and gravel deposits consists of predominantly derived artefacts (based on their physical condition – Hosfield 1999), of which over 50 per cent are bifaces. These artefacts have been recovered both as individual finds and larger assemblages numbering tens and hundreds (Wessex Archaeology 1993).

The Solent River therefore provides a 'deep time' data set, of a minimum 400,000 years duration, assuming an MIS-13 age for the Setley Plain gravels (Bridgland 2001) and an MIS-4 age for the Pennington upper gravels (Nicholls 1987), sub-divided into a series of *c.* 20–60,000-year archaeological palimpsests. These palimpsests take the form of individual terrace deposits, containing derived stone tools. Yet interpretation of these palimpsest data has traditionally

Table 13.2 Lower and Middle Palaeolithic artefacts in the Hampshire Basin

Artefact type	No.	Artefact type	No.
Bifaces	8584	Miscellaneous	156
Flakes	6240	Rough-outs	106
Retouched Flakes	235	Cores	174
Scrapers	9	Cleavers	1
Levallois Flakes	113	Chopper Cores	2
Levallois Cores	14	Flaked Nodules	1
Tortoise Cores	2	Total	15637

Source: Wessex Archaeology 1993.

been restricted to the discussion of regional presence/absence and the identification of morphological patterning within a typological framework (e.g. Wymer 1968; Roe 1981, 2001). One of the key reasons for these limited approaches concerns the unsystematic 'construction' of the archaeological record during the nineteenth and twentieth centuries. The collecting activities of amateur archaeologists and antiquarians and the localised distribution of aggregates extraction and economic development resulted in a regional archaeological record that is spatially and typologically biased (Hosfield 1999). Comparisons of sub-regional data sets must therefore acknowledge the different socio-economic conditions that influenced the extant archaeological data.

Population models

Hosfield (1999) and Ashton and Lewis (2002) have recently developed new applications for palimpsest data sets, focusing upon long-term demographic patterning. These population models acknowledge both the chronological structure of the palimpsest record, and the spatial and typological bias within the data. A specific case study is presented here, to illustrate these models. The analysis utilises palimpsest data sets in the modern region of Bournemouth to model hominin population histories within the wider Solent River system (Figure 13.2). The selection of the Bournemouth region reflected its history of antiquarian fieldwork, the presence of several findspots associated with the River Stour and the now-extinct River Solent (e.g. King's Park and Queen's Park in Boscombe; Bury 1923; Calkin and Green 1949; Wessex Archaeology 1993), the recent mapping of the terraces by Allen (1991) and Gibbard and Allen (1993), and the recent publication of a relatively robust geochronological model (Bridgland 2001).

As with the Middle Thames area of Ashton and Lewis (2002), the majority of artefacts from the Bournemouth area were collected by individuals rather than systematically excavated. In light of this rather unsystematic sampling history, a restricted study area was preferable, as it minimised the potential bias that could be introduced through localised collecting (Ashton and

Lewis 2002: 388). These individual antiquarians included C.H.O. Curtis of Bournemouth, who collected artefacts from Barton during the late nineteenth century, while J. Druitt collected artefacts from his home town of Bournemouth in the late nineteenth and early twentieth centuries (Hosfield 1999: Table 3.13). The work of A. H. Stevens, Dr H. P. Blackmore and Albert Way (and his son Norman) has also been documented (Wessex Archaeology 1993: 123).

Ashton and Lewis (2002) dealt with the problem of selective artefact collection (e.g. the sporadic collecting of flakes and cores), by utilising the numbers of bifaces, Levallois flakes and cores as a proxy for artefact discard rates and population. In my model, bifaces alone were utilised as a proxy, since the terrace deposits analysed were laid down prior to the first recognition of Levallois technique in the British Palaeolithic during marine isotope stage 8 (Bridgland 1996). Three terrace units were selected: the Setley Plain (stratotype SZ 305994: 42m), Old Milton (stratotype SZ 242929: 31m), and Taddiford Farm (SZ 259924: 26m) gravels (Allen and Gibbard 1993). The Mount Pleasant (stratotype SZ 296981: 36m) and Tom's Down (stratotype SU 450016: 28m) gravels (which stratigraphically lie between the other three terrace units) were excluded from this analysis as they are not preserved in the Bournemouth study area. Following the methodology of Ashton and Lewis (2002) therefore, an index of population density was constructed for the Setley Plain, Old Milton and Taddiford Farm terrace units.

The results were generated from the sites and artefact data presented in the Southern Rivers Palaeolithic Project (Wessex Archaeology 1993), and the methodology follows that of Ashton and Lewis (2002). The basic density values were initially adjusted to account for the differential time spans associated with the formation of each gravel unit, although it is recognised that gravel accumulation would not have been continuous during those periods. These densities were also recalculated to account for local variations in urbanisation, based on the Ordnance Survey 1" mapping, and quarrying, derived from the Southern Rivers Palaeolithic Project mapping (Wessex Archaeology 1993). The plots all indicate the same general pattern, however, with relatively small numbers of artefacts associated with the Setley Plain and Old Milton gravel, and relatively large quantities of material in the Taddiford Farm gravel. It is of course documented that much older artefacts can be reworked into younger and lower terrace aggradations. The observed pattern (low densities in the two oldest deposits and high densities in the youngest deposit) may therefore be partially exaggerated as a result of reworking. Nonetheless, the marked contrasts in densities between the three terrace units suggest that there is a genuine pattern, with a relatively dense phase (or phases) of artefact production and discard during the period associated with the deposition of the Taddiford Farm gravels (MIS-9).

Following Ashton and Lewis (2002), this model adopts artefact densities as a proxy for population sizes. The data therefore suggests relatively small populations during MIS-13 and MIS-11, followed by a significant increase in

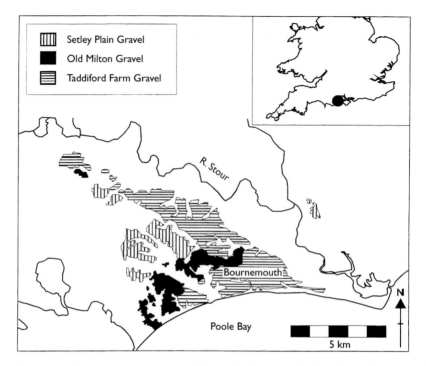

Figure 13.3 Distribution of the Setley Plain, Old Milton and Taddiford Farm Gravels in the Bournemouth area (after Allen and Gibbard 1993).

population during MIS-9, with all of these data relating to the area of the Solent River/River Stour confluence. The Shennan model (2001) would suggest that these population increases may be associated with successful technological innovation, and the first occurrence of Levallois technology in the deposits of the Solent River is associated with the MIS-9 Taddiford Farm gravels (Wessex Archaeology 1993; Bridgland 1996; Hosfield 1999). The link is not one of cause and effect between technological innovation and population increase, and it is stressed that these data alone do not explain the cause(s) of the apparent population increase. However, the larger populations present during MIS-9 may have provided the social framework and larger group sizes within which technological innovations and their successful transmission flourished. At the same time, Bridgland (1994, 1996) has demonstrated that the first appearance of Levallois technology during late MIS-9 and early MIS-8 is a robust pattern, occurring throughout the River Thames system and apparently in the Solent River system as well.[2] It might therefore be expected that a similar demographic pattern (a high peak during late MIS-9/early MIS-8) would occur in both the Solent River and Thames systems. Yet Ashton and Lewis (2002) have demonstrated that the population signature for the Middle Thames decreased markedly from MIS-11 onwards.

Table 13.3 Index of population variation in the Solent River/River Stour region during the late Middle Pleistocene

Terrace unit	MIS stage (after Bridgland 2001)	MIS duration	No. of bifaces	Terrace area (km²)	Biface density/km²	Biface density/ 100,000 years	Urban expansion until 1993 (km²)	Biface density over area of urban growth/ 100,000 years	Quarrying until 1993 (km²)	Biface density over area of quarrying/ 100,000 years
Setley Plain Gravel	13	50,000	14	3.97	3.53	7.06	3.97	7.06	0.02	1,400.00
Old Milton Gravel	11	63,000	13	5.62	2.31	3.67	5.57	3.70	0.04	515.87
Taddiford Farm Gravel	9	33,000	817	17.30	47.23	143.12	15.61	158.60	0.23	10,764.16

Overall therefore, the demographic patterns in the Solent River are interesting and may reflect trends in knowledge transmission and technological innovation. This is based on the apparent association between a notable peak in the demographic data during MIS-9 and the first appearance of Levallois technology, which has long been recognised as a highly significant technological change during the pre-Upper Palaeolithic of north-western Europe (e.g. Roe 1981). Following the Shennan (2001) model, it is suggested that the Levallois technological innovation was highly successful during MIS-9, and that its widespread adoption during this period is a reflection of the relatively large populations (and therefore efficient knowledge transmission mechanisms) of the time. It is noted that this model permits the possibility of numerous Levallois-type technological innovations prior to MIS-9, which were unsuccessful and short-lived as a result of small populations and therefore inefficient transmission mechanisms.

Yet it is clear that further testing of regional and sub-regional patterns in hominin demography (utilising artefact density as a proxy) are necessary. Moreover, this approach must consider three cautionary notes. First, improved understanding and modelling of vertical artefact derivation from older to younger terrace deposits is required, in order to improve the robusticity of these approaches. Second, the approach assumes that biface 'function' or 'functions' were consistent over long periods of Pleistocene time and/or that the frequency of biface production remained stable, irrespective of 'function'. This is possible, but recent evidence for biface use in butchery (Pitts and Roberts 1997) and wood-working (Dominguez-Rodrigo et al. 2001), use-wear studies and experimental archaeology (Keeley 1980; Jones 1980, 1981; Schick and Toth 1993; Pitts and Roberts 1997), variable patterns of immediate discard and reuse (Pitts and Roberts 1997) and social theories of biface use (Kohn and Mithen 1999; Gamble 1999) all suggest that the assumption may be an over-simplification. Third, the geochronological models for the Solent River lack absolute dates and are primarily based on the Bridgland (2001) model of terrace formation and the use of a diagnostic industry as a chronological marker. While the absence of biological data and biostratigraphical markers is a persistent problem (due to soil and sediment chemistry in the Solent River region), current developments in optically stimulated luminescence dating may result in more robust models in the near future.

I have shown therefore that regional palimpsest data sets (as represented by the fluvial deposits and derived artefact assemblages of the Solent River) can be employed to model hominin demography. Yet where does that leave us with respect to the individual's contribution to social processes? We are obviously dealing with generic rather than specific individuals, but testable mechanisms such as that of Shennan (2001) provide a framework through which to highlight the role of the generic individual. In linking population sizes and successful technological innovation, Shennan stresses the social processes of behavioural (tool-making) change and learning. Long-term fluctuations in demographic data can therefore be tracked and tested against the material record, potentially supporting propositions of changing social organisation and generic individual action. For example, the larger populations of the Solent River landscape in MIS-9 may be associated with distinctive social structures in which adults and children were involved in both parent/offspring- and adult/child-based processes of social learning and knowledge transmission.

Yet in using artefacts as a population proxy, the model presented above ignores a considerable body of potential information contained with the stone tool record that can be related to hominin behaviour and evolution. Unfortunately, the coarse resolution of regional and sub-regional terrace units dictates that only major technological innovations (such as the appearance of Levallois technique) can be modelled through long-term patterns in hominin demography. Finer-scale trends, such as the transitions from Clactonian to Acheulean technology within MIS-11 and MIS-9 (White and Schreve 2000) are more difficult to model with regional palimpsest data sets, since the derived artefacts within the terrace deposits cannot currently be divided between the earlier and later phases of the MIS-stages. Yet at the scale of individual palimpsest deposits, it may be possible to model the impact of individuals through high-resolution patterns of technological change. These approaches are explored in the following case study.

Fluvial landscapes: the River Axe

Although the Palaeolithic archaeology of south-west Britain is more renowned for its cave sites of Kent's Cavern (Campbell and Sampson 1971; Straw 1995, 1996) and Brixham Cave (Wymer 1999), the Middle Pleistocene fluvial deposits and associated lithic assemblage at Broom in the River Axe valley (Figure 13.1; Salter 1899, 1906; Ussher 1906; Woodward 1911; Reid Moir 1936; Green 1947; Green 1974, 1988; Stephens 1970a, 1970b, 1974, 1977; Shakesby and Stephens 1984; Campbell 1988; Marshall 2001) represent the most significant 'open site' in this region. The site is explored within this chapter as the structure of the fluvial sediments and the archaeology at Broom offer an opportunity to search for traces of individuals, as represented by long-term technological innovation (after Shennan 2001) and/or the short-term imposition of standardisation with respect to stone tool production.

The Broom 'site' was exposed during the commercial extraction of aggregates between the late nineteenth and mid twentieth centuries, in three pits (the Railway Ballast Pit, Pratt's Old Pit and Pratt's New Pit). Approximately 1,800 artefacts were collected from these pits, of which the majority are bifaces, predominantly knapped from chert with a small number of flint examples. The majority of the assemblage shows evidence of fluvial modification and transportation, although the degree of damage suggests that the artefacts were probably moved over hundreds rather than thousands of metres. It is stressed however that the assessment of fluvial modification and transportation of chert artefacts is complicated by the quality of the raw material and the focus of previous authors (e.g. Wymer 1968; Shackley 1974, 1975; Harding *et al.* 1987) upon flint artefacts in their investigations of stone tool movement in fluvial systems.

The fluvial sediments at Broom consist of at least 15 m of sands, gravels, silts and clays. These deposits have been traditionally divided into a tripartite sequence of lower gravels, the 'middle beds' (a mixture of gravels, sands, silts and clays), and upper gravels (Reid Moir 1936; Shakesby and Stephens 1984; Green 1988). Recent geomorphological research (e.g. Vandenberghe 1995, 2002; Maddy *et al.* 2001) has highlighted the apparent relationship between periods of fluvial activity (channel erosion and sedimentary aggradation) and periods of climatic instability. These phases appear to represent relatively short periods of the Middle Pleistocene climatic cycle, and are separated by long periods of relative quiescence and limited fluvial activity. The application of optically stimulated luminescence dating at Broom (Hosfield *et al.* in preparation) has indicated that the Broom sedimentary sequence may represent *at least* 20,000 years from top to bottom, and possibly rather more, up to 50,000–60,000 years. In this respect, the Broom terrace sediments represent a classic example of a relatively coarse minimum archaeological-stratigraphic unit and an archaeological palimpsest (Stern 1993). At a regional scale of analysis it is not possible to correlate units *within* the Broom sequence with deposits at other locations, since the absolute internal chronology of the deposits is unknown.

However, at the analytical scale of single exposures (in this case the deposits at Broom), it is possible to compare the three internal units, as their stratigraphical sequence can be demonstrated (Figure 13.4). Moreover, by adopting the current models of sporadic and episodic fluvial activity (e.g. Vandenberghe 1995, 2002; Maddy *et al.* 2001), it is suggested that the three sedimentary units (upper gravels, middle beds and lower gravels) at Broom are separated by significant periods of time. By extension, it is argued that the archaeology within these sedimentary units is also separated by significant time periods, while the accumulation of their encompassing sediments was a relatively rapid phenomena. It was therefore proposed that the three sedimentary units could form the framework for a higher-resolution examination of technological stability/change, based upon the archaeological content of each unit. It is stressed that the individual archaeological and sedimentary units are still archaeological palimpsests, since the distribution of the archaeological debris within each unit is unknown and cannot be assumed to have been deposited at a single moment.

Defining the archaeological content of each of the sedimentary units was based upon the archive of C. E. Bean (Green 1988), who documented the collection of over 1,000 stone tools from Pratt's Old Pit during the 1930s and early 1940s, and recorded valuable information concerning the stratigraphic provenance of many of the artefacts. Both Green (1988) and the current author

(Hosfield and Chambers 2003) have since divided the Bean collection, where possible, into stratigraphic units that were defined by the location of Bean's site datum and first floor level (Figure 13.5). The current stratigraphic sub-division of the assemblage identified three sub-samples, which were associated with the three major sedimentary units at Broom:

1   'Above datum' sample (20 bifaces) – associated with the Broom 'upper gravels'.
2   'Datum' sample (62 bifaces) – associated with the Broom 'middle beds'.
3   'Below datum' sample (34 bifaces) – associated with the Broom 'lower gravels'.

The structure of the sediments and archaeology at Broom therefore offer an opportunity to explore trends in long-term technological innovation (after Shennan 2001) and/or the short-term imposition of standardisation with respect to stone tool production. This sub-division of the Broom assemblage into stratigraphic units clearly makes a number of fundamental assumptions. These are identified here but dealt with in the following discussion of the evidence:

1   That the time-averaging associated with the individual archaeological samples is not of sufficient magnitude that any evidence for technological standardisation or innovation becomes invisible.
2   That the derived and reworked lithic artefacts are broadly contemporary with the sedimentary units within which they were ultimately deposited, and that material from single behavioural episodes does not occur in different samples.
3   That the traces of individuals will be evident in lithic technology.

Biface manufacturing and standardisation

Examination of the overall biface assemblage from Broom indicated an absence of clear standardisation in the production of bifacial stone tools (Hosfield and Chambers 2003). A range of categories were recorded for the bifaces: type (using the Wymer (1968) system); raw materials; blank form; tip type; butt type; edge profiles; and size (employing a weight index). While the majority of these categories demonstrated evidence for a dominant type (e.g. cordate/ovate bifaces; medium-grained chert; irregular rounded tips; trimmed flat butts; 100–500g in weight), the accompanying range of types evident in the assemblage hinted at considerable variation in technological practice and the apparent absence of imposed standardisation upon tool-making. These patterns contrast markedly with White's (1998) documentation of distinctive pointed/ovate biface assemblages across Southern Britain, suggested to relate to the types and quality of immediately available raw materials.

Examination of the individual biface sub-samples indicated that each of the samples bore a considerable resemblance to the overall Broom assemblage. In the majority of categories the dominant types were the same, and there was a similar range of variability in biface technology and typology within each of the samples. In other words, the samples demonstrate limited inter-sample variation, but considerable intra-sample (internal) variability. These data therefore indicate little evidence for technological change over the 20,000–60,000 year period associated with the Broom sedimentary sequence. Moreover, at the higher-resolution geochronological levels associated with each of the sub-samples, there is evidence for variation in technological practice and a lack of imposed standardisation (as was suggested above for the overall assemblage).

Social learning?

Do these patterns provide a window through which we can discuss the roles of the individual? The work of Shennan (2001) is of some assistance here, since

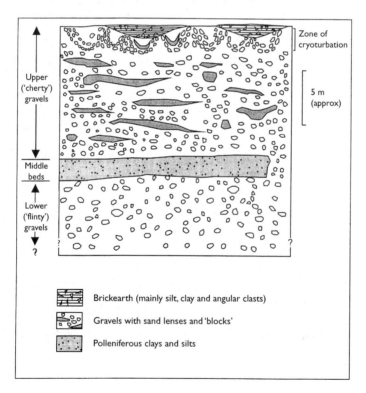

Figure 13.4 The Broom sedimentary sequence (lower 'flinty' gravels, middle beds (including polleniferous clays and silts), upper 'cherty' gravels). After Shakesby and Stephens 1984: Figure 2.

the model focuses upon technological innovation. The overall absence of long-term technological change might therefore be suggestive of small populations, within which successful innovations were relatively rare. With respect to the absence of imposed standardisation, Mithen's (1996a) model of group size, social learning and cultural traditions also provides a potentially useful framework. He proposed that in small groups the opportunities for social learning would be relatively limited. Consequently, knapping practices would be highly diverse due to the weakness or complete absence of cultural traditions (propagated through social learning). The Broom data could therefore be interpreted through this model, suggesting both small populations and the restricted involvement of individuals within social learning activities and processes.

The assumptions of this approach were identified above and can now be dealt with in more detail:

1   The magnitude of the time-averaging within the palimpsest samples. It is argued above that the deposition of the three sedimentary units (upper gravels, middle beds and lower beds) was rapid, interspersed with longer periods of relative fluvial inactivity. However, the magnitude of the time-averaging relates not only to the duration of the sedimentary events but also to the length of time over which archaeological materials were accumulating on the floodplain (prior to incorporation within the fluvial terrace sediments through entrainment, transport and deposition) since the last major sedimentary event.[3] The time interval is impossible

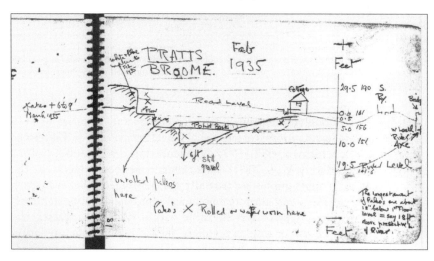

Figure 13.5 A schematic section of Pratt's Old Pit by C. E. Bean (February 1935). Note the location of the '1st floor' level and the site datum (at the road level by the cottage).

Table 13.4 Technological/typological categories present in the Broom biface assemblage

Biface type	Raw materials	Blank form
Cordate/ovate (188)	Medium-grained chert (309)	Flakes (103)
Cordate (122)	Fine-grained chert (187)	Cobble (96)
Pointed (80)	Coarse-grained chert (97)	Nodule (12)
Ovate (44)	Flint (46)	
Sub-cordate/ovate (39)	Quartz (1)	
Pointed/sub-cordate (39)		
Sub-cordate/cordate (29)		
Sub-cordate (27)		
Cleaver (13)		
Pointed/ficron (8)		
Ovate/flat-butted cordate (8)		
Ficron (8)		
and a range of other types		

Tip type[1]	Butt type	Edge profiles	Size (weight index)
Irregular rounded (274)	Cortex (126)	Straight;	Minimum (38)
Rounded (111)	Trimmed (513)	Sinuous;	Maximum (2437)
Ogee point (64)		S-twist combinations	Mean (408.33)
Lingulate point (32)			s.d. (243.33)
Basil point (29)			
Irregular pointed (27)			
Acute point (22)			
Cleaver (17)			
Pointed (9)			
Tranchet (7)			
Irregular tranchet (2)			
Rounded tranchet (1)			

Source: Hosfield and Chambers 2003.
[1] Caution is advised with respect to the interpretation of biface tips in derived assemblages, given the potential of these fragile biface elements to be damaged and/or modified during fluvial transport episodes.

to assess accurately, but probably represents several centuries or even millennia, following models of lateglacial fluvial behaviour (e.g. Cleveringa *et al.* 1988; Schirmer 1988, 1995; Vandenberghe 1995, 2002; Collins *et al.* 1996; Maddy *et al.* 2001). It is therefore acknowledged that the archaeological sub-samples are partially time-averaged. However, with respect to whether short-term technological innovation and/or standardisation is really absent or just invisible within these palimpsests, the similarity of the three samples points to the former and not the latter. If there had been distinctive, brief phases of innovation and/or standardisation, then differences between the samples might be expected (e.g. a dominance of pointed biface production in the youngest sample), yet such patterns are absent.

Table 13.5 Technological/typological categories present in the Broom biface sub-samples

	Sub-samples		
	Lower gravel	*Middle beds*	*Upper gravel*
Primary types	Cordate and cordate/ ovate bifaces	Cordate bifaces	Cordate/ovate bifaces
	Medium-grained chert	Medium-grained chert	Medium-grained chert
	Flake and cobble blanks	Flake and cobble blanks	Flake and cobble blanks
	Irregular rounded tips	Irregular rounded tips	Irregular rounded tips
	Trimmed butts	Trimmed butts	Trimmed butts
	Straight edge profiles	Straight edge profiles	Straight edge profiles
	400–600 g	200–500 g	200–500 g

Source: Hosfield and Chambers 2003.

2   Are the derived artefacts broadly contemporary with their sediments? It was indicated above that artefacts may lie upon floodplains for hundreds or thousands of years (during periods of fluvial inactivity) prior to incorporation within sediments during the next major aggradation phase. It is also argued however, that the levels of fluvial energy associated with the deposition of gravel units would have been sufficient to incorporate the majority of the extant archaeological material lying upon the floodplain and shallowly buried within near-surface sediments. Therefore, while the derived artefacts are not directly contemporary with their sediments, they do represent distinctive periods of time, perhaps dominated by fluvial quiescence, but curtailed by the deposition of a sedimentary unit.

3   Are individuals evident through lithic technology? It is worthwhile recalling that lithic technology may reflect only a small fraction of the hominin behavioural repertoire and its complexity. Moreover, the information concerning the individual in these archaeological palimpsests is severely handicapped by the absence of the specific contextual data with respect to tool use, through which innovative behavioural and technological strategies might be detected.

In summary, this case study has demonstrated that site-based palimpsest assemblages (as represented by the Broom bifaces) can be interrogated to explore mid-term (e.g. tens of millennia) patterns in tool-making and technological practice. As with the previous case study, however, can we relate these patterns to the individual? Once again we are dealing with generic individuals, and frameworks such as those provided by Shennan (2001) and Mithen (1996a) provide a means of exploring the roles of that category of individuals with respect to behavioural change and social learning. The Broom assemblage is characterised by an apparent absence of technological innovation over the mid-term and a lack of standardisation in tool-making throughout the time period represented. Following the arguments of Shennan (2001) and Mithen (1996a), these patterns can potentially be linked to small populations, which restricted social learning opportunities, both reducing the possibilities for successful and sustained innovations and producing weak or non-existent cultural traditions. Two key points are stressed however: first, that the arguments of Shennan (2001) and Mithen (1996a) are not the only ones that can be applied to these data. They are simply examples of the evolutionary theory from which the behaviour of generic individuals in particular situations can be modelled (Mithen 1993). And second, it is stressed that the interrogation of palimpsest data sets requires considerable understanding of (and the occasional assumption regarding) the geoarchaeological processes associated with the formation of the sediments and the incorporation of the archaeological materials.

Conclusion: seeking individuals

This chapter began by addressing two questions: how do individuals influence wider hominin society and behavioural evolution; and which elements of evolving hominin behaviour are evident in a palimpsest record? The manner in which individuals influence larger-scale social units and processes has received relatively little attention with respect to hunter-gatherer communities, where the focus has traditionally been upon the group as the unit of analysis (e.g. Clark 1992; Binford 2001). This partially reflects the chronological resolution associated with much of the archaeology dating to the earlier pre-historic periods – groups rather than individuals are commonly perceived as the instinctive analytical unit when dealing with time-averaged archaeological debris (e.g. Clark 1992: 107), despite Mithen's (1993) lucid critique of this approach. The search for individuals is also undermined by our inability to reach any sort of consensus as to whether we are dealing with essentially modern humans or some other type of social hominin (e.g. contrast Gamble (1995) and Roberts (1996)). At a practical level, archaeologists have repeatedly failed to relate the occasional archaeological 'moments in time' to long-term patterns in behavioural evolution, reflecting an absence of appropriate frameworks and analytical mechanisms. Finally, the apparent uniformity of material culture prior to the Upper Palaeolithic seems to have promoted the identification of traditions (e.g. represented by typological artefact groups) over individuals (e.g. represented by unique material culture such as grave goods or decorated technology). Yet it seems to me to be inevitable that individuals, whatever their specific character, must have played key roles within the hominin social sphere, through actions ranging from day-to-day social interactions to tech-nological innovation and changes to behavioural strategies (e.g. hunting or scavenging techniques). The problem has been, and remains, how to access those actions through both high- and low-resolution archaeological debris.

In his critique of the group-based approach, Mithen (1993) rightly highlights the problem that any individual will be a member of multiple groups, ranging from nuclear families and task-specific parties to mating systems and alliance networks. This approach can be adopted with respect to palimpsest data sets, to highlight the fundamental issue: what is the role of individual hominins? The answer is that individuals will have adopted countless roles, many of which are undetectable in the archaeological record, but from an archaeological perspective all of these roles are defined by the analytical focus and scale of our enquiries. Figure 13.6 offers an exploratory framework which defines some of these analytical foci, scales of analysis and the relationships between them. For example, at the scale of the primary context site and ecological time, the focus will be on the decision-making of generic (and occasionally even specific) individuals, with respect to short-term social processes such as food procurement and movements around the local landscape. The analytical methodologies associated with the investigation of these processes are well established (e.g. Roberts and Parfitt 1999). Yet at the scale of palimpsest data (both on- and off-site) and generational/evolutionary time, our understanding of generic individual involvement within processes of learning and transmission or behavioural evolution is seriously deficient. Moreover, the available analytical methodologies are also limited in scope. At first sight this is not surprising – assessing the role of individuals in long-term behavioural evolution or mid-term patterning in tool-making is neither straightforward nor intuitive. It is perhaps easy to think about generic individuals through the notion of innovators and inventors who leave their traces in the archaeological record as material signatures – a series of technological 'Eves (or Adams!)'. But this approach is rather disingenuous, and not only because it assumes a behavioural modernity in its notion of individual inventors. It also fails to draw any links between the different analytical scales. Rather it just looks for short-term aspects of behaviour *within* the palimpsest record. By contrast, the case studies presented here have tried to exploit the unique chronological longevity of the data, and explore analytical avenues that link the short, mid- and long terms.

The example presented here for the Solent River assumed a link between population size and rates of technological innovation, and suggested a possible long-term link between population growth and the first occurrence of Levallois technique, during MIS-9 in the Solent River region. Caution is advised however, since these results contrast markedly with those of Ashton and Lewis (2002) from the Middle Thames, where population is argued to have declined from MIS-11/10 onwards. Moreover, it is extremely difficult to assess absolute population sizes or densities on the basis of artefact proxies, since current understanding of frequencies of artefact production, use and discard during the Palaeolithic is extremely limited. Finally, since Bridgland (1994) has

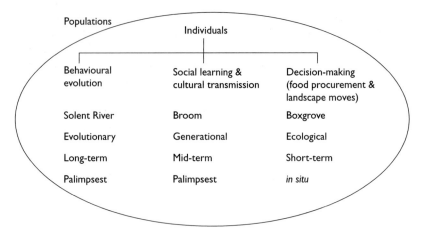

Figure 13.6 Individuals, behaviour and analytical scales – an exploratory framework.

suggested a Thames-wide MIS-9/8 age for the first appearance of Levallois, further rigorous testing of Shennan's (2001) arguments with respect to Levalloisian technology is required, through the modelling of population data across multiple river systems.

The second example explored higher-resolution patterns over the mid-term, with a view to exploring individual actions through evidence of technological change or imposed standardisation in tool-making. The Broom data however showed little evidence of either of these trends, potentially recalling Shennan's (2001) observation that:

> it appears possible that rates of successful technological innovation may have been correlated with population sizes and densities from the origins of hominin culture to the present. Is this the reason why handaxes barely changed for a million years?
>
> (Shennan 2001: 15)

However, it is stressed that evidence of short-lived technological change and imposed standardisation may be effectively 'invisible' within time-averaged deposits, and also that modern archaeologists may be failing to recognise significant typological and technological variation within lithic assemblages, and that they are actually far more heterogeneous than our classifications make them. Finally, it should also be noted that there are other archaeological palimpsests within which technological change and variability is far more evident (e.g. Swanscombe (Conway *et al.* 1996) and which could potential support the notions promoted by both Shennan (2001) and Mithen (1996a).

Finally, while it is not possible to directly identify specific individuals through their material debris within the palimpsest record – such identifications require fine-grained data sets, such as the Boxgrove knapping scatters

(Roberts and Parfitt 1999) – this is not a cause for despair. The concept of the generic individual (Mithen 1993), combined with models of mid- and long-term social processes, allows us to assess the contribution made by individuals to processes that continue over centuries and millennia. The most prominent of these models are currently concerned with issues of social learning and knowledge transmission (e.g. Shennan 2001; Mithen 1996a) and raise issues over the use of modern analogues with early hominins. However, what is not in doubt is that these approaches can be slotted into a framework that incorporates both the well-worn *in situ* short term and the palimpsest long term. I would suggest that a key need for the immediate future is to develop further models that explore processes of colonisation and demography from the perspective of individual action and engagement.

Acknowledgements

This research was funded by the Arts and Humanities Research Board (AHRB), a British Academy Postdoctoral Fellowship, and English Heritage (Aggregates Levy Sustainability Fund), all of whose support is very gratefully acknowledged. Particular thanks are expressed to Professor Clive Gamble, and also to Dr John McNabb, Dr Jennifer Heathcote and Dr Jenni Chambers for the numerous discussions regarding the research and ideas contained in this paper. All remaining errors and omissions are of course my own.

Notes

1   Primary context sites such as Boxgrove (Roberts and Parfitt 1999) and Caddington have produced the majority of waste flake and débitage material, through a combination of differential preservation conditions and the selective recovery of artefacts from secondary contexts.

2   It is stressed however that the development of Bridgland's (2001) geochronological model for the Solent River system is partially dependent on the assignment of the first apparance of Levallois technology to late MIS-9 and early MIS-8, so there is potentially something of a circular argument at play here.

3   This assumes that during major depositional phases, braided systems rework near-surface sediments (and their archaeological content) from the floodplain within a few decades (Gibbard and Lewin 2002: 189).

Chapter 14

Being modern in the Middle Stone Age

Individuals and innovation

C. Henshilwood and F. d'Errico

Introduction

Excavating and cataloguing the prehistory of western Europe was well advanced when the first spluttering attempts to explore Africa's distant past commenced. Much of this early exploration was in southern Africa. In 1929 Raymond Dart's description of the Taung child earned him derision in London. After all, and despite Darwin, the scientists of the day reasoned the origins of modern people lay in England, not that 'mysterious maw' that is Africa (Dowden 1995). At about the same time as Dart's discovery and into the 1950s the 'Stone Age' in South Africa became a passion for a few dedicated amateurs and professional archaeologists (e.g. Heese 1933; Goodwin and van Riet Lowe 1929; Jolly 1948; Malan 1955). European methodological and classificatory dogma predominated, as exemplified by the Abbé Breuil, the pope of prehistory in France (Heese n.d.). Most archaeological endeavour centred around the typology and chronological ordering of stone tools and their purported antiquity (e.g. Heese 1933; Jolly 1948). The people who had actually made these tools seemed largely forgotten or perhaps could not be recognised. In fact scant attention was paid during excavation to non-artefactual remains: unimportant bones, shells, etc. were simply tossed onto the spoilheap. This was a time for the groups-within-groups hierarchical pattern of Linnaean classification. It was not apparent to these early typologists that the classification of non-biological objects is purely arbitrary.

In the 1960s and 1970s, with a few exceptions (e.g. Singer and Wymer 1982; Klein 1972; Sampson 1974) the Middle Stone Age (<30 kyr) and earlier periods seemed an unpromising archaeological period in southern Africa. First, it was beyond the limits of radiocarbon dating; second, preservation of organics at most sites was poor and often only lithics remained. The newly fashionable study of extant hunter-gatherers and their relationship to the archaeological past in southern Africa seemed to hold much promise for interpreting archaeological sites and explaining the 'processes' that drove the lifeways of Later Stone Age (LSA) people. The 'processual' paradigm, as the name implies, was all about processes: 'within the processual view the aim is not to reach the

Indian behind the artefact but the system behind both Indian and artefact' (Flannery 1967). This view, reiterated by Binford (1982: 6), effectively sidelined the contribution of the individual to prehistory: 'the accuracy with which we are able to give meaning to the record is dependent upon our understanding of the *processes* which operated in the past to bring into being the observed patterning.' The paradigm of processual archaeology had led to descriptive empirical generalisations of archaelogical phenomena, but little understanding of why they took the form that they did.

The promise of post-processual archaeology in the 1980s was that the individual, or at least the cultural output of the individual, could be identified in the archaeological record. The basis for this theory-building, according to Whitelaw (1989: 2), is that general models could serve as a basis for building more specific theories, that then incorporated more and more elements of specific local context. Ultimately this would be brought down to the level of behaviour within a single culture or local group – so that eventually even individuals could be accommodated. In essence, he said, working out an understanding of human behaviour can be viewed as a process of working from the universal to the unique.

Beyond the comfort zone

Since the 1980s some very promising Middle Stone Age (MSA) sites in southern Africa have been subjected minutely to the archaeologists' thoughts, trowel and microscope. Documenting and discovering the sequence, economy and subsistence patterns of MSA people has produced some impressive results (e.g. Volman 1984; Singer and Wymer 1982; Deacon and Geleijnse 1988; Avery *et al.* 1997; Milo 1998; Wurz 2000). Finding human remains in MSA sites has also met with variable success (e.g. Rightmire and Deacon 1991; Singer and Wymer 1982; Avery *et al.* 1997; Henshilwood *et al.* 2001a; Grine and Henshilwood 2002). But overwhelmingly absent among these discoveries are the voices and lives of the people who made and used these things (Hall 2000). The promise of post-processualism has not become a reality in Stone Age studies in Africa. 'It is striking in the way in which archaeology – both in Africa and other parts of the world – returns repeatedly to a *comfort zone* of sequences, artefacts, plant remains, faunal assemblages and other collections of objects' (ibid., our emphasis).

Therefore it seems that the concept of the 'individual agent' as the source for economic and social life (Gamble and Porr this volume), the search for the individual in the archaeology of southern Africa has either been abandoned or ignored – but not quite. The LSA has provided more fertile ground for recognising the individual than has the MSA – mainly because our resolution of the former period is more defined and the evidence better preserved. At Dunefield Midden, an open LSA site on the western Cape coast, Parkington *et al.* (1992) recorded spatial patterning at the site, in particular around hearths.

The actions of individuals could be discerned in the way that artefacts and other debris were arranged around individual hearths and in the discard patterns associated with each hearth. Careful mapping of the Dunefield site allowed for some reconstruction (Henshilwood 1989: 164; Parkington *et al.* 1992) in the style of Glyn Isaac (1976).

On the basis of style or look-alike San rock paintings, Vinnicombe (1976: Figure 87) attempted with some sucess to detect the hand of the individual artist. Of course each depiction of an eland, shaman, etc. was painted by an individual, as was the manufacture of each handaxe or bone tool. But although we can recognise the individual in each and every artefact it is difficult to distinguish one individual from another because of an apparent sameness in the way many artefacts are produced. Bound within a cultural system it seems the individual becomes absorbed and his/her handiwork generally reflects cultural norms – seldom idiosyncracy.

Idiosyncracy is what Dowson (1988) looked for in San rock art. His concern was the cognitive contribution of individuals. During trance a shaman might experience a unique vision of the supernatural world (cf. Biesele 1978). When recounted, some of these mental images might be accepted as a novel representation of the spirit world. The vision of the individual shaman, if then depicted in rock art or experienced during trance by other shamans, may eventually become an intrinsic part of the San belief system. Expectation plays an integral part in 'out of body' experiences, hence the idiosyncratic images recalled by one shaman may eventually be experienced by other trancers. But as Dowson (1988) points out, not all idiosyncratic visions become accepted. So how then he asked would we recognise the individual? If, say, a novel vision is depicted in rock art this would leave an idiosyncratic legacy that while still a part of the San cognitive system is clearly different. Dowson (1988) accordingly looked for *sui generis* images in San rock art. Among these were a dying eland with leg extended, a human figure with zig-zag legs that terminate in fish tails and dancers juxtaposed with a bird. These are all metaphoric images associated with trance experience and yet they are unique. Each of these, he recognised, was the cognitive contribution of an individual. It must have been these individuals, and individuals like them both before and after, that shaped and crafted the complexity of human social cognition, the physical remains of which are the 'material culture' we now excavate. These are the embodied, social and active individuals (Gamble and Porr this volume) we hope to identify in this chapter.

Our brief is to provide insights into individuals from the MSA material record at Blombos Cave (BBC), South Africa; to identify not just the shadow of the individual among the 75–90 kyr stones and bones but to look for the individual agent or agents that acted as the source for social and economic life. Could the seemingly precocious assemblages in the upper MSA levels at BBC be attributed to the innovative behaviours of a few individuals? What factors in the southern Cape may have driven these developments that were later to become common at sites typically associated with modern human behaviour in the Eurasian Upper Palaeolithic sometime after 40 kyr?

Our approach in this chapter is first, to set the stage by presenting our interpretation of the role of the individual within the modern human behaviour debate and in cultural evolution. Second, we, re-examine some selected finds from the c. 75-kyr levels at BBC with the specific aim of identifying 'the individual at BBC'. In our final interpretation of the BBC individual we migrate from the observable to the unobservable, a step, 'that like religious devotion, requires a leap of faith' (Yellen 1977: 272).

Integrating the 'individual' within the 'modern' human behaviour debate

Genetic and fossil evidence suggests that humans were anatomically nearly modern in Africa by 160 kyr (e.g. Ingman et al. 2000; Cavalli-Sforza 2000; White et al. 2003). Key questions are whether anatomical and behavioural modernity developed in tandem, and what criteria, if any (Renfrew 1996), archaeologists should use to identify modern behaviour.

From both a theoretical and archaeological perspective there are diverse opinions for the definition of 'modern' human behaviour and the related terms 'fully' or 'partly'. Neanderthal populations living in Europe during OIS 3 produced a repertoire of cultural behaviours – personal ornaments, formal stone and bone tools, pigments, burials – which are generally considered as hallmarks of behavioural modernity (d'Errico et al. 1998; Zilhão and d'Errico 1999). This raises the question of whether behavioural modernity only emerged in our species or whether we have shared partially or completely these innovations with some of our ancestors (d'Errico 2003; d'Errico et al. 2003 in press).

It is probable that post c. 160 kyr the only hominid in Africa was anatomically modern H. sapiens, and behaviour changes during this period are therefore restricted to one species of hominid. Based on recently recovered evidence from African sites (e.g. Yellen et al. 1995; Vogelsang 1998; McBrearty and Brooks 2000; Henshilwood and Sealy 1997; Wurz 2000; Henshilwood et al. 2001a, 2001b; White et al. 2003; Stringer 2003) and on general theoretical grounds (cf. Chase and Dibble 1990; Gibson 1996; Renfrew 1996; Mellars 1996b; Foley and Lahr 1997) it is improbable that the MP/UP transition in Eurasia heralds the arrival of the earliest 'modern' human behaviour. As Gibson (1996) points out, it is implausible that a *sudden* change occurred in the brains of anatomically modern humans at the start of the UP, particularly in the absence of changes in external neural morphology at this time (also cf. Renfrew 1996; Foley and Lahr 1997; for a contra view cf. Klein 1995, 1999, 2000). That good evidence exists for cultural innovations in Eurasia at ~ 40 ka (e.g. Mellars 1996b) is not disputed, but clearly this scenario applies to Eurasia not to Africa. As Foley and Lahr (1997: 33) point out the UP symbolic explosion represents 'only one part of the potential for behavioural change within the modern human repertoire'. A number of authors have made the point that the development of 'modern' behaviours is likely to have been a vast and complex series of events that probably developed according to a mosaic pattern, and that the scale and repertoire of 'modern' behaviour in the Middle to Late Pleistocene is enormous (cf. Chase and Dibble 1990; Foley and Lahr 1997; Gibson 1996; Renfrew 1996; Deacon 1998; McBrearty and Brooks 2000). It has also been argued that this mosaic pattern may well include Neanderthals leading to a multiple species model for the origin of those advanced behaviours (d'Errico 2003). Neural reorganisation within the human brain over millenia, rather than as a punctuated event, may have led to periods of rapid innovation or stasis depending on selective criteria that favoured or disfavoured novelty and change. Rapid changes in MSA toolkits, for example between the MSA II and the Still Bay /Howiesons Poort (HP) in the southern Cape, may be one indicator of accumulated advances in cognitive abilities that manifest in novelty, perhaps initiated by creative individuals. Behaviour leading to the introduction of innovative ideas such as symbolic artefacts, a new subsistence skill, remodelling space within a living site or the creation of a finely worked bone point may act as a crucial marker for the recognition of 'modern' type behaviour in sites such as BBC.

An essential attribute of cognitively modern societies is their capacity to create symbolic systems and to reflect these visibly in their material culture. Recognition of distinct symbols that impart different meanings by members of a social group requires that the material representations show morphological variation that imparts to each an 'identity'. By identity we mean the collective aspect of the set of characteristics by which a symbolic item is recognisable or known. In the Christian faith for example the depiction of the cross has varied over two millennia but the various representations are recognisable as the same religious symbol. Symbols change through time because the original concepts are remodelled. Individuals play a major role in this process, either stimulating changes in the meanings of symbolic representations or experimenting with novel material expression of the same concepts. We may expect to find these mechanisms of cultural innovation operant even among early behaviourally modern societies since they too must have been able to transmit arbitrary systems of beliefs and innovations. In the archaeological record this should result in representations that are identifiable as instances of the same concept. Such representations may present morphological variability possibly attributed to the degree of freedom allowed to individuals responsible for their production, within societal norms, or to diachronic or regional changes within the symbolic tradition. Individual freedom is crucial for the evolution of a symbolic system and the degree of freedom may influence the rate of change in a system of beliefs. Innovation relates to individual freedom but if the innovator's social group does not accept the novelty it is likely to rapidly obsolesce. That same innovation may, however, if transmitted, be acceptable to and spread within other groups that adhere to the same symbolic system of beliefs. Invention of novel symbolic behaviours such as the realistic depictional representations found at Chauvet Cave or the complex musical instruments recovered at Aurignacian sites such as Geissenklösterle or Isturitz (Hahn and Münzel 1995; Lawson and d'Errico 2002) certainly implies a high degree of freedom granted to those individuals.

Towards a methodology: individuals by analogy

We have identified three different types of analogies we believe may be useful for identifying individual variation in the production of symbolic representations. Our first analogy is the identification of individually produced representations found in an archaeological context. For example, the distinct perforations and decorations (Figure 14.1) made on teeth extracted from the same animal and found at Aven des Iboussières identify the maker as one individual (d'Errico and Vanhaeren 2002).

Similarly, one individual using the same tool in a single session (Bosinski et al. 2001) made the schematic female representations on a number of rock slabs found at Gönnersdorf. Second, individual variability in the production of symbolic representations can be found within extant traditional societies. This approach assumes that analyses of symbol-bearing objects made by various individuals belonging to the same cultural system highlights personal interpretation of style within that group. Cross-cultural comparison of such variation provides an appropriate means of addressing the full range of individual variability in symbol-making and hence the identification of the prehistoric individual. An example is the study of personal style in the decoration of traditional ceramics amongst Ain Barda potters in Morocco and its application to the analysis of variation in Palaeolithic bone engravings (Ruiz Idarraga 2001). Analysis of modern artefacts used by a single person may identify unintentional signatures that may be used, when found in meaningful archaeological contexts, as a frame of reference to identify individual behaviour. A collection of pipes spotted at a dealer in a Bordeaux antique market show a specific bite pattern on the mouthpieces resulting from the unique chewing habit of the owner (Figure 14.2).

Our third analogy is provided by the analysis of modern personal variability in the experimental reproduction of past symbolic representations. This approach assumes that our ancestors shared our neuro-motor constraints and that our perceived contemporary exclusion from their cultural system does not significantly affect our capacity to mimic their technical behaviours and use modern variability to measure past individual performances (Figure 14.3). In this framework, experimental identification of diagnostic technical criteria provides information on the type of tool used, on possible changes of tools, on the chronology of the anthropogenic modifications, and on the time taken to produce them.

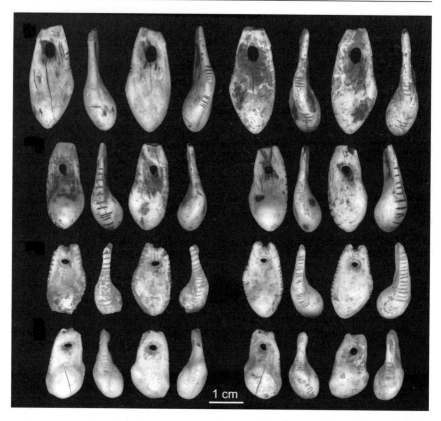

Figure 14.1 Paired red deer canines, recovered from the Aven des Iboussières multiple burials (*c.* 10 kyr). Each pair of canines was probably perforated and decorated by a single individual. Notice the similarity in the perforation size and manufacturing technique for each pair, as well as in the location, morphology and number of notches composing the decorations (modified after d'Errico and Vanhaeren 2002).

Application of these criteria to prehistoric engravings may allow, for example, identification of markings made by the same tool in a single session produced by an individual or, conversely, of engraved patterns made by different tools and possibly by different individuals. This information will help to compare technical behaviours in the production of similar symbolic representations and to evaluate the degree of freedom in each step of the production process. These technical choices, in particular when applied to a number of similar objects, may become integral to any argument on the significance of early symbolic behaviour. In a systematic process we can then generate a testable theory on the first stages of the development of this capacity. Examples of this approach are the study of Azilian and Magdalenian engravings

Figure 14.2 Collection of pipes with unique bite signature on the mouthpieces.

(d'Errico 1995; Fritz 2000) and the analysis of possible earlier symbolic representations such as the Berekhat Ram object and a fragment of engraved bone from Blombos (d'Errico and Nowell 2000; d'Errico *et al.* 2001).

Our discussion above shows, we believe, that methods to identify the individual do potentially exist. To date there has been very little formalisation and cross-application of these criteria to create an integrated body of knowledge relevant to the study of individuals and their role in past symbolic material culture. Building such testable theory in the future may identify key features or novel approaches that may highlight individual action and their creative contribution to cultural evolution.

The individual and cultural evolution

The MSA, *c.* 250 kyr to 100 kyr, in Africa is generally characterised as being a period of technological stasis where the forms and types of tools remain relatively unchanged. This 'fidelity of form' seems unaffected by environmental or ecological variation (Foley and Lahr 2003: 116). A key question is whether the archaeological record associated with anatomically modern humans (AMH) in southern Africa, or elsewhere, after *c.* 200 kyr provides evidence for a cognitive system undergoing change and, related to this question, can we make a link between phylogeny and technological modes? Space does not permit a detailed account of the archaeological evidence (see McBrearty and Brooks 2000 for a review) but it seems a variable mosaic pattern of cognitive advances associated with AMH can be detected. For example, at 160 kyr AMH in Ethiopia show evidence for deliberate treatement of the dead associated with

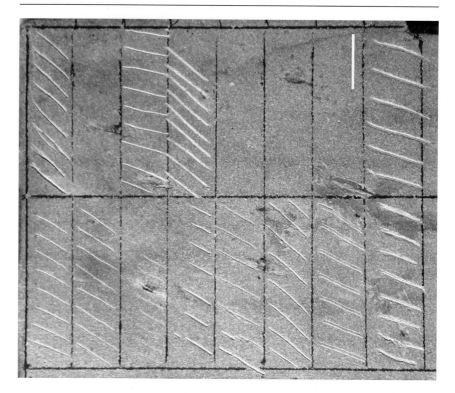

Figure 14.3 Oblique sets of lines produced by seven individuals of both sexes with a sharp flint point on a polished schist slab. A rectangle is the same size as the engraved facet on the SAM AA 8937 ochre from Blombos Cave. The objective of this experiment is to measure gestural variability in the production of the graphic elements that comprise the engraved patterns on ochre found at Blombos Cave. Scale = 5 mm.

modern type behaviour yet their lithic technology remains a mix of Achaeulean and MSA (Clark *et al.* 2003).

In the Near East at *c.* 90 kyr AMH at Skuhl and Qafzeh are associated with Mousterian technology similar to that of Neanderthals (Klein 2000). At Katanda in West Africa sophisticated bone harpoons are manufactured at *c.* 90 kyr (Yellen *et al.* 1995; Brooks *et al.* 1995). During the transition from Mode 2 to Mode 3 (Foley and Lahr 2003) there is directional change but the development of inter-assemblage variation is mainly the result of local style developing. The Still Bay dated at *c.* 75 kyr (Henshilwood *et al.* 2002; Jacobs *et al.* 2003a, 2003b) is specifically regarded by Foley and Lahr (2003: 121) as one example of local development. In southern Africa Wurz *et al.* (2003) demonstrate distinct technological changes in lithic style between the last interglacial MSA I period (*c.* 110–115 kyr) and the glacial MSA II (*c.* 94–85 kyr). They identify these MSA sub-stages as separate 'techno-traditions' and argue for volatility rather than stasis at the MSAI/II interface that can be extended to other parts of Africa. Cognitively modern behaviour, they contend, is associated with these observed changes in technological conventions at Klasies River Mouth.

We believe that the innovative technologies and social practices observed in the c. 90-kyr and later MSA levels at BBC are a part of a mosaic, a 'wind of change' across Africa that is associated with modifications to the cognitive capacities of AMH, the origins of which may date back at least 200 kyr. But what might have driven the development of innovative ideas at BBC and what selection criteria would have favoured their introduction? To address some of these questions we look, albeit briefly, to evolutionary theory, a field that is both complex and often deeply conflicting (Pearce 2002). Human culture can be minimally defined as socially transferred information that has material form stored as information in our brains.

Culture is also a shorthand for what makes humans unique (Foley and Lahr 2003: 122) although humans are not unique in possessing culture. Increasing field evidence suggests that some non-human animals maintain cultural traditions from social learning (Laland and Hoppit 2003) but the key difference between them and humans is they are unable to generate cumulative adaptation (Henrich and McElreath 2003). Local enhancement rather than imitation, in the strict sense, better describes chimp behaviourial learning where an individual will learn a trait on its own because of exposure to the conditions that allow for the trait to be acquired. By observing its mother fishing for termites a young chimp will acquire the behaviour, but this acquired 'culture' cannot be accumulated (Alvard 2003). Cultural behaviours are learned by humans via observational learning and local enhancement: they can imitate, modify and transmit the information they have learnt. The 'ratchet effect', described by Tomasello (1999) as the most distinctive characteristic of human cultural evolution, allows for the ideas and inventions of an individual to build on the ideas and inventions of others. Modifications to an artefact or a social practice made by one individual or a group of individuals may spread within the group, and then stay in place until some future individual or individuals make further modifications. The dynamics of the entire society of individuals which hosts ideas and inventions will determine which memes spread and which die (Gabora 1997: 5). The concept of individual creativity should not, however, obscure the fact that creativity is a collective affair that derives from within the group's cognitive system (see Shennan 2002). This is the point that Dowson (1988: 128) made when examining idiosyncracy or innovation in LSA rock art.

If the unique ability of humans to evolve complex cultural traditions, albeit over a very long period, allowed them to apparently penetrate a vacant 'cognitive niche' (Richerson and Boyd 1998: 15) then a crucial question concerns when the final evolutionary innovations that permitted this complexity first occurred. Another way of putting the question is when did the fully modern, culturally enhanced, human behavioural repertoire arise (cf. Alvard 2003: 141)? Richerson and Boyd (1998: 15) argue that is was 'rather late'. In their opinion the final signs of modern behaviour, recognisable in the archaeological record, occur within the last 100 kyr, although the fully developed capacity for cultural complexity was probably already in place long before this (also see Alvard 2003: 141). If the transition to behavioural modernity does date to *c.* 100 kyr it does not, in our opinion, signify the start of the 'cognitive revolution', any more than the UP in Europe was a 'revolution', as McBrearty and Brooks (2000) have elegantly argued. Rather, the route to human cultural complexity probably followed an intra-individual (Gabora 2001) selection process (not in the Darwinian sense) that resulted in many evolutionary cul-de-sacs – but it *was* a human trait that persisted. Perhaps our evolving cultural capacities depended first on some other adaptation which may have arisen for another reason entirely (Henrich and McElreath 2003: 127). For example it could have started with upright posture that freed the hands to make and carry artefacts. But there must be more to this evolutionary process, as selection would not favour the development of cognitive abilities to transmit complexities that do not yet exist – especially as observational learning requires expensive and complex cognitive machinery.

Language could not have evolved as a facilitator for a database of complex knowledge as in the absence of language the database did not yet exist (Alvard 2003: 143). Cultural complexity, like language, must have been a by-product to some other adaptation. Alvard (ibid.) suggests complex culture is an exaptation, a pre-existing characteristic that enhances the ability of a species to adapt to a change in its environment or way of living, that developed from more fundamental cognitive abilities. The emerging key hypothesis, according to Alvard (ibid.), is that the human ability to view others as the self is viewed – that is, as intentional agents – was the initial adaptation that subsequently led to the cultural complexity that characterises humanity. Whatever the cause or route it seems our species may have been the only one with a non-cognitive preadaptation necessary to permit the evolution of a capacity for complex culture (Richerson and Boyd 1998: 15).

The adaptive advantage of the acquired capacity for complex culture probably only became apparent when complex traditions began to evolve. Human adaptation to glacial environments, so-called variability selection (also see Potts 1996), may have favoured advanced cognitive abilities and social learning that allowed for rapid adjustment in variable environmental conditions (Alvard 2003: 142). Once the capacity for complex culture was in place, whether it was ecologically driven or not, the process that followed is unlikely to have been random. Unlike biology, the production of cultural novelty is never random but is generated and assimilated both strategically and contextually (Gabora 2001: 219). Innovation is a reflection of the accumulated knowledge of individuals, the circumstances they found themselves in, and the social structure in which they are embedded. Innovations will thus have a much better than chance probability of being fitter than their predecessors (see Shennan 2002; Boyd and Richerson 1985).

Case study: Blombos Cave

We use the material evidence recovered from the MSA levels at BBC to examine in more detail our methodology for studying idiosyncrasy and the individual.

Background

BBC, situated near Still Bay in the southern Cape (34025' S, 21013' E), is some 100 m from the coast and 35 m above sea level (Figure 14.4).

The site was excavated between 1991 and 2002. The upper ~ 80 cm of LSA deposits are radiocarbon dated at >2 ka (Henshilwood 1995). Sterile aeolian dune sand (~ 10–50 cm) separates the LSA from the MSA units (Henshilwood *et al.* 2001a, b). The upper MSA phase, named M1 (Figure 14.4), is typified by the presence of foliate bifacial points and conforms to the current definition for the Still Bay Industry (cf. Henshilwood *et al.* 2001a, b). Beneath the Still Bay phase is the M2 phase containing twenty-eight 'formal' bone tools (Henshilwood *et al.* 2001b). The production of the BBC bone tools results from a sequence of deliberate technical choices starting with blank selection up to the final shaping of the finished artefact. The lower MSA phase, M3, is rich in ochre and shellfish and the lithics most typical of an MSA II / Mossel Bay Industry (Henshilwood *et al.* 2001a, b).

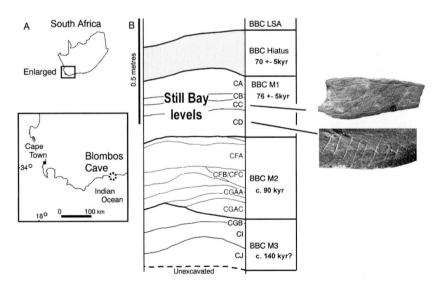

Figure 14.4 Location of Blombos Cave (A) and stratigraphy of the deposits (B). The provenance of the engraved ochres SAM AA 8937 and 8938 is indicated.

More than 2,000 pieces of ochre have been recovered from the M1 and M2 levels at BBC. Ochre was brought back to the site to be processed and used. Judging by the traces of utilisation most frequently encountered, the principal mode of use involved the production of powder. Traces of utilisation took two primary forms, grinding and scraping/incising. More than twenty crayons or crayon fragments were recovered and several stone tools have ochre thickly impregnated on their working edges.

Two engraved ochre pieces, recovered *in situ* from the M1 level, have already been described (Henshilwood *et al.* 2002). Eight others, potentially engraved, are under study. The former bear similar cross-hatched abstract designs engraved on the side of hematite slabs after their preparation by grinding. We have argued, on the basis of the complexity and similarity of the two designs as well as the consistency in the technical behaviours involved, that these two geometric motifs are very likely to be intentional symbolic images, the meaning of which is now unknown. However, we believe that to transmit this meaning would probably have relied on syntactical language because the designs are too complex for imitation alone (Henshilwood *et al.* 2002).

Dating the MSA levels

Two luminescence-based dating methods were applied to the BBC MSA layers (Henshilwood *et al.* 2002). Thermoluminescence (TL) dates were obtained for five burnt lithic samples from the MSA phase M1. The mean age for the lithic samples is 77 ± 6 kyr. To confirm the stratigraphic integrity, optically stimulated luminescence (OSL) dating was applied to the aeolian dune (BBC Hiatus) (Figure 14.4) that separates the LSA and MSA layers (cf. Henshilwood *et al.* 2002; Jacobs *et al.* 2003a, b). Multiple grain measurements using a single aliquot regenerative procedure yielded a depositional age of 69 ± 5 kyr. A second approach was to combine OSL signals from grains to generate synthetic aliquots. These provide a depositional age of 70 ± 5 kyr and confirm the antiquity of the upper MSA layers (Henshilwood *et al.* 2002; Jacobs *et al.* 2003a, b). The M2 levels have been similarly dated by the OSL method. Preliminary dates for these levels are *c.* 90 kyr (Jacobs pers. comm.). The age of the M3 levels are under investigation with a possible last interglacial date suggested (Jacobs pers. comm.).

Identifying the individual at BBC

Following from this general background we can now concentrate on identifying and extracting the individual, or individual behaviour, from the MSA material culture at BBC. We have selected two (see Henshilwood *et al.* 2002) of the ten potentially engraved ochres from the MSA to delimit individual variability in the production of abstract representations. Cross-hatched patterns are engraved

Figure 14.5 Left: view of flat side of the engraved ochre SAM AA 8937 showing facets produced by grinding and a removal scar with traces of scraping (scale = 5 mm); right: close-up view of a ground facet with sinuous engraved lines.

on the two pieces; SAM-AA 8937 (8937) comes from Layer CC and SAM-AA 8938 (8938) from Layer CD (Figures 14.4 and 14.5).

Both come from the M1 phase. We have identified a number of features related to the *chaîne opératoire* and to the type of representation that suggests these abstract designs represent a material expression of the same symbol. In each case a slab of ochre was chosen and, prior to engraving, one edge was ground to produce a rectangular level or near-level surface. This was achieved by moving the object across a coarse grindstone with a motion oblique to the main axis of the facet. The final stage of the grinding process was gentler, to homogenise the surface and reduce striations left by asperities during abrasion. A cross-hatched pattern consisting of two groups of intersecting parallel lines engraved oblique to the axis of the rectangle was made on each piece using similar motions. The engravers paid particular attention to filling the prepared space by starting and finishing each line close to the limits of the ground facet. One line bisects both designs horizontally and, on 8938, two supplementary lines, parallel to the first line, frame it.

Despite the remarkable similarities in the production of each design, behavioural differences appear that must be considered as individual interpretations in the production of the same symbol. The first difference relates to the degree of modification of the two blanks. While on the thicker slab, 8938, the ground facet and the engraving are the only anthropogenic modifications detected, on the smaller piece, 8937, both main aspects of the slab and most of its edges are shaped by grinding. On 8937 the remnants of a removal, made prior to grinding, was also intensively scraped (Figure 14.5). Importantly, another

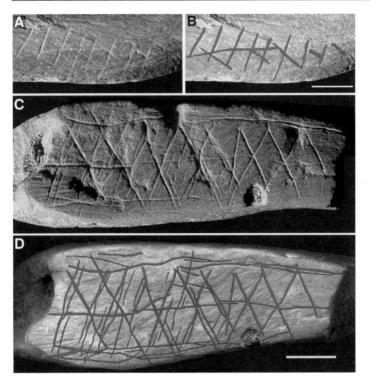

Figure 14.6 Photos and tracings of the engraved ochres from Blombos Cave. A–B: SAM AA 8937; C–D: SAM AA 8938.

engraving consisting of two sinuous, roughly parallel lines was made on a facet close to one end of the piece (Figure 14.6).

The second difference relates to the choice of raw material and its influence on the depicted design. On 8937 the ground facet appears too small to bear an engraving of the same level of complexity and with the same number of lines seen on 8938. The selection of the thinner piece of ochre (8937) by the maker can hardly be attributed to a lack of more appropriate blanks. Ochre slabs and fragments bigger than 8937, better suited to the production of a complex design, are common in the MSA layers (Henshilwood *et al.* 2001a), including Layer CC where the piece was found. Rather, the deliberate choice of a thinner blank is confirmed by the way in which the same design as that on 8938 has been accommodated within a far smaller space. The engraver of the 8937 design used a double strategy to succeed in this attempt. First, the design was miniaturised by engraving the oblique lines closer to one another than on 8938 and by making them much shorter. Second, the representation was simplified by keeping only the elements (and motions) that, to the maker, appeared crucial for recognition of the sign, namely a clearly identifiable set of oblique lines, then a second less accurate set and, finally, a rough and incomplete tracing of a middle line.

The third difference between 8937 and 8938 concerns the technical choices and skills of the two engravers. While the design on 8937 is composed of single stroke lines made with a sharp lithic point, that on 8938 was created with a more robust lithic point by alternating single stroke, double stroke and juxtaposed-joining lines. Although the 8938 design appears more elaborate, it seems the engraver was less capable or experienced. On 8938 the intersecting line sets are less parallels and not as straight as on 8937. In a number of cases grooves clearly intended to be double stroke lines on 8938 become either joining or parallel because of the engraver's inability to precisely locate the tool tip in the groove already made by the first passage of the tool or to keep it in an existing groove. The three lines framing and bisecting the oblique ones are particularly meaningful in this respect. All are composed of a juxtaposition of hardly parallel discontinous lines showing great variation in line dimension and depth. The hesitant character of the motions that have produced the two lines bounding the design might be attributed to the difficulty in engraving lines close to the facet edge. This reason cannot be applied to the line in the middle of the engraved surface, which is more certainly the expression of the engraver's ability to make continuous straight uniform lines.

Technological, stylistic and visual differences detected between these two objects are comparable, first, to that observed in symbolic representations made by a number of contemporary and historical traditional societies and second, in experimental engraved patterns of the same complexity. We believe this comparison can be made whatever the meaning and social function the engraved designs had to the makers and the group resident at BBC, and in spite of the lack of adapted analogies to demonstrate it. In other words, BBC individuals seem to adhere to their symbolic culture in a way similar to that of ethnographically known traditional societies. Transmission of socially shared representations guarantees their embodiment in the group's material culture. This transfer implies the parallel invention and transmission of traditional technical behaviours. The function of these behaviours is that of storing such representations more or less permanently, and making them visible and available for use in appropriate contexts.

Discussion: 'a leap of faith' from the data to the individual

In this chapter we have attempted to recognise the contributions of individuals at BBC, but the question remains: how great a role did the individual play in introducing innovative material culture or changing social structure in the the southern Cape or for that matter the MSA or Palaeolithic? The contribution of individuals in the evolution of cultural complexity is a topic addressed by a number of researchers (e.g. Gabora 1997, 2001; Richerson and Boyd 1998;

Pearce 2002; Alvard 2003). Most agree that the birth of a creative idea can only originate with an individual. A group of individuals may discuss the pros and cons of a new concept and each individual within the group may contribute but the final idea that is accepted by the group would have been generated by one individual, even if it came about through group input. Gabora's concept of an 'inkling' describes the action involved in individual creativity:

> An inkling, then, is a collapse on an association or relationship amongst memories or concepts that, although their distribution regions overlap, were stored there at different times, and have never before been simultaneously perturbed, and evoked in the same collapse. Though it is a reconstructed blend, something never actually experienced, it can still be said to have been evoked from memory. It's like getting a 'bite' on many fishing rods at once, and when you reel them in you get a fish that is a mixture of the characteristics of the various fish that bit.
>
> (Gabora 2000: 3)

Richerson and Boyd (1998: 14) suggest that the complexities of subsistence systems, artistic productions, languages, would have prohibited one individual from inventing them. Rather the incremental, marginal modifications of many innovators built up over many generations contributed to the complexity of human culture and behavioural modernity. They concur, however, that each increment to the human cultural repertoire, significant or not, is likely to have been the innovation of a single individual.

Innovation at Blombos Cave

If many researchers agree on the importance of the individual's role in the creation of cultural complexity then it seems pertinent to ask whether each of the innovative features observed at BBC, for example the bone points or the engraved ochre, could be the result of individual creativity? According to our argument above the answer must be yes – but whether one or all of these novel ideas occurred when the individual or individuals were resident at BBC, or even within a *c.* 90–75-kyr time frame, is more difficult to address. We suspect the likely answer is that all the innovations seen at BBC were part of a time-constrained Pan-MSA cognitive system that was prevalent, at least, within the southern Cape. For example, finely made silcrete bifacial points, almost identical to those at BBC, occur at cave sites hundreds of kilometres away in the Cederberg (Evans 1994) and on the Cape Peninsula (e.g. Schirmer 1975). However, the group or groups resident at BBC may have had some unique cultural features that were shared between areas, other groups or sites in close proximity to the site. Behavioural variability, expressed in material culture, is well described for extant hunter-gatherers (Blurton-Jones and Hawkes 1996). In almost all ethnographically known regions and historical periods humans have organised themselves into ascribed groups marked by arbitrary symbols (Henrich and McElreath 2003: 133). Could the BBC group have had ethnic markers that identified them as different from other groups and would this reflect in their material culture? Again, the answer is probably yes.

The style of making a bone tool or the particular pattern followed when inscribing a slab of ochre may have been specific to BBC residents or perhaps that area of the southern Cape. In the absence of knowing the range across which people and ideas moved, and due to the lack of excavated archaeological sites in the Cape that are reliably dated to the *c.* 90–75-kyr time period, it is difficult for us to be certain.

The timing of innovation

This leaves two further points to consider concerning innovation. First, why these innovations appeared at BBC when they did (i.e. *c.* 90–75 kyr) and second, if the model relating cultural complexity to ecological variability is correct, whether this would fit the environmental conditions present at BBC during the M1 and M2 occupations.

The timing of the first appearance of innovative material culture at BBC fits in with the scenario of cultural complexity being fully developed at about the end of the last interglacial. If cultural complexity was a phenomenon associated with advances in AMH cognitive abilities over much of Africa (see McBrearty and Brooks 2000 for further evidence) then AMH in the southern Cape are likely to have been similarly equipped, in a cognitive sense. The BBC innovations in the MSA appear to concur with similar advances in material culture in other parts of Africa (e.g. the bone harpoons at Katanda). Some are unusually novel, in particular the engraved ochre pieces. Could this relate to the ability of an individual to create an abstract concept within his/her brain and then materialise this through the constraints of an artistic medium? A distributed, content-addressable memory is a distinct trait of modern humans that allows for a reconstruction of events rather than simply the retrieval of information. Each time an item is recalled it is coloured by events that have taken place since the last recall and by current stimuli, goals and desires. Gabora (2000: 2) describes this as a reconstruction that enables the emergence of abstract concepts and is the wellspring of creativity. The creation of a mark, sign, abstract design, etc. on a material substance that retains meaning to the maker and/or others equates to information being stored outside the human brain. The advantages of having an external system for memory storage are obvious. The engraved ochre pieces from BBC, we believe, are intentional creations that had meaning to the individual maker/s and to others. The engravings were not a one-off 'doodle' or the idle 'scratching' of a bored indi-vidual but carried symbolic meaning that could be decoded, at least, by the immediate peer group of the maker/s. If only one individual at BBC possessed a mutation coding for an enlarged cognitive capacity that could now produce these abstract designs, then the expensive or complex bit of mental machinery required would serve no purpose (Richerson and Boyd 1998) unless other individuals in the group could interpret or benefit from the innovation. If they lacked the cognitive capacity for interpretation or imitation the innovation would die with the maker. We know this is not the case as engraved ochres are found in the *c.* 75-kyr levels at BBC but also in older layers. The concept of abstract design later became common, for example in European Upper Palaeolithic cave art. Distinctive innovations within a peer group or society, such as the engraved ochres at BBC or their ability to catch large fish, can often be traced to the actions of a few members, the cultural equivalent of the 'Founder Effect' in biology (Gabora 2001: 217). Subsequently, the average fitness of the initially innovative ideas gradually increases as agents modify ideas through further innovation, implement them as actions and imitate others whose ideas are fitter than their own (ibid.).

The next question is why the BBC innovations are not apparent at archaeological sites in the southern Cape after *c.* 75 kyr – did they suddenly die out at the end of the Still Bay phase? One answer may be that culture complexity and innovation is a heuristic strategy. Because of the speed with which cultural entities evolve, culturally derived needs may even change within the lifetime of a single individual (ibid.: 215). The fitness of the innovations at BBC at 75 kyr or 90 kyr may not have been selected during the following phase of the MSA in the region, the HP. Other innovations, such as the backed crescents and engravings on ostrich egg shell during the HP period instead came to the fore. The HP groups by *c.* 65 kyr had converged on novel ideas that, for them, had maximal fitness.

Cultural traditions are capable of sensitive adaptations to ecological change and local environment (Richerson and Boyd 1998). During the M1 and M2 phases it was relatively warm at BBC with moisture levels higher than during the Late Holocene (Henshilwood *et al.* 2001a). The nearby coastline provided a rich source of marine food as did the terrestrial plains, (Henshilwood and Sealy 1997; Henshilwood *et al.* 2001a) and ecological circumstances were probably conducive to population growth. Environmental conditions in the southern hemisphere deteriorated after *c.* 70 kyr (Kim *et al.* 1998; Lambeck *et al.* 2002). Both sea-levels and sea-surface temperatures on the southern Cape coast rapidly decreased after *c.* 70 kyr and by *c.* 65 kyr the shore had moved *c.* 50 km from its previous position (van Andel 1989). Population levels in the Cape at *c.* 90–75 kyr are unknown. However, the reduction in the number of archaeological sites after *c.* 60 kyr suggests a rapid decrease in population shortly after the onset of the cold Klasies Regression phase of the Last Glacial (Deacon and Deacon 1999; Klein 2000).

The climatic deterioration after the Still Bay occupation at BBC and the probable population decrease may also have contributed to the demise of the BBC innovations. Even given a capacity for complex traditions, the number of participants in a cultural system may be critical to the complexity that can be maintained (Richerson and Boyd 1998). The HP phase that followed has not produced evidence of engraved ochres, or bone tools or fishing, yet the associated lithic technology is considered precocious (Foley and Lahr 2003; Richerson and Boyd 1998). Interestingly, during the *c.* 55 kyr MSA III phase that postdates the HP period there is evidence of a lithic technology characteristic of the much earlier MSA II (*c.* 80 kyr). The innovations of the HP phase do not carry forward into this next MSA phase.

Clearly then the archaeological evidence from sites in the southern Cape tells us that the apparent behavioural precocity and/or innovative cultural material recorded in the M1 and M2 phases at BBC, and at HP sites, does not diffuse to later periods in the MSA. But successful diffusion is not necessarily a measure of cultural fitness. Evolutionary biologists have independent means of predicting which genetic variants are fit but archaeologists and anthropologists do not have this luxury when predicting cultural fitness. The evolution of complex traditions does not necessarily drive the evolution of still more sophisticated imitations or traditions. Richerson and Boyd (1998) point out that even among cognitively modern humans, the maintenance of complex traditions is not unproblematic. For example, Tasmanian isolation from Australia after the rise in Holocene sea-levels resulted in their toolkit shrinking in size and sophistication. Diamond (1978) argues that the Tasmanians were helpless to prevent an erosion of their more complex cultural traditions due to cultural drift. In a small population, with few people to reinvent them, complex skills are occasionally lost. Diamond's argument, we believe, can also be applied to explain variations in cultural complexity and perhaps even cultural culs-de-sac during the rise and fall of populations in southern Africa.

Another answer may be that innovations have not survived because of historical contingency. The survival of a cognitively modern human population is not only determined by long-term environmental and evolutionary trends but also by decisions taken by individuals. The smaller the population the more likely that valuable innovations may be lost as a consequence of stochastic events produced by inadequate choices. Historically, we see that strategic decisions taken at the moment of contact with other groups may lead to the survival or quick annihilation of entire societies and their material culture. There are no reasons to believe that it was otherwise in prehistory. Innovations that guarantee a better exploitation of resources or the maintenance of information within the group are not necessarily those determining its success in all circumstances.

Still another answer may lie in the fact that modern cultures evolve rapidly and transfer innovations via material items that do not necessarily survive in the archaeological record. A simple change in the location of sites in response to a climatic shift – from cave to open air for example – will result in the loss of worked bone. A change of media on which symbolic representation are made may survive in some cases (e.g. the engravings on ochre in the Still Bay and on ostrich egg shells in the HP), but disappear in others (e.g. carvings on wood or body painting). These apparent discontinuities will take the form, archaeologically, of regional phenomena, for example UP cave art in Europe, followed, chronologically and geographically, by scant evidence of this activity. This pattern may be erroneously interpreted as an evolutionary process punctuated by dramatic changes (or revolutions). It is therefore conceivable that the BBC innovations were not lost but stimulated comparable, albeit archaeologically undetectable, behaviours in both cultural offspring or neighbours. Of course the role of individuals in this process becomes crucial as they constitute the key for these stimuli becoming incorporated in a new cultural system.

In this chapter we have addressed some of the issues that surround individual contributions to cultural innovations in the MSA and those recovered from the MSA levels at BBC, the reasons for their introduction and the subsequent apparent discontinuity of some of these trends in the region. Examining all the processes that interact to generate the differential 'fitness' of cultural variants during the southern African MSA requires constructing a full-fledged theory of cultural evolution and the excavation of further *hard* evidence to back it up. The role of the individual in prehistory remains an enigma – but certainly an enigma worth pursuing if we hope to better understand how and when humans first become behaviourally modern.

Chapter 15

Concluding remarks
Context and the individual

Marcia-Anne Dobres

Palaeolithic studies of technology, social organisation and cognition have undergone an extraordinary intellectual and methodological shift over the past century, from evolutionary and typological concerns to extrasomatic questions of economy, function, resource procurement and biobehavioural adaptation. At long last, we have the ontological, interpretive and methodological means to 'people' the deep past, not at the rationalist (macro)scale championed by Adaptionists and Selectionists, but at the uniquely meaningful (micro)scale at which interpersonal and embodied social practice materialised communal belonging and personhood. It is an extraordinary conceptual advance in understanding the Lower and Middle Palaeolithic, to be able to ask thoughtful, systematic and legitimate questions about 'the individual', about agency, and about the mindfully and socially constituted hominid. The chapters in the volume demonstrate especially well that 'peopling' the deep past with individuals and intimate communities of practice is, simultaneously, an empirical question and a process of evolutionary importance. They also illustrate the necessity of taking materiality and sociality seriously when trying to explain material residues and model the evolutionary trajectory of our not-quite-human ancestors.

Why 'the individual' now?

The Introduction argues that this shift in explanatory interest is in part due to the accumulation of masses of controlled data that demand reinvestigation and reinterpretation. I'd also suggest that the nearly five decades of silence, explicitly imposed on positivist theoretical and epistemological grounds, has finally 'come to a head'. There are a number of converging reasons for forcing all but the most reticent of generalists to at last open the black box concerning agency and 'the individual' during the later Pleistocene. First, on an *ontological and theoretical basis*, long-held assertions that individuals, interpersonal relationships and intimate contexts of artefact-making and use are irrelevant to understanding the ebb and flow of macroscalar evolution have met their match in the well-reasoned introductions by Hopkinson and White, Porr, Field,

Hosfield, Petraglia *et al.*, and Gamble and Gaudzinski. Second, on *epistemological and methodological grounds*, the chapters by Gowlett, Sinclair and McNabb, Hosfield, Petraglia *et al.*, Pope and Roberts, Mania and Mania, Thieme, Adler and Conard, and Henshilwood and d'Errico ably demonstrate that should we wish to, we can indeed find empirically discernible traces of individual actions in the late Pleistocene archaeological record. With such empirical detail in hand, they also demonstrate that it is possible to explore anthropologically meaningful strategies of technical decision-making and personhood rather than steer off toward extrasomatic abstractions such as genetic fitness or selective advantage.

But the search for empirical traces of 'real' individual hominids is only part of what this volume is about. It is the *fallacy of misplaced concreteness* to believe that if we cannot discern the 'signature' traces of individual hands making or using a handaxe or dismembering an animal carcass, for example, then we cannot say anything worthwhile about the *role* of the hominid individual in the process of social reproduction and hominid evolution. But that's an empiricist's assertion. It's worth remembering that we cannot empirically 'see' the impact of the environment on physiobehavioral adaptations or gene pool frequency, nor do we actually 'see' the process of natural selection – yet we have no trouble conceptually linking all sorts of empirical patterns to such extrasomatic processes. So it is with processes of personhood, of mindfully constituted bodies, and of the role of the individual in the Palaeolithic body politic. This volume puts to an end claims that time-averaged and coarse-grained data are a stumbling block to exploring, for the later Pleistocene, questions of agency, meaning-making and social relations.

Lastly, virtually every one of these case studies is based on the indisputable premise that even the earliest hominids were a social and relational primate. Thus on *anthropological grounds* we can at long last make the case that it is *not* possible to understand supra-group evolutionary processes adequately without explicit concern as to how the somatic and sentient individual hominid contributed in that process – not as part of the genotype, not as a phenotypic expression of the species writ large, not as a mere 'unit' in the population or gene pool upon which natural selection operated – but through their meaning-fully constituted material and social engagement with the wider world (as Pope and Roberts, and Field cogently argue).

'Seeking' structure and agency in the Later Pleistocene – no 'cookbooks', please!

With 'the individual' in mind, several contributions get excellent mileage out of reanalysing well-preserved, data-rich assemblages in order to evaluate, at multiple geographic and temporal scales, the supposedly redundant nature of the Lower and Middle Palaeolithic/Stone Age. For some, the excessively uniform nature of these data is considered the 'proxy' of structure (tradition or cultural stability), while evidence of variability around identified norms is the 'proxy' of agency (the ego-centred individual or even personal style). Empirical traces of behavioural variability often serve as another kind of proxy, one signifying 'moments' of innovation or individual creativity that may have given rise to change of an evolutionary magnitude. For the time being, at least, this dichotomy seems to be the only way to imagine how individual hominids could have possibly contributed to the wholesale process of biocultural evolution. However, this need be only a short-lived *phase* in our intellectual and methodological growth in modelling a process far more complex, subtle and multiscal *a*r.

As Gamble and Gaudzinski correctly argue, we must understand that the hominid-to-human trajectory was about how individuals transformed and were transformed by their increasingly complex and multiscalar, but always physically mediated, relations with each other and with the external world. Thus in conjunction with our methodological zeal to find evidence of empirical individual hominids, we need also to model the *processes* by which phenomenal individuals *related* to each other, to their landscapes, to the environment, to the material world and to the intersection of lived and generational time. This, in turn, requires increased attention to the processual nature of empirical individuals *within* their body politic, and especially with how 'the individual' came to think and act in ways which promoted not just individuation, but also *collective sensibilities*. Put another way, archaeology needs explanatory frameworks and interpretive methodologies, grounded in rigorous materials analysis, that can overcome a long-standing and vexing multiscalar dilemma – how to make sense of extraordinarily long-lived technological traditions and/or macroscalar change in terms of the mindful body politic and the individuals constituting it. Especially promising in this regard are the case studies by Porr, Field, Sinclair and McNabb, Petraglia *et al.*, Pope and Roberts, Adler and Conard, Gamble and Gaudzinski and Henshilwood and d'Errico.

Thus, in pursuing the legitimate and necessary goal of understanding the individual hominid in context, we need to be wary of empiricist-driven methodological 'cookbooks' proffering one-size-fits-all lists of the vestiges of individual 'signatures' in the archaeological record, and recipes of patterns treated as quasi-ethnographic snapshots of Palaeolithic moments in time. For one thing, a cookbook approach is premised on the implicit (but false) assumption that 'exceptional sites' are required. But even Pompeii-like conditions of artefact preservation, such as at Boxgrove, Wallertheim and Isampur, do not automatically give us access to the *process* by which individual hominids were part of – or distinct from – their community. Understanding the *role* of the individual in hominid evolution, at social and temporal scales that transcend the micro/macro dichotomy, requires a focus on dynamic interpersonal, mindful and embodied *processes* and *relations*. What is critically important is that such dynamics do not necessarily derive from 'good' data, because the process is not *in* the data but in how we make sense of them. In order to *interpret* the material traces of 'real' individuals, and from these data understand their role(s) in ongoing streams of tradition and adaptation, we need to bring together a robust theoretical standpoint (regarding individuals, society, materiality and time) and appropriate strategies of materials analysis – alone, neither is sufficient. Indeed it is precisely because our analytic and explanatory limitations do not reside *in* data that Hosfield, in particular, can study the Acheulean hominid as an anthropologically meaningful social 'unit' with appeal to especially coarse-grained data – palimpsests. This is revolutionary.

Revolutionising the question of evolution: 'the individual' does make a difference

It is clear from the chapters presented here that it is possible, useful and necessary to ask about 'the individual hominid' and to conceptualise artefacts not as proxies of something else, but as a medium for materialising and negotiating social relationships, sensibility and individuality. What is truly revolutionary, however, is how subtly and cautiously the contributors *adapt* contemporary theories of agency and practice, which were specifically developed to explain modernity, to suit the uniqueness of archaeological questions about pre-modern hominids. By using empirical data as an independent restraint on 'anything goes' story-telling, these case studies provide nuanced and carefully reasoned models about a decidedly pre-modern kind of agency. And this, too, is revolutionary.

These case studies open up many exciting avenues for future research and pose important anthropological and processual questions about the deep past – questions which selectionist, adaptationist and similar extrasomatic perspectives are ill equipped to address. None forsake rigorous empirical study of the archaeological record, and several manage to reclaim 'bad' data long ignored by near-sighted empiricists. Moreover, they also provide robust *anthropological* reasons for measuring the lithic edge angles of PCTs and the thickness and length of flakes – not just because they can be measured, but because their statistical patterning is theoretically linked to aspects of individual and group skill, knowledge and social conditioning. Thus it is clear that when the question of 'the individual' is given prominence, empirical data can be used to link hand, mind and body to the social – peopled – context in with those actions took place. Thus as several chapters show, asking about the individual forces a more coherent and better justified use of empirical data – not for its own sake but for *anthropological* reasons. To my way of thinking, this is good science.

In this volume we also see the *integrated* use of local, regional, synchronic and diachronic patterns of material practice as a way of discerning different kinds of palaeoindividuals, networks of social relationships and even world-views for material living. Such patterns are used to explain how everyday material praxis was a key feature in the social reproduction of Acheulean and

Middle Stone Age hominids as well as a likely arena of culture change. Clearly, 'the individual' means different things to different contributors, but that does not indicate a weakness in this line of inquiry. Rather, such diversity indicates the likelihood that the process of individuation, the negotiation of social relationships, and various strategies of individual/group involvement with material 'taskscapes' in the later Pleistocene varied from place to place and from context to context. In this regard, one need only compare the tentative accounts proposed by Pope and Roberts with Petraglia *et al.* and Adler and Conard, and each of these with Sinclair and McNabb, Porr, Gamble and Gaudzinski or Henshilwood and d'Errico.

Rather than indicating different levels of success with data analysis, these various accounts tells us about the variety of hominid lifescapes practised during the Later Pleistocene. These are exactly the sort of theory-informed, empirically grounded and nuanced studies we need to explain how, in *human* terms, the Acheulean morphed into the Middle Palaeolithic and the Middle Stone Age. Not surprisingly, with their explicit focus on 'the individual,' practically every contributor is forced to rethink prevailing rationalistic models of Later Pleistocene economy, land use and tool-making as well as to challenge extrasocial approaches to data analysis. As Gamble and Gaudzinski note in particular, focusing on 'the individual' brings an entirely new concern to the study of resource procurement, land use and artefact manufacture – relationships.

Gamble and Porr's Introduction suggests that we need to 'amend' existing research questions about the Lower and Middle Palaeolithic to make room for the individual. With due respect, I think we must do far more than simply 'add and stir' individuals into the pot of materialist research strategies and paradigms specifically designed to explain extrasomatic biocultural evolution in terms of function, rationality and genetic fitness. Our existing paradigmatic pot has a very fat cookbook of analytic methods and explanatory models that, *by definition*, leave no room for the sentient, somatic and relational individual. And that is why this volume was compiled – to establish the necessity of, the methodologies for, and the models with which to reclaim the individual as something *more* than just a 'unit of analysis'.

But if we are going to accept that the processes of 'the individual', gender, agency, materiality, sociality and embodiment matter fundamentally to hominid evolution, then *their exploration must necessarily change our starting premises and choice of analytic methodologies*. It simply makes no sense to squeeze the individual into a paradigm with specially developed analytic methodologies that are not designed to account for mindful and somatic individuals. Thus what is *revolutionary* in the study of hominid evolution is not just asking about 'the individual', although this is a critical stage in that intellectual process – rather, it is in recognising that extrasomatic and adaptationist approaches are not up to the task and in developing strategies and frameworks which are.

As attempted in this volume, future Lower and Middle Palaeolithic research interested in 'the individual' must seek to understand *how* everyday and seemingly mundane material practice, undertaken by sentient and feeling individuals in socially charged settings, was the 'stuff' of both long-term stability and vast expanses of spatiotemporal change. The chapters in this volume provide ample inspiration – but should not be read as cookbooks for recipe-addicts. They ably demonstrate that current paradigms and explanations are unacceptably sterile, that the vagaries of the empirical record do not impose limitations on what we can and cannot know about the deep past, and that raising to prominence the question of the individual demands a far more complex and multifaceted appreciation of early hominids (no matter how small their brains). It follows, then, that we need to get beyond what Henshilwood and d'Errico call our 'comfort zone' and develop radically different intellectual and analytic strategies able to circumvent the multiscalar, paradigmatic, methodological and empirical dilemmas posed by taking seriously 'the individual hominid in context'.

Bibliography

Adam, K. D. 1951. Der Waldelefant von Lehringen – eine Jagdbeute des diluvialen Menschen. *Quartär* 5: 79–92.

Adler, D. S. 2002. Late Middle Palaeolithic Patterns of Lithic Reduction, Mobility, and Land Use in the Southern Caucasus. Unpublished PhD, Harvard University.

Adler, D. S., T. P. Prindiville, and N. J. Conard. 2003. Patterns of Spatial Organization and Land Use During the Eemian Interglacial in the Rhineland: New Data from Wallertheim, Germany. *Eurasian Prehistory* 1(2): 25–78.

Aiello, L. C. 1996. Hominine Preadaptations for Language and Cognition, in *Modelling the early human mind*. Edited by P. Mellars and K. Gibson, pp. 89–99. Cambridge: McDonald Institute Monographs.

Aiello, L. C., and P. Wheeler. 1995. The Expensive-tissue Hypothesis: The Brain and the Digestive System in Human and Primate Evolution. *Current Anthropology* 36: 199–221.

Alexandri, A. 1995. The Origins of Meaning, in *Interpreting Archaeology*. Edited by I. Hodder, M. Shanks, A. Alexandri, V. Buchli, J. Carman, J. Last, and G. Lucas, pp. 57–67. London: Routledge.

Allen, L. G. 1991. The Evolution of the Solent River System During the Pleistocene. Unpublished PhD, University of Cambridge.

Allen, L. G., and P. L. Gibbard. 1993. Pleistocene Evolution of the Solent River of Southern England. *Quaternary Science Reviews* 12: 503–428.

Alvard, M. S. 2003. The Adaptive Nature of Culture. *Evolutionary Anthropology* 12: 136–149.

Andresen, S. A., D. A. Bell, J. Hallos, T. R. J. Pumphrey, and J. A. J. Gowlett. 1997. Approaches to the Analysis of Evidence from the Acheulean Site of Beeches Pit, Suffolk, England, in *Archaeological Sciences 1995. Proceedings of a Conference on the Application of Scientific Techniques to the Study of Archaeology. Oxbow Monographs 64.* Edited by A. Sinclair, E. Slater, and J. Gowlett, pp. 389–394. Oxford: Oxbow Books.

Anklin, A., J.-M. Barnola, J. Beer, T. Blunier, K. Chappellaz, H. B. Clausen, D. Dahl-Jensen, W. Dansgaard, W. d. Angelis, R. J. Delmas, P. Duval, M. Fratta, A. Fuchs, K. Fuhrer, N. Gundestrup, C. Hammer, H. Oeschger, G. Orombelli, D. A. Peel, G. Raisbeck, D. Reynaud, C. Schott-Hvidberg, J. Schwander, H. Schoji, R. Souchez, B. Stauffer, J. P. Steffensen, M. Suevenard, A. Sveinbjornsdottir, T. Thorsteinsson, and E. W. Wolff. 1993. Climate Instability During the Last Interglacial Period Recorded in the GRIP Ice Core. *Nature* 364: 203–7.

Ashmore, W., and A. B. Knapp. Editors. 1999. *Archaeologies of Landscape: Contemporary Perspectives*. Oxford: Blackwell Publishers Ltd.

Ashton, N., and S. Lewis. 2002. Deserted Britain: Declining Populations in the British Late Middle Pleistocene. *Antiquity* 76: 388–96.

Ashton, N., S. G. Lewis, and S. Parfitt. Editors. 1998. *Excavations at the Lower Palaeolithic Site at East Farm, Barnham, Suffolk, 1989–1994*. London: British Museum Occasional Paper Number 125.

Austin, L. 1994. Life and Death of a Boxgrove Biface, in *Stories in Stone*. Edited by N. Ashton and A. David, pp. 119–25. London: Lithic Studies Society Occasional Paper 4, British Museum.

Avery, G., K. Cruz-Uribe, P. Goldberg, F. E. Grine, R. G. Klein, M. J. Lenardi, C. W. Marean, W. J. Rink, H. P. Shwarcz, A. I. Thackeray, and M. L. Wilson. 1997. The 1992–1993 Excavations at the Die Kelders Middle and Later Stone Age Cave Site, South Africa. *Journal of Field Archaeology* 24: 263–91.

Bailey, G. N. 1983. Concepts of Time in Quaternary Prehistory. *Annual Review of Anthropology* 12: 165–92.

Bar-Oz, G., D. S. Adler, M. T., N. Tushabramishvili, A. Belfer-Cohen, and O. Bar-Yosef. 2002. Middle and Upper Palaeolithic Foragers of the Southwest Caucasus: New Faunal Evidence from Western Georgia. *Archaeology, Ethnology and Anthropology of Eurasia* 4: 45–52.

Bar-Yosef, O., and S. L. Kuhn. 1999. The Big Deal About Blades: Laminar Technologies and Human Evolution. *American Anthropologist* 101: 322–38.

Bar-Yosef, O., and D. Pilbeam. Editors. 2000. *The Geography of Neandertals and Modern Humans in Europe and the Greater Mediterranean. Peabody Museum Bulletin 8*. Cambridge: Museum of Archaeology and Ethnology.

Barrett, J. 1987. Fields of Discourse: Reconstituting a Social Archaeology. *Critique of Anthropology* 7: 5–16.

———. 1994. *Fragments from Antiquity*. Oxford: Blackwell.

Barrett, J., R. Bradley, and M. Green. 1991. *Landscape, Monuments and Society: The Prehistory of Cranborne Chase*. Cambridge: Cambridge University Press.

Beaumont, P. 1999. *Pniel 6 (The Bend). Northern Cape. INQUA XV International Conference Field Guide*. Kimberley: McGregor Museum.

Behm-Blancke, G. 1960. *Altsteinzeitliche Rastplätze im Travertingebiet von Taubach, Weimar, Ehringsdorf. Alt-Thüringen 4*. Weimar: Herman Böhlaus Nachfolger.

Belfer-Cohen, A., and N. Goren-Inbar. 1994. Cognition and Communication in the Levantine Lower Palaeolithic. *World Archaeology* 26: 144–57.

Bender, B. 1978. Gatherer-hunter to Farmer: A Social Perspective. *World Archaeology* 10: 204–22.

Bergman, C. A., and M. B. Roberts. 1988. Flaking Technology at the Acheulean Site of Boxgrove, West Sussex (England). *Revue Archéologique de Picardie* 1–2: 105–13.

Bergman, C. A., M. B. Roberts, S. Collcutt, and P. Barlow. 1990. Refitting and Spatial Analysis of Artefacts from Quarry 2 at the Middle Pleistocene Acheulean Site of Boxgrove, West Sussex, England, in *The Big Puzzle*. Edited by E. Cziesla, S. Eickhoff, N. Arts, and D. Winter, pp. 265–81. Bonn: Holos.

Bettinger, R. 1991. *Hunter-gatherers: Archaeological and Evolutionary Theory*. New York: Plenum.

Biberson, P. 1961. *Le Paléolithique inférieur du Maroc Atlantique*. Vol. 17. Publications du Service des Antiquités du Maroc.

Biesele, M. 1978. Religion and Folklore, in *The Bushmen*. Edited by P. V. Tobias, pp. 162–72. Cape Town: Human & Rousseu.

Binford, L. R. 1964. A Consideration of Archaeological Research Design. *American Antiquity* 29: 425–41.

——. 1972. Contemporary Model Building: Paradigms and the Current State of Palaeolithic Research, in *Models in Archaeology*. Edited by D. L. Clarke, pp. 109–66. London: Methuen.

——. Editor. 1977. *For Theory Building in Archaeology*. New York: Academic Press.

——. 1978a. Dimensional Analysis of Behaviour and Site Structure: Learning from an Eskimo Hunting Stand. *American Antiquity* 43: 330–61.

——. 1978b. *Nunamiut Ethnoarchaeology*. New York: Academic Press.

——. 1980. Willow Smoke and Dogs Tails: Hunter-gatherer Settlement Systems and Archaeological Site Formation. *American Antiquity* 45: 4–20.

——. 1981a. *Bones: Ancient Men and Modern Myths*. New York: Academic Press.

——. 1981b. Behavioral Archaeology and the 'Pompeii Premise'. *Journal of Anthropological Research* 37: 195–208.

——. 1982. The Archaeology of Place. *Journal of Anthropological Archaeology* 1: 5–31.

——. 1983. *In Pursuit of the Past: Decoding the Archaeological Record*. London: Thames and Hudson.

——. 1984. *Faunal Remains from Klasies River Mouth*. New York: Academic Press.

——. 1985. Human Ancestors: Changing Views of their Behaviour. *Journal of Anthropological Archaeology* 4: 292–327.

——. 1989. Isolating the Transition to Cultural Adaptations: An Organizational Approach, in *The Emergence of Modern Humans. Biocultural Adaptations in the Later Pleistocene*. Edited by E. Trinkaus, pp. 18–41. Cambridge: Cambridge University Press.

——. 1991. When the Going Gets Tough, the Tough Get Going: Nunamiut Local Groups, Camping Patterns and Economic Organisation, in *Ethnoarchaeological Approaches to Mobile Campsites: Hunter-gatherer and Pastoralist Case Studies, International Monographs in Prehistory, Ethnoarchaeological Series 1*. Edited by C. S. Gamble and W. A. Boismier, pp. 25–138. Michigan: Ann Arbor.

——. 2001. *Constructing Frames of Reference: An Analytical Method for Archaeological Theory Building Using Ethnographic and Environmental Datasets*. Berkeley: University of California Press.

Binford, L. R., and N. Stone. 1986. Zhoukoudian: A Closer Look. *Current Anthropology* 27: 453–75.

Bird-David, N. 1999. 'Animism' Revisited: Personhood, Environment, and Relational Epistemology. *Current Anthropology* 40: 67–91.

Bishop, W. W. 1978. Geological Framework of the Kilombe Acheulian Site, Kenya, in *Geological Background to Fossil Man*. Edited by W. W. Bishop, pp. 329–36: Special Publication of the Geological Society 6.

Blackwell, B. A. B., S. Fevrier, J. I. B. Blickstein, K. Paddayya, M. Petraglia, R. Jhaldiyal, and A. R. Skinner. 2001. ESR Dating of an Acheulean Quarry Site at Isampur, India. *Journal of Human Evolution* 40: A3.

Blumenschine, R. J., and F. T. Masao. 1991. Living Sites at Olduvai Gorge, Tanzania? Preliminary Landscape Archaeology Results in the Basal Bed II Lake Margin Zone. *Journal of Human Evolution* 21: 451–62.

Blurton-Jones, N., and K. Hawkes. 1996. The Global Process and Local Ecology:

How Should we Explain Differences between the Hadza and the !Kung?, in *Cultural Diversity among Twentieth-Century Foragers.* Edited by S. Kent, pp. 159–87. Cambridge: Cambridge University Press.

Bocherens, H., D. Billiou, A. Mariotti, M. Patou-Mathis, M. Otte, D. Bonjean, and M. Toussaint. 1999. Palaeoenvironmental and Palaeodietary Implications of Isotopic Biogeochemistry of Last Interglacial Neanderthal and Mammal Bones in Scladina Cave (Belgium). *Journal of Archaeological Science* 26: 599–607.

Bodenhorn, B. 1988. Whales, Souls, Children and Other Things that Are 'Good to Share': Core Metaphors in a Contemporary Whaling Society. *Cambridge Anthropology* 13: 1–19.

Boëda, E. 1988. Le concept Levallois et évaluation de son champ d'application, in *L'Homme de Néanderthal, vol. 4: La technique.* Edited by L. Binford and J.-P. Rigaud, pp. 13–26. Liège: ERAUL 31. Etudes et recherches archaeologiques de l'Université de Liège.

Boëda, E., J.-M. Geneste, and L. Meignen. 1990. Identification de Chaînes Opératoires Lithiques du Paléolithique Ancien et Moyen. *Paleo* 2: 43–80.

Boesch, C., and H. Boesch. 1984. Mental Maps in Wild Chimpanzees: an Analysis of Hammer Transports for Nut Cracking. *Primates* 25: 160–70.

———. 1989. Hunting Behaviour of Wild Chimpanzees in Tai National Park. *American Journal of Physical Anthropology* 78: 547–73.

Boesch, C., and H. Boesch-Achermann. 2000. *The Chimpanzees of the Tai Forest: Behavioural Ecology and Evolution.* Oxford: Oxford University Press.

Boesch, C., and M. Tomasello. 1998. Chimpanzee and Human Cultures. *Current Anthropology* 39: 591–614.

Bogin, B., and B. H. Smith. 1996. Evolution of the Human Life Cycle. *American Journal of Human Biology* 8: 703–16.

Bogin, B. 1997. Evolutionary Hypotheses for Human Childhood. *Yearbook of Physical Anthropology* 40: 63–89.

Böhme, G. 1998. Neue Funde von Fischen, Amphibien und Reptilien aus dem Mittelpleistozän von Bilzingsleben. *Praehistoria Thuringica* 2: 96–107.

———. 2000. Reste von Fischen, Amphibien und Reptilien aus der Fundstelle Schöningen 12 bei Helmstedt (Niedersachsen) – Erste Ergebnisse. *Praehistoria Thuringica* 4: 18–27.

Bordes, F. 1961. Mousterian Cultures in France. *Science* 134: 803–10.

———. 1975. Sur la notion de sol d'habitat en préhistoire paléolithique. *Bulletin de la Société Préhistorique Française* 72: 139–44.

Bosinski, G. 1967. *Die mittelpaläolithischen Funde im westlischen Mitteleuropa. Fundamenta Reihe A/4.* Köln and Graz: Böhlau Verlag.

Bosinski, G., F. d'Errico, and P. Schiller. 2001. *Die Gravierten Frauendarstellungen Von Gönnersdorf. Der Magdalénien-Fundplatz Gönnersdorf, Band 8.* Stuttgart: Franz Steiner Verlag GMBH.

Boulding, K. E. 1956. General Systems Theory: The Skeleton of Science. *Management Science* 2: 197–208.

Bourdieu, P. 1977. *Outline of a Theory of Practice.* Cambridge: Cambridge University Press.

Bowen, D. Q., S. A. Hughes, G. A. Sykes, and G. M. Miller. 1989. Land-sea Correlations in the Pleistocene Based on Isoluecine Epimerization in Non-marine Molluscs. *Nature* 340: 49–51.

Boyd, R., and P. J. Richerson. 1985. *Culture and the Evolutionary Process*. Chicago: University of Chicago Press.

Boyle, K. V. 1990. *Upper Palaeolithic Faunas from South-West France: A Zoogeographic Perspective*. Oxford: British Archaeological Reports International Series 557.

——. 1997. Late Magdalenian Carcass Management Strategies: The Périgord Data. *Anthropozoologica* 25: 287–94.

Bradley, B. A., and C. G. Sampson. 1986. Analysis by Replication of two Acheulian Artefact Assemblages, in *Stone Age Prehistory: Essays In Memory of Charles McBurney*. Edited by G. N. Bailey and P. Callow, pp. 29–44. Cambridge: Cambridge University Press.

Bradley, R. 2002. *The Past in Prehistoric Societies*. London: Routledge.

Bräuer, G. 2001. The KNM-ER 3884 Hominid and the Emergence of Modern Anatomy in Africa, in *Humanity from African Naissance to Coming Millennia*. Edited by G. A. Doyle, pp. 191–7. Firenze: Firenze University Press.

Bridgland, D. R. 1994. *Quaternary of the Thames. Geological Conservation Series* 7. London: Chapman and Hall.

——. 1995. The Quaternary Sequence of the Eastern Thames Basin: Problems of Correlation, in *The Quaternary of the Lower Reaches of the Thames: Field Guide*. Edited by D. R. Bridgland, P. Allen, and B. A. Haggart, pp. 35–52. Durham: Quaternary Research Association.

——. 1996. Quaternary River Terrace Deposits as a Framework for the Lower Palaeolithic Record, in *The English Palaeolithic Reviewed*. Edited by C. S. Gamble and A. J. Lawson, pp. 23–39. Salisbury: Wessex Archaeology Ltd.

——. 1998. The Pleistocene History and Early Human Occupation of the River Thames Valley, in *Stone Age Archaeology: Essays in honour of John Wymer, Lithic Studies Society Occasional Paper 6*. Edited by N. Ashton, F. Healy, and P. Pettitt, pp. 29–37. Oxford: Oxbow Books.

——. 2000. River Terrace Systems in North-west Europe: An Archive of Environmental Change, Uplift and Early Human Occupation. *Quaternary Science Reviews* 19: 1293–303.

——. 2001. The Pleistocene Evolution and Palaeolithic Occupation of the Solent River, in *Palaeolithic Archaeology of the Solent River, Lithic Studies Society Occasional Paper 7*. Edited by F. F. Wenban-Smith and R. T. Hosfield, pp. 15–25. London: Lithic Studies Society.

Bridgland, D. R., and P. Allen. 1996. A Revised Model for Terrace Formation and Its Significance for the Lower Middle Pleistocene Thames Terrace Aggradations of North-east Essex, U.K., in *The Early Middle Pleistocene in Europe*. Edited by C. Turner, pp. 121–34. Rotterdam: Balkema.

Bridgland, D. R., and D. C. Schreve. 2001. River Terrace Formation in Synchrony with Long-term Climatic Fluctuation: Supporting Mammalian Evidence from Southern Britain, in *River Basins Sediments Systems: Archives of Environmental Change*. Edited by D. Maddy, M. Macklin, and J. Woodward, pp. 229–48. Rotterdam: Balkema.

Brody, H. 1981. *Maps and Dreams*. Vancouver: Douglas and McIntyre.

Brooks, A. S., D. M. Helgren, J. S. Cramer, A. Franklin, W. Hornyat, J. M. Keating, R. G. Klein, W. J. Rink, H. Schwarcz, J. N. L. Smith, K. Stewart, N. E. Todd, J. Verniers, and J. E. Yellen. 1995. Dating and Context of Three Middle Stone Age Sites with Bone Points in the Upper Semliki Valley, Zaire. *Science* 268: 548–53.

Bunn, H. T., J. W. K. Harris, G. L. Isaac, Z. Kaufulu, E. M. Kroll, K. Schick, N. Toth, and A. K. Behrensmeyer. 1980. FxJj50: An Early Pleistocene Site in Northern Kenya. *World Archaeology* 12: 109–36.

Burke, A. 1997. Incremental Analysis of Equid Teeth from Wallertheim, Germany, in *Reports for the Second Wallertheim Workshop*. Edited by N. J. Conard and A. W. Kandel, pp. 21–2. Tübingen: Institut für Ur- und Frühgeschichte Tübingen.

Bury, H. 1923. Some aspects of the Hampshire Plateau Gravels. *Proceedings of the Prehistoric Society of East Anglia* 4: 15–41.

——. 1926. The Rivers of the Hampshire Basin. *Proceedings of the Hampshire Field Club* 10: 1–12.

Butler, J. P. 1993. *Bodies that Matter: On the Discursive Limits of 'sex'*. New York & London: Routledge.

Byrne, R. 1995. *The Thinking Ape: Evolutionary Origins of Intelligence*. Oxford: Oxford University Press.

Byrne, R., and A. Whiten. 1988. *Machiavellian Intelligence: Social Experience and the Evolution of Intellect in Monkeys, Apes and Humans*. Oxford: Clarendon Press.

Cachel, S., and J. W. K. Harris. 1999. The Adaptive Zone of *Homo Erectus* from an African Perspective, in *Hominid Evolution. Lifestyles and Survival Strategies*. Edited by H. Ullrich, pp. 128–37. Gelsenkirchen/Schwelm: Edition Archaea.

Calkin, J. B., and J. F. N. Green. 1949. Palaeoliths and Terraces near Bournemouth. *Proceedings of the Prehistoric Society* 15: 21–37.

Callow, P. 1976. The Lower and Middle Palaeolithic of Britain and Adjacent Areas of Europe. Unpublished PhD, University of Cambridge.

Callow, P., and J. M. Cornford. Editors. 1986. *La Cotte de St. Brelade 1961–1978: Excavations by C. B. M. McBurney*. Norwich: Geo Books.

Campbell, J. B., and C. G. Sampson. 1971. A New Analysis of Kent's Cavern, Devonshire, England. *University of Oregon Anthropology Papers* 3: 1–40.

Campbell, S. S. 1988. *Quaternary of South-West England*. London: Chapman-Hall.

Carr, C. 1984. The Nature of Organization of Intrasite Archaeological Records and Spatial Analytical Approaches to Their Investigation. *Advances in Archaeological Method and Theory* 7: 103–222.

Carrithers, M. 1985. An Alternative Social History of the Self, in *The Category of the Person: Anthropology, Philosophy, History*. Edited by S. Lukes, pp. 234–256. Cambridge: Cambridge University Press.

——. 1996. Person, in *Encyclopedia of Social and Cultural Anthropology*. Edited by J. Spencer, pp. 419–23. London: Routledge.

Cavalli-Sforza, L. L. 2000. *Genes, People, and Languages*. New York: North Point Press.

Chapman, J. 2000. *Fragmentation in Archaeology: People, Places and Broken Objects in the Prehistory of South-eastern Europe*. London: Routledge.

Chase, P. G., and H. L. Dibble. 1990. On the Emergence of Modern Humans. *Current Anthropology* 31: 58–9.

Chatwin, C. P. 1936. *The Hampshire Basin and Adjoining Areas. British Regional Geology*. London: Department of Scientific and Industrial Research, HMSO.

Chavaillon, J., N. Chavaillon, F. Hours, and M. Piperno. 1979. From the Oldowan to the Middle Stone Age at Melka Kunture. *Quaternaria* 21: 87–114.

Childe, V. G. 1951. *Social Evolution*. London: Watts.

Clark, A. M. B. 1997. The Final Middle Stone Age at Rose Cottage Cave: A Distinct Industry in the Basutolian Ecozone. *South African Journal of Science* 93: 449–58.

Clark, G. A. 1992. A Comment on Mithen's Ecological Interpretation of Palaeolithic Art. *Proceedings of the Prehistoric Society* 58: 107–9.

Clark, J. D. 1987. Transitions: Homo Erectus and the Acheulean: the Ethiopian Sites of Gadeb and the Middle Awash. *Journal of Human Evolution* 16: 809–26.

——. 2001. *Kalambo Falls, Vol.3.* Cambridge: Cambridge University Press.

Clark, J. D., and C. V. Haynes. 1970. An Elephant Butchery Site at Mwanganda's Village, Karonga, Malawi and its Relevance for Palaeolithic Archaeology. *World Archaeology* 13: 390–411.

Clark, J. D., and H. Kurashina. 1979. Hominid Occupation of the East-central Highlands of Ethiopia in the Plio-Pleistocene. *Nature* 282: 33–9.

Clark, J. D., J. Beyene, G. Woldegabriel, W. K. Hart, P. R. Renne, H. Gilbert, A. Defleur, G. Suwa, S. Katoh, K. R. Ludwig, J. Boisserie, B. Asfaw, and T. D. White. 2003. Stratigraphic, Chronological and Behavioural Contexts of Pleistocene *Homo sapiens* from Middle Awash, Ethiopia. *Nature* 423: 747–52.

Clark, J. G. D. 1954. *Excavations at Star Carr.* Cambridge: Cambridge University Press.

Clark, P. J., and F. C. Evans. 1954. Distance to Nearest Neighbour as a Measure of Spatial Relationships in Populations. *Ecology* 35: 445–53.

Clayton, K. M. 1977. River Terraces, in *British Quaternary Studies: Recent Advances.* Edited by F. W. Shotton, pp. 153–68. Oxford: Clarendon Press.

Cleveringa, P., W. D. Gans, W. Huybrechts, and C. Verbruggen. 1988. Outline of River Adjustments in Small River Basins in Belgium and the Netherlands since the Upper Pleniglacial, in *Lake, Mire and River Environments During the Last 15000 Years.* Edited by G. Lang and C. Schluchter, pp. 123–32. Rotterdam: Balkema.

Close, A. E. 2000. Reconstructing Movement in Prehistory. *Journal of Archaeological Method and Theory* 7: 49–77.

Codrington, T. 1870. On the Superficial Deposits of the South of Hampshire and the Isle of Wight. *Quarterly Journal of the Geological Society* 26: 528–51.

Collins, P. E. F., I. M. Fenwick, M. Keith-Lucas, and P. Worsley. 1996. Late Devensian River and Floodplain Dynamics and Related Environmental Change in Northwest Europe, with Particular Reference to a Site at Woolhampton, Berkshire, England. *Journal of Quaternary Science* 11: 357–75.

Conard, N. J. 1990. Laminar Lithic Assemblages from the Last Interglacial Complex in Northwestern Europe. *Journal of Anthropological Research* 46: 243–62.

——. 1992. *Tönchesberg and its Position in the Palaeolithic Prehistory of Northern Europe. Monographien Römisch-Germanisches Zentralmuseum 20.* Bonn: Habelt Verlag.

——. 1994. On the Prospects for an Ethnography of Extinct Hominids. *Current Anthropology* 35: 281–82.

——. 1998. Middle Palaeolithic Settlement in the Rhineland, in *Middle Palaeolithic and Middle Stone Age Settlement Systems. Proceedings of the XIII Congress of the UISPP Vol. 6.* Edited by N. J. Conard and F. Wendorf, pp. 255–68. Forli: A.B.A.C.O. Editioni.

——. 2001a. The Future of Archaeology, in *Quo Vadis Archaeologica? Whither European Archaeology in the 21st Century.* Edited by Z. Koblyinski, pp. 106–17. Warsaw: Polish Academy of Sciences.

——. Editor. 2001b. *Settlement Dynamics of the Middle Palaeolithic and Middle Stone Age.* Tübingen: Kerns Verlag.

Conard, N. J., and D. S. Adler. 1997. Lithic Reduction and Hominid Behavior in the

Middle Palaeolithic of the Rhineland. *Journal of Anthropological Research* 53: 147–76.

Conard, N. J., and B. Fischer. 2000. Are there Recognizable Cultural Entities in the German Middle Palaeolithic?, in *Toward Modern Humans: the Yabrudian and Micoquian, 400–50 k-years ago*. Edited by A. Ronen and M. Weinstein-Evron, pp. 7–24. Oxford: Archaeopress.

Conard, N. J., and T. J. Prindiville. 2000. Middle Palaeolithic Hunting Economies in the Rhineland. *International Journal of Osteoarchaeology* 10: 286–309.

Conard, N. J., J. Preuß, R. Langohr, P. Haesaerts, T. Van Kolfschoten, B.-D. J., and A. Rebholz. 1995a. New Geological Research at the Middle Paleolithic Locality of Wallertheim in Rheinhessen. *Archäologisches Korrespondenzblatt* 25: 1–27.

Conard, N. J., D. S. Adler, D. T. Forrest, and P. J. Kaszas. 1995b. Preliminary Archaeological Results from the 1991–1993 Excavations in Wallertheim. *Archäologisches Korrespondenzblatt*: 13–27.

Conard, N. J., T. J. Prindiville, and D. S. Adler. 1998. Refitting Bones and Stones as a Means of Reconstructing Middle Paleolithic Subsistence in the Rhineland, in *XVIIIe Rencontres Internationales d'Archéologie et d'Histoire d'Antibes. Économie Préhistorique: Les Comportements de Subsistance au Paléolithique 23–25 October, 1997*. Edited by J.-P. Brugal, L. Meignen, and M. Patou-Mathis, pp. 273–90. Sophia Antipolis: Éditions APDCA.

Conway, B., J. McNabb, and N. Ashton. 1996. *Excavations at Barnfield Pit, Swanscombe 1968–1972. British Museum Occasional Paper No. 94*. London: British Museum.

Coope, G. R. 2001. Biostratigraphical Distinction of Interglacial Coelopteran Assemblages from Southern Britain Attributed to Oxygen Isotope Stages 5e and 7. *Quaternary Science Reviews* 20: 1717–22.

Cooper, C., H. Murphy, J. Mulvaney, and N. Peterson. 1981. *Aboriginal Australia – Exhibition Catalogue of the Australian Gallery Directors Council*. Sydney: National Library of Australia.

Cornford, J. M. 1986. Specialised Resharpening Techniques and Evidence of Handedness, in *La Cotte de St. Brelade 1961–1978: excavations by C. B. M. McBurney*. Edited by P. Callow and J. M. Cornford, pp. 337–53. Norwich: Geo Books.

Crompton, R. H., and J. A. J. Gowlett. 1993. Allometry and Multidimensional Form in Acheulean Bifaces from Kilombe, Kenya. *Journal of Human Evolution* 25: 175–99.

——. 1997. The Acheulean and the Sahara: Allometric Comparisons Between North and East African Sites, in *Archaeological Sciences 1995. Proceedings of a Conference on the Application of Scientific Techniques to the Study of Archaeology. Oxbow Monographs 64*. Edited by A. Sinclair, E. Slater, and J. Gowlett, pp. 400–5. Oxford: Oxbow Books.

Cziesla, E., S. Eickhoff, N. Arts, and D. Winter. Editors. 1990. *The Big Puzzle*. Bonn: Holos.

d'Errico, F. 1995. *L'Art Gravé Azilien. De La Technique à la Signification. Xxxième Supplément à Gallia-Préhistoire*. Paris: CNRS Editions.

d'Errico, F. 2003. The Invisible Frontier: A Multiple Species Model for the Origin of Behavioral Modernity. *Evolutionary Anthropology* 12: 188–202.

d'Errico, F., and A. Nowell. 2000. A New Look at the Berekhat Ram Figurine:

Implications for the Origins of Symbolism. *Cambridge Archaeological Journal* 10: 123–67.

d'Errico, F., and M. Vanhaeren. 2002. Criteria for Identifying Red Deer Age and Sex from their Canines: Application to Upper Palaeolithic and Mesolithic Ornaments. *Journal of Archaeological Science* 29: 3–34.

d'Errico, F., J. Zilhão, M. Julien, D. Baffier, and J. Pèlegrin. 1998. Neanderthal Acculturation in Western Europe? A Critical Review of the Evidence and its Interpretation. *Current Anthropology* 39: 1–44.

d'Errico, F., C. Henshilwood, and P. Nilssen. 2001. An Engraved Bone Fragment from ca. 75 Kyr Middle Stone Age Levels at Blombos Cave, South Africa. Implications for the Origin of Symbolism and Language. *Antiquity* 75: 309–18.

d'Errico, F., C. Henshilwood, G. Lawson, M. Vanhaeren, A.-M. Tillier, M. Soressi, F. Bresson, B. Maureille, A. Nowell, J. Lakarra, L. Backwell, and M. Julien. 2003. Archaeological Evidence for the Origins of Language, Symbolism and Music: An Alternative Multidisciplinary Perspective. *Journal of World Prehistory* 17: 1–70.

d'Errico, F., M. Julien, M. Liolios, M. Vanhaeren, and D. Baffier. 2003. Many Awls in our Argument: Bone Tool Manufacture and Use from the Chatelperronian and Aurignacian Layers of the Grotte du Renne at Arcy-sur-Cure, in *The Chronology of the Aurignacian and of the Transitional Technocomplexes: Dating, Stratigraphies, Cultural Implications.* Edited by J. Zilhão and F. d'Errico, pp. 247–70. Lisbon: Instituto Português De Arqueologia.

Damblon, F. In Press. Charcoal and Other Plant Macro-remains from Wallertheim (Mainz, Germany) and their Contribution to Middle Palaeolithic Environmental Reconstruction, in *The 1991–1994 Middle Paleolithic Excavations at Wallertheim, Tübingen Publications in Prehistory.* Edited by N. J. Conard. Tübingen: Kerns Verlag.

Dansgaard, W., S. J. Johnsen, H. B. Clausen, D. Dahl-Jensen, N. S. Gundestrup, C. U. Hammer, C. S. Hvidberg, J. P. Steffensen, A. E. Sveinbjörnsdottir, J. Jouzel, and G. Bond. 1993. Evidence for General Instability of Past Climate from a 250-kyr Ice-core Record. *Nature* 364: 218–20.

Darwin-Fox, W. 1862. When and How was the Isle of Wight Severed from the Mainland? *The Geologist* 5: 452–54.

David, F., and C. Farizy. 1994. Les vestiges osseux: étude archéozoologique, in *Hommes et Bisons du Paléolithique Moyen à Mauran.* Edited by C. Farizy, F. David, and J. Jaubert, pp. 177–303. Paris: CNRS.

Davies, W. 2001. A Very Model of a Modern Human Industry: New Perspectives on the Origins and Spread of the Aurignacian in Europe. *Proceedings of the Prehistoric Society* 67: 195–217.

Dawkins, R. 1976. *The Selfish Gene.* Oxford: Oxford University Press.

de la Torre, I., R. Mora, M. Domínguez-Rodrigo, L. Luque, and L. Alcalá. 2003. The Oldowan Industry of Peninj and its Bearing on the Reconstruction of the Technological Skills of Lower Pleistocene Hominids. *Journal of Human Evolution* 44: 203–24.

de Waal, F. 1982. *Chimpanzee Politics: Power and Sex among Apes.* London: Allen and Unwin.

———. 1998. *Chimpanzee Politics: Power and Sex among Apes.* Revised edition. Baltimore/London: Johns Hopkins University Press.

Deacon, H. J. 1998. Modern Human Emergence: An African Archaeological

Perspective, in *Dual Congress Proceedings, Colloquium 17, The Archaeology of Modern Human Origins.* Sun City, South Africa.

Deacon, H. J., and J. Deacon. 1999. *Human Beginnings in South Africa: Uncovering the Secrets of the Stone Age.* Claremont: David Philip Publishers Ltd.

Deacon, H. J., and V. B. Geleijnse. 1988. The Stratigraphy and Sedimentology of the Main Site Sequence, Klasies River, South Africa. *South African Archaeological Bulletin* 43: 5–14.

DeBono, H., and N. Goren-Inbar. 2001. Note of a Link between Acheulian Handaxes and the Levallois Method. *Journal of the Israel Prehistoric Society* 31: 9–23.

Deloze, V., P. Depaepe, J.-M. Gouédo, V. Krier, and J.-L. Locht. Editors. 1994. *Le Paléolithique moyen dans le nord du Sénonais (Yonne). Documents d'Archéologie Française* 47. Paris: Editions de la Maison des Sciences de L'Homme.

Dennell, R. 1997. The World's Oldest Spears. *Nature* 385: 767–8.

Dennett, D. 1991. *Consciousness Explained.* Harmondsworth: Penguin.

Depaepe, P. 1997. Analyses spatiales par repartition proportionnelle des artefacts: Premiers resultants sur deux sites du paléolithique moyen (Lailly 'Fond de Tournerie' et 'Molinons Grand Chanteloup', Yonne). *Bulletin de la Société Préhistorique Française* 94: 435–41.

———. 2001. A Comparison of Spatial Analyses of Three Mousterien Sites: New Methods, New Interpretations, in *Settlement Dynamics of the Middle Palaeolithic and Middle Stone Age.* Edited by N. J. Conard, pp. 337–60. Tübingen: Kerns Verlag.

Diamond, J. 1978. The Tasmanians: The Longest Isolation, the Simplest Technology. *Nature* 273: 185–6.

Dibble, H. L., and N. Rolland. 1992. On Assemblage Variability in the Middle Palaeolithic of Western Europe: History, Perspectives, and a New Synthesis, in *The Middle Palaeolithic: Adaptation, Behaviour, and Variability.* Edited by H. L. Dibble and P. Mellars, pp. 1–29. Philadelphia: The University Museum, University of Pennsylvania.

Diebel, K., and E. Pietrzeniuk. 1980. Pleistozäne Ostracoden aus dem Profil des Homo erectus-Fundortes bei Bilzingsleben. *Ethnographisch-Archäologische Zeitschrift* 21: 26–35.

Dix, J. K. 2001. The Geology of the Solent River System, in *Palaeolithic Archaeology of the Solent River, Lithic Studies Occasional Paper 7.* Edited by F. F. Wenban-Smith and R. T. Hosfield, pp. 7–14. London: Lithic Studies Society.

Dobres, M.-A. 2000. *Technology and Social Agency.* Oxford: Blackwell.

Dobres, M.-A., and C. R. Hoffman. 1994. Social Agency and the Dynamics of Prehistoric Technology. *Journal of Archaeological Method and Theory* 1: 211–58.

Dobres, M.-A., and J. Robb. Editors. 2000. *Agency in Archaeology.* London: Routledge.

Domínguez-Rodrigo, M. 2001. A Study of Carnivore Competition in Riparian and Open Habitats of Modern Savannas and its Implications for Hominid Behavioral Modelling. *Journal of Human Evolution* 40: 77–98.

Domínguez-Rodrigo, M., J. Serrallonga, J. Juan-Tresserras, L. Alcala, and L. Luque. 2001. Woodworking Activities by Early Humans: A Plant Residue Analysis on Acheulian Stone Tools from Peninj (Tanzania). *Journal of Human Evolution* 40: 289–99.

Domínguez-Rodrigo, M., I. de la Torre, L. Luque, L. Alcalá, R. Mora, J. Serrallonga, and V. Medina. 2002. The ST Site Complex at Peninj, West Lake Natron,

Tanzania: Implications for Early Hominid Behavioural Models. *Journal of Archaeological Science* 29: 639–65.

Donald, M. 1993. Précis of the Origin of the Modern Mind: Three States in the Evolution of Culture and Cognition. *Behavioral and Brain Sciences* 16: 737–91.

Dowden, R. 1995. Africa and its Art May be a PC Fiction Created by the West's Guilty Conscience, in *Spectator*, London.

Dowson, T. A. 1988. Revelations or Religious Reality: The Individual in San Rock Art. *World Archaeology* 20: 116–28.

Dunbar, R. I. M. 1996a. *Grooming, Gossip and the Evolution of Language*. London: Faber and Faber.

———. 1996b. On the Evolution of Language and Kinship, in *The Archaeology of Human Ancestry*. Edited by J. Steele and S. Shennan, pp. 380–96. London: Routledge.

———. 2003. The Social Brain: Mind, Language, and Society in Evolutionary Perspective. *Annual Review of Anthropology* 32: 163–81.

Edmonds, M. 1999. *Ancestral Geographies of the Neolithic: Landscapes, Monuments and Memory*. London: Routledge.

Efimenko, P. P. 1958. *Kostenki, I (in Russian)*. Moscow-Leningrad: NAUKA.

Elster, J. 1983. *Explaining Technical Change*. Cambridge: Cambridge University Press.

Evans, J. 1864. On Some Recent Discoveries of Flint Implements in Drift-Deposits in Hants and Wilts. *Quarterly Journal of the Geological Society* 20: 188–94.

Evans, U. 1994. Hollow Rock Shelter, A Middle Stone Age Site in the Cederberg. *South African Field Archaeology* 3: 63–72.

Everard, C. E. 1954. The Solent River: A Geomorphological Study. *Transactions of the Institute of British Geographers* 20: 41–58.

Féblot-Augustins, J. 1997. *La circulation des matières premières au Paléolithique*. Liège: ERAUL vol. 75.

———. 1999. Raw Material Transport Patterns and Settlement Systems in the European Lower and Middle Palaeolithic: Continuity, Change and Variability, in *The Middle Palaeolithic Occupation of Europe*. Edited by W. Roebroeks and C. Gamble, pp. 194–214. Leiden: European Science Foundation and University of Leiden.

Field, A. S. 2002. The Middle Pleistocene in Transition: Lithic Assemblages and Changing Social Relations between OIS 12 and 6 in Europe and Africa: Unpublished PhD thesis, University of Southampton.

Fischer, K. 1991. Wildrinderreste (Bovidae, Artiodactyla, Mammalia) aus dem mittelpleistozänen Holstein-Komplex von Bilzingsleben, in *Bilzingsleben IV. Homo erectus – seine Kultur und seine Umwelt*. Edited by K. Fischer, E. W. Guenther, W. D. Heinrich, D. Mania, R. Musil, and T. Nötzold, pp. 139–47. Berlin: Veröff. Landesmuseum Vorgeschichte, VEB Deutscher Verlag der Wissenschaften.

———. 1997. Vögel (Aves) und mittelgroße bis kleine Carnivoren (Mammalia) aus dem Holstein-Komplex von Bilzingsleben (Thüringen), in *Bilzingsleben IV. Homo erectus – seine Kultur und seine Umwelt*. Edited by F.-S.-U. Jena, pp. 183–88. Bad Homburg-Leipzig: Verlag Ausbildung und Wissen.

Fisher, J. W., and H. C. Strickland. 1991. Dwellings and fireplaces: keys to Efe Pygmy campsite structure, in *Ethnoarchaeological Approaches to Mobile Campsites: Hunter-gatherer and pastoralist case studies*, vol. 1, International Monographs in Prehistory

Ethnoarchaeological Series. Edited by C. S. Gamble and W. A. Boismier, pp. 215–36. Ann Arbor, Mich.: International Monographs in Prehistory.

Flannery, K. V. 1967. Culture History versus Cultural Process: A Debate in American Archaeology. *Scientific American* 217: 119–22.

Floss, H. 1994. *Rohmaterialversorgung im Paläolithikum des Mittelrheingebietes. Monographien des Römisch-Germanischen Zentralmuseums 21*. Bonn: Habelt Verlag.

Foley, R. A. 1981a. A Model of Regional Archaeological Structure. *Proceedings of the Prehistoric Society* 47: 1–17.

———. 1981b. *Off-Site Archaeology and Human Adaptation in Eastern Africa. British Archaeological Reports (International Series)*. Oxford: B. A. R.

———. Editor. 1984. *Hominid Evolution and Community Ecology*. New York: Academic Press.

———. 1987. *Another Unique Species. Patterns in Human Evolutionary Ecology*. Harlow/London: Longman.

———. 1991. How Useful is the Culture Concept in Early Hominid Studies?, in *The Origins of Human Behaviour*. Edited by R. A. Foley, pp. 25–38. London: Unwin Hyman.

———. 1999. Pattern and Process in Hominid Evolution, in *Structure and Contingency: Evolutionary Processes in Life and Human Society*. Edited by J. Bintliff, pp. 30–42. London: Leicester University Press.

———. 2001a. The Evolutionary Consequences of Increased Carnivory in Hominids, in *Meat-eating and Human Evolution*. Edited by C. B. Stanford and H. T. Bunn, pp. 305–29. Oxford: Oxford University Press.

———. 2001b. The Origin of Human Social Institutions. *Proceedings of the British Academy* 110: 171–95.

Foley, R. A., and M. M. Lahr. 1997. Mode 3 Technologies and the Evolution of Modern Humans. *Cambridge Archaeological Journal* 7: 3–36.

Foley, R. A., and M. M. Lahr. 2003. On Stony Ground: Lithic Technology, Human Evolution and the Emergence of Culture. *Evolutionary Anthropology* 12: 109–22.

Fowler, C. 2002. Body Parts: Personhood and Materiality in the Earlier Manx Neolithic, in *Thinking Through the Body: Archaeologies of Corporeality*. Edited by Y. Hamilakis, M. Pluciennik, and S. Tarlow, pp. 47–69. New York: Plenum.

Frenzel, B. 1973. *Climatic Fluctuations of the Ice Age*. Cleveland: Case Western Reserve University.

Fritz, C. 2000. *La Gravure Dans l'Art Mobilier Magdalénien, Du Geste À La Représentation*. Paris: Editions De La Maison Des Sciences De l'Homme.

Gabora, L. 1997. The Origin and Evolution of Culture and Creativity. *Journal of Memetics – Evolutionary Models of Information Transmission* 1.

———. 2000. Towards a Theory of Creative Inklings, in *Art, Technology and Consciousness*. Edited by R. Ascot: Intellect Press.

———. 2001. Cognitive Mechanisms Underlying the Origin and Evolution of Culture. Unpublished PhD, Vrije Universiteit Brussels.

Gabunia, L., A. Vekua, D. Lordkipanidze, C. C. I. Swisher, R. Ferring, A. Justus, M. Nioradze, M. Tvalchrelidze, S. C. Antón, G. Bosinski, O. Jöris, M.-A. de Lumley, G. Majsuradze, and G. Mouskhelishvili. 2000. Earliest Pleistocene Hominid Cranial Remains from Dmanisi, Georgia: Taxonomy, Geological Setting, and Age. *Science* 288: 1019–25

Gambier, D. 1992. Les populations magdaléniennes en France, in *Le peuplement*

Magdalénien. Edited by C.T.H.S., pp. 41–51. Paris: Actes du Colloque de Chancelade 10–15 Octobre 1988.

Gamble, C. S. 1986. *The Palaeolithic Settlement of Europe*. Cambridge: Cambridge University Press.

———. 1987. Man the Shoveler: Alternative Models for Middle Pleistocene Occupation in Northern Latitudes, in *The Pleistocene Old World: Regional Perspectives*. Edited by O. Soffer, pp. 81–98. New York: Plenum Press.

———. 1993. *Timewalkers: The Prehistory of Global Colonization*. Cambridge, Mass.: Harvard University Press.

———. 1995. Personality Most Ancient. *British Archaeology* 1.

———. 1996. Hominid Behaviour in the Middle Pleistocene; An English Perspective, in *The English Palaeolithic reviewed*. Edited by C. S. Gamble and A. J. Lawson, pp. 63–71. Salisbury: Trust for Wessex Archaeology.

———. 1998a. Handaxes and Palaeolithic individuals, in *Stone Age Archaeology: Essays in Honour of John Wymer*. Edited by N. Ashton, F. Healy, and P. Pettitt, pp. 105–9. Oxford: Oxbow Monograph 102.

———. 1998b. Palaeolithic Society and the Release from Proximity: A Network Approach to Intimate Relations. *World Archaeology* 29: 426–49.

———. 1999. *The Palaeolithic Societies of Europe*. Cambridge: Cambridge University Press.

———. 2001. *Archaeology: The Basics*. London: Routledge.

———. in press. Materiality and Symbolic Force: A Palaeolithic View of Sedentism, in *Rethinking Materiality*. Edited by E. DeMarrais, C. Gosden, C. Renfrew, and K. V. Boyle. Cambridge: McDonald Institute of Archaeological Research.

Gamble, C. S., and W. A. Boismier. Editors. 1991. *Ethnoarchaeological Approaches to Mobile Campsites: Hunter-gatherer and Pastoralist Case Studies*. International Monographs in Prehistory Ethnoarchaeological Series 1. Ann Arbor, Mich.: International Monographs in Prehistory.

Gamble, C. S., and E. K. Gittins. 2004. Social Archaeology and Origins Research: a Palaeolithic Perspective, in *Social Archaeology: A Companion*. Edited by R. Preucell and L. Meskell, pp. 96–118. Oxford: Blackwell.

Gamble, C. S., and J. Steele. 1998. Hominid Ranging Patterns and Dietary Strategies, *The Palaeoanthropology Society Meetings, Seattle, 1998*.

———. 1999. Hominid Ranging Patterns and Dietary Strategies, in *Hominid Evolution. Lifestyles and Survival Strategies*. Edited by H. Ullrich, pp. 396–409. Gelsenkirchen/Schwelm: Edition Archaea.

Gaudzinski, S. 1995a. Wisentjäger in Wallertheim: Zur Taphonomie einer mittelpaläolithischen Freilandstation in Rheinhessen. *Jahrbuch des Römisch-Germanischen Zentralmuseums*: 245–423.

———. 1995b. Wallertheim Revisited: A Reanalysis of the Fauna from the Middle Palaeolithic Site of the Wallertheim (Rheinhessen/Germany). *Journal of Archaeological Science* 22: 51–66.

———. 1996. Kärlich-Seeufer. Untersuchungen zu einer altpaläolithischen Fundstelle im Neuwieder Becken (Rheinland-Pfalz). Mit Beiträgen von F. Bittmann and H.-H. Leuschner. *Jahrbuch RGZM* 43: 3–239.

———. 1998. Knochen und Knochengeräte der mittelpaläolithischen Fundstelle Salzgitter Lebenstedt (Deutschland). *Jahrbuch des Römisch-Germanischen Zentralmuseums Mainz* 45: 163–220.

———. 1999a. The Faunal Record of the Lower and Middle Palaeolithic of Europe: Remarks on Human Interference, in *The Middle Palaeolithic Occupation of Europe*. Edited by W. Roebroeks and C. S. Gamble, pp. 215–33. Leiden: European Science Foundation and University of Leiden.

———. 1999b. Middle Palaeolithic Bone Tools from the Open-air Site Salzgitter Lebenstedt (Germany). *Journal of Archaeological Science* 26: 124–41.

Gaudzinski, S., and W. Roebroeks. 2000. Adults Only. Reindeer Hunting at the Middle Palaeolithic Site Salzgitter Lebenstedt, Northern Germany. *Journal of Human Evolution* 38: 497–521.

———. 2003. Profile analysis at Salzgitter-Lebenstedt. A Reply to Munson and Marean. *Journal of Human Evolution* 44: 275–81.

Gaudzinski, S., and E. Turner. Editors. 1999. *The Role of Early Humans in the Accumulation of European Lower and Middle Palaeolithic Bone Assemblages*. Mainz: Römisch-Germanisches Zentralmuseum 42.

Gell, A. 1992. *The Anthropology of Time: Cultural Constructions of Temporal Maps and Images*. Oxford: Berg.

———. 1998. *Art and Agency: Towards a New Anthropological Theory*. Oxford: Clarendon Press.

Geneste, J.-M. 1988a. Economie des resources lithiques dans le Moustérien du sud-ouest de la France, in *L'Homme de Néandertal, vol. 8: La subsistence*. Edited by M. Otte, pp. 75–97. Liège: ERAUL 35. Université de Liège.

———. 1988b. Systèmes d'approvisionnement en matières premières au Paléolithique moyen et au Paléolithique supérieur en Aquitaine, in *L'Homme de Néandertal*, vol. 8: La mutation. Edited by J. K. Kozlowski, pp. 61–70. Liège: ERAUL 35. Université de Liège.

Gero, J. 2000. Troubled Travels in Agency and Feminism, in *Agency in Archaeology*. Edited by M. A. Dobres and J. Robb, pp. 34–9. London: Routledge.

Gibbard, P. L. 1985. *The Pleistocene History of the Middle Thames Valley*. Cambridge: Cambridge University Press.

Gibbard, P. L., and J. Lewin. 2002. Climate and Related Controls on Inter-glacial Fluvial Sedimentation in Lowland Britain. *Sedimentary Geology* 151: 187–210.

Gibson, J. J. 1979. *The Ecological Approach to Visual Perception*. Hillsdale: Erlbaum Associates.

Gibson, K. 1996. The Biocultural Human Brain, in *Modelling the Early Human Mind*. Edited by P. Mellars and K. Gibson, pp. 33–46. Cambridge: McDonald Institute for Archaeological Research.

Gibson, K., and T. Ingold. Editors. 1993. *Tools, Language and Cognition in Human Evolution*. Cambridge: Cambridge University Press.

Giddens, A. 1981. *A Contemporary Critique of Historical Materialism*. London: Macmillan.

———. 1984. *The Constitution of Society: Outline of the Theory of Structuration*. Cambridge: Polity Press.

Gilman, A. 1984. Explaining the Upper Palaeolithic revolution, in *Marxist Perspectives in Archaeology*. Edited by M. Spriggs, pp. 115–26. Cambridge: Cambridge University Press.

Goffman, E. 1959. *The Presentation of Self in Everyday Life*. Garden City NY: Anchor Books.

Goodall, J. 1986. *The Chimpanzees of Gombe: Patterns of Behaviour*. Cambridge, Mass.: Belknap Press.

Goodwin, A. J. H., and C. V. R. Lowe. 1929. The Stone Age Cultures of South Africa. *Annals of the South African Museum* 27: 1–289.

Goring-Morris, A. N. 1987. *At the Edge: Terminal Pleistocene Hunter-gatherers in the Negev and Sinai*. Oxford: British Archaeological Reports International Series 361.

Gosden, C. 1994. *Social Being and Time*. Oxford: Blackwell.

Gowlett, J. A. J. 1978. Kilombe – an Acheulian Site Complex in Kenya, in *Geological Background to Fossil Man*, vol. 6. Edited by W. W. Bishop, pp. 337–60: Special Publication of the Geological Society.

———. 1984. Mental Abilities of Early Man: A Look at Some Hard Evidence, in *Hominid evolution and community ecology*. Edited by R. A. Foley, pp. 167–92. London: Academic Press.

———. 1988. A Case of Developed Oldowan in the Acheulean? *World Archaeology* 20: 13–26.

———. 1991. Kilombe – review of an Acheulean site complex, in *Approaches to understanding early hominid life-ways in the African savannah, vol. UISPP 11 Kongress Mainz 1987*. Edited by J. D. Clark, pp. 129–36. Bonn: Dr Rudolf Habelt.

———. 1993. Le site Acheuléen de Kilombe: stratigraphie, géochronologie, habitat et industrie lithique. *L'Anthropologie* 97: 69–84.

———. 1996a. Mental Abilities of Early *Homo*: Elements of Constraint and Choice in Rule Systems, in *Modelling the Early Human Mind*. Edited by P. Mellars and K. Gibson, pp. 191–215. Cambridge: McDonald Institute for Archaeological Research.

———. 1996b. Rule Systems in the Artefacts of Homo Erectus and early Homo Sapiens: Constrained or Chosen, in *Modelling the Early Human Mind*. Edited by P. Mellars and K. Gibson, pp. 191–215. Cambridge: McDonald Institute for Archaeological Research.

———. 1997. High Definition Archaeology: Ideas and Evaluation. *World Archaeology* 29: 151–71.

———. 1999. Lower and Middle Pleistocene Archaeology of the Baringo Basin, in *Late Cenozoic Environments and Hominid Evolution: A Tribute to Bill Bishop*. Edited by P. Andrews and P. Banham, pp. 123–41. London: Geological Society.

Gowlett, J. A. J., and R. H. Crompton. 1994. Kariandusi: Acheulean Morphology and the Question of Allometry. *African Archaeological Review* 12: 3–42.

Gowlett, J. A. J., and J. Hallos. 2000. Beeches Pit: Overview of the Archaeology, in *The Quaternary of Norfolk and Suffolk: Field Guide*. Edited by S. G. Lewis, C. A. Whiteman, and R. C. Preece, pp. 197–206. London: Quaternary Research Association.

Gowlett, J. A. J., J. C. Chambers, J. Hallos, and T. R. J. Pumphrey. 1998. Beeches Pit: First Views of the Archaeology of a Middle Pleistocene Site in Suffolk, UK, in European Context. Papers Presented at the International Symposium 'Lifestyles and Survival Strategies in Pliocene and Pleistocene Hominids', *Anthropologie* 36: 1–2, 91–7.

Gowlett, J. A. J., R. H. Crompton, and Y. Li. 2001. Allometric Comparisons between Acheulean and Sangoan Large Cutting Tools at Kalambo Falls, in *Kalambo Falls Prehistoric Site, Vol 3: The Earlier Cultures: Middle and Earlier Stone Age*. Edited by J. D. Clark, pp. 612–19. Cambridge: Cambridge University Press.

Graves-Brown, P. M. 1996. All Things Bright and Beautiful? Species, Ethnicity and Cultural Dynamics, in *Cultural Identity and Archaeology: The Construction of European Communities*. Edited by P. M. Graves-Brown, S. Jones, and C. Gamble, pp. 81–95. London: Routledge.

Grayson, D. K. 1983. *The Establishment of Human Antiquity*. New York: Academic Press.

Green, C. P. 1974. Pleistocene Gravels of the River Axe in South-western England, and their Bearing on the Southern Limit of Glaciation in Britain. *Geological Magazine* 111: 213–20.

Green, C. P. 1988. The Palaeolithic Site at Broom, Dorset, 1932–1941: From the Record of C. E. Bean Esq. F.S.A. *Proceedings of the Geologists' Association* 99: 173–80.

Green, C. P., and D. F. M. McGregor. 1980. Quaternary Evolution of the River Thames, in *The Shaping of Southern England*. Edited by D. K. C. Jones, pp. 177–202. London: Academic Press.

——. 1987. River Terraces: A Stratigraphic Record of Environmental Change, in *International Geomorphology 1986 Part I*. Edited by V. Gardiner, pp. 977–87. Chichester: Wiley.

Green, J. F. N. 1946. The Terraces of Bournemouth, Hampshire. *Proceedings of the Geologists' Association* 57: 82–101.

——. 1947. The High Platforms of East Devon. *Proceedings of the Geologists' Association* 52: 36–52.

Grene, M. 1969. Hierarchy: One Word, How Many Concepts?, in *Hierarchical Structures*. Edited by L. L. Whyte, A. G. Wilson, and D. Wilson, pp. 56–8. New York: Elsevier.

Grine, F. E., and C. S. Henshilwood. 2002. Additional Human Remains from Blombos Cave, South Africa (1999–2000 Excavations). *Journal of Human Evolution* 42: 293–302.

Grün, R., and P. Beaumont. 2001. Border Cave Revisited: a revised ESR chronology. *Journal of Human Evolution* 40: 467–82.

Haeckel, J. 1966. Die differenzierten Jäger und Sammler, in *Handbuch der Urgeschichte Bd. 1 – Ältere und mittlere Steinzeit*. Edited by K. J. Narr, pp. 407–18. Bern/München: Francke.

Hahn, J., and S. Münzel. 1995. Knochenflöten aus dem Aurignacien des Geißenklösterle bei Blaubeuren, Alb-Donau-Kreis, in *Fundberichte aus Baden-Württemberg Band 20 (Aufsätze)*, pp. 1–12. Stuttgart: Schweizerbart'sche Verlagsbuchhandlung.

Hall, M. 2000. Timeless Time – Africa and the World. *South African Association of Archaeologists Conference, Johannesburg, 2000*.

Hamilakis, Y., M. Pluciennik, and S. Tarlow. Editors. 2002a. *Thinking Through the Body: Archaeologies of Corporeality*. New York: Kluwer Academic/Plenum.

——. 2002b. Introduction: Thinking Through the Body, in *Thinking Through the Body: Archaeologies of Corporeality*. Edited by Y. Hamilakis, M. Pluciennik, and S. Tarlow, pp. 1–21. New York: Plenum.

Haneke, J., and M. Weidenfeller. In Press. Die Herkunft der Artefakte aus geologischer Sicht, in *The 1991–1994 Middle Paleolithic Excavations at Wallertheim, Tübingen Publications in Prehistory*. Edited by N. J. Conard. Tübingen: Kerns Verlag.

Harding, P., P. L. Gibbard, J. Lewin, M. G. Macklin, and E. H. Moss. 1987. The

Transport and Abrasion of Flint Handaxes in a Gravel-bed River, in *The Human Uses of Flint and Chert: Proceedings of the Fourth International Flint Symposium Held at Brighton Polytechnic, 15 April 1983*. Edited by G. d. Sieveking and M. H. Newcomer, pp. 115–26. Cambridge: Cambridge University Press.

Harris, M. 1968. *The Rise of Anthropological Theory*. New York: Crowell.

Hay, R. L. 1976. *Geology of the Olduvai Gorge: A Study of Sedimentation in a Semiarid Basin*. Berkeley: University of California Press.

Hayek, F. A. 1949. *Individualism and Economic Order*. Chicago: University of Chicago Press.

Hebig, W. 1983. Die Fischreste von Bilzingsleben. *Ethnographisch-Archäologische Zeitschrift* 24: 558–69.

Heese, C. H. 1933. *The Evolution of Palaeolithic Technique*. Vol. XI(2). *Annals of the University of Stellenbosch*. Cape Town: Nasionale Pers.

Heese, C. H. n.d. Archaeological Studies in the Cape Province. Riversdale.

Heinrich, W. D. 1997a. Zur Taphonomie, Paläoökologie und Biostratigraphie fossiler Kleinsäugerfaunen aus dem mittelpleistozänen Travertinkomplex Bilzingsleben II, in *Bilzingsleben V. Homo erectus – seine Kultur und seine Umwelt*. Edited by F.-S.-U. Jena, pp. 121–34. Bad Homburg-Leipzig: Verlag Ausbildung und Wissen.

———. 1997b. Über Trogontherium cuvieri (Mammalia, Rodentia: Castoridae) aus dem mittelpleistozänen Travertinkomplex Bilzingsleben II in Thüringen., in *Bilzingsleben V. Homo erectus – seine Kultur und seine Umwelt*. Edited by F.-S.-U. Jena, pp. 135–82. Bad Homburg-Leipzig: Verlag Ausbildung und Wissen.

———. 1998. Weitere Funde von Kleinsäugetieren aus dem Travertinkomplex Bilzingsleben II in Thüringen. *Praehistoria Thuringica* 2: 89–95.

Henke, W., and H. Rothe. 1999. *Stammgeschichte des Menschen. Eine Einführung*. Berlin/Heidelberg: Springer.

Henrich, J., and R. McElreath. 2003. The Evolution of Cultural Evolution. *Evolutionary Anthropology* 12: 123–35.

Henry, D. O. 1998. Intrasite Spatial Patterns and Behavioral Modernity: Indications from the Late Levantine Mousterian Rockshelter of Tor Faraj, Southern Jordan, in *Neandertals and Modern Humans in Western Asia*. Edited by T. Akazawa, K. Aoki, and O. Bar-Yosef, pp. 127–42. New York: Plenum Press.

Henshilwood, C. S. 1989. Home is Where the Hearth Is: A Spatial Study of Dunefields Midden. Unpublished Honours Thesis, University of Cape Town.

———. 1995. Holocene Archaeology of the Coastal Garcia State Forest, Southern Cape, South Africa. Unpublished PhD, University of Cambridge.

Henshilwood, C. S., and J. C. Sealy. 1997. Bone Artefacts from the Middle Stone Age at Blombos Cave, Southern Cape, South Africa. *Current Anthropology* 38: 890–5.

Henshilwood, C. S., J. C. Sealy, R. J. Yates, K. Cruz-Uribe, P. Goldberg, F. E. Grine, R. G. Klein, C. Poggenpoel, K. L. V. Niekerk, and I. Watts. 2001a. Blombos Cave, Southern Cape, South Africa: Preliminary Report on the 1992–1999 Excavations of the Middle Stone Age Levels. *Journal of Archaeological Science* 28: 421–8.

Henshilwood, C. S., F. E. d'Errico, C. W. Marean, R. G. Milo, and R. Yates. 2001b. An Early Bone Tool Industry from the Middle Stone Age at Blombos Cave, South Africa: Implications for the Origins of Modern Human Behaviour, Symbolism and Language. *Journal of Human Evolution* 41: 631–78.

Henshilwood, C. S., F. E. d'Errico, R. Yates, Z. Jacobs, C. Tribolo, G. A. T. Duller, N. Mercier, J. C. Sealy, H. Valladas, I. Watts, and A. G. Wintle. 2002. Emergence of Modern Human Behaviour: Middle Stone Age Engravings from South Africa. *Science* 295: 1278–80.

Hietala, H. Editor. 1984. *Intrasite Spatial Analysis in Archaeology.* Cambridge: Cambridge University Press.

Higgs, E. S. Editor. 1972. *Papers in Economic Prehistory.* Cambridge: Cambridge University Press.

——. Editor. 1975. *Palaeoeconomy.* Cambridge: Cambridge University Press.

Hill, K. 1982. Hunting and Human Evolution. *Journal of Human Evolution* 11: 521–44.

Hinde, R. A. 1976. Interactions, Relationships and Social Structure. *Man* 11: 1–17.

Hodder, I. 1982. *Symbols in Action: Ethnoarchaeological Studies of Material Culture.* Cambridge: Cambridge University Press.

Hoffecker, J. F. 2002. *Desolate Landscapes: Ice-age Settlement in Eastern Europe.* New Brunswick: Rutgers University Press.

Hooley, R. W. 1922. The History of the Drainage of the Hampshire Basin. *Papers and Proceedings of the Hampshire Field Club and Archaeological Society* 9: 151–72.

Hopkinson, T. 2001. The Middle Palaeolithic Leaf Points of Europe: An Ecological Geography. Unpublished PhD, University of Cambridge.

Hosfield, R. T. 1999. *The Palaeolithic of the Hampshire Basin: A Regional Model of Hominid Behaviour During the Middle Pleistocene. British Archaeological Reports (International Series).* Oxford: B. A. R.

Hosfield, R. T., and J. C. Chambers. 2003. *Case Study Investigation of the Broom and Dunbridge Lower Palaeolithic Assemblages.* Unpublished report (English Heritage ALSF Project 3361).

Hosfield, R. T., P. Toms, J. C. Chambers, and C. P. Green. In prep. Late Middle Pleistocene Dates from the Broom Palaeolithic Sites, Devon and Dorset, U.K.

Hublin, J.-J. 1984. The Fossil Man from Salzgitter Lebenstedt (FRD) and its Place in Human Evolution during the Pleistocene in Europe. *Zeitschrift für Morphologie und Anthropologie* 75: 45–56.

Humphrey, N. K. 1976. The Social Function of Intellect, in *Growing Points in Ethology.* Edited by P. Bateson and R. A. Hinde, pp. 303–17. Cambridge: Cambridge University Press.

Ingman, M., K. Kaessmann, S. Pääbo, and S. Gyllensten. 2000. Mitochondrial Genome Variation and the Origin of Modern Humans. *Nature* 408: 708–13.

Ingold, T. 1986. Prologue: Concerning the Hunter and his Spear, in *The Appropriation of Nature: Essays on Human Ecology and Social Relations.* Edited by T. Ingold, pp. 1–15. Manchester: Manchester University Press.

——. 1993a. The Temporality of the Landscape. *World Archaeology* 25: 152–73.

——. 1993b. Tool-use, sociality and intelligence, in *Tools, Language and Cognition in Human Evolution.* Edited by K. Gibson and T. Ingold, pp. 429–45. Cambridge: Cambridge University Press.

——. 2000a. Evolving Skills, in *Alas, Poor Darwin: Arguments Against Evolutionary Psychology.* Edited by H. Rose and S. Rose, pp. 273–97. New York: Harmony Books.

——. 2000b. *The Perception of the Environment: Essays in Livelihood, Dwelling and Skill.* London: Routledge.

Irving, L. 1972. *Arctic Life of Birds and Mammals, including Man.* New York and Heidelberg: Springer Verlag.

Isaac, G. L. I. 1967. Towards the Interpretation of Occupation Debris: Some Experiments and Observations. *Kroeber Anthropological Society Papers* 37: 31–57.

———. 1972. Early Phases of Human Behaviour: Models in Lower Palaeolithic Archaeology, in *Models in Archaeology.* Edited by D. L. Clarke, pp. 167–99. London: Methuen.

———. 1976. The Activities of Early African Hominids: A Review of Archaeological Evidence from the Time Span Two and a Half to One Million Years Ago, in *Human Origins: Louis Leakey and the East African Evidence.* Edited by G. Isaac and E. McCown, pp. 483–514. Menlo Park: Benjamin.

———. 1977. *Olorgesailie: Archaeological Studies of a Middle Pleistocene Lake Basin.* Chicago: University of Chicago Press.

———. 1978a. Food Sharing and Human Evolution: Archaeological Evidence from the Plio-Pleistocene of East Africa. *Journal of Archaeological Research* 34: 311–25.

———. 1978b. The Food Sharing Behaviour of Proto-human Hominids. *Scientific American* 238: 90–108.

———. 1981. Stone Age Visiting Cards: Approaches to the Study of Early Land Use Patterns, in *Pattern of the Past: Studies in Honour of David Clarke.* Edited by N. Hammond, G. Isaac, and I. Hodder, pp. 131–55. Cambridge: Cambridge University Press.

———. 1981. Archaeological Tests of Alternative Models of Early Hominid Behaviour: Excavation and Experiments, in *The Emergence of Man.* Edited by J. Z. Young, E. M. Jope, and K. P. Oakley, pp. 177–88. London: The Royal Society and the British Academy.

———. 1984. The Archaeology of Human Origins: Studies of the Lower Pleistocene in East Africa 1971–1981, in *Advances in Old World Archaeology 3.* Edited by F. Wendorf and A. Close, pp. 1–87. New York: Academic Press.

———. 1989a. *The Archaeology of Human Origins.* Edited by Barbara Isaac. Cambridge: Cambridge University Press.

———. 1989b. Towards the Interpretation of Occupation Debris: Some Experiments and Observations, in *The Archaeology of Human Origins: Papers by Glynn Isaac.* Edited by B. Isaac, pp. 191–205. Cambridge: Cambridge University Press.

Jacobs, Z., A. G. Wintle, and G. A. T. Duller. 2003a. Optical Dating of Dune Sand from Blombos Cave, South Africa: I – Multiple Grain Data. *Journal of Human Evolution* 44: 599–612.

Jacobs, Z., G. A. T. Duller, and A. G. Wintle. 2003b. Optical Dating of Dune Sand from Blombos Cave, South Africa: II – Single Grain Data. *Journal of Human Evolution* 44: 613–25.

James, W. 2003. *The Ceremonial Animal.* Oxford: Oxford University Press.

Jechorek, H. 2000. Die fossile Flora des Reinsdorf-Interglazials: Paläokarpologische Untersuchungen an mittelpleistozänen Ablagerungen im Braunkohlentagebau Schöningen. *Praehistoria Thuringica* 4: 7–17.

Jochim, M. A. 1976. *Hunter-Gatherer Settlement and Subsistence.* New York: Academic Press.

Johnson, A. W., and T. Earle. 1987. *The Evolution of Human Societies.* Stanford: Stanford University Press.

Johnson, M. 1999. *Archaeological Theory: An Introduction.* Oxford: Blackwell.

Jolly, K. 1948. The Development of the Cape Middle Stone Age in the Skildergat Cave, Fish Hoek. *South African Archaeological Bulletin* 2: 106–7.

Jones, A. 2001. Drawn from Memory: The Archaeology of Aesthetics and the Aesthetics of Archaeology in Earlier Bronze Age Britain and the Present. *World Archaeology* 33: 334–56.

Jones, K. T. 1993. The Archaeological Structure of a Short-term Camp, in *From Bones to Behavior: Ethnoarchaeological and Experimental Contributions to the Interpretation of Faunal Remains, Center for Archaeological Investigations, Occasional Papers 21*. Edited by J. Hudson, pp. 101–14. Carbondale: Southern Illinois University.

Jones, P. R. 1980. Experimental Butchery with Modern Stone Tools and its Relevance for Palaeolithic Archaeology. *World Archaeology* 12: 153–65.

——. 1981. Experimental Implement Manufacture and Use: A Case Study from Olduvai Gorge. *Philosphical Transactions of the Royal Society of London*: 189–95.

Jones, P. R. 1994. Results of experimental work in relation to the stone industries of Olduvai Gorge, in *Olduvai Gorge Volume 5; excavations in Beds III, IV and the Masek Beds, 1968–71*. Edited by M. D. Leakey and D. A. Roe, pp. 254–298. Cambridge: Cambridge University Press.

Julien, M., and J.-L. Rieu. Editors. 1999. *Occupations du Paléolithique supérieur dans le sud-est du Bassin parisien*. Documents d'Archéologique Française 78. Paris: Editions de la Maison des Sciences de l'Homme.

Keeley, L. 1980. *Experimental Determination of Stone Tool Uses: A Microwear Analysis*. Chicago: Chicago University Press.

Keen, D. H. 2001. Towards a Late Middle Pleistocene Non-marine Molluscan Biostratigraphy for the British Isles. *Quaternary Science Reviews* 20: 1657–65.

Kelly, R. 1983. Hunter-gatherer Mobility Strategies. *Journal of Anthropological Research* 39: 277–306.

Kelly, R. 1995. *The Foraging Spectrum: Diversity in Hunter-gatherer Lifeways*. Washington and London: Smithsonian Institution Press.

Kelly, R. 1992. Mobilty/Sedentism: Concepts, Archaeological Measures, and Effects. *Annual Reviews in Anthropology* 21: 43–66.

Kerrich, J. E. 1957. Statistical Note. *South African Archaeological Bulletin* 12: 137.

Key, C. A. 2000. The Evolution of Human Life History. *World Archaeology* 31: 329–50.

Kim, S.-J., T. J. Crowley, and A. Stossel. 1998. Local Orbital Forcing of Antarctic Climate Change During the Last Interglacial. *Science* 280: 728–30.

Kind, C.-J. 1985. *Die Verteilung von Steinartefakten in Grabungsflächen: ein Modell zur Organisation alt- und mittelsteinzeitlicher Siedlungsplätze*. Tübingen: Archaeologica Venatoria.

Kirch, P. V. 1984. *The Evolution of the Polynesian Chiefdoms*. Cambridge: Cambridge University Press.

Klein, R. G. 1972. Preliminary Report on the July Through September 1970 Excavations at Nelson Bay Cave, Plettenberg Bay (Cape Province, South Africa). *Palaeoecology of Africa* 6: 177–208.

——. 1995. Anatomy, Behavior and Modern Human Origins. *Journal of World Prehistory* 9: 167–98.

——. 1999. *The Human Career: Human Biological and Cultural Origins*, 2nd edition. Chicago: University of Chicago Press.

——. 2000. Archaeology and the Evolution of Human Behavior. *Evolutionary Anthropology* 9: 17–36.

Klein, R. G., and K. Cruz-Uribe. 1996. Exploitation of Large Bovids and Seals at Middle and Later Stone Age Sites in South Africa. *Journal of Human Evolution* 31: 315–34.

———. 2000. Middle and Late Stone Age Large Mammal and Tortoise Remains from Die Kelders Cave 1, Western Province, South Africa. *Journal of Human Evolution* 38: 169–95.

Kohn, M., and S. Mithen. 1999. Handaxes: Products of Sexual Selection? *Antiquity* 73: 518–26.

Kolen, J. 1999. Hominids without Homes: On the Nature of Middle Palaeolithic Settlement in Europe, in *The Middle Palaeolithic Occupation of Europe*. Edited by W. Roebroeks and C. S. Gamble, pp. 139–75. Leiden: European Science Foundation and University of Leiden.

Kroll, E. M., and T. D. Price. Editors. 1991. *The Interpretation of Archaeological Spatial Patterning*. New York: Plenum.

Kuhn, S. L. 1992. On Planning and Curated Technologies in the Middle Palaeolithic. *Journal of Anthropological Research* 48: 185–214.

———. 1994. Formal approach to the Design and Assembly of Mobile Toolkits. *American Antiquity* 59: 426–42.

———. 1995. *Mousterian Lithic Technology: An Ecological Perspective*. Princeton: Princeton University Press.

Kuman, K. 2003. Site Formation in the Early South African Stone Age Sites and its Influence on the Archaeological Record. *South African Journal of Science* 99: 251–4.

Kuman, K., M. Inbar, and R. J. Clarke. 1999. Palaeoenvironments and Cultural Sequence of the Florisbad Middle Stone Age Hominid Sites, South Africa. *Journal of Archaeological Science* 26: 1409–25.

Laland, K. N., and W. Hoppitt. 2003. Do Animals Have Culture? *Evolutionary Anthropology* 12: 150–9.

Lambeck, K., T. M. Esat, and E.-K. Potter. 2002. Links Between Climate and Sea Levels for the Past Three Million Years. *Nature* 419: 199–206.

Lamotte, A. Editor. 2001. *Les Industries à Bifaces de l'Europe du Nord-Ouest au Pléistocène Moyen. L'apport des données des gisements du bassin de la Somme, de l'Escaut et de la Baie de St-Brieuc*. Vol. 932. *BAR International Series*. Oxford: Archaeopress.

Laurat, T. 2000. Morphologie und Morphometrie spitzenartiger Steingeräte der altpaläolithischen Fundstelle Bilzingsleben (Thüringen). Unpublished Magister-Thesis, Universität Jena.

Lawson, G., and F. d'Errico. 2002. Microscopic, Experimental and Theoretical Reassessment of Upper Palaeolithic Bird-Bone Pipes from Isturitz, France: Ergonomics of Design, Systems of Notation and the Origins of Musical Traditions, in *Archaeology of Sound: origin and organisation*. Edited by E. Hickmann, A. D. Kilmer, and R. Eichmann, pp. 119–42. Rahden: Marie Leindorf GmbH.

Le Mort, F., and D. Gambier. 1992. Diversité du traitement des os humains au magdalénien: un exemple particulier le cas du gisement du Placard (Charente), in *Le peuplement Magdalénien*. Edited by C.T.H.S., pp. 29–40. Paris: Actes du Colloque de Chancelade 10–15 octobre 1988.

Leakey, M. D. 1971. *Olduvai Gorge: Excavations in Beds I and II 1960 – 1963*. Cambridge: Cambridge University Press.

Leakey, M. D., and J. M. Harris. Editors. 1987. *Laetoli: A Pliocene Site in Northern Tanzania*. Oxford: Clarendon Press.

Leenhardt, M. 1979. Do Kamo. Person and Myth in the Melanesian World. Chicago: University of Chicago Press.

Leroi-Gourhan, A. 1993. Gesture and Speech. Cambridge, Mass.: MIT Press.

Leroi-Gourhan, A., and M. Brézillon. 1966. L'habitation magdalénienne no. 1 de Pincevent près Montereau (Seine-et-Marne). Gallia Préhistorie 9: 263–365.

Lienhardt, G. 1961. Divinity and Experience: The Religion of the Dinka. Oxford: Clarendon Press.

——. 1985. Self: Public, Private. Some African Representations, in The Category of the Person: Anthropology, Philosophy, History. Edited by M. Carrithers, S. Collins, and S. Lukes, pp. 141–55. Cambridge: Cambridge University Press.

LiPuma, E. 1998. Modernity and Forms of Personhood in Melanesia, in Bodies and Persons: Comparative Perspectives from Africa and Melanesia. Edited by M. Lambek and A. Strathern, pp. 53–79. Cambridge: Cambridge University Press.

Little, M. G., R. R. Schneider, D. Kroon, B. Price, T. Bickert, and G. Wefer. 1997. Rapid Palaeoceanographic Changes in the Benguela Upwelling System for the Last 160,000 Years as Indicated by Abundances of Planktonic Foraminifera. Palaeogeography, Palaeoclimatology, Palaeoecology 130: 135–61.

Locht, J.-L. Editor. 2002. Bettencourt-Saint-Ouen (Somme); Cinq occupations paléolithique au début de la dernière glaciation. Documents d'Archéologie Française 90. Paris: Éditions de la Maison des sciences de l'Homme.

Maddy, D., D. R. Bridgland, and R. Westaway. 2001. Uplift-driven Valley Incision and Climate-controlled River Terrace Development in the Thames Valley, UK. Quaternary International 79: 23–36.

Mai, D. H. 1983. Die fossile Pflanzenwelt des interglazialen Travertins von Bilzingsleben, in Bilzingsleben II. Homo erectus – seine Kultur und seine Umwelt. Edited by D. H. Mai, D. Mania, T. Nötzold, V. Toepfer, E. Vlček, and W. D. Heinrich, pp. 45–129. Berlin: VEB Deutscher Verlag der Wissenschaften.

Malan, B. D. 1955. The Archaeology of Tunnel Cave and Skildergat Kop, Fish Hoek, Cape of Good Hope. South African Archaeology Bulletin 10: 3–9.

Mallik, R., N. Frank, A. Mangini, and G. A. Wagner. 2001. Präzise Th/U-Datierung archäologisch relevanter Travertinvorkommen Thüringens. Homo heidelbergensis von Mauer – Veröffentlichungen 1: 77–89.

Mania, D. 1983. Die Molluskenfauna des mittelpleistozänen Travertinkomplexes bei Bilzingsleben, in Bilzingsleben II. Homo erectus – seine Kultur und seine Umwelt. Edited by D. H. Mai, D. Mania, T. Nötzold, V. Toepfer, E. Vlček, and W. D. Heinrich, pp. 131–55. Berlin: VEB Deutscher Verlag der Wissenschaften.

——. 1991. Eiszeitarchäologische Forschungsarbeiten in den Tagebauen des Saale – Elbe-Gebietes. Veröffentlichungen des Museums für Ur- und Frühgeschichte Potsdam 25: 78–100.

——. 1993. Die Terrassen-Travertin-Sequenz von Bilzingsleben. Ein Beitrag zur Stratigraphie des Mittel- und Jungpleistozäns im Elbe-Saale-Gebiet. Ethnographisch-Archäologische Zeitschrift 34: 554–75.

——. 1994. Zu den Silexgeräten von Bilzingsleben (Altpaläolithikum, Mittelpleistozän). Ethnographisch-Archäologische Zeitschrift 34: 525–48.

——. 1995a. Die geologischen Verhältnisse im Gebiet von Schöningen, in Archäologische Ausgrabungen im Braunkohlentagebau Schöningen, Landkreis Helmstedt. Edited by H. Thieme and R. Maier, pp. 33–43. Hannover: Verlag Hahnsche Buchhandlung.

——. 1995b. The Earliest Occupation of Europe: The Elbe-Saale Region (Germany), in *The Earliest Occupation of Europe*. Edited by W. Roebroeks and T. v. Kolfschoten, pp. 85–101. Leiden: European Science Foundation and University of Leiden.

——. 1995c. Umwelt und Mensch am Beispiel von Bilzingsleben. *Etudes et recherches Archeologiques de l'Université de Liège* 62: 49–65.

——. 1997. Das Quartär des Saalegebietes und des Harzvorlandes unter besonderer Berücksichtigung der Travertine von Bilzingsleben – Ein Beitrag zur zyklischen Gliederung des eurasischen Quartärs, in *Bilzingsleben V. Homo erectus – seine Kultur und seine Umwelt*. Edited by F.-S.-U. Jena, pp. 23–103. Bad Homburg-Leipzig: Verlag Ausbildung und Wissen.

Mania, D., and D. H. Mai. 2001. Molluskenfaunen und Floren des Elbe-Saalegebietes während des mittleren Eiszeitalters. *Praehistoria Thuringica* 6/7: 49–91.

Mania, D., and U. Mania. 1988. Deliberate Engravings on Bone Artefacts of *Homo erectus*. *Rock Art Research* 5: 91–107.

——. 1997. Die schaberartigen Knochengeräte des Homo erectus von Bilzingsleben, in *Bilzingsleben V. Homo erectus – seine Kultur und seine Umwelt*. Edited by F.-S.-U. Jena, pp. 201–49. Bad Homburg-Leipzig: Verlag Ausbildung und Wissen.

——. 1998. Geräte aus Holz von der altpaläolithischen Fundstelle bei Bilzingsleben. *Praehistoria Thuringica* 2: 32–72.

——. 2002. Zür geologischen und archäologischen Fundsituation der menschlichen Fossilien von Bilzingsleben – The geological and archaeological find situation of fossil man of Bilzingsleben, in *Der fossile Mensch von Bilzingsleben. Bilzingsleben VI*. Edited by E. Vlček, D. Mania, and U. Mania, pp. 28–143. Weissbach: Beier & Beran.

Mania, D., M. Thomae, T. Litt, and T. Weber. 1990. *Neumark-Gröbern. Beiträge zur Jagd des Mittelpaläolithischen Menschen. Veröffentlichungen des Landesmuseums für Vorgeschichte Halle 43*. Berlin: Deutscher Verlag der Wissenschaften.

Marks, A. E., H. Hietala, and J. K. Williams. 2001. Tool Standardization in the Middle and Upper Palaeolithic: A Closer Look. *Cambridge Archaeological Journal* 11: 17–44.

Marriott, M. 1976. Hindu Transactions: Diversity without Dualism, in *Transactions and Meaning, ASA Essays in Anthropology 1*. Edited by B. Kapferer. Philadelphia: ISHI Publications.

Marshall, G. D., C. S. Gamble, and D. Roe. 2002. Lower Palaeolithic Technology, Raw Material and Population Ecology, York: Archaeological Data Service, AHDS. http://ads.ahds.ac.uk/catalogue/specColl/bifaces/index.cfm.

Marshall, G. D. 2001. The Broom Pits: A Review of Research and a Pilot Study of Two Acheulian Biface Assemblages, in *Palaeolithic Archaeology of the Solent River, Lithic Studies Society Occasional Paper 7*. Edited by F. F. Wenban-Smith and R. T. Hosfield, pp. 77–84. London: Lithic Studies Society.

Marwick, B. 2003. Pleistocene Exchange Networks as Evidence for the Evolution of Language. *Cambridge Archaeological Journal* 13: 67–81.

Mason, R. J. 1957. The Transvaal Middle Stone Age and Statistical Analysis. *South African Archaeological Bulletin* 12: 119–37.

——. 1962. *The Prehistory of the Transvaal*. Johannesburg: Witwatersrand University Press.

——. 1988. Cave of Hearths, Makapansgat, Transvaal, in *Archaeology Research Unit*

Occasional Paper No. 21. Johannesburg: University of Witwatersrand University Press.

Mauss, M. 1979. The Notion of Body Techniques, in *Sociology and Psychology: Essays.* Translated by Ben Brewster, pp. 97–123. London: Routledge and Kegan Paul.

——. 1985. A Category of the Human Mind: the Notion of Person; The Notion of Self, in *The Category of the Person. Anthropology, Philosophy, History.* Edited by M. Carrithers, S. Collins, and S. Lukes, pp. 1–25. New York: Cambridge University Press.

McBrearty, S., and A. S. Brooks. 2000. The Revolution that Wasn't: A New Interpretation of the Origin of Modern Humans. *Journal of Human Evolution* 39: 453–563.

McGrew, W. C. 1992. *Chimpanzee Material Culture: Implications for Human Evolution.* Cambridge: Cambridge University Press.

——. 1994. Tools Compared. The Material Culture, in *Chimpanzee Cultures.* Edited by R. W. Wrangham, W. C. McGrew, F. B. M. de Waal, and P. G. Heltne, pp. 25–39. Cambridge, MA/London: Harvard University Press.

McHenry, H. M. 1994. Tempo and Mode in Human Evolution. *Proceedings of the National Academy of Sciences* 91: 6780–6.

McPherron, S. P. 1994. A Reduction Model for Variability in Acheulian Biface Morphology. Unpublished PhD, University of Pennsylvania.

——. 1996. A Re-examination of the British Biface Data. *Lithics* 16: 47–63.

Meignen, L. 1993. *L'abri des Canalettes: Un habitat moustérien sur les grands Causses (Nant Aveyron). Fouilles 1980–1986.* Paris: Editions du C.N.R.S.

Mellars, P. A. 1996a. *The Neanderthal Legacy: An Archaeological Perspective From Western Europe.* Princeton: Princeton University Press.

——. 1996b. Symbolism, Language and the Neanderthal Mind, in *Modelling the Early Human Mind.* Edited by P. Mellars and K. Gibson, pp. 15–32. Cambridge: McDonald Institute for Archaeological Research.

Mellars, P. A., and K. Gibson. Editors. 1996. *Modelling the Early Human Mind.* Cambridge: McDonald Institute for Archaeological Research.

Meltzoff, A. 1995. Understanding the Intentions of Others: Re-enactment of Intended Acts by 18-month-old Children. *Developmental Psychology* 31: 838–50.

Miller, D. 1985. *Artefacts as Categories: A Study of Ceramic Variability in Central India.* Cambridge: Cambridge University Press.

Milo, R. G. 1998. Evidence for Hominid Predation at Klasies River Mouth, South Africa, and its Implications for the Behavior of Early Modern Humans. *Journal of Archaeological Science* 25: 99–133.

Mithen, S. 1993. Individuals, Groups and the Palaeolithic Record: A Reply to Clark. *Proceedings of the Prehistoric Society* 59: 393–98.

——. 1994. Technology and Society during the Middle Pleistocene: Hominid Group Size, Social Learning and Industrial Variability. *Cambridge Archaeological Journal* 4: 3–32.

——. 1996a. Social Learning and Cultural Tradition: Interpreting Early Palaeolithic Technology, in *The Archaeology of Human Ancestry.* Edited by J. Steele and S. Shennan, pp. 207–29. London: Routledge.

——. 1996b. *The Prehistory of the Mind: The Cognitive Origins of Art, Religion and Science.* London: Thames and Hudson.

Moore, H. 2000. Ethics and Ontology: Why Agents and Agency Matter, in *Agency in Archaeology*. Edited by M.-A. Dobres and J. Robb, pp. 259–63. London: Routledge.

Musil, R. 1991. Die Bären von Bilzingsleben – Die Pferde von Bilzingsleben, in *Bilzingsleben IV. Homo erectus – seine Kultur und seine Umwelt*. Edited by K. Fischer, E. W. Guenther, W. D. Heinrich, D. Mania, R. Musil, and T. Nötzold, pp. 103–30. Berlin: VEB Deutscher Verlag der Wissenschaften.

———. 1993. Unterschiede im Jagdwild der verschiedenen paläolithischen Kulturen unter besonderer Berücksichtigung von Bilzingsleben. *Ethnographisch-Archäologische Zeitschrift* 34: 601–7.

———. 2002. Morphologische und metrische Differenzen der Pferde von Bilzingsleben und Schöningen (Vorläufiger Bericht). *Praehistoria Thuringica* 8: 143–8.

Mussi, M. 1995. The Earliest Occupation of Europe: Italy, in *The Earliest Occupation of Europe*. Edited by W. Roebroeks and T. van Kolfschoten, pp. 27–49. Leiden: European Science Foundation and University of Leiden.

Nicholls, R. J. 1987. Evolution of the Upper Reaches of the Solent River and the Formation of Poole and Christchurch Bays, in *Wessex and the Isle of Wight: Field Guide*. Edited by K. E. Barber, pp. 99–114. Cambridge: Quaternary Research Association.

Nietzsche, F. 1954. Thus spoke Zarathustra: First Part, in *The Portable Nietzsche*. Edited by W. Kaufmann, pp. 121–91. New York: Viking Penguin.

Nishida, T., T. Hasegawa, H. Hayaki, Y. Takahata, and S. Uehara. 1992. Meat Sharing as a Coalition Strategy by an Alpha Male Chimpanzee?, in *Topics in Primatology*, Vol. 1, Human Origins. Proceedings of the XIII Congress International Primatological Society. Edited by T. Nishida, W. C. McGrew, P. Marler, M. Pickford, and F. de Waal, pp. 159–75. Tokyo: Tokyo University Press.

Nitecki, M. H. 1987. The Idea of Human Hunting, in *The Evolution of Human Hunting*. Edited by M. H. Nitecki and D. V. Nitecki, pp. 1–9. New York: Plenum Press.

Noble, W., and I. Davidson. 1996. *Human Evolution, Language and Mind*. Cambridge: Cambridge University Press.

Noll, M. P. 2000. Components of Acheulean Lithic Assemblage Variability at Olorgesailie, Kenya. Unpublished PhD, University of Illinois.

Noll, M. P., and M. D. Petraglia. 2003. Acheulean Bifaces and Early Human Behavioral Patterns in East Africa and South India, in *Multiple Approaches to the Study of Bifacial Technologies*. Edited by M. Soressi and H. L. Dibble, pp. 31–53. Philadelphia: University of Pennsylvania Press.

O'Connell, J. F. 1987. Alyawara Site Structure and its Archaeological Implications. *American Antiquity* 52: 74–108.

———. 1997. On Plio/Pleistocene Archaeological Sites and Central Places. *Current Anthropology* 38: 86–8.

O'Connell, J. F., K. Hawkes, and N. G. Blurton-Jones. 1999. Grandmothering and the Evolution of Homo Erectus. *Journal of Human Evolution* 36: 461–85.

O'Neill, R. V., D. L. DeAngelis, J. B. Waide, and T. F. H. Allen. 1986. *A Hierarchical Concept of Ecosystems*. Princeton, NJ: Princeton University Press.

Oakley, K. P., P. Andrews, L. H. Keeley, and J. D. Clark. 1977. A Reappraisal of the Clacton Spearpoint. *Proceedings of the Prehistoric Society* 43: 13–30.

Oliver, J. S., N. E. Sikes, and K. M. Stewart. 1994. *Early Hominid Behavioural Ecology*. New York: Academic Press.

Oppo, D. W., J. F. McManus, and J. L. Cullen. 1998. Abrupt Climate Events 500,000 to 340,000 Years Ago: Evidence from Subpolar North Atlantic Sediments. *Science* 279: 1335–8.

Orschiedt, J. 1999. *Manipulation an menschlichen Skelettresten: taphonomische Prozesse, Sekundarbestattungen oder Kannibalismus?* Tübingen: Mo Vince Verlag Urgeschichtliche Materialhefte 13.

Orwell, G. 1949. *1984*. Harmondsworth: Penguin Books.

Paddayya, K. 1982. *The Acheulian Culture of the Hunsgi Valley (Peninsular India): a Settlement System Perspective*. Poona: Deccan College Postgraduate and Research Institute.

——. The Acheulian Culture Project of the Hunsgi and Baichbal Valleys, Peninsular India, in *Human Roots: Africa and Asia in the Middle Pleistocene*. Edited by L. Barham and K. Robson-Brown, pp. 235–58. Bristol: Western Academic and Specialist Press Limited.

Paddayya, K., and R. Jhaldiyal. 1999. A New Acheulian Site at Kolihal: Hunsgi Valley, Karnataka. *Puratattva* 29: 1–7.

Paddayya, K., and M. D. Petraglia. 1993. Formation Processes of Acheulean Localities in the Hunsgi and Baichbal Valleys, Peninsular India, in *Formation Processes in Archaeological Context*. Edited by P. Goldberg, D. T. Nash, and M. D. Petraglia, pp. 61–82. Madison: Prehistory Press.

——. 1997. Isampur: An Acheulian Workshop in the Hunsgi Valley, Gulbarga District, Karnataka. *Man and Environment* 22: 95–100.

Paddayya, K., R. Jhaldiyal, and M. D. Petraglia. 2000. The Significance of the Acheulian Site of Isampur, Karnataka, in the Lower Palaeolithic of India. *Puratattva* 30: 1–24.

Paddayya, K., B. A. B. Blackwell, R. Jhaldiyal, M. D. Petraglia, S. Fevrier, D. A. Chaderton II, J. I. B. Blickstein, and A. R. Skinner. 2002. Recent Findings on the Acheulian of the Hunsgi and Baichbal Valleys, Karnataka, with Special Reference to the Isampur Excavation and its Dating. *Current Science* 83: 641–7.

Parkington, J., P. Nilsson, C. Reeler, and C. Henshilwood. 1992. Making Sense of Space at Dunefield Midden Campsite, Western Cape, South Africa. *South African Field Archaeology* 1: 63–70.

Pastoors, A. 2001. *Die mittelpaläolithische Freilandstation von Salzgitter-Lebenstedt: Genese der Fundstelle und Systematik der Steinbearbeitung*. Salzgitter: Salzgitter-Forschungen 3.

Pearce, T. 2002. Consciousness and the Archaeological Record. *The Ninth International Conference on Hunting and Gathering Societies, Edinburgh, Scotland, 2002*.

Peers, B. 2002. *Preliminary Report on the Archaeology of the Fisj Hoek – Noord Hoek Valley*. Unpublished Manuscript, South African Museum.

Petraglia, M. D. 1998. The Lower Paleolithic of India and its Bearing on the Asian Record, in *Early Human Behaviour in Global Context: The Rise and Diversity of the Lower Paleolithic Record*. Edited by M. D. Petraglia and R. Korisettar, pp. 343–90. New York: Routledge.

——. 2001. The Lower Palaeolithic of India and its Behavioural Significance, in *Human Roots: Africa and Asia in the Middle Pleistocene*. Edited by L. Barham and

K. Robson-Brown, pp. 217–33. Bristol: Western Academic and Specialist Press Limited.

Petraglia, M. D., P. LaPorta, and K. Paddayya. 1999. The first Acheulian Quarry in India: Stone Tool Manufacture, Biface Morphology, and Behaviors. *Journal of Anthropological Research* 55: 39–70.

Petraglia, M. D., J. Schuldenrein, and R. Korisettar. 2003. Landscapes, Activity, and the Acheulean to Middle Paleolithic Transition in the Kaladgi Basin, India. *Eurasian Prehistory* 1: 3–24.

Petit, P., J. Jouzel, D. Raynaud, N. I. Barkov, J.-M. Barnola, I. Basile, M. Benders, J. Chapellaz, M. Davis, G. Delaygue, M. Delmotte, V. M. Kotlyakov, M. Legrand, V. Y. Lipenkov, C. Lorius, L. Pepin, C. Ritz, E. Satlzman, and M. Stievenard. 1999. Climate and Atmospheric History of the Past 420,000 Years from the Vostok Ice Core, Antarctica. *Nature* 399: 429–36.

Pettitt, P. B. 2000. Neanderthal Lifecycles: Development and Social Phases in the Lives of the Last Archaics. *World Archaeology* 31: 351–66.

Pike-Tay, A. 1997. Incremental Analysis of Bovid and Cervid Teeth from Wallertheim, Germany, in *Reports for the Second Wallertheim Workshop*. Edited by N. J. Conard and A. W. Kandel, p. 69. Tübingen: Institut für Ur- und Frühgeschichte.

Pitts, M., and M. Roberts. 1997. *Fairweather Eden: Life in Britain Half a Million Years Ago as Revealed by the Excavations at Boxgrove*. London: Century.

Pope, M. 2002. The Significance of Biface-rich Assemblages: An Examination of Behavioural Controls on Lithic Assemblage Formation in the Lower Palaeolithic. Unpublished PhD, University of Southampton.

Porr, M. 2000. Signs of the Times. A Different Approach towards the Origins of Lower Palaeolithic Handaxes. *Archaeological Review from Cambridge* 17: 19–32.

Potts, R. 1988. *Early Hominid Activities at Olduvai*. New York: Aldine.

——. 1989. Olorgesailie: New Excavations and Findings in Early and Middle Pleistocene Toolmaking and the Transport of Resources. *Journal of Human Evolution* 18: 269–76.

——. 1993. Archaeological Interpretations of Early Hominid Behaviour and Ecology, in *The origins and Evolution of Humans and Humanness*. Edited by D. Rasmussen, pp. 49–74. Boston: Jones and Barlett Publishers.

——. 1994. Variables Versus Models of Early Hominid Land Use. *Journal of Human Evolution* 27: 7–24.

——. 1996. *Humanity's Descent: The Consequences of Ecological Instability*. New York: William Morrow & Co.

Potts, R., A. K. Behrensmeyer, and P. Ditchfield 1999. Palaeolandscape Variation and Early Pleistocene Hominid Activities: Members 1 and 7, Olorgesailie Formation, Kenya. *Journal of Human Evolution* 37: 747–88.

Preece, R. C. 2001. Molluscan Evidence for Differentiation of Interglacials within the 'Cromerian Complex'. *Quaternary Science Reviews* 20: 1643–56.

Proctor, R. N. 2003. Three Roots of Human Recency: Molecular Anthropology, the Refigured Acheulean, and the UNESCO Response to Auschwitz. *Current Anthropology* 44: 213–39.

Raymo, M. E., K. Ganley, S. Carter, D. W. Oppo, and J. McManus. 1998. Millennial-scale Climate Instability during the Early Pleistocene Epoch. *Nature* 392: 699–702.

Raynal, J.-P., and J.-P. Texier. 1989. Decouverte d'Acheuléen ancien dans la Carrière Thomas 1 à Casablanca et problème de l'ancienneté de la présence humaine au Maroc. *Comptes Rendus Academie des Sciences Paris* 308 (Serie II): 1743–49.

Reader, S. M., and K. N. Laland. 2002. Social Intelligence, Innovation, and Enhanced Brain Size in Primates. *Proceedings of the National Academy of Sciences* 99: 4436–41.

Reid, C. 1893. A Fossiliferous Pleistocene Deposit at Stone on the Hampshire Coast. *Quarterly Journal of the Geological Society of London* 49: 325–9.

———. 1898. *The Geology of the Country around Bournemouth*, 1st edition. *Memoir of the Geological Survery of England and Wales.* London: HMSO.

———. 1902a. *The Geology of the Country around Ringwood. Memoir of the Geological Survey of England and Wales.* London: HMSO.

———. 1902b. *The Geology of the Country around Southampton. Memoir of the Geological Survey of England and Wales.* London: HMSO.

Reid Moir, J. 1936. Ancient Man in Devon. *Proceedings of the Devon Archaeological Exploraiton Society* 2: 264–75.

Renfrew, C. 1972. *The Emergence of Civilisation: the Cyclades and the Aegean in the Third Millennium BC.* London: Methuen.

———. 1996. The Sapient Behaviour Paradox, in *Modelling the Early Human Mind.* Edited by P. Mellars and K. Gibson, pp. 11–14. Cambridge: McDonald Institute for Archaeological Research.

Révillion, S., and A. Tuffreau. Editors. 1994. *Les Industries Laminaires au Paléolithique Moyen. Centre national de la recherche scientifique 18.* Paris: Éditions du C.N.R.S.

Richards, M., P. Pettitt , E. Trinkaus, F. H. Smith, M. Paunovic, and I. Karavanic. 2000. Neanderthal Diet at Vindija and Neanderthal Predation: The Evidence from Stable Isotopes. *Proceedings National Academy of Sciences USA* 97: 7663–6.

Richerson, P., and R. Boyd. 1998. The Pleistocene and the Origins of Human Culture: Built for Speed. *The 5th Biannual Symposium on the Science of Behaviour: Behaviour, Evolution and Culture, Mexico, University of Guadalajara, 1998.*

Rieder, H. 2000. Die altpaläolithischen Wurfspeere von Schöningen, ihre Erprobung und ihre Bedeutung für die Lebensumwelt des Homo erectus. *Praehistoria Thuringica* 5: 68–75.

Rigaud, J.-P. Editor. 1988. *La Grotte Vaufrey à Cenac et Saint-Julien (Dordogne): Paléoenvironments, chronologie et activités humaines. Mémoires de la Société Préhistorique Française 19.* Paris.

Rightmire, G. P., and H. J. Deacon. 1991. Comparative Studies of Late Pleistocene Human Remains from Klasies River Mouth, South Africa. *Journal of Human Evolution* 20: 131–56.

Roberts, M. B. 1986. Excavation of a Lower Palaeolithic Site at Amey's Eartham Pit, Boxgrove, West Sussex: A Preliminary Report. *Proceedings of the Prehistoric Society* 52: 215–45.

———. 1996. 'Man the Hunter' Returns at Boxgrove. *British Archaeology* 18.

Roberts, M. B., and S. A. Parfitt. 1999. *Boxgrove: A Middle Pleistocene Hominid Site at Eartham Quarry, Boxgrove, West Sussex.* London: English Heritage.

Roberts, M. B., and M. I. Pope. In prep. *The Raised Beach Mapping Project*: English Heritage Monograph.

Roberts, M. B., C. S. Gamble, and D. R. Bridgland. 1995. The Earliest Occupation of Europe: The British Isles, in *The Earliest Occupation of Europe*. Edited by W. Roebroeks and T. van Kolfschoten, pp. 165–91. Leiden: European Science Foundation and University of Leiden.

Roberts, M. B., S. A. Parfitt, M. I. Pope, and F. F. Wenban-Smith. 1997. Boxgrove, West Sussex: Rescue Excavations of a Lower Palaeolithic Landsurface (Boxgrove Project B, 1989–91). *Proceedings of the Prehistoric Society* 63: 303–58.

Roberts, M. B., S. A. Parfitt, and M. I. Pope. In prep. *Boxgrove: A Middle Pleistocene Hominid Site at Eartham Quarry, Boxgrove, West Sussex. Volume 2*. London: English Heritage.

Roche, H., J.-P. Brugal, D. Lefèvre, S. Ploux, and P.-J. Texier. 1988. Isenya: état des recherc ies sur un nouveau site acheuléen d'Afrique orientale. *African Archaeological Review* 6: 27–55.

Roche, H., A. Delanges, J.-P. Brugal, C. Feibel, M. Kibunjia, V. Mouree, and P.-J. Texier. 1999. Early Hominid Stone Tool Production and Technical Skill 2.34 Myr Ago in West Turkana, Kenya. *Nature* 399: 57–60.

Rodseth, L., R. W. Wrangham, A. Harrigan, and B. B. Smuts. 1991. The Human Community as a Primate Society. *Current Anthropology* 32: 221–54.

Roe, D. A. 1968. British Lower and Middle Palaeolithic Handaxe Groups. *Proceedings of the Prehistoric Society* 34: 1–82.

———. 1981. *The Lower and Middle Palaeolithic Periods in Britain*. London: Routledge and Kegan Paul.

———. 1994. A Metrical Analysis of Selected Sets of Handaxes and Cleavers from Olduvai Gorge, in *Olduvai Gorge Volume 5; Excavations in Beds III, IV and the Masek Beds, 1968–71*. Edited by M. D. Leakey and D. A. Roe, pp. 146–234. Cambridge: Cambridge University Press.

———. 2001. Some Earlier Palaeolithic Find-spots of Interest in the Solent Region, in *Palaeolithic Archaeology of the Solent River, Lithic Studies Society Occasional Paper 7*. Edited by F. F. Wenban-Smith and R. T. Hosfield, pp. 47–56. London: Lithic Studies Society.

Roebroeks, W. 1988. *From Find Scatters to Early Hominid Behavior: A Study of Middle Paleolithic Riverside Settlements at Maastricht-Belvédère (The Netherlands). Vol. 21. Analecta Praehistorica Leidensia*. Leiden: University of Leiden.

———. 2001. Hominid Behaviour and the Earliest Occupation of Europe: An Exploration. *Journal of human evolution* 41: 437–61.

Roebroeks, W., and R. Corbey. 2001. Biases and Double Standards in Palaeo-anthropology, in *Studying Human Origins: Disciplinary History and Epistemology*. Edited by R. Corbey and W. Roebroeks, pp. 67–76. Amsterdam: Amsterdam University Press.

Roebroeks, W., and C. S. Gamble. Editors. 1999. *The Middle Palaeolithic Occupation of Europe*. Leiden: European Science Foundation and University of Leiden.

Roebroeks, W., and A. Tuffreau. 1999. Palaeoenvironment and Settlement Patterns of the Northwest European Middle Palaeolithic, in *The Middle Palaeolithic Occupation of Europe*. Edited by W. Roebroeks and C. S. Gamble, pp. 121–38. Leiden: European Science Foundation and University of Leiden.

Roebroeks, W., J. Kolen, and E. Rensink. 1988. Planning Depth, Anticipation and the Organization of Middle Palaeolithic Technology: The 'Archaic Natives' Meet Eve's Descendants. *Helinium* 28: 17–34.

Roebroeks, W., N. Conard, and T. van Kolfschoten. 1992a. Dense Forests, Cold

Steppes, and the Palaeolithic Settlement of Northern Europe. *Current Anthropology* 33: 551–86.

Roebroeks, W., D. De Loecker, P. Hennekens, and M. van Ieperen. 1992b. 'A Veil of Stones': On the Interpretation of an Early Middle Palaeolithic Low Density Scatter at Maastricht-Belvédère (The Netherlands). *Analecta Praehistorica Leidensia* 25: 1–16.

Rolland, N. 1995. Levallois Technique Emergence: Single or Multiple? A Review of the Euro-African Record, in *The Definition and Interpretation of Levallois Technology*. Edited by H. L. Dibble and O. Bar-Yosef, pp. 333–59. Madison: Prehistory Press.

Rolland, N., and H. L. Dibble. 1990. A New Synthesis of Middle Palaeolithic Variability. *American Antiquity* 55: 480–99.

Rose, J. 1979. River Terraces and Sea Level Change. *Brighton Polytechnic Geographic Society Magazine* 3: 13–30.

Rose, J., C. Turner, G. R. Coope, and M. D. Bryan. 1980. Channel Changes in a Lowland River Catchment over the Last 13,000 Years, in *Timescales in Geomorphology*. Edited by R. A. Cullingford, D. A. Davidson, and J. Lewin, pp. 159–75. Chichester: John Wiley & Sons Ltd.

Rose, S., R. C. Lewontin, and L. J. Kamin. 1984. *Not in our Genes: Biology, Ideology and Human Nature*. London: Pantheon.

Rousseau, D.-D., J.-J. Puisségur, and J. P. Lautridou. 1990. Biogeography of the Pleistocene Pleniglacial Malacofaunas in Europe: Stratigraphic and Climatic Implications. *Palaeogeography, Palaeoclimatology, Palaoecology* 80: 7–23.

Roux, V. 1999. Ethnoarchaeology and the Generation of Referential Models: The Case of Harappan Carnelian Beads, in *Ethno-analogy and the Reconstruction of Prehistoric Artefact Use and Production, Urgeschichtliche Materialhefte 14*. Edited by L. R. Owen and M. Porr, pp. 153–69. Tübingen: Mo Vince Verlag.

Roux, V., B. Bril, and G. Dietrich. 1995. Skills and Learning Difficulties Involved in Stone Knapping: The Case of Stone-bead Knapping in Khambhat, India. *World Archaeology* 27: 63–87.

Ruff, C. B. 1991. Climate and Body Shape in Hominid Evolution. *Journal of Human Evolution* 21: 81–105.

Ruiz Idarraga, R. 2001. Metodologia Del Analisis Del Arte Paleolitico: Al Autoria Y El Estilo Del Grupo. Unpublished PhD, University de Deusto.

Russell, B. 1921. *The Analysis of Mind*. London: Allen and Unwin.

Sackett, J. R. 1982. Approaches to Style in Lithic Archaeology. *Journal of Anthropological Archaeology* 1: 59–112.

Salter, A. E. 1899. Pebbly and Other Gravels in Southern England. *Proceedings of the Geologists' Association* 15: 264–86.

——. 1906. *The Geology of the Country near Sidmouth and Lyme Regis*, 1st edition. *Memoir of the British Geological Survey, Sheet 326 & 340*. London: HMSO.

Sampson, C. G. 1974. *The Stone Age Archaeology of Southern Africa*. New York: Academic Press.

Santonja, M., and P. Villa. 1990. The Lower Paleolithic of Spain and Portugal. *Journal of World Prehistory* 4: 45–94.

Sartre, J.-P. 1962. *The Transcendence of the Ego: An Existentialist Theory of Consciousness*. New York: Noonday Press.

Scheer, A. 1993. The Organization of Lithic Resource Use During the Gravettian in

Germany, in *Before Lascaux: The Complex Record of the Early Upper Palaeolithic*. Edited by H. Knecht, A. Pike-Tay, and R. White, pp. 193–210. Boca Raton: CRC Press.

Schick, K. D. 1987. Modeling the Formation of Early Stone Age Artifact Concentrations. *Journal of Human Evolution* 16: 789–807.

———. 1992. Geoarchaeological Analysis of an Acheulean Site at Kalambo Falls, Zambia. *Geoarchaeology* 7: 1–26.

Schick, K. D. 1994. The Movius Line Reconsidered, in *Integrative Paths to the Past*. Edited by R. S. Corruccini and R. L. Ciochon, pp. 569–96. Englewood Cliffs, NJ: Prentice-Hall.

Schick, K. D., and J. D. Clark. 2003. Biface Technological Development and Variability in the Acheulean Industrial Complex in the Middle Awash Region of the Afar Rift, Ethiopia, in *Multiple Approaches to the Study of Bifacial Technologies*. Edited by M. Soressi and H. L. Dibble, pp. 1–30. Philadelphia: University of Pennsylvania Press.

Schick, K. D., and N. Toth. 1993. *Making Silent Stones Speak: Human Evolution and the Dawn of Technology*. London: Phoenix.

Schiegl, S. In Press. Analysis of Ash-derived Opal Phytoliths in the Sediments from the Hearth of Wallertheim A, in *The 1991–1994 Middle Paleolithic Excavations at Wallertheim, Tübingen Publications in Prehistory*. Edited by N. J. Conard. Tübingen: Kerns Verlag.

Schirmer, G. R. 1975. *An Analysis of Lithic Material from Dale Rose Parlour, Trappies Kop Bay, Cape Peninsula. Unpublished Archaeology Additional Report*. Cape Town: University of Cape Town.

Schirmer, W. 1988. Holocene Valley Development on the Upper Rhine and Main, in *Lake, Mire and River Environments During the Last 15,000 years*. Edited by G. Lang and C. Schluchter, pp. 153–60. Rotterdam: Balkema.

———. 1995. Valley Bottoms in the Late Quaternary, in *Late Quaternary and Present-day Fluvial Processes in Central Europe*. Edited by J. Hagedom, pp. 27–51. Berlin: Gebrüder Borntraeger.

Schlanger, N. 1996. Understanding Levallois: Lithic Technology and Cognitive Archaeology. *Cambridge Archaeological Journal* 6: 231–54.

Schoch, W. H. 1995. Hölzer aus der Fundschicht 1 des altpaläolithischen Fundplatzes Schöningen 12 (Reinsdorf-Interglazial), in *Archäologische Ausgrabungen im Braunkohlentagebau Schöningen, Landkreis Helmstedt*. Edited by H. Thieme and R. Maier, pp. 73–84. Hannover: Verlag Hahnsche Buchhandlung.

Schreve, D. C. 1997. Mammalian Biostratigraphy of the Later Middle Pleistocene in Britain. Unpublished PhD, University of London.

———. 2001a. Mammalian Evidence from Middle Pleistocene Fluvial Sequences for Complex Environmental Change at the Oxygen Isotope Sub-stage Level. *Quaternary International* 79: 65–74.

———. 2001b. Differentiation of the British Late Middle Pleistocene Interglacials: the Evidence from Mammalian Biostratigraphy. *Quaternary Science Reviews* 20: 693–705.

Schultz, H., U. v. Rad, and H. Erlenkeuser. 1998. Correlation between Arabian Sea and Greenland Climate Oscillations of the Past 110,000 years. *Nature* 393: 54–7.

Schwarcz, H. P., R. Grun, A. G. Latham, D. Mania, and K. Brunnacker. 1988. The Bilzingsleben Archaeological Site: New Dating Evidence. *Archaeometry* 30: 5–17.

Shackleton, N. J. 1987. Oxygen Isotopes, Ice Volume and Sea Level. *Quaternary Science Reviews* 6: 183–90.

Shackley, M. L. 1974. Stream Abrasion of Flint Implements. *Nature* 248: 501–2.

——. 1975. A Study of the Mousterian of Acheulian Tradition Industries of Southern Britain. Unpublished PhD, University of Southampton.

Shakesby, R. A., and N. Stephens. 1984. The Pleistocene Gravels of the Axe Valley, Devon. *Report of the Transactions of the Devon Association for the Advancement of Science* 116: 77–88.

Shanks, M., and C. Tilley. 1987a. *Re-constructing Archaeology: Theory and Practice*, 2nd edition. London: Routledge.

——. 1987b. *Social Theory and Archaelogy*. London: Polity.

Shennan, S. 2002. *Genes, Memes and Human History: Darwinian Archaeology and Cultural Evolution*. London: Thames and Hudson.

Shennan, S. J. 1993. After Social Evolution: A New Archaeological Agenda?, in *Archaeological Theory: Who Sets the Agenda?* Edited by N. Yoffee and A. Sherratt, pp. 53–59. Cambridge: Cambridge University Press.

——. 2001. Demography and Cultural Innovation: A Model and Some Implications for the Emergence of Modern Human Culture. *Cambridge Archaeological Journal* 11: 5–16.

Shipman, P., G. Foster, and M. Schoeninger. 1984. Burnt Bones and Teeth: An Experimental Study of Colour, Morphology, Crystal Structure and Shrinkage. *Journal of Archaeological Science* 11: 307–25.

Shipton, C. 2003. Sociality and Cognition in the Acheulean: A Case Study on the Hunsgi-Baichbal Basin, Karnataka, India. Unpublished PhD, University of Cambridge.

Sinclair, A. 2000. Constellations of Knowledge: Human Agency and Material Affordance in Lithic Technology, in *Agency in Archaeology*. Edited by M.-A. Dobres and J. Robb, pp. 196–212. London: Routledge.

Singer, R., and J. Wymer. 1982. *The Middle Stone Age at Klasies River Mouth in South Africa*. Chicago: Chicago University Press.

Smith, M. A., M. Spriggs, and B. Frankhauser. 1993. *Sahul in Review: Pleistocene Archaeology in Australia, New Guinea and Island Melanesia*. Canberra: Department of Prehistory Research School of Pacific Studies.

Smolla, G. 1953. Gab es eine prälithische Periode in der Kulturgeschichte der Menschheit? *Tribus* 1952/1953: 75–103.

Speth, J. D., and K. Spielmann. 1983. Energy Source, Protein Metabolism and Hunter-gatherer Subsistence Strategies. *Journal of Anthropological Archaeology* 2: 1–31.

Stapert, D., and M. Street. 1997. High Resolution or Optimum Resolution? Spatial Analysis of the Federmesser Site at Andernach. *World Archaeology* 29: 172–94.

Steele, J., and S. Shennan. Editors. 1996. *The Archaeology of Human Ancestry: Power, Sex and Tradition. Theoretical Archaeology group (TAG)*. London: Routledge.

Stephens, N. 1970a. The Lower Severn Valley, in *The Glaciations of Wales and Adjoining Regions*. Edited by C. A. Lewis, pp. 267–314. Harlow: Longmans.

——. 1970b. The West Country and Southern Ireland, in *The Glaciations of Wales and Adjoining Regions*. Edited by C. A. Lewis, pp. 267–314. Harlow: Longmans.

——. 1974. The Chard Area and the Axe Valley Sections, in *Field Handbook for the*

Quaternary Research Association Easter Meeting 1974. Edited by A. Straw, pp. 46–51. Exeter: Quaternary Research Association.

——. 1977. The Axe Valley, in *INQUA Congress Guidebook for Excursions, A6 and C6, South-West England.* Edited by D. N. Mottershead, pp. 24–29. Norwich: Geo Abstracts Ltd.

Stern, N. 1993. The Structure of the Lower Pleistocene Archaeological Record: A Case Study from the Koobi Fora Formation. *Current Anthropology* 34: 201–25.

——. 1994. The Implications of Time-averaging for Reconstructing the Land-use Patterns of Early Tool-using Hominids. *Journal of Human Evolution* 27: 89–105.

Stevenson, M. G. 1991. Beyond the Formation of Hearth-Associated Artifact Assemblages, in *The Interpretation of Archaeological Spatial Patterning.* Edited by E. M. Kroll and T. D. Price, pp. 269–99. New York: Plenum Press.

Steward, J. H. 1936. The Economic and Social Basis of Primitive Bands, in *Essays in Anthropology Presented to A. L. Kroeber.* Edited by R. H. Lowie, pp. 331–50. Berkeley: University of California Press.

Stiles, D. 1998. Raw Material as Evidence for Human Behaviour in the Lower Pleistocene: The Olduvai Case, in *Early Human Behaviour in Global Context.* Edited by M. D. Petraglia and R. Korisettar, pp. 133–50. London: Routledge.

Stiner, M. C. 1993. Modern Human Origins – Faunal Perspectives. *Annual Review of Anthropology* 22: 55–82.

——. 1994. *Honor among Thieves: A Zooarchaeological Study of Neandertal Ecology.* New Jersey: Princeton University Press.

——. 2002. Carnivory, Coevolution, and the Geographic Spread of the Genus Homo. *Journal of Archaeological Research* 10: 1–63.

Stout, D. 2002. Skill and Cognition in Stone Tool Production: An Ethnographic Case Study from Irian Jaya. *Current Anthropology* 43: 693–722.

Strathern, M. 1988. *The Gender of the Gift: Problems with Women and Problems with Society in Melanesia.* Berkeley: University of California Press.

Straw, A. 1995. Kent's Cavern – Whence and Whither. Pengelly Centenary Lecture III. *Transactions and Proceedings of the Torquay Natural History Society* 21: 129–211.

——. 1996. The Quaternary Record of Kent's Cavern: A Brief Reminder and Update. *Quaternary Newsletter* 80: 17–25.

Stringer, C. B. 2003. Human Evolution: Out of Ethiopia. *Nature* 423: 742–7.

Stringer, C. B., E. Trinkaus, M. B. Roberts, S. A. Parfitt, and R. I. Macphail. 1998. The Middle Pleistocene Human Tibia from Boxgrove. *Journal of Human Evolution* 34: 509–47.

Stutz, A. J. 2002. Polarizing Microscopy Identification of Chemical Diagenesis in Archaeological Cementum. *Journal of Archaeological Science* 29: 1327–47.

Svoboda, J., V. Lozek, and E. Vlček. 1996. *Hunters between East and West: The Palaeolithic of Moravia.* New York: Plenum Press.

Swanson, E. H. 1970. Pleistocene Geochronology in the New Forest. *Bulletin of the Institute of Archaeology, University of London* 8: 55–100.

Szabo, B. J., C. McKinney, T. S. Dalbey, and K. Paddayya. 1990. On the Age of the Acheulian Culture of the Hunsgi-Baichbal Valleys, Peninsular India. *Bulletin of the Deccan College Postgraduate and Research Institute* 50: 317–21.

Taborin, Y. 1992. Les espaces d'acheminement de certains coquillages Magdaléniens, in *Le peuplement Magdalénien*. Edited by C.T.H.S., pp. 417–29. Paris: Actes du Colloque de Chancelade 10–15 Octobre 1988.

Thackeray, A. I. 1989. Changing Fashions in the Middle Stone Age: The Stone Artefact Sequence from Klasies River Main Site, South Africa. *The African Archaeological Review* 7: 33–57.

———. 1992. The Middle Stone Age South of the Limpopo River. *Journal of World Prehistory* 6: 385–440.

Thackeray, A. I., and A. J. Kelly. 1988. A Technological and Typological Analysis of Middle Stone Age Assemblages Antecedent to the Howieson's Poort at Klasies River Main Site. *South African Archaeological Bulletin* 43: 15–26.

Thieme, H. 1995a. Der altpaläolithische Fundplatz Schöningen 13 I (Holstein-Interglazial), in *Archäologische Ausgrabungen im Braunkohlentagebau Schöningen, Landkreis Helmstedt*. Edited by H. Thieme and R. Maier, pp. 57–61. Hannover: Verlag Hahnsche Buchhandlung.

———. 1995b. Die altpaläolithischen Fundschichten Schöningen 12 (Reinsdorf-Interglazial), in *Archäologische Ausgrabungen im Braunkohlentagebau Schöningen, Landkreis Helmstedt*. Edited by H. Thieme and R. Maier, pp. 62–72. Hannover: Verlag Hahnsche Buchhandlung.

———. 1995c. Ein altpaläolithischer Lagerplatz aus der Zeit des Urmenschen von Schöningen 13 II (Reinsdorf-Interglazial), in *Archäologische Ausgrabungen im Braunkohlentagebau Schöningen, Landkreis Helmstedt*. Edited by H. Thieme and R. Maier, pp. 95–106. Hannover: Verlag Hahnsche Buchhandlung.

———. 1996. Altpalaolithische Wurfspeere aus Schöningen, Niedersachsen – ein Vorbericht. *Archäologisches Korrespondenzblatt* 26: 377–93.

———. 1997. Lower Palaeolithic Hunting Spears from Germany. *Nature* 385: 807–10.

———. 1998. Altpaläolithische Wurfspeere aus Schöningen, Niedersachsen. *Praehistoria Thuringica* 2: 22–31.

———. 1999a. Altpaläolithische Holzgeräte aus Schöningen, Ldkr. Helmstedt. Bedeutsame Funde zur Kulturentwicklung des frühen Menschen. *Germania* 77: 451–87.

———. 1999b. Ein angekohlter Holzstab vom altpaläolithischen Fundplatz Schöningen 13 II-4, in *Den Bogen spannen . . . Festschrift für B. Gramsch. Beiträge zur Ur- und Frühgeschichte Mitteleuropas 20*. Edited by E. Cziesla, T. Kersting, and S. Pratsch, pp. 15–27. Weißbach: Beier & Beran.

Thieme, H., and R. Maier. 1995. *Archäologische Ausgrabungen im Braunkohlentagebau Schöningen, Landkreis Helmstedt*. Hannover: Verlag Hahnsche Buchhandlung.

Thieme, H., and D. Mania. 1993. 'Schöningen 12' – ein mittelpleistozänes Interglazialvorkommen im Nordharzvorland mit paläolithischen Funden. *Ethnographisch-Archäologische Zeitschrift* 34: 610–19.

Thieme, H., and S. Veil. 1985. Neue Untersuchungen zum eemzeitlichen Elefanten-Jagdplatz Lehringen, Ldkr. Verden. *Die Kunde* 36: 11–58.

Thieme, H., D. Mania, B. Urban, and T. van Kolfschoten. 1993. Schöningen (Nordharzvorland). Eine altpaläolithische Fundstelle aus dem mittleren Eiszeitalter. *Archäologisches Korrespondenzblatt* 23: 147–63.

Thissen, J. 1986. Ein weiterer Fundplatz der Westwandfundschicht (B1) von Rheindahlen. *Archäologisches Korrespondenzblatt* 16: 111–21.

Thomas, J. 1991. *Rethinking the Neolithic*. Cambridge: Cambridge University Press.

———. 1996. *Time, Culture and Identity: An Interpretive Archaeology*. London: Routledge.

——. 2002. Archaeology's Humanism and the Materiality of the Body, in *Thinking through the Body. Archaeologies of Corporeality*. Edited by Y. Hamilakis, M. Pluciennik, and S. Tarlow, pp. 29–45. New York: Plenum.

Tilley, C. 1994. *A Phenomenology of Landscape: Places, Paths and Monuments*. Oxford: Berg.

——. 1996. *An Ethnography of the Neolithic*. Cambridge: Cambridge University Press.

Tobias, P. V. 1971. Human Skeletal Remains from the Cave of Hearths, Makapansgat. *American Journal of Physical Anthropology* 34: 335–67.

——. 1999. Biological Equipment, Environment and Survival in the Australopithecine World, in *Hominid Evolution. Lifestyles and Survival Strategies*. Edited by H. Ullrich, pp. 55–71. Gelsenkirchen/Schwelm: Edition Archaea.

Tode, A. 1953. Die Untersuchung der paläolithischen Freilandstation von Salzgitter-Lebenstedt. *Eiszeitalter und Gegenwart* 3: 144–220.

——. 1982. *Der Altsteinzeitliche Fundplatz Salzgitter-Lebenstedt*. Köln: Böhlau Verlag.

Toepfer, V. 1983. Ein Oberkieferfragment des Löwen aus dem Travertinkomplex von Bilzingsleben, in *Bilzingsleben II. Homo erectus – seine Kultur und seine Umwelt*. Edited by D. H. Mai, D. Mania, T. Nötzold, V. Toepfer, E. Vlček, and W. D. Heinrich, pp. 163–73. Berlin: VEB Deutscher Verlag der Wissenschaften.

Tomasello, M. 1994. The Question of Chimpanzee Culture, in *Chimpanzee Cultures*. Edited by R. W. Wrangham, W. C. McGrew, F. B. M. de Waal, and P. G. Heltne, pp. 301–17. Cambridge, MA/London: Harvard University Press.

——. 1999. *The Cultural Origins of Human Cognition*. Cambridge, Mass.: Harvard University Press.

Tomasello, M., and J. Call. 1997. *Primate Cognition*. Oxford: Oxford University Press.

Toren, C. 1999. *Mind, Materiality and History: Explorations in Fijian Ethnography*. London: Routledge.

Torrence, R. 1989a. Tools as Optimal Solutions, in *Time, Energy and Stone Tools*. Edited by R. Torrence, pp. 1–6. Cambridge: Cambridge University Press.

——. 1989b. Re-tooling: Towards a Behavioural Theory of Stone Tools, in *Time, Energy and Stone Tools*. Edited by R. Torrence, pp. 57–66. Cambridge: Cambridge University Press.

Toth, N., and K. Schick. 1993. Early Stone Industries and Inferences Regarding Language and Cognition, in *Tools, Language and Cognition in Human Evolution*. Edited by K. R. Gibson and T. Ingold, pp. 346–62. Cambridge: Cambridge University Press.

Tuffreau, A. 1992. Middle Palaeolithic Settlement in Northern France, in *The Middle Palaeolithic: Adaptation, Behaviour, and Variability*, 1st edition, Vol. 4. Edited by H. L. Dibble and P. Mellars, pp. 59–75. Philadelphia: The University Museum, University of Pennsylvania.

Tuffreau, A., and P. Antoine. 1995. The Earliest Occupation of Europe: Continental Northwestern Europe, in *The Earliest Occupation of Europe*. Edited by W. Roebroeks and T. van Kolfschoten, pp. 147–63. Leiden: European Science Foundation and University of Leiden.

Tuffreau, A., and J.-P. Bouchet. 1985. Le gisement acheuléen de la Vallée du Muid à Gouzeaucourt (Nord). *Bulletin de la Société Préhistorique Française* 82: 291–306.

Tuffreau, A., A. Lamotte, and J.-L. Marcy. 1997. Land-use and Site Function in Acheulean Complexes of the Somme Valley. *World Archaeology* 29: 225–41.

Turq, A. 1999. Reflections on the Middle Palaeolithic of the Aquitaine Basin, in *The Middle Palaeolithic Occupation of Europe*. Edited by W. Roebroeks and C. S. Gamble, pp. 107–20. Leiden: European Science Foundation and University of Leiden.

Urban, B. 1993. Mittelpleistozäne Interglaziale im Tagebau Schöningen. *Archäologische Zeitschrift* 34: 620–22.

——. 1995. Palynological Evidence of Younger Middle Pleistocene Interglacials (Holsteinian, Reinsdorf and Schöningen) in the Schöningen Open-cast Lignite Mine (East Lower Saxony, Germany). *Meded. Rijks Geol. Dienst* 52: 175–86.

——. 1997. Grundzüge der eiszeitlichen Klima- und Vegetationsgeschichte in Mitteleuropa, in *Homo heidelbergensis von Mauer. Das Auftreten des Menschen in Europa*. Edited by A. Wagner and K. W. Beinhauer, pp. 240–63. Heidelberg: Universitätsverlag Winter.

Urban, B., H. Thieme, and H. Elsner. 1988. Biostratigraphische, quartärgeologische und urgeschichtliche Befunde aus dem Tagebau 'Schöningen', Ldkr. Helmstedt. *Zeitschrift der deutschen geologischen Gesellschaft* 139: 123–54.

Urban, B., R. Lenhard, D. Mania, and B. Albrect. 1991a. Mittelpleistozän im Tagebau Schöningen, Ldkr. Helmstedt. *Zeitschrift der deutschen geologischen Gesellschaft* 142: 351–72.

Urban, B., H. Elsner, A. Hölzer, D. Mania, and B. Albrecht. 1991b. Eine eem- und frühweichselzeitliche Abfolge im Tagebau Schöningen, Landkreis Helmstedt. *Eiszeitalter und Gegenwart* 41: 85–99.

Ussher, W. A. E. 1906. *The Geology of the Country between Wellington and Chard. Memoir of the British Geological Survey, Sheet 311*. London: HMSO.

Van Andel, T. H. 1989. Late Pleistocene Sea Levels and the Human Exploitation of the Shore and Shelf of Southern South Africa. *Journal of Field Archaeology* 16: 133–54.

van der Made, J. 1998. A Preliminary Note on the Cervids from Bilzingsleben. *Praehistoria Thuringica* 2: 108–22.

——. 2000. A Preliminary Note on the Rhinos from Bilzingsleben. *Praehistoria Thuringica* 4: 41–64.

van Kolfschoten, T. 1993. Die Vertebraten des Interglazials von Schöningen 12. *Ethnographisch-Archäologische Zeitschrift* 34: 623–8.

——. 1995. Faunenreste des altpaläolithischen Fundplatzes Schöningen 12 (Reinsdorf-Interglazial), in *Archäologische Ausgrabungen im Braunkohlentagebau Schöningen, Landkreis Helmstedt*. Edited by H. Thieme and R. Maier, pp. 85–94. Hannover: Verlag Hahnsche Buchhandlung.

Van Peer, P. 1992. *The Levallois Reduction Strategy. Monographs in World Archaeology No. 13*. Madison: Prehistory Press.

van Riet Lowe, C. 1945. The Evolution of the Levallois Technique in South Africa. *Man* 45: 49–59.

van Schaik, C. P., and G. R. Pradhan. 2003. A Model for Tool-use Traditions in Primates: Implications for the Coevolution of Culture and Cognition. *Journal of Human Evolution* 44: 645–64.

van Schaik, C. P., M. Ancrenaz, G. Borgen, B. Galdikas, C. D. Knott, I. Singleton, A. Suzuki, S. S. Utami, and M. Merrill. 2003. Orangutan cultures and the evolution of material culture. *Science* 299: 102–5.

Vandenberghe, J. 1993. Changing Fluvial Processes under Changing Periglacial

Conditions, in *Geormorphology and Geoecology*. Edited by I. Douglas and J. Hagedorn, pp. 17–28. Berlin: Gebrüder Borntraeger.

———. 1995. Timescales, Climate and River Development. *Quaternary Science Reviews* 14: 631–8.

———. 2002. The Relation between Climate and River Processes, Landforms and Deposits during the Quaternary. *Quaternary International* 91: 17–23.

Vaquero, M., and I. Pastó 2001. The Definition of Spatial Units in Middle Palaeolithic Sites: The Hearth-related Assemblages. *Journal of Archaeological Science* 28: 209–20.

Velegrakis, A. F. 1994. Aspects of Morphology and Sedimentology of a Transgressional Embayment System: Poole and Christchurch Bays, Southern England. Unpublished PhD, University of Southampton.

Velegrakis, A. F., J. K. Dix, and M. B. Collins. 1999. Late Quaternary Evolution of the Upper Reaches of the Solent River, Southern England, Based upon Marine Geophysical Evidence. *Journal of the Geological Society of London* 156: 73–87.

Villa, P. 1990. Torralba and Aridos: Elephant Exploitation in Middle Pleistocene Spain. *Journal of Human Evolution* 19: 299–309.

Vinnicombe, P. 1976. *People of the Eland*. Pietermaritzburg: University of Natal Press.

Vlček, E. 1978. A New Discovery of Homo Erectus in Central Europe. *Journal of Human Evolution* 7: 39–251.

———. 2002. Der fossile Mensch von Bilzingsleben – The Fossil Man of Bilzingsleben, in *Der fossile Mensch von Bilzingsleben. Bilzingsleben VI*. Edited by E. Vlček, D. Mania, and U. Mania, pp. 145–392. Weissbach: Beier & Beran.

Vogelsang, R. 1998. *Middle Stone Age Fundstellen in Südwest-Namibia*. Köln: Heinrich-Barth-Institut.

Volman, T. P. 1984. Early Prehistory of Southern Africa, in *Southern African Prehistory and Palaeoenvironments*. Edited by R. G. Klein, pp. 169–220. Rotterdam: A. A. Balkema.

Wagner, E. 1995. Cannstatt I. Großwildjäger im Travertingebiet. Forschungen und Berichte zur Vor- und Frühgeschichte in Baden-Württemberg 61. Unpublished PhD, University of Stuttgart.

Walker, A., and R. E. Leakey. 1993. *The Nariokotome Homo Erectus Skeleton*. Cambridge, Mass.: Harvard University Press.

Weißmüller, W. 2003. Von Gestaltungsfreiheit und Standardisierungszwang: Zum Zeichencharakter paläolithischer Silexartefakte, in *Spuren und Botschaften: Interpretationen materieller Kultur*. Edited by U. Veit, T. L. Kienlin, C. Kümmel, and S. Schmidt, pp. 173–85. Münster: Waxmann.

Wenban-Smith, F. F. 2000. Typology and Technology, in *The Palaeolithic Site at Red Barns, Portchester, Hampshire: Bifacial Technology, Raw Material Quality and the Organisation of Archaic Behaviour*. Edited by F. F. Wenban-Smith, C. S. Gamble, and A. M. ApSimon, pp. 243–8. Proceedings of the Prehistoric Society 66.

Wenban-Smith, F. F., C. S. Gamble, and A. ApSimon. 2000. The Lower Palaeolithic Site at Red Barns, Portchester: Bifacial Technology, Raw Material Quality, and the Organisation of Archaic Behaviour. *Proceedings of the Prehistoric Society* 66: 209–56.

Wessex Archaeology 1993. *The Southern Rivers Palaeolithic Project: Report No. 1, 1991–1992. The Upper Thames Valley, the Kennet Valley and the Upper Solent Drainage System*. Salisbury: Wessex Archaeology.

Wheeler, R. E. M. 1954. *Archaeology from the Earth.* Harmonsdworth: Penguin Books.

White, H. J. O. 1912. *The Geology of the Country around Winchester and Stockbridge. Memoir of the Geological Survey of England and Wales.* London: HMSO.

———. 1915. *The Geology of the Country near Lymington and Portsmouth. Memoir of the Geological Survey of England and Wales.* London: HMSO.

———. 1917. *The Geology of the Country around Bournemouth,* 2nd edition. *Memoir of the Geological Survey of Great Britain.* London: HMSO.

———. 1921. *A Short Account of the Geology of the Isle of Wight. Memoir of the Geological Survey of England and Wales.* London: HMSO.

White, M. J. 1996. Biface Variability and Human Behaviour in the Earlier Palaeolithic: A Study from South-Eastern England. Unpublished PhD, University of Cambridge.

———. 1998. On the Significance of Acheulean Biface Variability in Southern Britain. *Proceedings of the Prehistoric Society* 64: 15–44.

———. 2000. The Clactonian Question: On the Interpretation of Core and Flake Assemblages in the British Lower Palaeolithic. *Journal of World Prehistory* 14: 1–63.

White, M. J., and N. Ashton. 2003. Lower Palaeolithic Core Technology and the Origins of the Levallois Method in North-Western Europe. *Current Anthropology* 44: 598–609.

White, M. J., and P. B. Pettitt. 1995. Technology of Early Palaeolithic Western Europe: Innovation, Variability and a Unified Framework. *Lithics* 16: 27–40.

White, M. J., and S. J. Plunkett. in press. *Miss Layard Excavates: A Palaeolithic Site at Foxhall Road, Ipswich, 1903–1905.* Bristol: WASP.

White, M. J., and D. C. Schreve. 2000. Island Britain – Peninsula Britain: Palaeogeography, Colonisation and the Lower Palaeolithic Settlement of the British Isles. *Proceedings of the Prehistoric Society* 66: 1–28.

White, T. D., B. Asfaw, D. DeGusta, H. Gilbert, G. D. Richards, G. Suwa, and F. C. Howell. 2003. Pleistocene Homo Sapiens from Middle Awash, Ethiopia. *Nature* 423: 742–7.

Whitelaw, T. 1989. The Social Organisation of Space in Hunter-Gatherer Communities: Some Implications for Social Inference in Archaeology. Unpublished PhD, University of Cambridge.

Whiten, A., J. Goodall, W. C. McGrew, T. Nishida, V. Reynolds, Y. Sugiyama, C. E. G. Tutin, R. W. Wrangham, and C. Boesch. 1999. Cultures in Chimpanzees. *Nature* 399: 682–5.

Wiessner, P. 1983. Style and Social Information in Kalahari San Projectile Points. *American Antiquity* 48: 253–76.

———. 1984. Reconsidering the Behavioural Basis for Style: A Case Study among the Kalahari San. *Journal of Anthropological Archaeology* 3: 190–234.

Wishart, D. 1999. *ClustanGraphics Primer: A Guide to Cluster Analysis.* Edinburgh: Clustan Limited.

Wobst, H. M. 1977. Stylistic Behaviour and Information Exchange, in *Papers for the Director: Research Essays in Honor of James B. Griffin,* Vol. 61, *Anthropological papers.* Edited by C. E. Cleland, pp. 317–42: Museum of Anthropology, University of Michigan.

———. 2000. Agency in (spite of) Material Culture, in *Agency in Archaeology.* Edited by M.-A. Dobres and J. Robb, pp. 40–50. London: Routledge.

Woodward, H. B. 1911. *The Geology of the Country near Sidmouth and Lyme Regis*, 2nd edition. *Memoir of the British Geological Survey, Sheet 326 and 340*. London: HMSO.

Wrangham, R. W. 1979. Sex Differences in Chimpanzee Dispersion, in *The Great Apes*. Edited by D. A. Hamburg and T. D. McCown, pp. 481–9. Menlo Park: Benjamin.

Wurz, S. 2000. The Middle Stone Age at Klasies River, South Africa. Unpublished PhD, University of Stellenbosch.

Wurz, S., N. J. L. Roux, S. Gardner, and H. J. Deacon. 2003. Discriminating Between the End Products of the Earlier Middle Stone Age Sub-Stages at Klasies River using Biplot Methodology. *Journal of Archaeological Science* 30: 1107–26.

Wymer, J. J. 1968. *Lower Palaeolithic Archaeology in Britain as represented by the Thames Valley*. London: John Baker.

——. 1999. *The Lower Palaeolithic Occupation of Britain*. Salisbury: Wessex Archaeology and English Heritage.

Wynn, T. 1989. *The Evolution of Spatial Competence*. Urbana: University of Illinois Press.

——. 1993a. Layers of Thinking in Tool Behaviour, in *Tools, Language and Cognition in Human Evolution*. Edited by K. Gibson and T. Ingold, pp. 389–406. Cambridge: Cambridge University Press.

——. 1993b. Two Developments in the Mind of Early Homo. *Journal of Anthropological Archaeology* 12: 299–322.

——. 1995. Handaxe Enigmas. *World Archaeology* 27: 10–24.

——. 1999. The Evolution of Tools and Symbolic Behaviour, in *Handbook of Human Symbolic Evolution*. Edited by A. Lock and C. R. Peters, pp. 263–87. Oxford: Blackwell Publishers.

Wynn, T., and W. C. McGrew. 1989. An Ape's View of the Oldowan. *Man (NS)* 24: 383–98.

Wynn, T., and F. Tierson. 1990. Regional Comparison of the Shapes of Later Acheulean Handaxes. *American Anthropologist* 92: 73–84.

Yates, T. 1990. Jacques Derrida: 'There is Nothing Outside of the Text', in *Reading Material Culture*. Edited by C. Tilley, pp. 206–80. Oxford: Blackwell.

Yellen, J. E. 1977. *Archaeological Approaches to the Present. Models for Reconstructing the Past*. New York: Academic Press.

——. 1996. Behavioural and Taphonomic Patterning at Katanda 9: A Middle Stone Age Site, Kivu Province, Zaire. *Journal of Archaeological Science* 23: 915–32.

Yellen, J. E., A. S. Brooks, E. Cornelissen, M. J. Mehlman, and K. Stewart. 1995. A Middle Stone Age Worked Bone Industry from Katanda, Upper Semliki Valley, Zaire. *Science*: 553–6.

Zeuner, F. E. 1958. *Dating the Past: An Introduction to Geochronology*, 4th edition. London: Methuen & Co. Ltd.

Zilhão, J., and F. d'Errico. 1999. The Chronology and Taphonomy of the Earliest Aurignacian and its Implications for the Understanding of Neandertal Extinction. *Journal of World Prehistory* 13: 1–68.

Index

Abric Romaní 150

abstract: concept 261, 266; design 256, 262; notions 114; thought 106, 109, 113, 129

accumulation 29, 40–41, 43–44, 47, 128, 136, 148, 162–163, 165, 167–168, 173–174, 214, 234; of artefacts 42–43, 49, 85; *see also* carnivore(s)

Acheulean 13–16, 19, 21–22, 26–27, 32, 37, 41–45, 47, 50, 52–53, 63–64, 66, 72, 74–75, 80, 83, 91, 93, 95–96, 162, 179–186, 197–198, 210, 212, 214, 217–219, 268–269; activities 202; African 53; behaviour 30; British 23–26; contexts 214; early 51, 92; hominid 268; hominins 211, 213–214, 216, 218–219; individual 16; industries 207; Late 207, 211; mind 207; populations 218; society 198, 208, 211–212, 215–216; technology 214, 217; Upper 174; *see also* biface, handaxe

action 8–9, 15, 17, 21–22, 29, 30, 31, 33, 34, 35, 36, 38, 41–42, 45, 49–51, 66, 69, 71–74, 77–78, 84, 91, 93, 109, 113, 129, 134, 153, 156, 162, 168, 173, 176, 207, 218, 220, 240, 268; collective 4, 33; context for 21; deliberate 176; group 221; habitual 162; hominin 135, 198, 208; human 11, 32, 197; individual 8, 19, 97, 133, 135–136, 139, 154, 194, 198, 202, 218–219, 221, 225, 233, 242–243, 251, 266;

of individuals 246; knowledgeable 26; principles of 21, 26–28; sequence 16, 51, 177; social 87, 163, 165, 173–174; technological 193; templates for 14

activity 100, 103–104, 109, 115, 129–131, 149–150, 158, 165, 214, 219, 237; areas 81, 87, 101, 114, 264; carnivore 141; fluvial 234; individual 197; zone(s) 100–102; *see also* carnivore, cultural, hominid, hominin, human, reduction, subsistence

actor(s) 8, 9, 69, 79, 173, 262; knowledgeable 156, 175; social 8, 68, 76; *see also* economic

adaptability 91

adaptation 1–3, 5, 20, 75, 78, 110, 114, 152, 161, 213, 219, 221, 254, 262, 268; adaptationist 265, 268–269; ape grade 73–75; biobehavioural 265; cultural 100, 102, 104, 114; cumulative 253; genetic 8; psychobehvaioural 266

adaptive 13, 96–97; factors 73; process 197; strategies 129, 156; system 15, 159; *see also* landscape

affordances 20, 81, 96

Africa 6, 44, 75–76, 177, 179, 208, 217, 244, 247, 251, 253, 261; East 207; South 180–181, 184, 191–192; southern 179–180, 193–194, 244–245, 252, 263; West 252

African: datasets, 63; East 50, 52, 115; ESA 179; LSA 194; sites 64; South